Toward the Open Field

Toward the Open Field

Poets on the Art of Poetry, 1800–1950

EDITED BY MELISSA KWASNY

Wesleyan University Press • Middletown, Connecticut

Published by Wesleyan University Press,
Middletown, CT 06459
This collection © 2004 by Wesleyan University Press
Introduction and headnotes © 2004 by Melissa Kwasny
Copyright notices for all other materials are listed
on the permissions page

Printed in the United States of America
Design & Composition by Chris Crochetière,
BW&A Books, Inc., Durham, NC

5   4   3   2   1

Library of Congress Cataloging-in-Publication Data

Toward the open field : poets on the art of poetry,
1800–1950 / edited by Melissa Kwasny.
     p. cm.
Includes bibliographical references (p.).
ISBN 0-8195-6606-3 (alk. paper) —
ISBN 0-8195-6607-1 (pbk. : alk. paper)
1. Poetry—History and criticism.
I. Kwasny, Melissa, 1954–
PN1064.T68 2004
809.1—dc22   2004041913

permissions

for Robert Baker

contents

III. The Poem as a Field of Action, 1918–1950

introduction

Field: where something is planted, where something occurs, a playing field or a scene where the battle is waged, as William Carlos Williams says, "the poem as a field of action."[1] The field can be viewed from without—the field of physics, the field of poetics—or from within—the "verse-field" as identified by Walt Whitman as early as 1891,[2] the open field of composition, the site of the poem itself. This book traces the unfolding of a field poetic in both senses, primarily within the British and the American traditions, from the romantic period through the end of the modernist period in the years immediately following the Second World War. In doing so, it perhaps points to the open field of poetic practice and theory in our own time: the polyphonic, diversified, and—depending on one's viewpoint—playing field or battlefield that is the state of contemporary poetry, characterized by a multitude of experiments in form and subject. The term *open field* can be employed to refer to a poem whose form is determined not by traditional metrical or rhyme schemes but by the development, in one sense or another, of what Stéphane Mallarmé calls an "individual intonation."[3] Here I propose to use it as a general term for a range of modern poetic forms that, from the romantic period on, have been variously designated as organic form, free verse, open form, the prose poem, and the scored page, among many others. These terms all refer to a kind of patterning (at the level of line, syntax, rhythm, diction, even punctuation) shaped not by inherited conventions but rather by the specific demands of the individual poem, or poet, or subject.

This anthology intends to trace a movement *from conventional form to exploratory field,* and to do so, not by presenting the work of literary historians but by collecting some of the important prose works of poets themselves. This is not to disparage the role of critics or to suggest that a poet's interpretation of poetic practice is necessarily truer or more authentic. Indeed, some of these poets—Samuel Taylor Coleridge and T. S. Eliot come first to mind—were among the foremost critics of their time, having a lasting impact on literary criticism. In addition, what poets say they are doing and what they do in their poems are not always the same thing. As Coleridge points out, William Wordsworth does not write in the vernacular of the shepherds or the leech gatherer. "And I reflect with de-

light," he writes, " how little a mere theory, though of his own workman-
ship, interferes with the processes of genuine imagination in a man of true
poetic genius."[4] Nevertheless, these prose works have had substantive impact on the poetry of their time and continue to be relevant, whether for
the insight they provide into a particular poet's decisions, made, for all
practical purposes, in solitude, or for the light they cast on broader cultural movements, as expressed in André Breton's *Manifesto of Surrealism*
or Charles Baudelaire's definition of the dandy.

Form is rarely, if ever, divisible from its content, and so, this collection also
traces the changing notions of what a poem is, what a poet is, and why we
read a poem. Because many of these notions have their origins in the romantic revolution of the late eighteenth and early nineteenth centuries,
the book begins there, in 1802, with Wordsworth's "Preface" to the *Lyrical
Ballads*. It proceeds through a hundred and fifty years of an English-language
tradition—and a few of the European poetries that greatly influenced it
—on its way from the romantic break with the Augustan or neoclassical
poem through the more open forms of the last century. Literary history, of
course, is messy and interpretive. I have not tried to frame a trajectory according to ideas of linearity, of one idea supplanting another, but have
simply ordered the essays in the chronological sequence in which they
were first published. That this places Paul Valéry, traditionally considered
a symbolist, after the *Manifesto of Surrealism* should not so much be cause for
alarm as evidence of the nonlinearity of poetic activity—and the fact that
Valéry stopped writing poetry for twenty years in despair of ever emulating
Mallarmé.

This anthology is intended for poets and students of poetry. It does not
aim to trace a strict line of inheritance, to propose an unfamiliar interpretation of this fairly canonical representation of texts, nor to posit or defend theories of influence. In any art, each generation must make anew
the language so that the world is seen fresh, so that, as Shelley writes,
echoing Coleridge, we may purge "from our inward sight the film of familiarity which obscures from us the wonder of our being."[5] Each age has
its ideals and aspirations which demand new forms of expression. Though
Walt Whitman writes in his preface to *Leaves of Grass* that "the cleanest
expression is that which finds no sphere worthy of itself and makes one,"[6]
this is itself a claim variously repeated throughout the romantic and modernist periods. Everywhere in this collection is the echoing of ideas, an
"*over-and-overing*," to borrow a term from Gerard Manley Hopkins.[7]

These prefaces, introductions, essays, apologies, letters, and manifestos allow the reader to be privy to one of the great extended and now public conversations by poets about the poetry they are writing—or think they are writing—in a dynamic period of literary experimentation.

I. Form as Proceeding, 1802 to 1883

The first part of this book begins with Wordsworth's preface to the 1802 edition of *The Lyrical Ballads,* one of the more famous manifestos in poetry, marking, as it does, the advent of the romantic revolution in English verse. The poems and critical writings of Wordsworth and Coleridge, his coauthor of the *Ballads,* were crucial in the romantic redefinition of poetry and the poet, one which, two hundred years later, is internalized to such an extent that it seems to need little defense. The belief in the need for a simple, common diction, for the poem's rhythm to reflect the sense of the poet thinking and feeling—Wordsworth's "fluxes and refluxes of the mind"[8]—these concepts seem intrinsic to the definition of poetry itself. And the poet? According to Wordsworth, he is a "man speaking to men," and yet, a man more refined, more passionate, more capable of binding "together by passion and knowledge the vast empire of human society."[9] This elevated conception of the poet, now Poet, secularized priest of what John Keats (a generation later) calls "the Powers of the Imagination,"[10] remains rather more common today than one might think.

Although Wordsworth and Coleridge both continued to write in ballad meter and in blank verse—as did Shelley, Keats, Emerson, and Dickinson—something was amiss. Gradually, and then with a surprising suddenness in the middle of the nineteenth century, a range of formal innovations emerged: a loosening of meter in favor of speech rhythms, the abandonment of exact rhyme, a distrust of conventional figurative language, and an increasing emphasis on idiosyncratic patterning, as in Dickinson's use of capitalization, dashes, and off-rhyme, Whitman's breakthrough to free verse, and Hopkins's development of sprung rhythm. Evident in these prose works is how the poets themselves understood the struggle to replace traditional form with a form that proceeds out of their individual concerns.

Form as Proceeding

Coleridge, in 1812, was the first to use the term "organic form" in relation to a poetics that determined its form naturally instead of arbitrarily, what he would define later as "form as proceeding, and. shape as superinduced."[11] In 1855, Walt Whitman also laid claim to poems which would grow "as unerringly and loosely as lilacs or roses on a bush, and take shapes as compact as the shapes of chestnuts and oranges and melons and pears, and shed the perfume impalpable to form."[12] Neither of these poets was against form per se. "The expunging of Augustan by Romantic form," as Donald Wesling states, "was by no means an abandonment of form. Rather, there was a shifting of formal values and an invention of new types of patterning."[13] Dickinson developed a highly idiosyncratic variation on traditional rhythm ("[I] could not drop the Bells whose jingling cooled my Tramp"),[14] while Hopkins spent a lifetime studying other models, in particular from the Anglo-Saxon, and invented an entirely new way of counting stress, one which he named sprung rhythm. That it was a struggle is evidenced by the preoccupation in many of these prose works with analyzing, and trying to justify, meter. Hopkins speaks of unmetered poetry disparagingly, calling it "prose bewitched."[15] (And Mina Loy, forty years later, adopts the phrase as a banner of modernism: "Poetry is prose bewitched.")[16] Wordsworth justifies its use by stating that meter tempers emotion which would otherwise be too unnerving. It would take until 1855 and Walt Whitman's first edition of *Leaves of Grass* for the reins of the pentameter to be loosened.

A form that proceeds naturally rather than arbitrarily tends to put more pressure on the process of the poem's making than a poem in which the form is decided beforehand. It demands a willingness to experiment. The poem has to be able to make its way with a bit of uncertainty, what Keats, in a famous letter, calls" negative capability."[17] What is a poem if it cannot be defined by outward form? It is in this part of the book that we see poets beginning to explore questions of interiority, as well as the imperative to experimentation that it demands. We will see the attempt to define and redefine the poem, often in relation to what it is not. "For it is not metres, but a metre-making argument that makes a poem," Emerson says,[18] while Shelley removes the definition from matters of meter altogether, claiming that anything poetic is a poem and that musicians, painters, even historians are also poets.

"I write in metre," Coleridge says, "because I am about to use a language different from that of prose."[19] If poetry does not have a recognizable form, if it is not written in a different language, what is it that will distinguish it from prose and from the increasingly popular novels of the nineteenth century? This question, and its contradictory answers, surfaces again and again. "No, it is plain that metre, rhythm, rhyme, and all the structure which is called verse both necessitates and engenders a difference in diction and in thought," Hopkins writes in an early essay entitled "Poetic Theory,"[20] while Wordsworth argues in his preface that there can be no essential difference because "the same human blood circulates through the veins of them both."[21]

The Role of the Poet

"What is Poetry?—is so nearly the same question with, what is a poet?—that the answer to the one is involved in the solution of the other," writes Coleridge.[22] The breaking of the pentameter (as Ezra Pound later put it) involved not only a critique of meter or rhythm or placement of the line, but analogously, a fundamental critique of the purpose of making a poem. If one believes in a form underlying form, in the inner dictates of the poem rather than in those dictated by an outside authority, one must begin to rely on an inner authority (self-reliance, individualism, a diffusion and enlargement of the concept of the self). The poet is no longer the wordsmith of old, a teller of traditional stories and aphorism, but an individual in his or her own right, intent on the self's testimony. In Shelley we see an insistence that a poem not function as a moral treatise; he affirms the poem's independence of—and the poet's imaginative freedom from—any external authority of church or state. Emerson claims for the poet almost supernatural authority—"The poet alone knows astronomy, chemistry, vegetation and animation"[23]—as does Keats: "My Imagination is a Monastry and I am its Monk."[24]

The changing role or roles of the poet, inseparable from changing and sometimes conflicting notions of identity, are mapped in the letters and essays of this part. The idea that form should reflect a personal rhythm, shaped by the individual imagination, implies that the poet has a self worthy of giving testimony, of expressing its individual "emotion recollected in tranquility"[25] or disclosing a distinctive vision. And yet, as these essays show, at the same time that the creative self is being celebrated, it is being subtly undermined in ways that anticipate the concerns of later modernist poets. Keats complains about the "wordsworthian or egotistical sublime,"[26] seeking other stances, the most famous of which is the chameleon poet, an image with which Keats figures the poet's capacity to adopt the feelings and concerns of multiple identities. Whitman claims that he contains multitudes. And Hopkins, with whom this section ends, literally embodies the tension between priest and poet, tradition and invention, outer and inner authority; surprisingly, this devout Catholic may in important respects be closer than any of the other poets in this part to the sort of melancholy, ennui, and alienation voiced in Baudelaire's verse and prose.

II. Crise de Vers, 1859 to 1945

"For I bring news—the most amazing and unprecedented news," Stéphane Mallarmé said in a lecture at Oxford in 1894. "We have been experimenting with verse."[27] Although Whitman was known to the French soon after *Leaves of Grass* was published, and Edgar Allen Poe's poetic theories—influenced by his reading of Coleridge—were translated by Charles Baudelaire, the French had already been experimenting with ways of loosening the alexandrine—their own equivalent of the pentameter. Their experiments have had a profound impact on poetry internationally and have proven greatly instructive to the subsequent English language poets of modernism.

Part II contains a small selection of prose works written in languages other than English—predominantly French—by poets whose poems and critical thinking speak to and extend the central concerns of the romantic writers and who here serve as spokesmen for two of the most influential avant-garde movements of the modern period: symbolism and surrealism. The part begins with excerpts from Baudelaire's *The Painter of Modern Life,* an essay that introduces themes common in most of the essays of this period, above all the uncertain role of the poet (and the poem) when confronted with the tragedies of the French Revolution, the rise of industrial capitalism, the overcrowding of the cities, and the growing power of a bourgeois class largely indifferent to art—in short, when confronted with modernity.

A broad gulf in tone separates Whitman's *Leaves of Grass,* published in 1855, and Baudelaire's *Fleurs du Mal,* published two years later. To move from Whitman's sense of possibility to the alienation and, at times, desperation of Baudelaire and his fellow déclassés—including Arthur Rimbaud and Mallarmé—is to recognize a poet at odds with, alienated from his or her culture, a condition that, at the same time, creates a demand for change. Although Mallarmé wrote that "the crisis in poetry lies less in [questions of form] than in certain new states of our poetic mind,"[28] this was a period of extreme experimentation and exploration in form, a period in which the French invented the prose poem as well as their own version of free verse. As Guillaume Apollinaire proclaims in his essay, *The New Spirit and the Poets*, "How could the poet not be interested in these investigations which can lead to new discoveries in thought and lyricism?"[29]

Crisis in Poetry

By 1894, when Mallarmé brought his news to Oxford, the French had already complicated the romantic conundrum of the distinction between verse and prose with the creation of the prose poem. Aloysius Betrand's collection, *Gaspard de la Nuit*, appeared in 1842. Baudelaire began writing the poems which would comprise *Le Spleen de Paris* in 1855 and, although Rimbaud's book of prose poems, *Illuminations*, did not appear until 1886, he was writing them in the 1870s. Breaking the meter was more difficult for the French, writing in a tradition characterized by strict metrical conventions, yet Baudelaire, Mallarmé, Rimbaud, and Laforgue were also the authors of some of the first free verse or vers libre—poems written without traditional end-stopped rhyme and recognizable meter (although it is not the only or most characteristic of the forms they wrote in). Mallarmé in the meantime was utilizing the new technology of typography to score the poem on the page, a practice Apollinaire would name "visual lyricism."[30]

For Mallarmé, who called ordinary speech "no more than a commercial approach to reality,"[31] the turn to experimentation was also a turning away from the everyday understanding of communication as a simple "exchange of" or "commerce in" words. Symbolism, the movement he was eventually to represent more "purely" than any other poet of his time, renounces mere description or representation of material reality in favor of symbols that might evoke or suggest the mystery of the invisible world of spirit. "It is not *description* which can unveil the efficacy and beauty of monuments, seas, or the human face in all their maturity and native state, but rather evocation, *allusion, suggestion*," Mallarmé writes.[32] The symbolists' aim was to develop a "pure poetry," distinguishable in diction and intention from the basic impurity of human speech, "a language within a language," as Valéry claims,[33] and one that would, in its emphasis on interior form and abstraction, pattern itself after music, whether the Wagnerian opera that fascinated the French symbolists or the Andalusian flamenco loved by Federico García Lorca. As Walter Pater—an English symbolist who had a significant influence on the young Eliot and Pound—wrote *in The Renaissance:* "All art aspires to the condition of music."[34]

The growing belief in "this poem which is a poem and nothing more—this poem written solely for the poem's sake" (as Edgar Allen Poe wrote in "The Poetic Principle,"[35] an essay of great importance to Baudelaire) would refocus the poet's attention on the formal, rather than didactic, elements of the poem itself, an emphasis that would contribute to a new philosophy of aestheticism, an insistence on *l'art pour l'art* (art for art's sake). Valéry's story about the conversation between Mallarmé and Edgar Degas is emblematic; having listened to the painter tell of how he always had had ideas for a poem but had never been able to write one, Mallarmé responds by saying that poems are made not of ideas but of words.[36] This emphasis on the linguistic substance of the poem later comes to be echoed by Williams Carlos Willams, perhaps the most decidedly antisymbolist of all modernist poets: "A poem is a small (or large) machine made of words."[37] This heightened concern to "free" the poem from traditional "descriptive" and "mimetic" tasks is expressed by poets of radically different orientations throughout this entire (symbolist, modernist, avant-gardist) period.

In many of these essays, there is an increasing scrutiny and analysis of the process of making a poem, and a searching for ways in which the writing of a poem could break the bounds of linear thought and instead become a means of exploration or self-discovery or liberation. "Poetry became an adventure," Aimé Césaire proclaims. "At the end of the road: clairvoyance and knowledge."[38] Toward this aim, Rimbaud calls for a "long, prodigious, and rational *disordering* of *all the senses*."[39] Lorca courts the *duende*, a source of inspiration not to be called on externally as one would a muse, but which must be "roused in the very cells of the blood."[40] The surrealist experiments with automatic writing and collage were concerned with devel-

oping new processes by which the poet could move outside not only traditional forms of art but also traditional forms of thought, accessing dream,
chance, and the unconscious. "If the depths of our mind contain within it
strange forces capable of augmenting those on the surface," Breton writes in
his *Manifesto of Surrealism*, "there is every reason to seize them."[41]

The Role of the Poet

In his essay "The Painter of Modern Life," Baudelaire postulates a role
for the modern poet in terms of the artist Constantin Guys. Guys is characterized as a flaneur who, much like Whitman, throws himself into the
midst of the modern crowd and yet, keeps himself aloof from it. "Observer, philosopher, *flâneur*,"[42] the poet as imagined by Baudelaire differs
from Wordsworth's "man speaking to men" by the distance he or she
keeps from them; in this way, the flaneur is also a member of an elite, not
an isolated prophet or a lonely visionary—the typical romantic stance—
but an artist, a dandy, an aristocrat by virtue of sensitivity, as well as by an
"air of coldness which comes from an unshakeable determination not to
be moved."[43] Consequently, Baudelaire's modern artist is also an aesthete
who views his or her life as a work of art, contemplating the crowd merely
as material. For the artist is, as well, a craftsman, concerned with a knowledge of the processes and materials of art.

And yet the flaneur is not solipsistic; he or she is a keen observer of
modern life, more akin to Keats's chameleon poet than a "wordsworthian
or egotistical sublime." With ironic detachment from the world paradoxically comes a weakening of the self, a kind of impersonality or depersonalization that appears in many of these essays. Baudelaire writes that he is
"an 'I' with an insatiable appetite for the 'not-I'";[44] Rimbaud says, "Car Je
est un autre" (For I is someone else);[45] and Mallarmé, though not at all
interested in representing modern life, seeks the loss of self in the mysterious movements of language itself: "If the poem is to be pure, the poet's
voice must be stilled and the initiative taken by the words themselves."[46]
In an effort to inhabit the voice—or voices—of the not-I, to still the voice
of personality, these poets adopt many masks, from Baudelaire's flaneur
and Rimbaud's personae through Lorca's singer overcome with *duende*,
with the spirit of the music itself.

III. The Poem as a Field of Action, 1918 to 1950

The modern poem, Wallace Stevens wrote, is "the poem of the mind in the act of finding / what will suffice. It has not always had / To find: the scene was set; it repeated what / Was in the script."[47] By the end of World War I, the script was gone. In 1922, the year that Breton was declaring Dada dead and announcing the birth of surrealism, T. S. Eliot was publishing *The Wasteland,* editions of Ezra Pound's *Cantos* had begun to appear, and William Carlos Williams had published *Kora in Hell.* These highly experimental poems, along with those of H.D., Richard Aldington, Wyndham Lewis, and many others would establish the Anglo strain of what has come to be called modernism.

Many of the concerns of the French symbolists and surrealist movements would carry over into the poetry of the English modernists: extreme prosodic experimentation and an intense analysis of the means and processes of making a poem, of the formal aspects of language itself. Imagism, vorticism, objectivism, in these movements, like the continental movements beforehand, is evident the question of what constitutes poetic form when traditional form is gone, and consequently, an increasing scrutiny placed on those tools of expression other than meter and rhyme: image, voice, line, word, down to, in Gertrude Stein, the function of parts of speech, and of punctuation.

In an effort to, as Louis Zukofsky said, 'think clearly then about poetry"[48] in the aftermath of a catastrophic world war and the signs of an impending second one, the growth of fascism and pervasive economic crisis, and an increasing alienation of the individual from society, these essays place an emphasis not only on the field where the world and the imagination intersect—in the poem—but also in what come to be divergent definitions of the real. In a rapidly changing world, the poet, too, must be redefined and reinvented. There is a distrust of the individual testimony of the romantic soul, and a further unfolding of the symbolist emphasis on poetic "impersonality," as Eliot calls it,[49] an often fragmentary voice—and often voices—which would speak *through* the poem for the depersonalized voices of the modern age. What will suffice? "Nothing is good save the new," writes William Carlos Williams,[50] and yet, in these essays we also see conflicting stances toward the new, from Eliot's defense of European literary tradition to Langston Hughes's repudiation of it, from Marianne Moore's pairing of feeling and precision to Olson's praise of progress and speed.

The Poem as a Field of Action

The section begins with Pound's "A Retrospect," a compilation of essays and notes, some of which had appeared previously, which was published in 1918, five years after imagism had been "created" by Pound, H.D., and Richard Aldington. "To break the pentameter, that was the first heave," Pound will write later in *The Cantos*,[51] but at this point he is just as concerned (as were other modernist poets) with the tendency of free verse to become "as prolix and verbose as any of the flaccid varieties that preceded it."[52] Imagism was a movement in which clear, precise, direct images were to lend to a poem in free verse the sort of structure once supplied by meter and rhyme. Further, the imagist poem, as defined by Pound, was without ornament, without extra words, and without metaphor per se. ("The natural object is always the *adequate* symbol.")[53] The imagist poem, then, aimed for concreteness, economy, and directness; the emphasis on "objectivity" was proposed as a corrective to the excessive "subjectivity" of romantic and postromantic poetry.

Indeed, the qualities of the imagist poem would inform much of subsequent modernist poetry. "*Impossible* to communicate anything but particulars,"[54] Zukofsky writes in his 1931 essay on objectivism, a name that later came to define a group of American poets which included Zukofsky, Charles Reznikoff, George Oppen, Lorine Niedecker, Carl Rakosi, and, to some extent, William Carlos Williams. (Basil Bunting, an English poet, is often associated with this group as well.) "Thinking with the things as they exist," Zukofsky writes,[55] and even Wallace Stevens, whose poems are completely unlike those of the objectivists, claims that "The imagination loses vitality as it ceases to adhere to what is real."[56]

If form is no longer imposed from without, how then does it manifest? The pressure of the real often makes itself heard, in this selection of essays, as an insistence not only on the concrete image but on changing notions of rhythm, in particular on alternative yet concrete ways to measure it. Williams and Hughes search for rhythms determined by speech and the particularly American rhythms of blues and jazz. Hughes, like many of the poets writing in the Harlem Renaissance of the 1910s through 1930s, uses dialect, aiming to capture the lively vernacular of African American people on the streets of New York, and he frames many of his poems as blues songs. Olson proposes a way to measure the line by the breath. And Stein suggests the poet go by way of "the inner life of sentences and paragraphs,"[57] the developing syntactical energies of the poem as it is being written. This attention to the formal aspects of the poem sometimes emerges as a kind of constructivism—the viewing of the poem as an object, a machine, a mechanism that is made, and yet processual, too, the poem as a register of heightened perception. "This object in process," Zukofsky writes, "The poem as a job."[58]

This new kind of poem as job to be accomplished—or discovery to be enacted—demands from the poet a new level of awareness at the minute sites where the poet makes his or her decisions, during the very process of the writing of the poem. Thus, the poem, in many of these essays, is posited not as a representation of reality, but as its own reality. The poems become, as Charles Altieri writes, presentations, not representations, "in other words, become something like physical correlates for the nature of consciousness."[59] Composition by field, Olson calls it, where the poet "can go by no track other than the one the poem under hand declares, for itself."[60] Or as Zukofsky says, poems are "acts upon particulars."[61]

Many of these poets were already experimenting with forms that would cross the boundary between prose and poetry that so preoccupied many of the previous poets in this collection. Pound, Eliot, Williams, Zukofsky, and Olson all included prose or prosaic elements in their longer works. Marianne Moore's poems written in syllabics often undermined poetic rhythm in sentences that sound similar to prose. The prose poem entered American poetry with Stein's *Tender Buttons*, published in 1914, and Williams's *Kora in Hell*, published in 1920. In fact, Stein begins the lecture included here with the question itself: what is poetry and what is prose? For her, the difference is reduced to the level of parts of speech: poetry having to do with nouns and prose with verbs, with poetry "really loving the name of anything."[62]

The Role of the Poet

In the third part of this volume, the romantic conception of the poet as visionary or prophet, of individual soul crying out its testimony, often transforms into a view of the poet as master craftsman, orchestrator of multiple voices, creator of necessary and supreme fictions. The use of personae and collages made of (often disjunctive) images and quotations appears in the work of many of these poets, so that often—passages in Eliot, Pound, Stevens, Moore, Williams, and Zukofsky come to mind—the "I" which was so important in romantic testimony literally disappears. What replaces it is the sense of a wider ranging, more dispersed identity cast across literary and political history, whether in the ancient courts of Confucius or the streets and cabarets of New York's Harlem, "the direct response," Mina Loy writes, "of the poet's mind to the modern world of varieties in which he finds himself."[63]

Like Baudelaire's dandy or Breton's surrealist, the modern poet of these essays is often alienated from the dominant culture and formulating his or her role in opposition to it—one thinks of Hughes, doubly alienated by virtue of being a poet and being black—preoccupied, and in conflicting relationship with, the intersection of the world and the poem. Hughes, Eliot, Loy, Pound, and Zukofsky were all formal innovators *and* passionately engaged with the politics of their times. "What I want to emphasize," Williams writes in a late "Statement" on measure for Cid Corman, "is that I do not consider anything I have put down there as final. There will be other experiments but all will be directed toward the discovery of a new measure, I repeat, a new measure by which may be ordered our poems as well as our lives."[64] Whether that new measure comes from the voice of the disenfranchised—"the eternal tom-tom beating in the Negro soul"[65]—or an imagination which has "lived all of the last two thousand years,"[66] there is an insistence that the new poet must be in the world, "not a charioteer," as Stevens writes, "traversing vacant space."[67]

The emphasis on the real is inseparable from this sense of commitment, this effort to get the poem away from romantic solipsism and back to the concrete realities of objects and people and places. Eliot calls for a late symbolist "Impersonal theory of poetry," likening the poet to the sliver of platinum that acts as catalyst in the reaction needed to make sulfuric acid, a catalyst, however, that remains "unmoved" by the process.[68] "Objectivism," Olson writes, "is the getting rid of the lyrical interference of the individual as ego. . . . For a man is himself an object . . in a larger field of objects."[69]

✳

"If one thinks of the literal root of the word verse, 'a line, furrow, turning—*vertere*, to turn . . . ,' he will come to a sense of 'free verse' as that instance of writing in poetry which 'turns' upon an occasion intimate with, in fact, the issue of, its own nature," writes Robert Creeley in an essay first published in 1969, where this anthology ends.[70] Indeed, for poets it is no longer possible to avoid making a decision about form, a decision that is personal and at the same time informed by the history of poetics, whether that decision is to employ traditional forms or not. After 1950, the field explodes with new visions, new forms, and new roles for the poet. In fact, when we, as Stevens did, attempt to "construct the figure of a poet, a possible poet,"[71] the figure will include those who are not men, who are not white or European, who are not heterosexual or privileged by class as many of the poets in this collection were.

Black Mountain, the New York School, the San Francisco Renaissance and the Beats, the Black Arts movement, the feminist work of poets such as Adrienne Rich and Audre Lorde, Deep Image, language poetry, performance poetry: the currents of exploration delineated in this anthology, often serving as points of departure and contention, have been further unfolded, questioned, and complicated in these more recent poetries. The process of discovery, the movement of invention, is after all the very spirit of these currents in modern poetry: "The poem of the mind in the act of finding / What will suffice."[72] The poet of each age travels outside the established literary conventions to gather those concrete materials and speech patterns which promise to reanimate the power and relevance of poetry, perhaps, as Rimbaud said, to "define the amount of the unknown awakening in the universal soul of his time."[73] It is the great gift of these prose works that in them we can eavesdrop on the process.

ENDNOTES

1. William Carlos Williams. "The Poem as a Field of Action," in *Selected Essays* (New York: New Directions, 1954), 280.

2. Walt Whitman, *Leaves of Grass and Other Writings,* edited by Michael Moon (New York: Norton, 2002), 451.

3. Stéphane Mallarmé, "Music and Literature," in *Selected Prose Poems, Essays and Letters,* translated by Bradford Cook (Baltimore: John Hopkins University Press, 1956), 44.

4. Samuel Taylor Coleridge, *Biographia Literaria; or, Biographical Sketches of*

My Literary Life and Opinions, edited by John Calvin Metcalf (New York: Macmillan, 1926), 228.

5. Percy Bysshe Shelley, "A Defence of Poetry," in *Shelley's Defence of Poetry / Browning's Essay on Shelley,* edited by L. Winstanley (Boston: D. C. Heath, 1911), 53.

6. Walt Whitman, "Preface to the 1855 Edition of *Leaves of Grass,*" in *Collected Poems and Selected Prose,* edited by James E. Miller Jr. (Boston: Houghton Mifflin, 1959), 418.

7. Gerard Manley Hopkins, "Poetry and Verse," in *The Notebooks and Papers of Gerard Manley Hopkins,* edited by Humphry House (Oxford: Oxford University Press, 1937), 249.

8. William. Wordsworth, *Lyrical Ballads: The Text of the 1789 Edition with the Additional 1800 Poems and the Prefaces,* edited by R. L. Brett and A. R. Jones (London: Methuen, 1965), 247.

9. Wordsworth, 259.

10. John Keats, *Letters of John Keats,* edited by Robert Gittings (Oxford: Oxford University Press, 1970), 27.

11. Samuel Taylor Coleridge, "On Poesy or Art," in *Biographia Literaria with Aesthetic Essays,* edited by J. Shawcross (London: Oxford University Press, 1907), 262.

12. Whitman, "Preface," 415.

13. Donald Wesling, *The New Poetics: Poetic Form since Coleridge and Wordsworth* (Lewisburg: Bucknell University Press, 1985).

14. Emily Dickinson, *Letters of Emily Dickinson,* edited by Thomas H. Johnson (Cambridge, Mass.: Harvard University Press, 1986), 408.

15. Gerard Manley Hopkins, "To Robert Bridges," in *A Hopkins Reader,* edited by John Pick (Garden City: Image, 1966), 175.

16. Mina Loy, *The Lost Lunar Baedeker,* edited by Roger L. Conover (New York: Noonday, 1996), 157.

17. Keats, 43.

18. Ralph Waldo Emerson, "The Poet," in *The Selected Writings of Ralph Waldo Emerson* (New York: Modern Library, 1992), 290.

19. Coleridge, 236.

20. Hopkins, "Poetic Theory," in *A Hopkins Reader,* 136.

21. Wordsworth, 254.

22. Coleridge, 197.

23. Emerson, 296.

24. Keats, 390.

25. Wordsworth, 266.

26. Keats, 157.

27. Mallarmé, 44.

28. Stéphane Mallarmé, "Crisis in Poetry," in *Selected Prose Poems, Essays and Letters*, 39.

29. Guillaume Apollinaire, "The New Spirit and the Poets," in *Selected Writings*, translated by Roger Shattuck (New York: New Directions, 1971), 227.

30. Apollinaire, 228.

31. Stéphane Mallarmé, "Crisis in Poetry," 34.

32. Ibid., 40.

33. Paul Valéry, "Poetry and Abstract Thought," in *The Art of Poetry*, translated by Denise Folliot (Princeton: Princeton University Press, 1989), 148.

34. Walter Pater, *The Renaissance: Studies in Art and Poetry*, edited by Donald E. Hill (Berkeley: University of California Press, 1980), 106.

35. Edgar Allen Poe, "The Poetic Principle," in *Works of Edgar Allen Poe*, vol. 4 (New York: Harper, 1849), 7.

36. Valéry, 147.

37. Williams, "Author's Introduction, to *The Wedge*," 256.

38. Aimé Césaire, "Poetry and Knowledge," translated by A. James Arnold, in *Lyric and Dramatic Poetry* (Charlottesville: University of Virginia Press, 1990), xlii–lvi.

39. Arthur Rimbaud, *Collected Poems*, translated by Oliver Bernard (New York: Penguin, 1962), 10.

40. Federico García Lorca, "Theory and Function of the Duende," *in Poetics of the New American Poetry*, edited by Donald Allen and Warren Tallman (New York: Grove Press, 1973), 93.

41. André Breton, "Manifesto of Surrealism," in *Manifestoes of Surrealism*, translated by Richard Seaver and Helen R. Lane (Ann Arbor: University of Michigan Press, 1972), 10.

42. Charles Baudelaire, *The Painter of Modern Life and Other Essays*, translated by Jonathan Mayne (New York: DaCapo Press, 1986), 4.

43. Ibid., 29.

44. Ibid., 9.

45. Rimbaud, 6.

46. Mallarmé, "Crisis in Poetry," 40.

47. Wallace Stevens, " Of Modern Poetry," in *The Palm at the End of the Mind* (New York: Vintage, 1990), 174.

48. Louis Zukofsky, "Poetry," in *Prepositions +: The Collected Critical Essays* (Middletown, Conn.: Wesleyan University Press, 2000), 7.

49. T. S. Eliot, "Tradition and the Individual Talent," in *Selected Essays* (New York: Harcourt, Brace and World, 1960), 11.

50. Williams, "Prologue to Kora in Hell," 21.

51. Ezra Pound, *The Cantos of Ezra Pound* (New York: New Directions, 1971), 538.

52. Ezra Pound, "A Retrospect," in *Literary Essays,* edited by T. S. Eliot (New York: New Directions, 1968), 3.

53. Ibid., 5.

54. Zukofsky, "An Objective," 24.

55. Ibid., 20.

56. Wallace Stevens, "The Noble Rider and the Sound of Words," in *The Necessary Angel: Essays on Reality and the Imagination* (New York: Vintage, 1951), 6.

57. Gertrude Stein, "Poetry and Grammar," in *Lectures in America* (New York: Vintage, 1975), 222.

58. Zukofsky, "An Objective," 23.

59. Charles Altieri, "What Modernism Offers the Contemporary Poet," in *What Is a Poet,.* edited by Hank Lazer (Tuscaloosa: University of Alabama Press, 1987), 53.

60. Charles Olson, "Projective Verse," in *Selected Writings,* edited by Robert Creeley (New York: New Directions, 1966), 16.

61. Zukofsky, "An Objective," 26.

62. Stein, 232.

63. Loy, 158.

64. Williams, "On Measure and Statement for Cid Corman," 340.

65. Langston Hughes, "The Negro Artist and the Racial Mountain," in *The Nation,* June 23, 1926.

66. Stevens, "The Noble Rider," 23.

67. Ibid..

68. Eliot, 7.

69. Olson, 24.

70. Robert Creeley, "A Note Apropos Free Verse," in *Collected Essays of Robert Creeley* (Berkeley: University of California Press, 1989), 492.

71. Stevens, "The Noble Rider," 23.

72. Stevens, "Of Modern Poetry," 174.

73. Rimbaud, 13.

Toward the Open Field

I. Form as Proceeding
1802–1883

William Wordsworth, "Preface" to the Second Edition of *The Lyrical Ballads*, 1802

When *The Lyrical Ballads*, containing poems by William Wordsworth and Samuel Taylor Coleridge, was first published anonymously in 1798, it met with widespread condemnation and parody. The poems, which included such important work as Wordsworth's "Lines" ("Tintern Abbey") and Coleridge's *Rime of the Ancient Mariner*, were thought of as anti-classical and even vulgar in their choice of common subjects and ordinary themes and in their claim for a diction stripped of high-blown poeticisms and arbitrary form (one parody, a ballad entitled "Goody Grizzle and her Ass," was signed "Rusticus"). When the *Ballads* were reprinted in 1800, Wordsworth included a preface as their defense, and, in 1802, expanded it to include his answer to the question "What is a Poet?" The "Preface" is considered the first manifesto of romanticism in English.

❋

Preface

The First Volume of these Poems has already been submitted to general perusal. It was published, as an experiment, which, I hoped, might be of some use to ascertain, how far, by fitting to metrical arrangement a selection of the real language of men in a state of vivid sensation, that sort of pleasure and that quantity of pleasure may be imported, which a Poet may rationally endeavour to impart.

I had formed no very inaccurate estimate of the probable effect of those Poems: I flattered myself that they who should be pleased with them would read them with more than common pleasure: and on the other hand, I was well aware, that by those who should dislike them they would be read with more than common dislike. The result has differed from my expectation in this only, that I have pleased a greater number, than I ventured to hope I should please.

For the sake of variety, and from a consciousness of my own weakness,

I was induced to request the assistance of a Friend, who furnished me with the Poems of the ANCIENT MARINER, the FOSTER-MOTHER'S TALE, the NIGHTINGALE, the DUNGEON, and the poem entitled LOVE. I should not, however, have requested this assistance, had I not believed that the Poems of my Friend would in a great measure have the same tendency as my own, and that, though there would be found a difference, there would be found no discordance in the colours of our style; as our opinions on the subject of poetry do almost entirely coincide.

Several of my Friends are anxious for the success of these Poems from a belief, that, if the views with which they were composed were indeed realized, a class of Poetry would be produced, well adapted to interest mankind permanently, and not unimportant in the multiplicity, and in the quality of its moral relations: and on this account they have advised me to prefix a systematic defence of the theory, upon which the poems were written. But I was unwilling to undertake the task, because, I knew that on this occasion the Reader would look coldly upon my arguments, since I might be suspected of having been principally influenced by the selfish and foolish hope of *reasoning* him into an approbation of these particular Poems: and I was still more unwilling to undertake the task, because adequately to display my opinions, and fully to enforce my arguments would require a space wholly disproportionate to the nature of a preface. For to treat the subject with the clearness and coherence, of which I believe it susceptible, it would be necessary to give a full account of the present state of the public taste in this country, and to determine how far this taste is healthy or depraved; which, again, could not be determined, without pointing out, in what manner language and the human mind act and react on each other, and without retracing the revolutions, not of literature alone, but likewise of society itself. I have therefore altogether declined to enter regularly upon this defence; yet I am sensible, that there would be some impropriety in abruptly obtruding upon the Public, without a few words of introduction, Poems so materially different from those, upon which general approbation is at present bestowed.

It is supposed, that by the act of writing in verse an Author makes a formal engagement that he will gratify certain known habits of association; that he not only thus apprizes the Reader that certain classes of ideas and expressions will be found in his book, but that others will be carefully excluded. This exponent or symbol held forth by metrical language must in different æras of literature have excited very different expectations: for example, in the age of Catullus, Terence, and Lucretius and that of Statius or Claudian; and in our own country, in the age of Shakespeare and Beaumont and Fletcher, and that of Donne and Cowley, or Dryden, or Pope. I will not take upon me to determine the exact import of the promise which by the act of writing in verse an Author, in the present day, makes to his Reader; but I am certain it will appear to many persons that I have not fulfilled the terms of an engagement thus voluntarily contracted. They who have been accustomed to the gaudiness and inane phraseology of many modern writers, if they persist in reading this book to its conclusion, will, no doubt, frequently have to struggle with feelings of strangeness and awkwardness: they will look round for poetry, and will be induced to inquire by what species of courtesy these attempts can be permitted to assume that title. I hope therefore the Reader will not censure me, if I attempt to state what I have proposed to myself to perform; and also, (as far as the limits of a preface will permit) to explain some of the chief reasons which have determined me in the choice of my purpose: that at least he may be spared any unpleasant feeling of disappointment, and that I myself may be protected from the most dishonorable accusation which can be brought against an Author, namely, that of an indolence which prevents him from endeavouring to ascertain what is his duty, or, when his duty is ascertained, prevents him from performing it.

The principal object, then, which I proposed to myself in these Poems was to chuse incidents and situations from common life, and to relate or describe them, throughout, as far as was possible, in a selection of language really used by men; and, at the same time, to throw over them a certain colouring of imagination, whereby ordinary things should be presented to the mind in an unusual way; and further, and above all, to make these incidents and situations interesting by tracing in them, truly though not ostentatiously, the primary laws of our nature: chiefly as far as regards the manner in which we associate ideas in a state of excitement. Low and rustic life was generally chosen, because in that condition, the essential passions of the heart find a better soil in which they can attain their maturity, are less under restraint, and speak a plainer and more emphatic language; because in that condition of life our elementary feelings co-exist in a state of greater simplicity, and consequently may be more accurately contemplated, and more forcibly communicated; because the manners of rural life germinate from those elementary feelings; and from the necessary character of rural occupations, are more easily comprehended; and are more durable; and lastly, because in that condition the passions of men are incorporated with the beautiful and permanent forms of nature. The language, too, of these men is adopted (purified indeed from what appear to be its real defects, from all lasting and rational causes of dislike or disgust) because such men hourly communicate with the best objects from which the best part of language is originally derived; and because, from their rank in society and the sameness and narrow circle of their intercourse, being less under the influence of social vanity they convey their feelings and notions in simple and unelaborated expressions. Accordingly, such a language, arising out of repeated experience and regular feelings, is a more permanent, and a far more philosophical language, than that which is frequently substituted for it by Poets, who think that they are conferring honour upon themselves and their art, in proportion as they separate themselves from the sympathies of men, and indulge in arbitrary and capricious habits of expression, in order to furnish food for fickle tastes, and fickle appetites, of their own creation.*

I cannot, however, be insensible of the present outcry against the triviality and meanness both of thought and language, which some of my contemporaries have occasionally introduced into their metrical compositions; and I acknowledge, that this defect, where it exists, is more dishonorable to the Writer's own character than false refinement or arbitrary innovation, though I should contend at the same time that it is far less pernicious in the sum of its consequences. From such verses the Poems in these volumes will be found distinguished at least by one mark of difference, that each of them has a worthy *purpose*. Not that I mean to say, that I always began to write with a distinct purpose formally conceived; but I believe that my habits of meditation have so formed my feelings, as that my descriptions of such objects as strongly excite those feelings, will be found to carry along with them a *purpose*. If in this opinion I am mistaken, I can have little right to the name of a Poet. For all good poetry is the spontaneous overflow of powerful feelings; but though this be true, Poems to which any value can be attached, were never produced on any variety of subjects but by a man who, being possessed of more than unusual organic sensibility, had also thought long and deeply. For our con-

---

*It is worth while here to observe that the affecting parts of Chaucer are almost always expressed in language pure and universally intelligible even to this day.

tinued influxes of feeling are modified and directed by our thoughts, which are indeed the representatives of all our past feelings; and, as by contemplating the relation of these general representatives to each other we discover what is really important to men, so, by the repetition and continuance of this act, our feelings will be connected with important subjects, till at length, if we be possessed of much sensibility, such habits of mind will be produced, that, by obeying blindly and mechanically the impulses of those habits, we shall describe objects, and utter sentiments, of such a nature and in such connection with each other, that the under-standing of the being to whom we address ourselves, if he be in a health-ful state of association, must necessarily be in some degree enlightened, and his affections ameliorated.

❈

I have said that each of these poems has a purpose. I have also informed my Reader what this purpose will be found principally to be: namely to il-lustrate the manner in which our feelings and ideas are associated in a state of excitement. But, speaking in language somewhat more appropri-ate, it is to follow the fluxes and refluxes of the mind when agitated by the great and simple affections of our nature. This object I have endeavoured in these short essays to attain by various means; by tracing the maternal passion through many of its more subtle windings, as in the poems of the IDIOT BOY and the MAD MOTHER; by accompanying the last struggles of a human being, at the approach of death, cleaving in solitude to life and society, as in the Poem of the FORSAKEN INDIAN; by shewing, as in the Stanzas entitled WE ARE SEVEN, the perplexity and obscurity which in childhood attend our notion of death, or rather our utter inability to admit that notion; or by displaying the strength of fraternal, or to speak more philosophically, of moral attachment when early associated with the great and beautiful objects of nature, as in THE BROTHERS; or, as in the incident of SIMON LEE, by placing my Reader in the way of receiving from ordinary moral sensations another and more salutary impression than we are accustomed to receive from them. It has also been part of my general purpose to attempt to sketch characters under the influence of less impassioned feelings, as in the two April mornings, the Fountain, the OLD MAN TRAVELLING, THE TWO THIEVES, &c. characters of which the elements are simple, belonging rather to nature than to manners, such as exist now, and will probably always exist, and which from their constitution may be distinctly and profitably contemplated. I will not abuse the indulgence of my Reader by dwelling longer upon this subject; but it is proper that I should mention one other circumstance which distinguishes these Poems from the popular Poetry of the day; it is this, that the feeling therein developed gives importance to the action and situation, and not the action and situation to the feeling. My meaning will be rendered perfectly intelligible by referring my Reader to the Poems entitled POOR SUSAN and the CHILDLESS FATHER, particularly to the last Stanza of the latter Poem.

❋

I will not suffer a sense of false modesty to prevent me from asserting, that I point my Reader's attention to this mark of distinction, far less for the sake of these particular Poems than from the general importance of the subject. The subject is indeed important! For the human mind is capable of being excited without the application of gross and violent stimulants; and he must have a very faint perception of its beauty and dignity who does not know this, and who does not further know, that one being is elevated above another, in proportion as he possesses this capability. It has therefore appeared to me, that to endeavour to produce or enlarge this capability is one of the best services in which, at any period, a Writer can be engaged; but this service, excellent at all times, is especially so at the present day. For a multitude of causes, unknown to former times, are now acting with a combined force to blunt the discriminating powers of the mind, and unfitting it for all voluntary exertion to reduce it to a state of almost savage torpor. The most effective of these causes are the great national events which are daily taking place, and the encreasing accumulation of men in cities, where the uniformity of their occupations produces a craving for extraordinary incident, which the rapid communication of intelligence hourly gratifies. To this tendency of life and manners the literature and theatrical exhibitions of the country have conformed themselves. The invaluable works of our elder writers, I had almost said the works of Shakespear and Milton, are driven into neglect by frantic novels, sickly and stupid German Tragedies, and deluges of idle and extravagant stories in verse.–When I think upon this degrading thirst after outrageous stimulation, I am almost ashamed to have spoken of the feeble effort with which I have endeavoured to counteract it; and, reflecting upon the magnitude of the general evil, I should be oppressed with no dishonorable melancholy, had I not a deep impression of certain inherent and indestructible qualities of the human mind, and likewise of certain powers in the great and permanent objects that act upon it which are equally inherent and indestructible; and did I not further add to this impression a belief, that the time is approaching when the evil will be systematically opposed, by men of greater powers, and with far more distinguished success.

❋

Having dwelt thus long on the subjects and aim of these Poems, I shall request the Reader's permission to apprize him of a few circumstances relating to their *style*, in order, among other reasons, that I may not be censured for not having performed what I never attempted. The Reader will find that personifications of abstract ideas rarely occur in these volumes; and, I hope, are utterly rejected as an ordinary device to elevate the style, and raise it above prose. I have proposed to myself to imitate, and, as far as is possible, to adopt the very language of men; and assuredly such personifications do not make any natural or regular part of that language. They are, indeed, a figure of speech occasionally prompted by passion, and I have made use of them as such; but I have endeavoured utterly to reject them as a mechanical device of style, or as a family language which Writers in metre seem to lay claim to by prescription. I have wished to keep my Reader in the company of flesh and blood, persuaded that by so doing I shall interest him. I am, however, well aware that others who pursue a different track may interest him likewise; I do not interfere with their claim, I only wish to prefer a different claim of my own. There will also be found in these volumes little of what is usually called poetic diction; I have taken as much pains to avoid it as others ordinarily take to produce it; this I have done for the reason already alleged, to bring my language near to the language of men, and further, because the pleasure which I have proposed to myself to impart is of a kind very different from that which is supposed by many persons to be the proper object of poetry. I do not know how without being culpably particular I can give my Reader a more exact notion of the style in which I wished these poems to be written than by informing him that I have at all times endeavoured to look steadily at my subject, consequently, I hope that there is in these Poems little falsehood of description, and that my ideas are expressed in language fitted to their respective importance. Something I must have gained by this practice, as it is friendly to one property of all good poetry, namely, good sense; but it has necessarily cut me off from a large portion of phrases and figures of speech which from father to son have long been regarded as the common inheritance of Poets. I have also thought it expedient to restrict myself still further, having abstained from the use of many expressions, in themselves proper and beautiful, but which have been foolishly repeated by bad Poets, till such feelings of disgust are connected with them as it is scarcely possibly by any art of association to overpower.

❋

If in a Poem there should be found a series of lines, or even a single line, in which the language, though naturally arranged and according to the strict laws of metre, does not differ from that of prose, there is a numerous class of critics, who, when they stumble upon these prosaisms as they call them, imagine that they have made a notable discovery, and exult over the Poet as over a man ignorant of his own profession. Now these men would establish a canon of criticism which the Reader will conclude he must utterly reject, if he wishes to be pleased with these volumes. And it would be a most easy task to prove to him, that not only the language of a large portion of every good poem, even of the most elevated character, must necessarily, except with reference to the metre, in no respect differ from that of good prose, but likewise that some of the most interesting parts of the best poems will be found to be strictly the language of prose, when prose is well written. The truth of this assertion might be demonstrated by innumerable passages from almost all the poetical writings, even of Milton himself. I have not space for much quotation; but, to illustrate the subject in a general manner, I will here adduce a short composition of Gray, who was at the head of those who by their reasonings have attempted to widen the space of separation betwixt Prose and Metrical composition, and was more than any other man curiously elaborate in the structure of his own poetic diction.

> In vain to me the smiling mornings shine,
> And reddening Phoebus lifts his golden fire:

The birds in vain their amorous descant join,
Or chearful fields resume their green attire:
These ears alas! for other notes repine;
A different object do these eyes require;
My lonely anguish melts no heart but mine;
And in my breast the imperfect joys expire;
Yet Morning smiles the busy race to cheer,
And new-born pleasure brings to happier men;
The fields to all their wonted tribute bear;
To warm their little loves the birds complain.
I fruitless mourn to him that cannot hear
And weep the more because I weep in vain.

It will easily be perceived that the only part of this Sonnet which is of any value is the lines printed in Italics: it is equally obvious, that, except in the rhyme, and in the use of the single word "fruitless" for fruitlessly, which is so far a defect, the language of these lines does in no respect differ from that of prose.

By the foregoing quotation I have shewn that the language of Prose may yet be well adapted to Poetry; and I have previously asserted that a large portion of the language of every good poem can in no respect differ from that of good Prose. I will go further. I do not doubt that it may be safely affirmed, that there neither is, nor can be, any essential difference between the language of prose and metrical composition. We are fond of tracing the resemblance between Poetry and Painting, and accordingly, we call them Sisters: but where shall we find bonds of connection sufficiently strict to typify the affinity betwixt metrical and prose composition? They both speak by and to the same organs; the bodies in which both of them are clothed may be said to be of the same substance, their affections are kindred and almost identical, not necessarily differing even in degree;* Poetry sheds no tears "such as Angels weep," but natural and

---

*I here use the word "Poetry" (though against my own judgment) as opposed to the word Prose, and synonomous with metrical composition. But much confusion has been introduced into criticism by this contradistinction of Poetry and Prose, instead of the more philosophical one of Poetry and Matter of fact, or Science. The only strict antithesis to Prose is Metre; nor is this, in truth, a *strict* antithesis; because lines and passages of metre so naturally occur in writing prose, that it would be scarcely possible to avoid them, even were it desirable.

human tears; she can boast of no celestial Ichor that distinguishes her vital juices from those of prose; the same human blood circulates through the veins of them both.

If it be affirmed that rhyme and metrical arrangement of themselves constitute a distinction which overturns what I have been saying on the strict affinity of metrical language with that of prose, and paves the way for other artificial distinctions which the mind voluntarily admits, I answer that the language of such Poetry as I am recommending is, as far as is possible, a selection of the language really spoken by men; that this selection, wherever it is made with true taste and feeling, will of itself form a distinction far greater than would at first be imagined, and will entirely separate the composition from the vulgarity and meanness of ordinary life; and, if metre be superadded thereto, I believe that a dissimilitude will be produced altogether sufficient for the gratification of a rational mind. What other distinction would we have? Whence is it to come? And where is it to exist? Not, surely, where the Poet speaks through the mouths of his characters: it cannot be necessary here, either for elevation of style, or any of its supposed ornaments: for, if the Poet's subject be judiciously chosen, it will naturally, and upon fit occasion, lead him to passions the language of which, if selected truly and judiciously, must necessarily be dignified and variegated, and alive with metaphors and figures. I forbear to speak of an incongruity which would shock the intelligent Reader, should the Poet interweave any foreign splendour of his own with that which the passion naturally suggests: it is sufficient to say that such addition is unnecessary. And, surely, it is more probable that those passages, which with propriety abound with metaphors and figures, will have their due effect, if, upon other occasions where the passions are of a milder character, the style also be subdued and temperate.

❋

But, as the pleasure which I hope to give by the Poems I now present to the Reader must depend entirely on just notions upon this subject, and, as it is in itself of the highest importance to our taste and moral feelings, I cannot content myself with these detached remarks. And if, in what I am about to say, it shall appear to some that my labour is unnecessary, and that I am like a man fighting a battle without enemies, I would remind such persons, that, whatever may be the language outwardly holden by men, a practical faith in the opinions which I am wishing to establish is almost unknown. If my conclusions are admitted, and carried as far as they must be carried if admitted at all, our judgments concerning the works of the greatest Poets both ancient and modern will be far different from what they are at present, both when we praise, and when we censure: and our moral feelings influencing, and influenced by these judgments will, I believe, be corrected and purified.

❊

Taking up the subject, then, upon general grounds, I ask what is meant by the word Poet? What is a Poet? To whom does he address himself? And what language is to be expected from him? He is a man speaking to men; a man, it is true, endued with more lively sensibility, more enthusiasm and tenderness, who has a greater knowledge of human nature, and a more comprehensive soul, than are supposed to be common among mankind; a man pleased with his own passions and volitions, and who rejoices more than other men in the spirit of life that is in him; delighting to contemplate similar volitions and passions as manifested in the goings-on of the Universe, and habitually impelled to create them where he does not find them. To these qualities he has added a disposition to be affected more than other men by absent things as if they were present; an ability of conjuring up in himself passions, which are indeed far from being the same as those produced by real events, yet (especially in those parts of the general sympathy which are pleasing and delightful) do more nearly resemble the passions produced by real events, than anything which, from the motions of their own minds merely, other men are accustomed to feel in themselves; whence, and from practice, he has acquired a greater readiness and power in expressing what he thinks and feels, and especially those thoughts and feelings which, by his own choice, or from the structure of his own mind, arise in him without immediate external excitement.

❊

But, whatever portion of this faculty we may suppose even the greatest Poet to possess, there cannot be a doubt but that the language which it will suggest to him, must, in liveliness and truth, fall far short of that which is uttered by men in real life, under the actual pressure of those passions, certain shadows of which the Poet thus produces, or feels to be produced, in himself. However exalted a notion we would wish to cherish of the character of a Poet, it is obvious, that, while he describes and imitates passions, his situation is altogether slavish and mechanical, compared with the freedom and power of real and substantial action and suffering. So that it will be the wish of the Poet to bring his feelings near to those of the persons whose feelings he describes, nay, for short spaces of time perhaps, to let himself slip into an entire delusion, and even confound and identify his own feelings with theirs; modifying only the language which is thus suggested to him, by a consideration that he describes for a particular purpose, that of giving pleasure. Here, then, he will apply the principle on which I have so much insisted, namely, that of selection; on this he will depend for removing what would otherwise be painful or disgusting in the passion; he will feel that there is no necessity to trick out or to elevate nature: and, the more industriously he applies this principle, the deeper will be his faith that no words, which his fancy or imagination can suggest, will be to be compared with those which are the emanations of reality and truth.

✳

But it may be said by those who do not object to the general spirit of these remarks, that, as it is impossible for the Poet to produce upon all occasions language as exquisitely fitted for the passion as that which the real passion itself suggests, it is proper that he should consider himself as in the situation of a translator, who deems himself justified when he substitutes excellences of another kind for those which are unattainable by him; and endeavours occasionally to surpass his original, in order to make some amends for the general inferiority to which he feels that he must submit. But this would be to encourage idleness and unmanly despair. Further, it is the language of men who speak of what they do not understand; who talk of Poetry as of a matter of amusement and idle pleasure; who will converse with us as gravely about a *taste* for Poetry, as they express it, as if it were a thing as indifferent as a taste for Rope-dancing, or Frontiniac or Sherry. Aristotle, I have been told, hath said, that Poetry is the most philosophic of all writing: it is so: its object is truth, not individual and local, but general, and operative; not standing upon external testimony, but carried alive into the heart by passion; truth which is its own testimony, which gives strength and divinity to the tribunal to which it appeals, and receives them from the same tribunal. Poetry is the image of man and nature. The obstacles which stand in the way of the fidelity of the Biographer and Historian, and of their consequent utility, are incalculably greater than those which are to be encountered by the Poet who has an adequate notion of the dignity of his art. The Poet writes under one restriction only, namely, that of the necessity of giving immediate pleasure to a human Being possessed of that information which may be expected from him, not as a lawyer, a physician, a mariner, an astronomer or a natural philosopher, but as a Man. Except this one restriction, there is no object standing between the Poet and the image of things; between this, and the Biographer and Historian there are a thousand.

*

Nor let this necessity of producing immediate pleasure be considered as a degradation of the Poet's art. It is far otherwise. It is an acknowledgment of the beauty of the universe, an acknowledgment the more sincere, because it is not formal, but indirect; it is a task light and easy to him who looks at the world in the spirit of love: further, it is a homage paid to the native and naked dignity of man, to the grand elementary principle of pleasure, by which he knows, and feels, and lives, and moves. We have no sympathy but what is propagated by pleasure: I would not be misunderstood; but wherever we sympathize with pain it will be found that the sympathy is produced and carried on by subtle combinations with pleasure. We have no knowledge, that is, no general principles drawn from the contemplation of particular facts, but what has been built up by pleasure, and exists in us by pleasure alone. The Man of Science, the Chemist and Mathematician, whatever difficulties and disgusts they may have had to struggle with, know and feel this. However painful may be the objects with which the Anatomist's knowledge is connected, he feels that his knowledge is pleasure; and where he has no pleasure he has no knowledge. What then does the Poet? He considers man and the objects that surround him as acting and re-acting upon each other, so as to produce an infinite complexity of pain and pleasure: he considers man in his own nature and in his ordinary life as contemplating this with a certain quantity of immediate knowledge, with certain convictions, intuitions, and deductions which by habit become of the nature of intuitions; he considers him as looking upon this complex scene of ideas and sensations, and finding every where objects that immediately excite in him sympathies which, from the necessities of his nature, are accompanied by an overbalance of enjoyment.

❋

To this knowledge which all men carry about with them, and to these sympathies in which without any other discipline than that of our daily life we are fitted to take delight, the Poet principally directs his attention. He considers man and nature as essentially adapted to each other, and the mind of man as naturally the mirror of the fairest and most interesting qualities of nature. And thus the Poet, prompted by this feeling of pleasure which accompanies him through the whole course of his studies, converses with general nature with affections akin to those, which, through labour and length of time, the Man of Science has raised up in himself, by conversing with those particular parts of nature which are the objects of his studies. The knowledge both of the Poet and the Man of Science is pleasure; but the knowledge of the one cleaves to us as a necessary part of our existence, our natural and unalienable inheritance; the other is a personal and individual acquisition, slow to come to us, and by no habitual and direct sympathy connecting us with our fellow-beings. The Man of Science seeks truth as a remote and unknown benefactor; he cherishes and loves it in his solitude: the Poet, singing a song in which all human beings join with him, rejoices in the presence of truth as our visible friend and hourly companion. Poetry is the breath and finer spirit of all knowledge: it is the impassioned expression which is in the countenance of all Science. Emphatically may it be said of the Poet, as Shakespeare hath said of man, "that he looks before and after." He is the rock of defence of human nature; an upholder and preserver, carrying every where with him relationship and love. In spite of difference of soil and climate, of language and manners, of laws and customs, in spite of things silently gone out of mind and things violently destroyed, the Poet binds together by passion and knowledge the vast empire of human society, as it is spread over the whole earth, and over all time. The objects of the Poet's thoughts are every where; though the eyes and sense of man are, it is true, his favorite guides, yet he will follow wheresoever he can find an atmosphere of sensation in which to move his wings. Poetry is the first and last of all knowledge—it is as immortal as the heart of man. If the labours of men of Science should ever create any material revolution, direct or indirect, in our condition, and in the impressions which we habitually receive, the Poet will sleep then no more than at present, but he will be ready to follow the steps of the Man of Science, not only in those general indirect effects, but he will be at his side, carrying sensation into the midst of the objects of the Science itself. The remotest discoveries of the Chemist, the Botanist, or Mineralogist, will be as proper objects of the Poet's art as any upon which it can be employed, if the time should ever come when these things shall be familiar to us, and the relations under which they are contemplated by the followers of these respective Sciences shall be manifestly and palpably material to us as enjoying and suffering beings. If the time should ever come when what is now called Science, thus familiarized to men, shall be ready to put on, as it were, a form of flesh and blood, the Poet will lend his divine spirit to aid the transfiguration, and will welcome the Being thus produced, as a dear and genuine inmate of the household of man.–It is not, then, to be supposed that any one, who holds that sublime notion of Poetry which I have attempted to convey, will break in upon the sanctity and truth of his pictures by transitory and accidental ornaments, and endeavour to excite admiration of himself by arts, the necessity of which must manifestly depend upon the assumed meanness of his subject.

❋

What I have thus far said applies to Poetry in general; but especially to those parts of composition where the Poet speaks through the mouths of his characters; and upon this point it appears to have such weight that I will conclude, there are few persons of good sense, who would not allow that the dramatic parts of composition are defective, in proportion as they deviate from the real language of nature, and are coloured by a diction of the Poet's own, either peculiar to him as an individual Poet, or belonging simply to Poets in general, to a body of men who, from the circumstance of their compositions being in metre, it is expected will employ a particular language.

❋

It is not, then, in the dramatic parts of composition that we look for this distinction of language; but still it may be proper and necessary where the Poet speaks to us in his own person and character. To this I answer by referring my Reader to the description which I have before given of a Poet. Among the qualities which I have enumerated as principally conducing to form a Poet, is implied nothing differing in kind from other men, but only in degree. The sum of what I have there said is, that the Poet is chiefly distinguished from other men by a greater promptness to think and feel without immediate external excitement, and a greater power in expressing such thoughts and feelings as are produced in him in that manner. But these passions and thoughts and feelings are the general passions and thoughts and feelings of men. And with what are they connected? Undoubtedly with our moral sentiments and animal sensations, and with the causes which excite these; with the operations of the elements and the appearances of the visible universe; with storm and sunshine, with the revolutions of the seasons, with cold and heat, with loss of friends and kindred, with injuries and resentments, gratitude and hope, with fear and sorrow. These, and the like, are the sensations and objects which the Poet describes, as they are the sensations of other men, and the objects which interest them. The Poet thinks and feels in the spirit of the passions of men. How, then, can his language differ in any material degree from that of all other men who feel vividly and see clearly? It might be *proved* that it is impossible. But supposing that this were not the case, the Poet might then be allowed to use a peculiar language when expressing his feelings for his own gratification, or that of men like himself. But Poets do not write for Poets alone, but for men. Unless therefore we are advocates for that admiration which depends upon ignorance, and that pleasure which arises from hearing what we do not understand, the Poet must descend from this supposed height, and, in order to excite rational sympathy, he must express himself as other men express themselves. To this it may be added, that while he is only selecting from the real language of men, or which amounts to the same thing, composing accurately in the spirit of such selection, he is treading upon safe ground, and we know what we are to expect from him. Our feelings are the same with respect to metre; for, as it may be proper to inform the Reader, the distinction of metre is regular and uniform, and not like that which is produced by what is usually called poetic diction, arbitrary, and subject to infinite caprices upon which no calculation whatever can be made. In the one case, the

Reader is utterly at the mercy of the Poet respecting what imagery or diction he may choose to connect with the passion, whereas, in the other, the metre obeys certain laws, to which the Poet and Reader both willingly submit because they are certain, and because no interference is made by them with the passion but such as the concurring testimony of ages has shewn to heighten and improve the pleasure which co-exists with it.

❋

It will now be proper to answer an obvious question, namely, why, professing these opinions have I written in verse? To this, in addition to such answer as is included in what I have already said, I reply in the first place, because, however I may have restricted myself, there is still left open to me what confessedly constitutes the most valuable object of all writing whether in prose or verse, the great and universal passions of men, the most general and interesting of their occupations, and the entire world of nature, from which I am at liberty to supply myself with endless combinations of forms and imagery. Now, supposing for a moment that whatever is interesting in these objects may be as vividly described in prose, why am I to be condemned, if to such description I have endeavoured to superadd the charm, which, by the consent of all nations, is acknowledged to exist in metrical language? To this, by such as are unconvinced by what I have already said, it may be answered, that a very small part of the pleasure given by Poetry depends upon the metre, and that it is injudicious to write in metre, unless it be accompanied with the other artificial distinctions of style with which metre is usually accompanied, and that by such deviation more will be lost from the shock which will be thereby given to the Reader's associations, than will be counterbalanced by any pleasure which he can derive from the general power of numbers. In answer to those who still contend for the necessity of accompanying metre with certain appropriate colours of style in order to the accomplishment of its appropriate end, and who also, in my opinion, greatly under-rate the power of metre in itself, it might perhaps, as far as relates to these Poems, have been almost sufficient to observe that poems are extant, written upon more humble subjects, and in a more naked and simple style than I have aimed at, which poems have continued to give pleasure from generation to generation. Now, if nakedness and simplicity be a defect, the fact here mentioned affords a strong presumption that poems somewhat less naked and simple are capable of affording pleasure at the present day; and, what I wished *chiefly* to attempt, at present, was to justify myself for having written under the impression of this belief.

❋

But I might point out various causes why, when the style is manly, and the subject of some importance, words metrically arranged will long continue to impart such a pleasure to mankind as he who is sensible of the extent of that pleasure will be desirous to impart. The end of Poetry is to produce excitement in coexistence with an overbalance of pleasure. Now, by the supposition, excitement is an unusual and irregular state of the mind; ideas and feelings do not in that state succeed each other in accustomed order. But, if the words by which this excitement is produced are in themselves powerful, or the images and feelings have an undue proportion of pain connected with them, there is some danger that the excitement may be carried beyond its proper bounds. Now the co-presence of something regular, something to which the mind has been accustomed in various moods and in a less excited state, cannot but have great efficacy in tempering and restraining the passion by an intertexture of ordinary feeling, and of feeling not strictly and necessarily connected with the passion. This is unquestionably true, and hence, though the opinion will at first appear paradoxical, from the tendency of metre to divest language in a certain degree of its reality, and thus to throw a sort of half consciousness of unsubstantial existence over the whole composition, there can be little doubt but that more pathetic situations and sentiments, that is, those which have a greater proportion of pain connected with them, may be endured in metrical composition, especially in rhyme, than in prose. The metre of the old ballads is very artless; yet they contain many passages which would illustrate this opinion, and, I hope, if the following Poems be attentively perused, similar instances will be found in them. This opinion may be further illustrated by appealing to the Reader's own experience of the reluctance with which he comes to the re-perusal of the distressful parts of Clarissa Harlowe, or the Gamester. While Shakespeare's writings, in the most pathetic scenes, never act upon us as pathetic beyond the bounds of pleasure—an effect which, in a much greater degree than might at first be imagined, is to be ascribed to small, but continual and regular impulses of pleasurable surprise from the metrical arrangement.–On the other hand (what it must be allowed will much more frequently happen) if the Poet's words should be incommensurate with the passion, and inadequate to raise the Reader to a height of desirable excitement, then, (unless the Poet's choice of his metre has been grossly injudicious) in the feelings of pleasure which the Reader has been accustomed to connect with metre in general, and in the feeling, whether chearful or melancholy, which he has been accustomed to connect with that particular movement of metre, there will be found something which will greatly contribute to impart passion to the words, and to effect the complex end which the Poet proposes to himself.

※

If I had undertaken a systematic defence of the theory upon which these poems are written, it would have been my duty to develope the various causes upon which the pleasure received from metrical language depends. Among the chief of these causes is to be reckoned a principle which must be well known to those who have made any of the Arts the object of accurate reflection; I mean the pleasure which the mind derives from the perception of similitude in dissimilitude. This principle is the great spring of the activity of our minds, and their chief feeder. From this principle the direction of the sexual appetite, and all the passions connected with it take their origin: It is the life of our ordinary conversation; and upon the accuracy with which similitude in dissimilitude, and dissimilitude in similitude are perceived, depend our taste and our moral feelings. It would not have been a useless employment to have applied this principle to the consideration of metre, and to have shown that metre is hence enabled to afford much pleasure, and to have pointed out in what manner that pleasure is produced. But my limits will not permit me to enter upon this subject, and I must content myself with a general summary.

※

I have said that Poetry is the spontaneous overflow of powerful feelings: it takes its origin from emotion recollected in tranquillity: the emotion is contemplated till by a species of reaction the tranquillity gradually disappears, and an emotion, kindred to that which was before the subject of contemplation, is gradually produced, and does itself actually exist in the mind. In this mood successful composition generally begins, and in a mood similar to this it is carried on; but the emotion, of whatever kind and in whatever degree, from various causes is qualified by various pleasures, so that in describing any passions whatsoever, which are voluntarily described, the mind will upon the whole be in a state of enjoyment. Now, if Nature be thus cautious in preserving in a state of enjoyment a being thus employed, the Poet ought to profit by the lesson thus held forth to him, and ought especially to take care, that whatever passions he communicates to his Reader, those passions, if his Reader's mind be sound and vigorous, should always be accompanied with an overbalance of pleasure. Now the music of harmonious metrical language, the sense of difficulty overcome, and the blind association of pleasure which has been previously received from works of rhyme or metre of the same or similar construction, an indistinct perception perpetually renewed of language closely resembling that of real life, and yet, in the circumstance of metre, differing from it so widely, all these imperceptibly make up a complex feeling of delight, which is of the most important use in tempering the painful feeling which will always be found intermingled with powerful descriptions of the deeper passions. This effect is always produced in pathetic and impassioned poetry; while, in lighter compositions, the ease and gracefulness with which the Poet manages his numbers are themselves confessedly a principal source of the gratification of the Reader. I might perhaps include all which it is *necessary* to say upon this subject by affirming what few persons will deny, that, of two descriptions, either of passions, manners, or characters, each of them equally well executed, the one in prose and the other in verse, the verse will be read a hundred times where the prose is read once. We see that Pope by the power of verse alone, has contrived to render the plainest common sense interesting, and even frequently to invest it with the appearance of passion. In consequence of these convictions I related in metre the Tale of GOODY BLAKE and HARRY GILL, which is one of the rudest of this collection. I wished to draw attention to the truth that the power of the human imagination is sufficient to produce such changes even in our physical nature as might almost appear miraculous. The truth is an important one; the fact (for it is a *fact*) is a valuable illustration of it. And I have the satisfaction of knowing that it has been communicated to many hundreds of people who would never have heard of it, had it not been narrated as a Ballad, and in a more impressive metre than is usual in Ballads.

※

Having thus explained a few of the reasons why I have written in verse, and why I have chosen subjects from common life, and endeavoured to bring my language near to the real language of men, if I have been too minute in pleading my own cause, I have at the same time been treating a subject of general interest; and it is for this reason that I request the Reader's permission to add a few words with reference solely to these particular poems, and to some defects which will probably be found in them. I am sensible that my associations must have sometimes been particular instead of general, and that, consequently, giving to things a false importance, sometimes from diseased impulses I may have written upon unworthy subjects; but I am less apprehensive on this account, than that my language may frequently have suffered from those arbitrary connections of feelings and ideas with particular words and phrases, from which no man can altogether protect himself. Hence I have no doubt, that, in some instances feelings even of the ludicrous may be given to my Readers by expressions which appeared to me tender and pathetic. Such faulty expressions, were I convinced they were faulty at present, and that they must necessarily continue to be so, I would willingly take all reasonable pains to correct. But it is dangerous to make these alterations on the simple authority of a few individuals, or even of certain classes of men; for where the understanding of an Author is not convinced, or his feelings altered, this cannot be done without great injury to himself; for his own feelings are his stay and support, and if he sets them aside in one instance, he may be induced to repeat this act till his mind loses all confidence in itself, and becomes utterly debilitated. To this it may be added, that the Reader ought never to forget that he is himself exposed to the same errors as the Poet, and perhaps in a much greater degree: for there can be no presumption in saying, that it is not probable he will be so well acquainted with the various stages of meaning through which words have passed, or with the fickleness or stability of the relations of particular ideas to each other; and above all, since he is so much less interested in the subject, he may decide lightly and carelessly.

※

Long as I have detained the Reader, I hope he will permit me to caution him against a mode of false criticism which has been applied to Poetry in which the language closely resembles that of life and nature. Such verses have been triumphed over in parodies of which Dr. Johnson's Stanza is a fair specimen.

> "I put my hat upon my head,
> And walk'd into the Strand,
> And there I met another man
> Whose hat was in his hand."

Immediately under these lines I will place one of the most justly admired stanzas of the "*Babes* in the Wood."

> "These pretty Babes with hand in hand
> Went wandering up and down;
> But never more they saw the Man
> Approaching from the Town."

In both these stanzas the words, and the order of the words, in no respect differ from the most unimpassioned conversation. There are words in both, for example, "the Strand," and "the Town," connected with none but the most familiar ideas; yet the one stanza we admit as admirable, and the other as a fair example of the superlatively contemptible. Whence arises this difference? Not from the metre, not from the language, not from the order of the words; but the *matter* expressed in Dr. Johnson's stanza is contemptible. The proper method of treating trivial and simple verses to which Dr. Johnson's stanza would be a fair parallelism is not to say, this is a bad kind of poetry, or this is not poetry; but this wants sense; it is neither interesting in itself, nor can *lead* to any thing interesting; the images neither originate in that sane state of feeling which arises out of thought, nor can excite thought or feeling in the Reader. This is the only sensible manner of dealing with such verses: Why trouble yourself about the species till you have previously decided upon the genus? Why take pains to prove than an Ape is not a Newton when it is self-evident that he is not a man?

I have one request to make of my Reader, which is, that in judging these Poems he would decide by his own feelings genuinely, and not by reflection upon what will probably be the judgment of others. How common is it to hear a person say, "I myself do not object to this style of composition or this or that expression, but to such and such classes of people it will appear mean or ludicrous." This mode of criticism, so destructive of all sound unadulterated judgment, is almost universal: I have therefore to request, that the Reader would abide independently by his own feelings, and that if he finds himself affected he would not suffer such conjectures to interfere with his pleasure.

❋

If an Author by any single composition has impressed us with respect for his talents, it is useful to consider this as affording a presumption, that, on other occasions where we have been displeased, he nevertheless may not have written ill or absurdly; and, further, to give him so much credit for this one composition as may induce us to review what has displeased us with more care than we should otherwise have bestowed upon it. This is not only an act of justice, but in our decisions upon poetry especially, may conduce in a high degree to the improvement of our own taste: for an *accurate* taste in poetry, and in all the other arts, as Sir Joshua Reynolds has observed, is an *acquired* talent, which can only be produced by thought and a long continued intercourse with the best models of composition. This is mentioned, not with so ridiculous a purpose as to prevent the most inexperienced Reader from judging for himself, (I have already said that I wish him to judge for himself;) but merely to temper the rashness of decision, and to suggest, that, if Poetry be a subject on which much time has not been bestowed, the judgment may be erroneous; and that in many cases it necessarily will be so.

❋

I know nothing would have so effectually contributed to further the end which I have in view as to have shewn of what kind the pleasure is, and how that pleasure is produced, which is confessedly produced by metrical composition essentially different from what I have here endeavoured to recommend: for the Reader will say that he has been pleased by such composition; and what can I do more for him? The power of any art is limited; and he will suspect, that if I propose to furnish him with new friends, it is only upon condition of his abandoning his old friends. Besides, as I have said, the Reader is himself conscious of the pleasure which he has received from such composition, composition to which he has peculiarly attached the endearing name of Poetry; and all men feel an habitual gratitude, and something of an honorable bigotry for the objects which have long continued to please them; we not only wish to be pleased, but to be pleased in that particular way in which we have been accustomed to be pleased. There is a host of arguments in these feelings; and I should be the less able to combat them successfully, as I am willing to allow, that, in order entirely to enjoy the Poetry which I am recommending, it would be necessary to give up much of what is ordinarily enjoyed. But, would my limits have permitted me to point out how this pleasure is produced, I might have removed many obstacles, and assisted my Reader in perceiving that the powers of language are not so limited as he may suppose; and that it is possible that poetry may give other enjoyments, of a purer, more lasting, and more exquisite nature. This part of my subject I have not altogether neglected; but it has been less my present aim to prove, that the interest excited by some other kinds of poetry is less vivid, and less worthy of the nobler powers of the mind, than to offer reasons for presuming, that, if the object which I have proposed to myself were adequately attained, a species of poetry would be produced, which is genuine poetry; in its nature well adapted to interest mankind permanently, and likewise important in the multiplicity and quality of its moral relations.

❋

From what has been said, and from a perusal of the Poems, the Reader will be able clearly to perceive the object which I have proposed to myself: he will determine how far I have attained this object; and, what is a much more important question, whether it be worth attaining; and upon the decision of these two questions will rest my claim to the approbation of the public.

Samuel Taylor Coleridge, Chapter 14 of *Biographia Literaria*, 1817, and "On Poesy or Art," 1818

Samuel Taylor Coleridge, author of *The Rime of the Ancient Mariner*, and the mysterious, unfinished "Kubla Khan," as well as memorable shorter poems such as "Frost at Midnight" and "Dejection: An Ode," was a great friend, and for a time, a neighbor of Wordsworth's in Somerset. *Biographia Literaria*, Coleridge's literary biography, or biography of critical ideas, was intended, at least initially, to be a preface to a book of poems, though it eventually spanned twenty-four chapters. The *Biographia* is worth reading in its entirety, especially for Coleridge's attempt to create a set of standards with which to judge poetry and for the four-chapter affirmation of and argument with Wordsworth's "Preface," the first chapter of which is included here.

Also included is "On Poesy or Art," an essay in which Coleridge examines the philosophical underpinnings of his theory of organic form. Influenced by his reading of the work of German romantic writers, particularly A. W. Schlegel's lectures on Shakespeare, Coleridge first articulated his theory in a lecture that he gave around 1812 at the Surrey Institution of London. In his notes for this lecture, he writes: "No work of true Genius dare want its appropriate Form—neither indeed is there any danger of this—as it must not, so neither can it, be lawless—for it is even this that constitutes it Genius—the power of acting creatively under laws of its own origination . . . The form is mechanic when on any given material we impress a predetermined form, not necessarily arising out of the properties of the material—as when to a mass of wet clay we give whatever shape we wish it to retain when hardened—The organic form on the other hand is innate, it shapes as it develops itself from within, and the fullness of its development is one & the same with the perfection of its outward Form. Such is the Life, such the form." Coleridge's theory argues for the breaking of arbitrary forms of meter and rhyme, providing a basis for future experimentations in free verse.

Chapter XIV

Occasion of the Lyrical Ballads, and the objects originally proposed—Preface to the second edition—The ensuing controversy, its causes and acrimony—Philosophic definitions of a Poem and Poetry with scholia.

During the first year that Mr. Wordsworth and I were neighbours, our conversations turned frequently on the two cardinal points of poetry, the power of exciting the sympathy of the reader by a faithful adherence to the truth of nature, and the power of giving the interest of novelty by the modifying colours of the imagination. The sudden charm, which accidents of light and shade, which moon-light or sunset diffused over a known and familiar landscape, appeared to represent the practicability of combining both. These are the poetry of nature. The thought suggested itself—(to which of us I do not recollect)—that a series of poems might be composed of two sorts. In the one, the incidents and agents were to be, in part at least, supernatural; and the excellence aimed at was to consist in the interesting of the affections by the dramatic truth of such emotions, as would naturally accompany such situations, supposing them real. And real in this sense they have been to every human being who, from what ever source of delusion, has at any time believed himself under supernatural agency. For the second class, subjects were to be chosen from ordinary life; the characters and incidents were to be such as will be found in every village and its vicinity, where there is a meditative and feeling mind to seek after them, or to notice them, when they present themselves.

In this idea originated the plan of the LYRICAL BALLADS; in which it was agreed, that my endeavours should be directed to persons and characters supernatural, or at least romantic; yet so as to transfer from our inward nature a human interest and a semblance of truth sufficient to procure for these shadows of imagination that willing suspension of disbelief for the moment, which constitutes poetic faith. Mr. Wordsworth, on the other hand, was to propose to himself as his object, to give the charm of novelty to things of every day, and to excite a feeling analogous to the supernatural, by awakening the mind's attention to the lethargy of custom, and directing it to the loveliness and the wonders of the world before us; an inexhaustible treasure, but for which, in consequence of the film of familiarity and selfish solicitude, we have eyes, yet see not, ears that hear not, and hearts that neither feel nor understand.

With this view I wrote THE ANCIENT MARINER, and was preparing among other poems, THE DARK LADIE, and the CHRISTABEL, in which I should have more nearly realized my ideal, than I had done in my first attempt. But Mr. Wordsworth's industry had proved so much more successful, and the number of his poems so much greater, that my compositions, instead of forming a balance, appeared rather an interpolation of heterogeneous matter. Mr. Wordsworth added two or three poems written in his own character, in the impassioned, lofty, and sustained diction, which is characteristic of his genius. In this form the LYRICAL BALLADS were published; and were presented by him, as an experiment, whether subjects, which from their nature rejected the usual ornaments and extra-colloquial style of poems in general, might not be so managed in the language of ordinary life as to produce the pleasurable interest, which it is the peculiar business of poetry to impart. To the second edition he added a preface of considerable length; in which, notwithstanding some passages of apparently a contrary import, he was understood to contend for the extension of this style to poetry of all kinds, and to reject as vicious and indefensible all phrases and forms of speech that were not included in what he (unfortunately, I think, adopting an equivocal expression) called the language of real life. From this preface, prefixed to poems in which it was impossible to deny the presence of original genius, however mistaken its direction might be deemed, arose the whole long-continued controversy. For from the conjunction of perceived power with supposed heresy I explain the inveteracy and in some instances, I grieve to say, the acrimonious passions, with which the controversy has been conducted by the assailants.

Had Mr. Wordsworth's poems been the silly, the childish things, which they were for a long time described as being: had they been really distinguished from the compositions of other poets merely by meanness of language and inanity of thought; had they indeed contained nothing more than what is found in the parodies and pretended imitations of them; they must have sunk at once, a dead weight, into the slough of oblivion, and have dragged the preface along with them. But year after year increased the number of Mr. Wordsworth's admirers. They were found too not in the lower classes of the reading public, but chiefly among young men of strong sensibility and meditative minds; and their admiration (inflamed perhaps in some degree by opposition) was distinguished by its intensity, I might almost say, by its religious fervour. These facts, and the intellectual energy of the author, which was more or less consciously felt, where it was outwardly and even boisterously denied, meeting with sentiments of aversion to his opinions, and of alarm at their consequences, produced an eddy of criticism, which would of itself have borne up the poems by the violence with which it whirled them round and round. With many parts of this preface in the sense attributed to them and which the words undoubtedly seem to authorize, I never concurred; but on the contrary objected to them as erroneous in principle, and as contradictory (in appearance at least) both to other parts of the same preface, and to the author's own practice in the greater part of the poems themselves. Mr. Wordsworth in his recent collection has, I find, degraded this prefatory disquisition to the end of his second volume, to be read or not at the reader's choice. But he has not, as far as I can discover, announced any change in his poetic creed. At all events, considering it as the source of a controversy, in which I have been honoured more than I deserve by the frequent conjunction of my name with his, I think it expedient to declare once for all, in what points I coincide with the opinions supported in that preface, and in what points I altogether differ. But in order to render myself intelligible I must previously, in as few words as possible, explain my views, first, of a Poem; and secondly, of Poetry itself, in kind, and in essence.

The office of philosophical disquisition consists in just distinction; while it is the privilege of the philosopher to preserve himself constantly aware, that distinction is not division. In order to obtain adequate notions of any truth, we must intellectually separate its distinguishable parts; and this is the technical process of philosophy. But having so done, we must then restore them in our conceptions to the unity, in which they actually co-exist; and this is the result of philosophy. A poem contains the same elements as a prose composition; the difference therefore must consist in a different combination of them, in consequence of a different object being proposed. According to the difference of the object will be the difference of the combination. It is possible, that the object may be merely to facilitate the recollection of any given facts or observations by artificial arrangement; and the composition will be a poem, merely because it is distinguished from prose by metre, or by rhyme, or by both conjointly. In this, the lowest sense, a man might attribute the name of a poem to the well-known enumeration of the days in the several months;

"Thirty days hath September,
April, June, and November," &c.

and others of the same class and purpose. And as a particular pleasure is found in anticipating the recurrence of sounds and quantities, all compositions that have this charm super-added, whatever be their contents, *may* be entitled poems.

So much for the superficial form. A difference of object and contents supplies an additional ground of distinction. The immediate purpose may be the communication of truths; either of truth absolute and demonstrable, as in works of science; or of facts experienced and recorded, as in history. Pleasure, and that of the highest and most permanent kind, may result from the attainment of the end; but it is not itself the immediate end. In other works the communication of pleasure may be the immediate purpose; and though truth, either moral or intellectual, ought to be the ultimate end, yet this will distinguish the character of the author, not the class to which the work belongs. Blest indeed is that state of society, in which the immediate purpose would be baffled by the perversion of the proper ultimate end; in which no charm of diction or imagery could exempt the BATHYLLUS even of an Anacreon, or the ALEXIS of Virgil, from disgust and aversion!

But the communication of pleasure may be the immediate object of a work not metrically composed; and that object may have been in a high degree attained, as in novels and romances. Would then the mere superaddition of metre, with or without rhyme, entitle *these* to the name of poems? The answer is, that nothing can permanently please, which does not contain in itself the reason why it is so, and not otherwise. If metre be super-added, all other parts must be made consonant with it. They must be such, as to justify the perpetual and distinct attention to each part, which an exact correspondent recurrence of accent and sound are calculated to excite. The final definition then, so deduced, may be thus worded. A poem is that species of composition, which is opposed to works of science, by proposing for its *immediate* object pleasure, not truth; and from all other species—(having *this* object in common with it)—it is discriminated by proposing to itself such delight from the *whole*, as is compatible with a distinct gratification from each component *part*.

Controversy is not seldom excited in consequence of the disputants attaching each a different meaning to the same word; and in few instances has this been more striking, than in disputes concerning the present subject. If a man chooses to call every composition a poem, which is rhyme, or measure, or both, I must leave his opinion uncontroverted. The distinction is at least competent to characterize the writer's intention. If it were subjoined, that the whole is likewise entertaining or affecting, as a tale, or as a series of interesting reflections, I of course admit this as another fit ingredient of a poem, and an additional merit. But if the definition sought for be that of a *legitimate* poem, I answer, it must be one, the parts of which mutually support and explain each other; all in their proportion harmonizing with, and supporting the purpose and known influences of metrical arrangement. The philosophic critics of all ages coincide with the ultimate judgment of all countries, in equally denying the praises of a just poem, on the one hand, to a series of striking lines or distiches, each of which, absorbing the whole attention of the reader to itself, becomes disjoined from its context, and forms a separate whole, instead of a harmonizing part; and on the other hand, to an unsustained composition, from which the reader collects rapidly the general result unattracted by the component parts. The reader should be carried forward, not merely or chiefly by the mechanical impulse of curiosity, or by a restless desire to arrive at the final solution; but by the pleasurable activity of mind excited by the attractions of the journey itself. Like the motion of a serpent, which the Egyptians made the emblem of intellectual power; or like the path of sound through the air;—at every step he pauses and half recedes, and from the retrogressive movement collects the force which again carries him onward. *Præcipitandus est liber spiritus,* says Petronius most happily. The epithet, *liber,* here balances the preceding verb; and it is not easy to conceive more meaning condensed in fewer words.

But if this should be admitted as a satisfactory character of a poem, we have still to seek for a definition of poetry. The writings of Plato, and Jeremy Taylor, and Burnet's Theory of the Earth, furnish undeniable proofs that poetry of the highest kind may exist without metre, and even without the contradistinguishing objects of a poem. The first chapter of Isaiah—(indeed a very large portion of the whole book)—is poetry in the most emphatic sense; yet it would be not less irrational than strange to assert, that pleasure, and not truth was the immediate object of the prophet. In short, whatever specific import we attach to the word, Poetry, there will be found involved in it, as a necessary consequence, that a poem of any length neither can be, nor ought to be, all poetry. Yet if an harmonious whole is to be produced, the remaining parts must be preserved in keeping with the poetry; and this can be no otherwise effected than by such a studied selection and artificial arrangement, as will partake of one, though not a peculiar property of poetry. And this again can be no other than the property of exciting a more continuous and equal attention than the language of prose aims at, whether colloquial or written.

My own conclusions on the nature of poetry, in the strictest use of the word, have been in part anticipated in some of the remarks on the Fancy and Imagination in the early part of this work. What is poetry?—is so nearly the same question with, what is a poet?—that the answer to the one is involved in the solution of the other. For it is a distinction resulting from the poetic genius itself, which sustains and modifies the images, thoughts, and emotions of the poet's own mind.

The poet, described in ideal perfection, brings the whole soul of man into activity, with the subordination of its faculties to each other according to their relative worth and dignity. He diffuses a tone and spirit of unity, that blends, and (as it were) *fuses*, each into each, by that synthetic and magical power, to which I would exclusively appropriate the name of Imagination. This power, first put in action by the will and understanding, and retained under their irremissive, though gentle and unnoticed, control, *laxis effertur habenis*, reveals itself in the balance or reconcilement of opposite or discordant qualities: of sameness, with difference; of the general with the concrete; the idea with the image; the individual with the representative; the sense of novelty and freshness with old and familiar objects; a more than usual state of emotion with more than usual order; judgment ever awake and steady self-possession with enthusiasm and feeling profound or vehement; and while it blends and harmonizes the natural and the artificial, still subordinates art to nature; the manner to the matter; and our admiration of the poet to our sympathy with the poetry. Doubtless, as Sir John Davies observes of the soul—(and his words may with slight alteration be applied, and even more appropriately, to the poetic Imagination)—

Doubtless this could not be, but that she turns
Bodies to *spirit* by sublimation strange,
As fire converts to fire the things it burns,
As we our food into our nature change.

From their gross matter she abstracts *their* forms,
And draws a kind of quintessence from things;
Which to her proper nature she transforms
To bear them light on her celestial wings.

Thus does she, when from *individual states*
She doth abstract the universal kinds;
Which then re-clothed in divers names and fates
Steal access through the senses to our minds.

Finally, Good Sense is the Body of poetic genius, Fancy its Drapery, Motion its Life, and Imagination the Soul that is everywhere, and in each; and forms all into one graceful and intelligent whole.

On Poesy or Art

Man communicates by articulation of sounds, and paramountly by the memory in the ear; nature by the impression of bounds and surfaces on the eye, and through the eye it gives significance and appropriation, and thus the conditions of memory, or the capability of being remembered, to sounds, smells, &c. Now Art, used collectively for painting, sculpture, architecture and music, is the mediatress between, and reconciler of, nature and man. It is, therefore, the power of humanizing nature, of infusing the thoughts and passions of man into every thing which is the object of his contemplation; color, form, motion, and sound, are the elements which it combines, and it stamps them into unity in the mould of a moral idea.

The primary art is writing;—primary, if we regard the purpose abstracted from the different modes of realizing it, those steps of progression of which the instances are still visible in the lower degrees of civilization. First, there is mere gesticulation; then rosaries or *wampum;* then picture-language; then hieroglyphics, and finally alphabetic letters. These all consist of a translation of man into nature, of a substitution of the visible for the audible.

The so called music of savage tribes as little deserves the name of art for the understanding, as the ear warrants it for music. Its lowest state is a mere expression of passion by sounds which the passion itself necessitates;— the highest amounts to no more than a voluntary reproduction of these sounds in the absence of the occasioning causes, so as to give the pleasure of contrast,—for example, by the various outcries of battle in the song of security and triumph. Poetry also is purely human; for all its materials are from the mind, and all its products are for the mind. But it is the apotheosis of the former state, in which by excitement of the associative power passion itself imitates order, and the order resulting produces a pleasureable passion, and thus it elevates the mind by making its feelings the object of its reflexion. So likewise, whilst it recalls the sights and sounds that had accompanied the occasions of the original passions, poetry impregnates them with an interest not their own by means of the passions, and yet tempers the passion by the calming power which all distinct images exert on the human soul. In this way poetry is the preparation for art, inasmuch as it avails itself of the forms of nature to recall, to express, and to modify the thoughts and feelings of the mind. Still, however, poetry can only act through the intervention of articulate speech, which is so peculiarly human, that in all languages it constitutes the ordinary phrase by which man and nature are contradistinguished. It is the original force of the word "brute," and even "mute" and "dumb" do not convey the absence of sound, but the absence of articulated sounds.

As soon as the human mind is intelligibly addressed by an outward image exclusively of articulate speech, so soon does art commence. But please to observe that I have laid particular stress on the words "human mind,"—meaning to exclude thereby all results common to man and all other sentient creatures, and consequently confining myself to the effect produced by the congruity of the animal impression with the reflective powers of the mind; so that not the thing presented, but that which is represented by the thing, shall be the source of the pleasure. In this sense nature itself is to a religious observer the art of God; and for the same cause art itself might be defined as of a middle quality between a thought and a thing, or, as I said before, the union and reconciliation of that which is nature with that which is exclusively human. It is the figured language of thought, and is distinguished from nature by the unity of all the parts in one thought or idea. Hence nature itself would give us the impression of a work of art, if we could see the thought which is present at once in the whole and in every part; and a work of art will be just in proportion as it adequately conveys the thought, and rich in proportion to the variety of parts which it holds in unity.

If, therefore, the term "mute" be taken as opposed not to sound but to articulate speech, the old definition of painting will in fact be the true and best definition of the Fine Arts in general, that is, *muta poesis,* mute poesy, and so of course poesy. And, as all languages perfect themselves by a gradual process of desynonymizing words originally equivalent, I have cherished the wish to use the word "poesy" as the generic or common term, and to distinguish that species of poesy which is not *muta poesis* by its usual name "poetry"; while of all the other species which collectively form the Fine Arts, there would remain this as the common definition,—that they all, like poetry, are to express intellectual purposes, thoughts, conceptions, and sentiments which have their origin in the human mind,— not, however, as poetry does, by means of articulate speech, but as nature or the divine art does, by form, color, magnitude, proportion, or by sound, that is, silently or musically.

Well! it may be said—but who has ever thought otherwise? We all know that art is the imitatress of nature. And, doubtless, the truths which I hope to convey would be barren truisms, if all men meant the same by the words "imitate" and "nature." But it would be flattering mankind at large, to presume that such is the fact. First, to imitate. The impression on the wax is not an imitation, but a copy, of the seal; the seal itself is an imitation. But, further, in order to form a philosophic conception, we must seek for the kind, as the heat in ice, invisible light, &c., whilst, for practical purposes, we must have reference to the degree. It is sufficient that philosophically we understand that in all imitation two elements must coexist, and not only coexist, but must be perceived as coexisting. These two constituent elements are likeness and unlikeness, or sameness and difference, and in all genuine creations of art there must be a union of these disparates. The artist may take his point of view where he pleases, provided that the desired effect be perceptibly produced,—that there be likeness in the difference, difference in the likeness, and a reconcilement of both in one. If there be likeness to nature without any check of difference, the result is disgusting, and the more complete the delusion, the more loathsome the effect. Why are such simulations of nature, as wax-work figures of men and women, so disagreeable? Because, not finding the motion and the life which we expected, we are shocked as by a falsehood, every circumstance of detail, which before induced us to be interested, making the distance from truth more palpable. You set out with a supposed reality and are disappointed and disgusted with the deception; whilst, in respect to a work of genuine imitation, you begin with an acknowledged total difference, and then every touch of nature gives you the pleasure of an approximation to truth. The fundamental principle of all this is undoubtedly the horror of falsehood and the love of truth inherent in the human breast. The Greek tragic dance rested on these principles, and I can deeply sympathize in imagination with the Greeks in this favorite part of their theatrical exhibitions, when I call to mind the pleasure I felt in beholding the combat of the Horatii and Curiatii most exquisitely danced in Italy to the music of Cimarosa.

Secondly, as to nature. We must imitate nature! yes, but what in nature, —all and every thing? No, the beautiful in nature. And what then is the beautiful? What is beauty? It is, in the abstract, the unity of the manifold, the coalescence of the diverse; in the concrete, it is the union of the shapely (*formosum*) with the vital. In the dead organic it depends on regularity of form, the first and lowest species of which is the triangle with all its modifications, as in crystals, architecture, &c.; in the living organic it is not mere regularity of form, which would produce a sense of formality; neither is it subservient to any thing beside itself. It may be present in a disagreeable object, in which the proportion of the parts constitutes a whole; it does not arise from association, as the agreeable does, but sometimes lies in the rupture of association; it is not different to different individuals and nations, as has been said, nor is it connected with the ideas of the good, or the fit, or the useful. The sense of beauty is intuitive, and beauty itself is all that inspires pleasure without, and aloof from, and even contrarily to, interest.

If the artist copies the mere nature, the *natura naturata*, what idle rivalry! If he proceeds only from a given form, which is supposed to answer to the notion of beauty, what an emptiness, what an unreality there always is in his productions, as in Cipriani's pictures! Believe me, you must master the essence, the *natura naturans*, which presupposes a bond between nature in the higher sense and the soul of man.

The wisdom in nature is distinguished from that in man by the co-instantaneity of the plan and the execution; the thought and the product are one, or are given at once; but there is no reflex act, and hence there is no moral responsibility. In man there is reflexion, freedom, and choice; he is, therefore, the head of the visible creation. In the objects of nature are presented, as in a mirror, all the possible elements, steps, and processes of intellect antecedent to consciousness, and therefore to the full development of the intelligential act; and man's mind is the very focus of all the rays of intellect which are scattered throughout the images of nature. Now so to place these images, totalized, and fitted to the limits of the human mind, as to elicit from, and to superinduce upon, the forms themselves the moral reflexions to which they approximate, to make the external internal, the internal external, to make nature thought, and thought nature,—this is the mystery of genius in the Fine Arts. Dare I add that the genius must act on the feeling, that body is but a striving to become mind,—that it is mind in its essence!

In every work of art there is a reconcilement of the external with the internal; the conscious is so impressed on the unconscious as to appear in it; as compare mere letters inscribed on a tomb with figures themselves constituting the tomb. He who combines the two is the man of genius; and for that reason he must partake of both. Hence there is in genius itself an unconscious activity; nay, that is the genius in the man of genius. And this is the true exposition of the rule that the artist must first eloign himself from nature in order to return to her with full effect. Why this? Because if he were to begin by mere painful copying, he would produce masks only, not forms breathing life. He must out of his own mind create forms according to the severe laws of the intellect, in order to generate in himself that co-ordination of freedom and law, that involution of obedience in the prescript, and of the prescript in the impulse to obey, which assimilates him to nature, and enables him to understand her. He merely absents himself for a season from her, that his own spirit, which has the same ground with nature, may learn her unspoken language in its main radicals, before he approaches to her endless compositions of them. Yes, not to acquire cold notions—lifeless technical rules—but living and life-producing ideas, which shall contain their own evidence, the certainty that they are essentially one with the germinal causes in nature,—his consciousness being the focus and mirror of both,—for this does the artist for a time abandon the external real in order to return to it with a complete sympathy with its internal and actual. For of all we see, hear, feel and touch the substance is and must be in ourselves; and therefore there is no alternative in reason between the dreary (and thank heaven! almost impossible) belief that every thing around us is but a phantom, or that the life which is in us is in them likewise; and that to know is to resemble, when we speak of objects out of ourselves, even as within ourselves to learn is, according to Plato, only to recollect;—the only effective answer to which, that I have been fortunate to meet with, is that which Pope has consecrated for future use in the line—

"And coxcombs vanquish Berkeley with a grin!"

The artist must imitate that which is within the thing, that which is active through form and figure, and discourses to us by symbols—the *Natur-geist*, or spirit of nature, as we unconsciously imitate those whom we love; for so only can he hope to produce any work truly natural in the object and truly human in the effect. The idea which puts the form together cannot itself be the form. It is above form, and is its essence, the universal in the individual, or the individuality itself,—the glance and the exponent of the indwelling power.

Each thing that lives has its moment of self-exposition, and so has each period of each thing, if we remove the disturbing forces of accident. To do this is the business of ideal art, whether in images of childhood, youth, or age, in man or in woman. Hence a good portrait is the abstract of the personal; it is not the likeness for actual comparison, but for recollection. This explains why the likeness of a very good portrait is not always recognized; because some persons never abstract, and amongst these are especially to be numbered the near relations and friends of the subject, in consequence of the constant pressure and check exercised on their minds by the actual presence of the original. And each thing that only appears to live has also its possible position of relation to life, as nature herself testifies, who where she cannot be, prophesies her being in the crystallized metal, or the inhaling plant.

The charm, the indispensable requisite, of sculpture is unity of effect. But painting rests in a material remoter from nature, and its compass is therefore greater. Light and shade give external, as well as internal, being even with all its accidents, whilst sculpture is confined to the latter. And here I may observe that the subjects chosen for works of art, whether in sculpture or painting, should be such as really are capable of being expressed and conveyed within the limits of those arts. Moreover they ought to be such as will affect the spectator by their truth, their beauty, or their sublimity, and therefore they may be addressed to the judgement, the senses, or the reason. The peculiarity of the impression which they may make, may be derived either from color and form, or from proportion and fitness, or from the excitement of the moral feelings; or all these may be combined. Such works as do combine these sources of effect must have the preference in dignity.

Imitation of the antique may be too exclusive, and may produce an injurious effect on modern sculpture;—1st, generally, because such an imitation cannot fail to have a tendency to keep the attention fixed on externals rather than on the thought within;—2ndly, because, accordingly, it leads the artist to rest satisfied with that which is always imperfect, namely, bodily form, and circumscribes his view of mental expression to the ideas of power and grandeur only;—3rdly, because it induces an effort to combine together two incongruous things, that is to say, modern feelings in antique forms;—4thly, because it speaks in language, as it were, learned and dead, the tones of which, being unfamiliar, leave the common spectator cold and unimpressed;—and lastly, because it necessarily causes a neglect of thoughts, emotions and images of profounder interest and more exalted dignity, as motherly, sisterly, and brotherly love, piety, devotion, the divine become human,—the Virgin, the Apostle, the Christ. The artist's principle in the statue of a great man should be the illustration of departed merit; and I cannot but think that a skilful adoption of modern habiliments would, in many instances, give a variety and force of effect which a bigoted adherence to Greek or Roman costume precludes. It is, I believe, from artists finding Greek models unfit for several important modern purposes, that we see so many allegorical figures on monuments and elsewhere. Painting was, as it were, a new art, and being unshackled by old models it chose its own subjects, and took an eagle's flight. And a new field seems opened for modern sculpture in the symbolical expression of the ends of life, as in Guy's monument, Chantrey's children in Worcester Cathedral, &c.

Architecture exhibits the greatest extent of the difference from nature which may exist in works of art. It involves all the powers of design, and is sculpture and painting inclusively. It shews the greatness of man, and should at the same time teach him humility.

Music is the most entirely human of the fine arts, and has the fewest *analoga* in nature. Its first delightfulness is simple accordance with the ear; but it is an associated thing, and recalls the deep emotions of the past with an intellectual sense of proportion. Every human feeling is greater and larger than the exciting cause,—a proof, I think, that man is designed for a higher state of existence; and this is deeply implied in music, in which there is always something more and beyond the immediate expression.

With regard to works in all the branches of the fine arts, I may remark that the pleasure arising from novelty must of course be allowed its due place and weight. This pleasure consists in the identity of two opposite elements, that is to say—sameness and variety. If in the midst of the variety there be not some fixed object for the attention, the unceasing succession of the variety will prevent the mind from observing the difference of the individual objects; and the only thing remaining will be the succession, which will then produce precisely the same effect as sameness. This we experience when we let the trees or hedges pass before the fixed eye during a rapid movement in a carriage, or, on the other hand, when we suffer a file of soldiers or ranks of men in procession to go on before us without resting the eye on any one in particular. In order to derive pleasure from the occupation of the mind, the principle of unity must always be present, so that in the midst of the multeity the centripetal force be never suspended, nor the sense be fatigued by the predominance of the centrifugal force. This unity in multeity I have elsewhere stated as the principle of beauty. It is equally the source of pleasure in variety, and in fact a higher term including both. What is the seclusive or distinguishing term between them?

Remember that there is a difference between form as proceeding, and shape as superinduced;—the latter is either the death or the imprisonment of the thing;—the former is its self-witnessing and self-effected sphere of agency. Art would or should be the abridgment of nature. Now the fulness of nature is without character, as water is purest when without taste, smell, or color; but this is the highest, the apex only,—it is not the whole. The object of art is to give the whole *ad hominem;* hence each step of nature hath its ideal, and hence the possibility of a climax up to the perfect form of a harmonized chaos.

To the idea of life victory or strife is necessary; as virtue consists not simply in the absence of vices, but in the overcoming of them. So it is in beauty. The sight of what is subordinated and conquered heightens the strength and the pleasure; and this should be exhibited by the artist either inclusively in his figure, or else out of it, and beside it to act by way of supplement and contrast. And with a view to this, remark the seeming identity of body and mind in infants, and thence the loveliness of the former; the commencing separation in boyhood, and the struggle of equilibrium in youth: thence onward the body is first simply indifferent; then demanding the translucency of the mind not to be worse than indifferent; and finally all that presents the body as body becoming almost of an excremental nature.

John Keats, *Selected Letters,* 1817 and 1818

John Keats's letters—to his brothers, his friends, his publishers, and his fiancée, Fanny Brawne—provide an intimate portrait of a struggling young poet in the generation after the birth of English romanticism. Amid the dross of family news and literary gossip, are drafts of poems and a record of Keats's developing ideas on poetics. "Negative Capability," "the camelion [chameleon] poet," "the holiness of the heart's affections," "the sense of beauty": many of our most commonplace notions of a poem and a poet were coined by Keats in his letters. What is immediately apparent is his steadfast conviction in his calling, and his devotion to this calling as one of almost religious significance. "My Imagination is a Monastry and I am its Monk," he writes to Percy Bysshe Shelley in August 1820.

The letters included here are written to his brothers, Tom and George, his publisher, John Taylor, and Taylor's reader, Richard Woodhouse, during the years Keats was working on his long poems *Endymion*, *Hyperion*, and *The Eve of St. Agnes*. The next year, Keats produced all his great odes, including "Ode to Autumn," "Ode to a Nightingale," and "Ode to Psyche." In 1820, he contracted tuberculosis; he died, at the age of twenty-six, the following spring in Rome, on his way to visit Shelley.

❋

Letters

Hampstead Sunday
22 December [1817]
My dear Brothers
I must crave your pardon for not having written ere this & & I saw Kean return to the public in Richard III, & finely he did it, & at the request of Reynolds I went to criticise his Luke in Riches—the critique is in todays champion, which I send you with the Examiner in which you will find very proper lamentation on the obsoletion of christmas Gambols &

pastimes: but it was mixed up with so much egotism of that drivelling nature that pleasure is entirely lost. Hone the publisher's trial, you must find very amusing; & as Englishmen very encouraging—his *Not Guilty* is a thing, which not to have been, would have dulled still more Liberty's Emblazoning—Lord Ellenborough has been paid in his own coin—Wooler & Hone have done us an essential service—I have had two very pleasant evenings with Dilke yesterday & today; & am at this moment just come from him & feel in the humour to go on with this, began in the morning, & from which he came to fetch me. I spent Friday evening with Wells & went the next morning to see *Death on the Pale horse.* It is a wonderful picture, when West's age is considered; But there is nothing to be intense upon; no women one feels mad to kiss; no face swelling into reality. the excellence of every Art is its intensity, capable of making all disagreeables evaporate, from their being in close relationship with Beauty & Truth—Examine King Lear & you will find this examplified throughout; but in this picture we have unpleasantness without any momentous depth of speculation excited, in which to bury its repulsiveness—The picture is larger than Christ rejected—I dined with Haydon the sunday after you left, & had a very pleasant day, I dined too (for I have been out too much lately) with Horace Smith & met his two brothers with Hill & Kingston & one Du Bois, they only served to convince me, how superior humour is to wit in respect to enjoyment—These men say things which make one start, without making one feel, they are all alike; their manners are alike; they all know fashionables; they have a mannerism in their very eating & drinking, in their mere handling a Decanter—They talked of Kean & his low company—Would I were with that company instead of yours said I to myself! I know such like acquaintance will never do for me & yet I am going to Reynolds, on wednesday—Brown & Dilke walked with me & back from the Christmas pantomime. I had not a dispute but a disquisition with Dilke, on various subjects; several things dovetailed in my mind, & at once it struck me, what quality went to form a Man of Achievement especially in Literature & which Shakespeare posessed so enormously—I mean *Negative Capability,* that is when man is capable of being in uncertainties, Mysteries, doubts, without any irritable reaching after fact & reason—Coleridge, for instance, would let go by a fine isolated verisimilitude caught from the Penetralium of mystery, from being incapable of remaining content with half knowledge. This pursued through Volumes would perhaps take us no further than this, that with a great poet the sense of Beauty overcomes every other consideration, or rather obliterates all consideration.

Shelley's poem is out & there are words about its being objected too, as much as Queen Mab was. Poor Shelley I think he has his Quota of good qualities, in sooth la!! Write soon to your most sincere friend & affectionate Brother

    John

❀

Hampstead 27 Feby—

My dear Taylor,

Your alteration strikes me as being a great improvement—the page looks much better. And now I will attend to the Punctuations you speak of—the comma should be at *soberly,* and in the other passage the comma should follow *quiet,* . I am extremely indebted to you for this attention and also for your after admonitions—It is a sorry thing for me that any one should have to overcome Prejudices in reading my Verses—that affects me more than any hypercriticism on any particular Passage. In *Endymion* I have most likely but moved into the Go-cart from the leading strings. In Poetry I have a few Axioms, and you will see how far I am from their Centre. 1st I think Poetry should surprise by a fine excess and not by Singularity—it should strike the Reader as a wording of his own highest thoughts, and appear almost a Remembrance—2nd Its touches of Beauty should never be half way therby making the reader breathless instead of content: the rise, the progress, the setting of imagery should like the Sun come natural natural too him—shine over him and set soberly although in magnificence leaving him in the Luxury of twilight—but it is easier to think what Poetry should be than to write it—and this leads me on to another axiom. That if Poetry comes not as naturally as the Leaves to a tree it had better not come at all. However it may be with me I cannot help looking into new countries with 'O for a Muse of fire to ascend!'—If Endymion serves me as a Pioneer perhaps I ought to be content. I have great reason to be content, for thank God I can read and perhaps understand Shakespeare to his depths, and I have I am sure many friends, who, if I fail, will attribute any change in my Life and Temper to Humbleness rather than to Pride—to a cowering under the Wings of great Poets rather than to a Bitterness that I am not appreciated. I am anxious to get Endymion printed that I may forget it and proceed. I have coppied the 3rd Book and have begun the 4th. On running my Eye over the Proofs—I saw one Mistake I will notice it presently and also any others if there be any—There should be no comma in 'the raft branch down sweeping from a tall Ash top'—I have besides made one or two alteration and also altered the 13 Line Page 32 to make sense of it as you will see. I will take care the Printer shall not trip up my Heels—There should be no dash after Dryope in the Line 'Dryope's lone lulling of her Child. Remember me to Percy Street.

your sincere and oblig^{d} friend,

John Keats—

P.S. You shall have a short Preface in good time—

❋

27 October 1818

My dear Woodhouse,

Your Letter gave me a great satisfaction; more on account of its friendliness, than any relish of that matter in it which is accounted so acceptable in the 'genus irritabile' The best answer I can give you is in a clerklike manner to make some observations on two principle points, which seem to point like indices into the midst of the whole pro and con, about genius, and views and atchievements and ambition and cœtera. 1st As to the poetical Character itself, (I mean that sort of which, if I am any thing, I am a Member; that sort distinguished from the wordsworthian or egotistical sublime; which is a thing per se and stands alone) it is not itself—it has no self—it is every thing and nothing—It has no character—it enjoys light and shade; it lives in gusto, be it foul or fair, high or low, rich or poor, mean or elevated—It has as much delight in conceiving an Iago as an Imogen. What shocks the virtuous philosoper, delights the camelion Poet. It does no harm from its relish of the dark side of things any more than from its taste for the bright one; because they both end in speculation. A Poet is the most unpoetical of any thing in existence; because he has no Identity—he is continually [informing]—and filling some other Body—The Sun, the Moon, the Sea and Men and Women who are creatures of impulse are poetical and have about them an unchangeable attribute—the poet has none; no identity—he is certainly the most unpoetical of all God's Creatures. If then he has no self, and if I am a Poet, where is the Wonder that I should say I would write no more? Might I not at that very instant been cogitating on the Characters of saturn and Ops? It is a wretched thing to confess; but is a very fact that not one word I ever utter can be taken for granted as an opinion growing out of my identical nature—how can it, when I have no nature? When I am in a room with People if I ever am free from speculating on creations of my own brain, then not myself goes home to myself: but the identity of every one in the room begins to to press upon me that, I am in a very little time anhilated—not only among Men; it would be the same in a Nursery of children: I know not whether I make myself wholly understood: I hope enough so to let you see that no dependence is to be placed on what I said that day.

In the second place I will speak of my views, and of the life I purpose to myself—I am ambitious of doing the world some good: if I should be spared that may be the work of maturer years—in the interval I will assay to reach to as high a summit in Poetry as the nerve bestowed upon me will suffer. The faint conceptions I have of Poems to come brings the blood frequently into my forehead—All I hope is that I may not lose all interest in human affairs—that the solitary indifference I feel for applause even from the finest Spirits, will not blunt any acuteness of vision I may have. I do not think it will—I feel assured I should write from the mere yearning and fondness I have for the Beautiful even if my night's labours should be burnt every morning and no eye ever shine upon them. But even now I am perhaps not speaking from myself; but from some charac-ter in whose soul I now live. I am sure however that this next sentence is from myself. I feel your anxiety, good opinion and friendliness in the highest degree, and am
    Your's most sincerely,
    John Keats

Percy Bysshe Shelley, "A Defence of Poetry," 1820

At the turn of the nineteenth century, English poetry was emerging from a neoclassical or Augustan age when all contemporary work was to be judged by its conformity, or lack of, to the rules of the Greek and Latin classics. Yet England was rapidly moving away from the ancient world. It was beginning its age of colonial expansion and had seen the French Revolution end in disillusionment. Mechanization had begun to have a major impact on people's lives with the inventions of the steam engine, iron smelting, the telegraph. It was an age, too, of mechanistic philosophies that stressed reason over imagination—Hobbes, Locke, Descartes. To counter this, the poets, influenced as well by philosophers like Kant, took as their task not only a redefinition of what a poem is and should do, but a critique of society itself.

Written in 1820, the year before Keats died of tuberculosis, and two years before Shelley himself drowned off Italy's coast at age thirty, this quintessential romantic essay picks up on many of the aforementioned themes: an elevated definition both of what is a poem and a poet. What Coleridge called, in his *Biographia Literaria,* Fancy and Imagination, Shelley distinguishes as Reason (analysis) and Imagination (synthesis), arguing that poetry has as its practice the process of creation rather than the mere association of images.

Shelley's "Defence" was in fact a response to Thomas Love Peacock's essay "The Four Ages of Poetry," an essay that included an attack on contemporary poets. Countering the familiar charge of amorality leveled against the romantic poets—for Shelley, as well as Wordsworth, Keats, and others, the imagination had taken over the role of the church, its power a secularization of the divine—Shelley insists in this essay on the value of poetry, a value more powerful than that of moral doctrine.

❁

A Defence of Poetry

PART I

According to one mode of regarding those two classes of mental action, which are called reason and imagination, the former may be considered as mind contemplating the relations borne by one thought to another, however produced, and the latter, as mind acting upon those thoughts so as to colour them with its own light, and composing from them, as from elements, other thoughts, each containing within itself the principle of its own integrity. The one is the τo ποιειν, or the principle of synthesis, and has for its objects those forms which are common to universal nature and existence itself; the other is the τo λογιζειν, or principle of analysis, and its action regards the relations of things simply as relations; considering thoughts, not in their integral unity, but as the algebraical representations which conduct to certain general results. Reason is the enumeration of qualities already known; imagination is the perception of the value of those qualities, both separately and as a whole. Reason respects the differences, and imagination the similitudes of things. Reason is to imagination as the instrument to the agent, as the body to the spirit, as the shadow to the substance.

Poetry, in a general sense, may be defined to be "the expression of the imagination": and poetry is connate with the origin of man. Man is an instrument over which a series of external and internal impressions are driven, like the alternations of an ever-changing wind over an Æolian lyre, which move it by their motion to ever-changing melody. But there is a principle within the human being, and perhaps within all sentient beings, which acts otherwise than in the lyre, and produces not melody alone, but harmony, by an internal adjustment of the sounds or motions thus excited to the impressions which excite them. It is as if the lyre could accommodate its chords to the motions of that which strikes them, in a determined proportion of sound; even as the musician can accommodate his voice to the sound of the lyre. A child at play by itself will express its delight by its voice and motions; and every inflexion of tone and every gesture will bear exact relation to a corresponding antitype in the pleasurable impressions which awakened it; it will be the reflected image of that impression; and as the lyre trembles and sounds after the wind has died away, so the child seeks, by prolonging in its voice and motions the duration of the effect, to prolong also a consciousness of the cause. In relation to the objects which delight a child, these expressions are, what poetry is to higher objects. The savage (for the savage is to ages what the child is to years) expresses the emotions produced in him by surrounding objects in a similar manner; and language and gesture, together with plastic or pictorial imitation, become the image of the combined effect of those objects, and of his apprehension of them. Man in society, with all his passions and his pleasures, next becomes the object of the passions and pleasures of man; an additional class of emotions produces an augmented treasure of expressions; and language, gesture, and the imitative arts, become at once the representation and the medium, the pencil and the picture, the chisel and the statue, the chord and the harmony. The social sympathies, or those laws from which, as from its elements, society results, begin to develop themselves from the moment that two human beings co-exist; the future is contained within the present, as the plant within the seed; and equality, diversity, unity, contrast, mutual dependence, become the principles alone capable of affording the motives according to which the will of a social being is determined to action, inasmuch as he is social; and constitute pleasure in sensation, virtue in sentiment, beauty in art, truth in reasoning, and love in the intercourse of kind. Hence men, even in the infancy of society, observe a certain order in their words and actions, distinct from that of the objects and the impressions represented by them, all expression being subject to the laws of that from which it proceeds. But let us dismiss those more general considerations which might involve an inquiry into the principles of society itself, and restrict our view to the manner in which the imagination is expressed upon its forms.

In the youth of the world, men dance and sing and imitate natural objects, observing in these actions, as in all others, a certain rhythm or order. And, although all men observe a similar, they observe not the same order, in the motions of the dance, in the melody of the song, in the combinations of language, in the series of their imitations of natural objects. For there is a certain order or rhythm belonging to each of these classes of mimetic representation, from which the hearer and the spectator receive an intenser and purer pleasure than from any other: the sense of an approximation to this order has been called taste by modern writers. Every man in the infancy of art, observes an order which approximates more or less closely to that from which this highest delight results: but the diversity is not sufficiently marked, as that its gradations should be sensible, except in those instances where the predominance of this faculty of approximation to the beautiful (for so we may be permitted to name the relation between this highest pleasure and its cause) is very great. Those in whom it exists in excess are poets, in the most universal sense of the word; and the pleasure resulting from the manner in which they express the influence of society or nature upon their own minds, communicates itself to others, and gathers a sort of reduplication from that community. Their language is vitally metaphorical; that is, it marks the before unapprehended relations of things and perpetuates their apprehension, until the words which represent them, become, through time, signs for portions or classes of thoughts instead of pictures of integral thoughts; and then if no new poets should arise to create afresh the associations which have been thus disorganized, language will be dead to all the nobler purposes of human intercourse. These similitudes or relations are finely said by Lord Bacon to be "the same footsteps of nature impressed upon the various subjects of the world"[1]—and he considers the faculty which perceives them as the storehouse of axioms common to all knowledge. In the infancy of society every author is necessarily a poet, because language itself is poetry; and to be a poet is to apprehend the true and the beautiful, in a word, the good which exists in the relation, subsisting, first between existence and perception, and secondly between perception and expression. Every original language near to its source is in itself the chaos of a cyclic poem: the copiousness of lexicography and the distinctions of grammar are the works of a later age, and are merely the catalogue and the form of the creations of poetry.

But poets, or those who imagine and express this indestructible order, are not only the authors of language and of music, of the dance, and architecture, and statuary, and painting: they are the institutors of laws, and the founders of civil society, and the inventors of the arts of life, and the teachers, who draw into a certain propinquity with the beautiful and the true, that partial apprehension of the agencies of the invisible world which is called religion. Hence all original religions are allegorical, or susceptible of allegory, and, like Janus, have a double face of false and true. Poets, according to the circumstances of the age and nation in which they appeared, were called, in the earlier epochs of the world, legislators, or prophets: a poet

---

[1] De Augment. Scient., cap. I, lib. iii.

essentially comprises and unites both these characters. For he not only beholds intensely the present as it is, and discovers those laws according to which present things ought to be ordered, but he beholds the future in the present, and his thoughts are the germs of the flower and the fruit of latest time. Not that I assert poets to be prophets in the gross sense of the word, or that they can foretell the form as surely as they foreknow the spirit of events: such is the pretence of superstition, which would make poetry an attribute of prophecy, rather than prophecy an attribute of poetry. A poet participates in the eternal, the infinite, and the one; as far as relates to his conceptions, time and place and number are not. The grammatical forms which express the moods of time, and the difference of persons, and the distinction of place, are convertible with respect to the highest poetry without injuring it as poetry; and the choruses of Æschylus, and the book of Job, and Dante's Paradise, would afford, more than other writings, examples of this fact, if the limits of this essay did not forbid citation. The creations of sculpture, painting, and music are illustrations still more decisive.

Language, colour, form, and religious and civil habits of action, are all the instruments and materials of poetry; they may be called poetry by that figure of speech which considers the effect as a synonyme of the cause. But poetry in a more restricted sense expresses those arrangements of language, and especially metrical language, which are created by that imperial faculty, whose throne is curtained within the invisible nature of man. And this springs from the nature itself of language, which is a more direct representation of the actions and passions of our internal being, and is susceptible of more various and delicate combinations, than colour, form, or motion, and is more plastic and obedient to the control of that faculty of which it is the creation. For language is arbitrarily produced by the imagination, and has relation to thoughts alone; but all other materials, instruments, and conditions of art have relations among each other, which limit and interpose between conception and expression. The former is as a mirror which reflects, the latter as a cloud which enfeebles, the light of which both are mediums of communication. Hence the fame of sculptors, painters, and musicians, although the intrinsic powers of the great masters of these arts may yield in no degree to that of those who have employed language as the hieroglyphic of their thoughts, has never equalled that of poets in the restricted sense of the term; as two performers of equal skill will produce unequal effects from a guitar and a harp. The fame of legislators and founders of religions, so long as their institutions last, alone seems to exceed that of poets in the restricted sense; but it can scarcely be a question, whether, if we deduct the celebrity which their flattery of the gross opinions of the vulgar usually conciliates, together with that which belonged to them in their higher character of poets, any excess will remain.

We have thus circumscribed the word poetry within the limits of that art which is the most familiar and the most perfect expression of the faculty itself. It is necessary, however, to make the circle still narrower, and to determine the distinction between measured and unmeasured language; for the popular division into prose and verse is inadmissible in accurate philosophy.

Sounds as well as thoughts have relation both between each other and towards that which they represent, and a perception of the order of those relations has always been found connected with a perception of the order of the relations of thoughts. Hence the language of poets has ever affected a certain uniform and harmonious recurrence of sound, without which it were not poetry, and which is scarcely less indispensable to the communication of its influence, than the words themselves, without reference to that peculiar order. Hence the vanity of translation; it were as wise to cast a violet into a crucible that you might discover the formal principle of its colour and odour, as seek to transfuse from one language into another the creations of a poet. The plant must spring again from its seed, or it will bear no flower—and this is the burthen of the curse of Babel.

An observation of the regular mode of the recurrence of harmony in the language of poetical minds, together with its relation to music, produced metre, or a certain system of traditional forms of harmony and language. Yet it is by no means essential that a poet should accommodate his language to this traditional form, so that the harmony, which is its spirit, be observed. The practice is indeed convenient and popular, and to be preferred, especially in such composition as includes much action: but every great poet must inevitably innovate upon the example of his predecessors in the exact structure of his peculiar versification. The distinction between poets and prose-writers is a vulgar error. The distinction between philosophers and poets has been anticipated. Plato was essentially a poet—the truth and splendour of his imagery, and the melody of his language, are the most intense that it is possible to conceive. He rejected the measure of the epic, dramatic, and lyrical forms, because he sought to kindle a harmony in thoughts divested of shape and action, and he forebore to invent any regular plan of rhythm which would include, under determinate forms, the varied pauses of his style. Cicero sought to imitate the cadence of his periods, but with little success. Lord Bacon was a poet.[1] His language has a sweet and majestic rhythm, which satisfies the sense, no less than the almost super-human wisdom of his philosophy satisfies the intellect; it is a strain which distends, and then bursts the circumference of the reader's mind, and pours itself forth together with it into the universal element with which it has perpetual sympathy. All the authors of revolutions in opinion are not only necessarily poets as they are inventors, nor even as their words unveil the permanent analogy of things by images which participate in the life of truth; but as their periods are harmonious and rhythmical, and contain in themselves the elements of verse; being the echo of the eternal music. Nor are those supreme poets, who have employed traditional forms of rhythm on account of the form and action of their subjects, less capable of perceiving and teaching the truth of things, than those who have omitted that form. Shakespeare, Dante, and Milton (to confine ourselves to modern writers) are philosophers of the very loftiest power.

A poem is the very image of life expressed in its eternal truth. There is this difference between a story and a poem, that a story is a catalogue of detached facts, which have no other connection than time, place, circumstance, cause and effect; the other is the creation of actions according to the unchangeable forms of human nature, as existing in the mind of the Creator, which is itself the image of all other minds. The one is partial, and applies only to a definite period of time, and a certain combination of events which can never again recur; the other is universal, and contains within itself the germ of a relation to whatever motives or actions have place in the possible varieties of human nature. Time, which destroys the beauty and the use of the story of particular facts, stripped of the poetry which should invest them, augments that of poetry, and for ever develops new and wonderful applications of the eternal truth which it contains. Hence epitomes have been called the moths of just history; they eat out the poetry of it. A story of particular facts is as a mirror which obscures and distorts that which should be made beautiful: poetry is a mirror which makes beautiful that which is distorted.

---

[1] See the Filum Labyrinthi, and the Essay on Death particularly.

The parts of a composition may be poetical, without the composition as a whole being a poem. A single sentence may be considered as a whole, though it may be found in the midst of a series of unassimilated portions; a single word even may be a spark of inextinguishable thought. And thus all the great historians, Herodotus, Plutarch, Livy, were poets; and although the plan of these writers, especially that of Livy, restrained them from developing this faculty in its highest degree, they made copious and ample amends for their subjection, by filling all the interstices of their subjects with living images.

Having determined what is poetry, and who are poets, let us proceed to estimate its effect upon society.

Poetry is ever accompanied with pleasure: all spirits on which it falls open themselves to receive the wisdom which is mingled with its delight. In the infancy of the world, neither poets themselves nor their auditors are fully aware of the excellence of poetry: for it acts in a divine and unapprehended manner, beyond and above consciousness; and it is reserved for future generations to contemplate and measure the mighty cause and effect in all the strength and splendour of their union. Even in modern times, no living poet ever arrived at the fulness of his fame; the jury which sits in judgment upon a poet, belonging as he does to all time, must be composed of his peers: it must be impanneled by Time from the selectest of the wise of many generations. A poet is a nightingale, who sits in darkness and sings to cheer its own solitude with sweet sounds; his auditors are as men entranced by the melody of an unseen musician, who feel that they are moved and softened, yet know not whence or why. The poems of Homer and his contemporaries were the delight of infant Greece; they were the elements of that social system which is the column upon which all succeeding civilisation has reposed. Homer embodied the ideal perfection of his age in human character; nor can we doubt that those who read his verses were awakened to an ambition of becoming like to Achilles, Hector, and Ulysees: the truth and beauty of friendship, patriotism, and persevering devotion to an object, were unveiled to the depths in these immortal creations: the sentiments of the auditors must have been refined and enlarged by a sympathy with such great and lovely impersonations, until from admiring they imitated, and from imitation they identified themselves with the objects of their admiration. Nor let it be objected, that these characters are remote from moral perfection, and that they can by no means be considered as edifying patterns for general imitation. Every epoch, under names more or less specious, has deified its peculiar errors; Revenge is the naked idol of the worship of a semi-barbarous age; and Self-deceit is the veiled image of unknown evil, before which luxury and satiety lie prostrate. But a poet considers the vices of his contemporaries as the temporary dress in which his creations must be arrayed, and which cover without concealing the eternal proportions of their beauty. An epic or dramatic personage is understood to wear them around his soul, as he may the ancient armour or the modern uniform around his body; whilst it is easy to conceive a dress more graceful than either. The beauty of the internal nature cannot be so far concealed by its accidental vesture, but that the spirit of its form shall communicate itself to the very disguise, and indicate the shape it hides from the manner in which it is worn. A majestic form and graceful motions will express themselves through the most barbarous and tasteless costume. Few poets of the highest class have chosen to exhibit the beauty of their conceptions in its naked truth and splendour; and it is doubtful whether the alloy of costume, habit, etc., be not necessary to temper this planetary music for mortal ears.

The whole objection, however, of the immorality of poetry rests upon a misconception of the manner in which poetry acts to produce the moral improvement of man. Ethical science arranges the elements which poetry has created, and propounds schemes and proposes examples of civil and domestic life: nor is it for want of admirable doctrines that men hate, and despise, and censure, and deceive, and subjugate one another. But poetry acts in another and diviner manner. It awakens and enlarges the mind itself by rendering it the receptacle of a thousand unapprehended combinations of thought. Poetry lifts the veil from the hidden beauty of the world, and makes familiar objects be as if they were not familiar; it reproduces all that it represents, and the impersonations clothed in its Elysian light stand thenceforward in the minds of those who have once contemplated them, as memorials of that gentle and exalted content which extends itself over all thoughts and actions with which it co-exists. The great secret of morals is love; or a going out of our nature, and an identification of ourselves with the beautiful which exists in thought, action, or person, not our own. A man, to be greatly good, must imagine intensely and comprehensively; he must put himself in the place of another and of many others; the pains and pleasures of his species must become his own. The great instrument of moral good is the imagination; and poetry administers to the effect by acting upon the cause. Poetry enlarges the circumference of the imagination by replenishing it with thoughts of ever new delight, which have the power of attracting and assimilating to their own nature all other thoughts, and which form new intervals and interstices whose void for ever craves fresh food. Poetry strengthens the faculty which is the organ of the moral nature of man, in the same manner as exercise strengthens a limb. A poet therefore would do ill to embody his own conceptions of right and wrong, which are usually those of his place and time, in his poetical creations, which participate in neither. By this assumption of the inferior office of interpreting the effect, in which perhaps after all he might acquit himself but imperfectly, he would resign a glory in a participation in the cause. There was little danger that Homer, or any of the eternal poets, should have so far misunderstood themselves as to have abdicated this throne of their widest dominion. Those in whom the poetical faculty, though great, is less intense, as Euripides, Lucan, Tasso, Spenser, have frequently affected a moral aim, and the effect of their poetry is diminished in exact proportion to the degree in which they compel us to advert to this purpose.

Homer and the cyclic poets were followed at a certain interval by the dramatic and lyrical poets of Athens, who flourished contemporaneously with all that is most perfect in the kindred expressions of the poetical faculty; architecture, painting, music, the dance, sculpture, philosophy, and we may add, the forms of civil life. For although the scheme of Athenian society was deformed by many imperfections which the poetry existing in chivalry and Christianity has erased from the habits and institutions of modern Europe; yet never at any other period has so much energy, beauty, and virtue been developed; never was blind strength and stubborn form so disciplined and rendered subject to the will of man, or that will less repugnant to the dictates of the beautiful and the true, as during the century which preceded the death of Socrates. Of no other epoch in the history of our species have we records and fragments stamped so visibly with the image of the divinity in man. But it is poetry alone, in form, in action, or in language, which has rendered this epoch memorable above all others, and the storehouse of examples to everlasting time. For written poetry existed at that epoch simultaneously with the other arts, and it is an idle inquiry to demand which gave and which received the light, which all, as from a common focus, have scattered over the darkest periods of succeeding time. We know no more of cause and effect than a constant conjunction of events: poetry is ever found to co-exist with whatever other arts contribute to the happiness and perfection of man. I appeal to what has already been established to distinguish between the cause and the effect.

It was at the period here adverted to, that the drama had its birth; and however a succeeding writer may have equalled or surpassed those few great specimens of the Athenian drama which have been preserved to us, it is indisputable that the art itself never was understood or practised according to the true philosophy of it, as at Athens. For the Athenians employed language, action, music, painting, the dance, and religious institutions, to produce a common effect in the representation of the highest idealisms of passion and of power; each division in the art was made perfect in its kind by artists of the most consummate skill, and was disciplined into a beautiful proportion and unity one towards the other. On the modern stage a few only of the elements capable of expressing the image of the poet's conception are employed at once. We have tragedy without music and dancing; and music and dancing without the highest impersonations of which they are the fit accompaniment, and both without religion and solemnity. Religious institution has indeed been usually banished from the stage. Our system of divesting the actor's face of a mask, on which the many expressions appropriated to his dramatic character might be moulded into one permanent and unchanging expression, is favourable only to a partial and inharmonious effect; it is fit for nothing but a monologue, where all the attention may be directed to some great master of ideal mimicry. The modern practice of blending comedy with tragedy, though liable to great abuse in point of practice, is undoubtedly an extension of the dramatic circle; but the comedy should be as in King Lear, universal, ideal, and sublime. It is perhaps the intervention of this principle which determines the balance in favour of King Lear against the Œdipus Tyrannus or the Agamemnon, or, if you will, the trilogies with which they are connected; unless the intense power of the choral poetry, especially that of the latter, should be considered as restoring the equilibrium. King Lear, if it can sustain this comparison, may be judged to be the most perfect specimen of the dramatic art existing in the world; in spite of the narrow conditions to which the poet was subjected by the ignorance of the philosophy of the drama which has prevailed in modern Europe. Calderon, in his religious Autos, has attempted to fulfil some of the high conditions of dramatic representation neglected by Shakespeare;

such as the establishing a relation between the drama and religion, and the accommodating them to music and dancing; but he omits the observation of conditions still more important, and more is lost than gained by the substitution of the rigidly-defined and ever-repeated idealisms of a distorted superstition for the living impersonations of the truth of human passion.

But I digress.—The connexion of scenic exhibitions with the improvement or corruption of the manners of men, has been universally recognised; in other words, the presence or absence of poetry in its most perfect and universal form has been found to be connected with good and evil in conduct or habit. The corruption which has been imputed to the drama as an effect, begins, when the poetry employed in its constitution ends: I appeal to the history of manners whether the periods of the growth of the one and the decline of the other have not corresponded with an exactness equal to any example of moral cause and effect.

The drama at Athens, or wheresoever else it may have approached to its perfection, ever co-existed with the moral and intellectual greatness of the age. The tragedies of the Athenian poets are as mirrors in which the spectator beholds himself, under a thin disguise of circumstance, stript of all but that ideal perfection and energy which every one feels to be the internal type of all that he loves, admires, and would become. The imagination is enlarged by a sympathy with pains and passions so mighty, that they distend in their conception the capacity of that by which they are conceived; the good affections are strengthened by pity, indignation, terror and sorrow; and an exalted calm is prolonged from the satiety of this high exercise of them into the tumult of familiar life: even crime is disarmed of half its horror and all its contagion by being represented as the fatal consequence of the unfathomable agencies of nature; error is thus divested of its wilfulness; men can no longer cherish it as the creation of their choice. In a drama of the highest order there is little food for censure or hatred; it teaches rather self-knowledge and self-respect. Neither the eye nor the mind can see itself, unless reflected upon that which it resembles. The drama, so long as it continues to express poetry, is as a prismatic and many-sided mirror, which collects the brightest rays of human nature and divides and reproduces them from the simplicity of these elementary forms, and touches them with majesty and beauty, and multiplies all that it reflects, and endows it with the power of propagating its like wherever it may fall.

But in periods of the decay of social life, the drama sympathizes with that decay. Tragedy becomes a cold imitation of the form of the great masterpieces of antiquity, divested of all harmonious accompaniment of the kindred arts; and often the very form misunderstood, or a weak attempt to teach certain doctrines, which the writer considers as moral truths; and which are usually no more than specious flatteries of some gross vice or weakness, with which the author, in common with his auditors, are infected. Hence what has been called the classical and domestic drama. Addison's "Cato" is a specimen of the one; and would it were not superfluous to cite examples of the other! To such purposes poetry cannot be made subservient. Poetry is a sword of lightning, ever unsheathed, which consumes the scabbard that would contain it. And thus we observe that all dramatic writings of this nature are unimaginative in a singular degree; they affect sentiment and passion, which, divested of imagination, are other names for caprice and appetite. The period in our own history of the grossest degradation of the drama is the reign of Charles II, when all forms in which poetry had been accustomed to be expressed became hymns to the triumph of kingly power over liberty and virtue. Milton stood alone illuminating an age unworthy of him. At such periods the calculating principle pervades all the forms of dramatic exhibition, and poetry ceases to be expressed upon them. Comedy loses its ideal universality: wit succeeds to humour; we laugh from self-complacency and triumph, instead of pleasure; malignity, sarcasm, and contempt succeed to sympathetic merriment; we hardly laugh, but we smile. Obscenity, which is ever blasphemy against the divine beauty in life, becomes, from the very veil which it assumes, more active if less disgusting: it is a monster for which the corruption of society for ever brings forth new food, which it devours in secret.

The drama being that form under which a greater number of modes of expression of poetry are susceptible of being combined than any other, the connexion of poetry and social good is more observable in the drama than in whatever other form. And it is indisputable that the highest perfection of human society has ever corresponded with the highest dramatic excellence; and that the corruption or the extinction of the drama in a nation where it has once flourished, is a mark of a corruption of manners, and an extinction of the energies which sustain the soul of social life. But, as Machiavelli says of political institutions, that life may be preserved and renewed, if men should arise capable of bringing back the drama to its principles. And this is true with respect to poetry in its most extended sense: all language, institution and form, require not only to be produced but to be sustained: the office and character of a poet participates in the divine nature as regards providence, no less than as regards creation.

Civil war, the spoils of Asia, and the fatal predominance first of the Macedonian, and then of the Roman arms, were so many symbols of the extinction or suspension of the creative faculty in Greece. The bucolic writers, who found patronage under the lettered tyrants of Sicily and Egypt, were the latest representatives of its most glorious reign. Their poetry is intensely melodious; like the odour of the tuberose, it overcomes and sickens the spirit with excess of sweetness; whilst the poetry of the preceding age was as a meadow-gale of June, which mingles the fragrance of all the flowers of the field, and adds a quickening and harmonising spirit of its own which endows the sense with a power of sustaining its extreme delight. The bucolic and erotic delicacy in written poetry is correlative with that softness in statuary, music and the kindred arts, and even in manners and institutions, which distinguished the epoch to which I now refer. Nor is it the poetical faculty itself, or any misapplication of it, to which this want of harmony is to be imputed. An equal sensibility to the influence of the senses and the affections is to be found in the writings of Homer and Sophocles: the former, especially, has clothed sensual and pathetic images with irresistible attractions. Their superiority over these succeeding writers consists in the presence of those thoughts which belong to the inner faculties of our nature, not in the absence of those which are connected with the external: their incomparable perfection consists in a harmony of the union of all. It is not what the erotic poets have, but what they have not, in which their imperfection consists. It is not inasmuch as they were poets, but inasmuch as they were not poets, that they can be considered with any plausibility as connected with the corruption of their age. Had that corruption availed so as to extinguish in them the sensibility to pleasure, passion, and natural scenery, which is imputed to them as an imperfection, the last triumph of evil would have been achieved. For the end of social corruption is to destroy all sensibility to pleasure; and, therefore, it is corruption. It begins at the imagination and the intellect as at the core, and distributes itself thence as a paralysing venom, through the affections into the very appetites, until all become a torpid mass in which hardly sense survives. At the approach of such a period, poetry ever addresses itself to those faculties which are the last to be destroyed, and its voice is heard, like the footsteps of Astræa, departing from the world. Poetry ever communicates all the pleasure which men are capable of receiving: it is ever still the light of life; the source of whatever of beautiful or generous or true can have place in an evil time. It will readily be confessed that those among the luxurious citizens of Syracuse and Alexandria, who were delighted with the poems of Theocritus, were less cold, cruel, and sensual than the remnant of their tribe. But corruption must utterly have destroyed the fabric of human society before poetry can ever cease. The sacred links of that chain have never been entirely disjoined, which descending through the minds of many men is attached to those great minds, whence as from a magnet the invisible effluence is sent forth, which at once connects, animates, and sustains the life of all. It is the faculty which contains within itself the seeds at once of its own and of social renovation. And let us not circumscribe the effects of the bucolic and erotic poetry within the limits of the sensibility of those to whom it was addressed. They may have perceived the beauty of those immortal compositions, simply as fragments and isolated portions: those who are more finely organised, or, born in a happier age, may recognise them as episodes to that great poem, which all poets, like the co-operating thoughts of one great mind, have built up since the beginning of the world.

The same revolutions within a narrower sphere had place in ancient Rome; but the action and forms of its social life never seem to have been perfectly saturated with the poetical element. The Romans appear to have considered the Greeks as the selectest treasuries of the selectest forms of manners and of nature, and to have abstained from creating in measured language, sculpture, music, or architecture, anything which might bear a particular relation to their own condition, whilst it should bear a general one to the universal constitution of the world. But we judge from partial evidence, and we judge perhaps partially. Ennius, Varro, Pacuvius, and Accius, all great poets, have been lost. Lucretius is in the highest, and Virgil in a very high sense, a creator. The chosen delicacy of expressions of the latter, are as a mist of light which conceal from us the intense and exceeding truth of his conceptions of nature. Livy is instinct with poetry. Yet Horace, Catullus, Ovid, and generally the other great writers of the Virgilian age, saw man and nature in the mirror of Greece. The institutions also, and the religion of Rome, were less poetical than those of Greece, as the shadow is less vivid than the substance. Hence poetry in Rome seemed to follow, rather than accompany, the perfection of political and domestic society. The true poetry of Rome lived in its institutions; for whatever of beautiful, true, and majestic, they contained, could have sprung only from the faculty which creates the order in which they consist. The life of Camillus, the death of Regulus; the expectation of the senators, in their godlike state, of the victorious Gauls; the refusal of the republic to make peace with Hannibal, after the battle of Cannæ, were not the consequences of a refined calculation of the probable personal advantage to result from such a rhythm and order in the shows of life, to those who were at once the poets and the actors of these immortal dramas. The imagination beholding the beauty of this order, created it out of itself according to its own idea; the consequence was empire, and the reward ever-living fame. These things are not the less poetry, *quia carent vate sacro*. They are the episodes of that cyclic poem written by Time upon the memories of men. The Past, like an inspired rhapsodist, fills the theatre of everlasting generations with their harmony.

At length the ancient system of religion and manners had fulfilled the circle of its revolutions. And the world would have fallen into utter anarchy and darkness, but that there were found poets among the authors of the Christian and chivalric systems of manners and religion, who created forms of opinion and action never before conceived; which, copied into the imaginations of men, became as generals to the bewildered armies of their thoughts. It is foreign to the present purpose to touch upon the evil produced by these systems: except that we protest, on the ground of the principles already established, that no portion of it can be attributed to the poetry they contain.

It is probable that the poetry of Moses, Job, David, Solomon, and Isaiah had produced a great effect upon the mind of Jesus and his disciples. The scattered fragments preserved to us by the biographers of this extraordinary person, are all instinct with the most vivid poetry. But his doctrines seem to have been quickly distorted. At a certain period after the prevalence of a system of opinions founded upon those promulgated by him, the three forms into which Plato had distributed the faculties of mind underwent a sort of apotheosis, and became the object of the worship of the civilised world. Here it is to be confessed that "Light seems to thicken," and

> "The crow makes wing to the rooky wood,
> Good things of day begin to droop and drowse,
> And night's black agents to their preys do rouse."

But mark how beautiful an order has sprung from the dust and blood of this fierce chaos! how the world, as from a resurrection, balancing itself on the golden wings of knowledge and of hope, has reassumed its yet unwearied flight into the heaven of time. Listen to the music, unheard by outward ears, which is as a ceaseless and invisible wind, nourishing its everlasting course with strength and swiftness.

The poetry in the doctrines of Jesus Christ, and the mythology and institutions of the Celtic conquerors of the Roman Empire, outlived the darkness and the convulsions connected with their growth and victory, and blended themselves in a new fabric of manners and opinion. It is an error to impute the ignorance of the dark ages to the Christian doctrines or the predominance of the Celtic nations. Whatever of evil their agencies may have contained sprang from the extinction of the poetical principle, connected with the progress of despotism and superstition. Men, from causes too intricate to be here discussed, had become insensible and selfish: their own will had become feeble, and yet they were its slaves, and thence the slaves of the will of others: lust, fear, avarice, cruelty, and fraud, characterised a race amongst whom no one was to be found capable of *creating* in form, language, or institution. The moral anomalies of such a state of society are not justly to be charged upon any class of events immediately connected with them, and those events are most entitled to our approbation which could dissolve it most expeditiously. It is unfortunate for those who cannot distinguish words from thoughts, that many of these anomalies have been incorporated into our popular religion.

It was not until the eleventh century that the effects of the poetry of the Christian and chivalric systems began to manifest themselves. The principle of equality had been discovered and applied by Plato in his Republic, as the theoretical rule of the mode in which the materials of pleasure and of power produced by the common skill and labour of human beings ought to be distributed among them. The limitations of this rule were asserted by him to be determined only by the sensibility of each, or the utility to result to all. Plato, following the doctrines of Timæus and Pythagoras, taught also a moral and intellectual system of doctrine, comprehending at once the past, the present, and the future condition of man. Jesus Christ divulged the sacred and eternal truths contained in these views to mankind, and Christianity, in its abstract purity, became the exoteric expression of the esoteric doctrines of the poetry and wisdom of antiquity. The incorporation of the Celtic nations with the exhausted population of the south, impressed upon it the figure of the poetry existing in their mythology and institutions. The result was a sum of the action and reaction of all the causes included in it; for it may be assumed as a maxim that no nation or religion can supersede any other without incorporating into itself a portion of that which it supersedes. The abolition of personal and domestic slavery, and the emancipation of women from a great part of the degrading restraints of antiquity, were among the consequences of these events.

The abolition of personal slavery is the basis of the highest political hope that it can enter into the mind of man to conceive. The freedom of women produced the poetry of sexual love. Love became a religion, the idols of whose worship were ever present. It was as if the statues of Apollo and the Muses had been endowed with life and motion, and had walked forth among their worshippers; so that earth became peopled by the inhabitants of a diviner world. The familiar appearance and proceedings of life became wonderful and heavenly, and a paradise was created as out of the wrecks of Eden. And as this creation itself is poetry, so its creators were poets; and language was the instrument of their art: "Galeotto fù il libro, e chi lo scrisse." The Provençal Trouveurs, or inventors, preceded Petrarch, whose verses are as spells, which unseal the inmost enchanted fountains of delight which is in the grief of love. It is impossible to feel them without becoming a portion of that beauty which we contemplate: it were superfluous to explain how the gentleness and the elevation of mind connected with these sacred emotions can render men more amiable, more generous and wise, and lift them out of the dull vapours of the little world of self. Dante understood the secret things of love even more than Petrarch. His *Vita Nuova* is an inexhaustible fountain of purity of sentiment and language: it is the idealised history of that period, and those intervals of his life which were dedicated to love. His apotheosis of Beatrice in Paradise, and the gradations of his own love and her loveliness, by which as by steps he feigns himself to have ascended to the throne of the Supreme Cause, is the most glorious imagination of modern poetry. The acutest critics have justly reversed the judgment of the vulgar, and the order of the great acts of the "Divine Drama," in the measure of the admiration which they accord to the Hell, Purgatory, and Paradise. The latter is a perpetual hymn of everlasting love. Love, which found a worthy poet in Plato alone of all the ancients, has been celebrated by a chorus of the greatest writers of the renovated world; and the music has penetrated the caverns of society, and its echoes still drown the dissonance of arms and superstition. At successive intervals, Ariosto, Tasso, Shakespeare, Spenser, Calderon, Rousseau, and the great writers of our own age, have celebrated the dominion of love, planting as it were trophies in the human mind of that sublimest victory over sensuality and force. The true relation borne to each other by the sexes into which human kind is distributed, has become less misunderstood; and if the error which confounded diversity with inequality of the powers of the two sexes has been partially recognised in the opinions and institutions of modern Europe, we owe this great benefit to the worship of which chivalry was the law, and poet the prophets.

The poetry of Dante may be considered as the bridge thrown over the stream of time, which unites the modern and ancient world. The distorted notions of invisible things which Dante and his rival Milton have idealised, are merely the mask and the mantle in which these great poets walk through eternity enveloped and disguised. It is a difficult question to determine how far they were conscious of the distinction which must have subsisted in their minds between their own creeds and that of the people. Dante at least appears to wish to mark the full extent of it by placing Riphæus, whom Virgil calls *justissimus unus,* in Paradise, and observing a most heretical caprice in his distribution of rewards and punishments. And Milton's poem contains within itself a philosophical refutation of that system, of which, by a strange and natural antithesis, it has been a chief popular support. Nothing can exceed the energy and magnificence of the character of Satan as expressed in "Paradise Lost." It is a mistake to suppose that he could ever have been intended for the popular personification of evil. Implacable hate, patient cunning, and a sleepless refinement of device to inflict the extremest anguish on an enemy, these things are evil; and, although venial in a slave, are not to be forgiven in a tyrant; although redeemed by much that ennobles his defeat in one subdued, are marked by all that dishonours his conquest in the victor. Milton's Devil as a moral being is as far superior to his God, as one who perseveres in some purpose which he has conceived to be excellent in spite of adversity and torture, is to one who in the cold security of undoubted triumph inflicts the most horrible revenge upon his enemy, not from any mistaken notion of inducing him to repent of a perseverance in enmity, but with the alleged design of exasperating him to deserve new torments. Milton has so far violated the popular creed (if this shall be judged to be a violation) as to have alleged no superiority of moral virtue to his God over his Devil. And this bold neglect of a direct moral purpose is the most decisive proof of the supremacy of Milton's genius. He mingled as it were the elements of human nature as colours upon a single pallet, and arranged them in the composition of his great picture according to the laws of epic truth; that is, according to the laws of that principle by which a series of actions of the external universe and of intelligent and ethical beings is calculated to excite the sympathy of succeeding generations of mankind. The Divina Commedia and Paradise Lost have conferred upon modern mythology a systematic form; and when change and time shall have added one more superstition to the mass of those which have arisen and decayed upon the earth, commentators will be learnedly employed in elucidating the religion of ancestral Europe, only not utterly forgotten because it will have been stamped with the eternity of genius.

Homer was the first and Dante the second epic poet: that is, the second poet, the series of whose creations bore a defined and intelligible relation to the knowledge and sentiment and religion of the age in which he lived, and of the ages which followed it, developing itself in correspondence with their development. For Lucretius had limed the wings of his swift spirit in the dregs of the sensible world; and Virgil, with a modesty that ill became his genius, had affected the fame of an imitator, even whilst he created anew all that he copied; and none among the flock of mock-birds, though their notes were sweet, Apollonius Rhodius, Quintus Calaber, Nonnus, Lucan, Statius, or Claudian, have sought even to fulfil a single condition of epic truth. Milton was the third epic poet. For if the title of epic in its highest sense be refused to the Æneid, still less can it be conceded to the Orlando Furioso, the Gerusalemme Liberata, the Lusiad, or the Fairy Queen.

Dante and Milton were both deeply penetrated with the ancient religion of the civilised world; and its spirit exists in their poetry probably in the same proportion as its forms survived in the unreformed worship of modern Europe. The one preceded and the other followed the Reformation at almost equal intervals. Dante was the first religious reformer, and Luther surpassed him rather in the rudeness and acrimony, than in the boldness of his censures of papal usurpation. Dante was the first awakener of entranced Europe; he created a language, in itself music and persuasion, out of a chaos of inharmonious barbarisms. He was the congregator of those great spirits who presided over the resurrection of learning; the Lucifer of that starry flock which in the thirteenth century shone forth from republican Italy, as from a heaven, into the darkness of the benighted world. His very words are instinct with spirit; each is as a spark, a burning atom of inextinguishable thought; and many yet lie covered in the ashes of their birth, and pregnant with the lightning which has yet found no conductor. All high poetry is infinite; it is as the first acorn, which contained all oaks potentially. Veil after veil may be undrawn, and the inmost naked beauty of the meaning never exposed. A great poem is a fountain for ever overflowing with the waters of wisdom and delight; and after one person and one age has exhausted all its divine effluence which their peculiar relations enable them to share, another and yet another succeeds, and new relations are ever developed, the source of an unforeseen and an unconceived delight.

The age immediately succeeding to that of Dante, Petrarch, and Boccaccio, was characterised by a revival of painting, sculpture, and architecture. Chaucer caught the sacred inspiration, and the superstructure of English literature is based upon the materials of Italian invention.

But let us not be betrayed from a defence into a critical history of poetry and its influence on society. Be it enough to have pointed out the effects of poets, in the large and true sense of the word, upon their own and all succeeding times.

But poets have been challenged to resign the civic crown to reasoners and mechanists, on another plea. It is admitted that the exercise of the imagination is most delightful, but it is alleged that that of reason is more useful. Let us examine as the grounds of this distinction what is here meant by utility. Pleasure or good, in a general sense, is that which the consciousness of a sensitive and intelligent being seeks, and in which, when found, it acquiesces. There are two kinds of pleasure, one durable, universal, and permanent; the other transitory and particular. Utility may either express the means of producing the former or the latter. In the former sense, whatever strengthens and purifies the affections, enlarges the imagination, and adds spirit to sense, is useful. But a narrower meaning may be assigned to the word utility, confining it to express that which banishes the importunity of the wants of our animal nature, the surrounding men with security of life, the dispersing of the grosser delusions of superstition, and the conciliating such a degree of mutual forbearance among men as may consist with the motives of personal advantage.

Undoubtedly the promoters of utility, in this limited sense, have their appointed office in society. They follow the footsteps of poets, and copy the sketches of their creations into the book of common life. They make space, and give time. Their exertions are of the highest value, so long as they confine their administration of the concerns of the inferior powers of our nature within the limits due to the superior ones. But whilst the sceptic destroys gross superstitions, let him spare to deface, as some of the French writers have defaced, the eternal truths charactered upon the imaginations of men. Whilst the mechanist abridges, and the political economist combines labour, let them beware that their speculations, for want of correspondence with those first principles which belong to the imagination, do not tend, as they have in modern England, to exasperate at once the extremes of luxury and want. They have exemplified the saying, "To him that hath, more shall be given; and from him that hath not, the little that he hath shall be taken away." The rich have become richer, and the poor have become poorer; and the vessel of the state is driven between the Scylla and Charybdis of anarchy and despotism. Such are the effects which must ever flow from an unmitigated exercise of the calculating faculty.

It is difficult to define pleasure in its highest sense; the definition involving a number of apparent paradoxes. For, from an inexplicable defect of harmony in the constitution of human nature, the pain of the inferior is frequently connected with the pleasures of the superior portions of our being. Sorrow, terror, anguish, despair itself, are often the chosen expressions of an approximation to the highest good. Our sympathy in tragic fiction depends on this principle; tragedy delights by affording a shadow of the pleasure which exists in pain. This is the source also of the melancholy which is inseparable from the sweetest melody. The pleasure that is in sorrow is sweeter than the pleasure of pleasure itself. And hence the saying, "It is better to go to the house of mourning, than to the house of mirth." Not that this highest species of pleasure is necessarily linked with pain. The delight of love and friendship, the ecstasy of the admiration of nature, the joy of the perception and still more of the creation of poetry, is often wholly unalloyed.

The production and assurance of pleasure in this highest sense is true utility. Those who produce and preserve this pleasure are poets or poetical philosophers.

The exertions of Locke, Hume, Gibbon, Voltaire, Rousseau[1] and their disciples, in favour of oppressed and deluded humanity, are entitled to the gratitude of mankind. Yet it is easy to calculate the degree of moral and intellectual improvement which the world would have exhibited, had they never lived. A little more nonsense would have been talked for a century or two; and perhaps a few more men, women, and children burnt as heretics. We might not at this moment have been congratulating each other on the abolition of the Inquisition in Spain. But it exceeds all imagination to conceive what would have been the moral condition of the world if neither Dante, Petrarch, Boccaccio, Chaucer, Shakespeare, Calderon, Lord Bacon, nor Milton, had ever existed; if Raphael and Michael Angelo had never been born; if the Hebrew poetry had never been translated; if a revival of the study of Greek literature had never taken place; if no monuments of ancient sculpture had been handed down to us; and if the poetry of the religion of the ancient world had been extinguished together with its belief. The human mind could never, except by the intervention of these excitements, have been awakened to the invention of the grosser sciences, and that application of analytical reasoning to the aberrations of society, which it is now attempted to exalt over the direct expression of the inventive and creative faculty itself.

We have more moral, political, and historical wisdom than we know how to reduce into practice; we have more scientific and economical knowledge than can be accommodated to the just distribution of the produce which it multiplies. The poetry in these systems of thought is concealed by the accumulation of facts and calculating processes. There is no want of knowledge respecting what is wisest and best in morals, government, and political economy, or at least, what is wiser and better than what men now practise and endure. But we let *"I dare not* wait upon *I would,* like the poor cat in the adage."* We want the creative faculty to imagine that which we know; we want the generous impulse to act that which we imagine; we want the poetry of life: our calculations have outrun conception; we have eaten more than we can digest. The cultivation of those sciences which have enlarged the limits of the empire of man over the external world, has, for want of the poetical faculty, proportion-

---

[1] Although Rousseau had been thus classed, he was essentially a poet. The others, even Voltaire, were mere reasoners.

ally circumscribed those of the internal world; and man, having enslaved the elements, remains himself a slave. To what but a cultivation of the mechanical arts in a degree disproportioned to the presence of the creative faculty, which is the basis of all knowledge, is to be attributed the abuse of all invention for abridging and combining labour, to the exasperation of the inequality of mankind? From what other cause has it arisen that the discoveries which should have lightened, have added a weight to the curse imposed on Adam? Poetry, and the principle of Self, of which money is the visible incarnation, are the God and Mammon of the world.

The functions of the poetical faculty are two-fold; by one it creates new materials of knowledge, and power, and pleasure; by the other it engenders in the mind a desire to reproduce and arrange them according to a certain rhythm and order which may be called the beautiful and the good. The cultivation of poetry is never more to be desired than at periods when, from an excess of the selfish and calculating principle, the accumulation of the materials of external life exceed the quantity of the power of assimilating them to the internal laws of human nature. The body has then become too unwieldy for that which animates it.

Poetry is indeed something divine. It is at once the centre and circumference of knowledge; it is that which comprehends all science, and that to which all science must be referred. It is at the same time the root and blossom of all other systems of thought; it is that from which all spring, and that which adorns all; and that which, if blighted, denies the fruit and the seed, and withholds from the barren world the nourishment and the succession of the scions of the tree of life. It is the perfect and consummate surface and bloom of all things; it is as the odour and the colour of the rose to the texture of the elements which compose it, as the form and splendour of unfaded beauty to the secrets of anatomy and corruption. What were virtue, love, patriotism, friendship—what were the scenery of this beautiful universe which we inhabit; what were our consolations on this side of the grave—and what were our aspirations beyond it, if poetry did not ascend to bring light and fire from those eternal regions where the owl-winged faculty of calculation dare not ever soar? Poetry is not like reasoning, a power to be exerted according to the determination of the will. A man cannot say, "I will compose poetry." The greatest poet even cannot say it; for the mind in creation is as a fading coal, which some invisible influence, like an inconstant wind, awakens to transitory brightness; this power arises from within, like the colour of a flower which fades and changes as it is developed, and the conscious portions of our natures are unprophetic either of its approach or its departure. Could this influence be durable in its original purity and force, it is impossible to predict the greatness of the results; but when composition begins, inspiration is already on the decline, and the most glorious poetry that has ever been communicated to the world is probably a feeble shadow of the original conceptions of the poet. I appeal to the greatest poets of the present day, whether it is not an error to assert that the finest passages of poetry are produced by labour and study. The toil and the delay recommended by critics can be justly interpreted to mean no more than a careful observation of the inspired moments, and an artificial connexion of the spaces between their suggestions by the intertexture of conventional expressions; a necessity only imposed by the limitedness of the poetical faculty itself: for Milton conceived the "Paradise Lost" as a whole before he executed it in portions. We have his own authority also for the muse having "dictated" to him the "unpremeditated song." And let this be an answer to those who would allege the fifty-six various readings of the first line of the "Orlando Furioso." Compositions so produced are to poetry what mosaic is to painting. This instinct and intuition of the poetical faculty is still more observable in the plastic and pictorial arts; a great statue or picture grows under the power of the artist as a child in the mother's womb; and the very mind which directs the hands in formation is incapable of accounting to itself for the origin, the graduations, or the media of the process.

Poetry is the record of the best and happiest moments of the happiest and best minds. We are aware of evanescent visitations of thought and feeling sometimes associated with place or person, sometimes regarding our own mind alone, and always arising unforeseen and departing unbidden, but elevating and delightful beyond all expression: so that even in the desire and the regret they leave, there cannot but be pleasure, participating as it does in the nature of its object. It is as it were the interpenetration of a diviner nature through our own; but its footsteps are like those of a wind over the sea, which the coming calm erases, and whose traces remain only as on the wrinkled sands which pave it. These and corresponding conditions of being are experienced principally by those of the most delicate sensibility and the most enlarged imagination; and the state of mind produced by them is at war with every base desire. The enthusiasm of virtue, love, patriotism, and friendship is essentially linked with such emotions; and whilst they last, self appears as what it is, an atom to a universe. Poets are not only subject to these experiences as spirits of the most refined organisation, but they can colour all that they combine with the evanescent hues of this ethereal world; a word, a trait in the representation of a scene or a passion will touch the enchanted chord, and reanimate, in those who have ever experienced these emotions, the sleeping, the cold, the buried image of the past. Poetry thus makes immortal all that is best and most beautiful in the world; it arrests the vanishing apparitions which haunt the interlunations of life, and veiling them, or in language or in form, sends them forth among mankind, bearing sweet news of kindred joy to those with whom their sisters abide—abide, because there is no portal of expression from the caverns of the spirit which they inhabit into the universe of things. Poetry redeems from decay the visitations of the divinity in man.

Poetry turns all things to loveliness; it exalts the beauty of that which is most beautiful, and it adds beauty to that which is most deformed; it marries exultation and horror, grief and pleasure, eternity and change; it subdues to union under its light yoke all irreconcilable things. It transmutes all that it touches, and every form moving within the radiance of its presence is changed by wondrous sympathy to an incarnation of the spirit which it breathes: its secret alchemy turns to potable gold the poisonous waters which flow from death through life; it strips the veil of familiarity from the world, and lays bare the naked and sleeping beauty, which is the spirit of its forms.

All things exist as they are perceived: at least in relation to the percipient. "The mind is at its own place, and of itself can make a heaven of hell, a hell of heaven." But poetry defeats the curse which binds us to be subjected to the accident of surrounding impressions. And whether it spreads its own figured curtain, or withdraws life's dark veil from before the scene of things, it equally creates for us a being within our being. It makes us the inhabitants of a world to which the familiar world is a chaos. It reproduces the common universe of which we are portions and percipients, and it purges from our inward sight the film of familiarity which obscures from us the wonder of our being. It compels us to feel that which we perceive, and to imagine that which we know. It creates anew the universe, after it has been annihilated in our minds by the recurrence of impressions blunted by reiteration. It justifies the bold and true words of Tasso—*Non merita nome di creatore, se non Iddio ed il Poeta.*

A poet, as he is the author to others of the highest wisdom, pleasure, virtue, and glory, so he ought personally to be the happiest, the best, the wisest, and the most illustrious of men. As to his glory, let time be challenged to declare whether the fame of any other institutor of human life be comparable to that of a poet. That he is the wisest, the happiest, and the best, inasmuch as he is a poet, is equally incontrovertible: the greatest poets have been men of the most spotless virtue, of the most consummate prudence, and, if we would look into the interior of their lives, the most fortunate of men: and the exceptions, as they regard those who possessed the poetic faculty in a high yet inferior degree, will be found on consideration to confine rather than destroy the rule. Let us for a moment stoop to the arbitration of popular breath, and usurping and uniting in our own persons the incompatible characters of accuser, witness, judge, and executioner, let us decide without trial, testimony, or form, that certain motives of those who are "there sitting where we dare not soar," are reprehensible. Let us assume that Homer was a drunkard, that Virgil was a flatterer, that Horace was a coward, that Tasso was a madman, that Lord Bacon was a peculator, that Raphael was a libertine, that Spenser was a poet laureate. It is inconsistent with this division of our subject to cite living poets, but posterity has done ample justice to the great names now referred to. Their errors have been weighed and found to have been dust in the balance; if their sins "were as scarlet, they are now white as snow"; they have been washed in the blood of the mediator and redeemer, Time. Observe in what a ludicrous chaos the imputations of real or fictitious crime have been confused in the contemporary calumnies against poetry and poets; consider how little is, as it appears—or appears, as it is; look to your own motives, and judge not, lest ye be judged.

Poetry, as has been said, differs in this respect from logic, that it is not subject to the control of the active powers of the mind, and that its birth and recurrence have no necessary connexion with the consciousness or will. It is presumptuous to determine that these are the necessary conditions of all mental causation, when mental effects are experienced unsusceptible of being referred to them. The frequent recurrence of the poetical power, it is obvious to suppose, may produce in the mind a habit of order and harmony correlative with its own nature and with its effects upon other minds. But in the intervals of inspiration, and they may be frequent without being durable, a poet becomes a man, and is abandoned to the sudden reflux of the influences under which others habitually live. But as he is more delicately organised than other men, and sensible to pain and pleasure, both his own and that of others, in a degree unknown to them, he will avoid the one and pursue the other with an ardour proportioned to this difference. And he renders himself obnoxious to calumny, when he neglects to observe the circumstances under which these objects of universal pursuit and flight have disguised themselves in one another's garments.

But there is nothing necessarily evil in this error, and thus cruelty, envy, revenge, avarice, and the passions purely evil, have never formed any portion of the popular imputations on the lives of poets.

I have thought it most favourable to the cause of truth to set down these remarks according to the order in which they were suggested to my mind, by a consideration of the subject itself, instead of observing the formality of a polemical reply; but if the view which they contain be just, they will be found to involve a refutation of the arguers against poetry, so far at least as regards the first division of the subject. I can readily conjecture what should have moved the gall of some learned and intelligent writers who quarrel with certain versifiers; I confess myself, like them, unwilling to be stunned by the Theseids of the hoarse Codri of the day. Bavius and Mævius undoubtedly are, as they ever were, insufferable persons. But it belongs to a philosophical critic to distinguish rather than confound.

The first part of these remarks has related to poetry in its elements and principles; and it has been shown, as well as the narrow limits assigned them would permit, that what is called poetry, in a restricted sense, has a common source with all other forms of order and of beauty, according to which the materials of human life are susceptible of being arranged, and which is poetry in an universal sense.

The second part will have for its object an application of these principles to the present state of the cultivation of poetry, and a defence of the attempt to idealise the modern forms of manners and opinions, and compel them into a subordination to the imaginative and creative faculty. For the literature of England, an energetic development of which has ever preceded or accompanied a great and free development of the national will, has arisen as it were from a new birth. In spite of the low-thoughted envy which would undervalue contemporary merit, our own will be a memorable age in intellectual achievements, and we live among such philosophers and poets as surpass beyond comparison any who have appeared since the last national struggle for civil and religious liberty. The most unfailing herald, companion, and follower of the awakening of a

great people to work a beneficial change in opinion or institution, is poetry. At such periods there is an accumulation of the power of communicating and receiving intense and impassioned conceptions respecting man
and nature. The persons in whom this power resides, may often, as far as
regards many portions of their nature, have little apparent correspondence
with that spirit of good of which they are the ministers. But even whilst
they deny and abjure, they are yet compelled to serve, the power which is
seated on the throne of their own soul. It is impossible to read the compositions of the most celebrated writers of the present day without being
startled with the electric life which burns within their words. They measure the circumference and sound the depths of human nature with a comprehensive and all-penetrating spirit, and they are themselves perhaps the
most sincerely astonished at its manifestations; for it is less their spirit
than the spirit of the age. Poets are the hierophants of an unapprehended
inspiration; the mirrors of the gigantic shadows which futurity casts upon
the present; the words which express what they understand not; the trum-
pets which sing to battle, and feel not what they inspire; the influence
which is moved not, but moves. Poets are the unacknowledged legislators
of the world.

Ralph Waldo Emerson, "The Poet," 1844

Although it was Wordsworth, Coleridge, Schlegel, and other Europeans who were calling for an end to the mechanical regularity imposed by inherited meter and traditional forms, they could not accomplish the freedom they longed for. They could not break the meter that kept them tied to centuries of tradition of English verse, a struggle we see reflected in the recurring attention paid, in these essays, to the difference between poetry and prose. (Without meter, what makes it a poem?) In hindsight, it seems inevitable that the revolutionary step toward free verse would be a step across the Atlantic.

"Why should not we also enjoy an original relation to the universe? Why should not we have a poetry and philosophy of insight and not of tradition, and a religion by revelation to us, and not the history of theirs?" Ralph Waldo Emerson asks in one of his first essays, "Nature." Coming to maturity after the Revolutionary War, his was a generation struggling to define a distinctly American identity. "The Poet," published in 1844, but widely given as a lecture beforehand, is Emerson's call to arms for a poetry to reflect this identity, one of individualism and self-reliance, energy and process, and transcendence of, not adherence to, tradition.

Emerson was a reader of both Coleridge and Wordsworth and had met both of them in Europe in 1831. But in "The Poet," Emerson brings many of the ideas of romanticism to his countrymen in his particularly American translation. The quest for common themes and language in England would become, in the heroism of America, a triumph of content over form, of enthusiasm (Emerson's word for inspiration) over meter. Though a poet himself, Emerson was unable in his poetry to accomplish what he envisioned. He was, like Coleridge, searching for his Wordsworth.

❋

The Poet

A moody child and wildly wise
Pursued the game with joyful eyes,
Which chose, like meteors, their way,
And rived the dark with private ray:
They overleapt the horizon's edge,
Searched with Apollo's privilege;
Through man, and woman, and sea, and star
Saw the dance of nature forward far;
Through worlds, and races, and terms, and times
Saw musical order, and pairing rhymes.

Olympian bards who sung
Divine ideas below,
Which always find us young,
And always keep us so.

Those who are esteemed umpires of taste are often persons who have acquired some knowledge of admired pictures or sculptures, and have an inclination for whatever is elegant; but if you inquire whether they are beautiful souls, and whether their own acts are like fair pictures, you learn that they are selfish and sensual. Their cultivation is local, as if you should rub a log of dry wood in one spot to produce fire, all the rest remaining cold. Their knowledge of the fine arts is some study of rules and particulars, or some limited judgment of color or form, which is exercised for amusement or for show. It is a proof of the shallowness of the doctrine of beauty as it lies in the minds of our amateurs, that men seem to have lost the perception of the instant dependence of form upon soul. There is no doctrine of forms in our philosophy. We were put into our bodies, as fire is put into a pan to be carried about; but there is no accurate adjustment between the spirit and the organ, much less is the latter the germination of the former. So in regard to other forms, the intellectual men do not believe in any essential dependence of the material world on thought and volition. Theologians think it a pretty air-castle to talk of the spiritual meaning of a ship or a cloud, of a city or a contract, but they prefer to come again to the solid ground of historical evidence; and even the poets are contented with a civil and conformed manner of living, and to write poems from the fancy, at a safe distance from their own experience. But the highest minds of the world have never ceased to explore the double meaning, or shall I say the quadruple or the centuple or much more manifold meaning, of every sensuous fact; Orpheus, Empedocles, Heraclitus, Plato, Plutarch, Dante, Swedenborg, and the masters of sculpture, picture and poetry. For we are not pans and barrows, nor even porters of the fire and torch-bearers, but children of the fire, made of it, and only the same divinity transmuted and at two or three removes, when we know least about it. And this hidden truth, that the fountains whence all this river of Time and its creatures floweth are intrinsically ideal and beautiful, draws us to the consideration of the nature and functions of the Poet, or the man of Beauty; to the means and materials he uses, and to the general aspect of the art in the present time.

The breadth of the problem is great, for the poet is representative. He stands among partial men for the complete man, and apprises us not of his wealth, but of the common wealth. The young man reveres men of genius, because, to speak truly, they are more himself than he is. They receive of the soul as he also receives, but they more. Nature enhances her beauty, to the eye of loving men, from their belief that the poet is beholding her shows at the same time. He is isolated among his contemporaries by truth and by his art, but with this consolation in his pursuits, that they will draw all men sooner or later. For all men live by truth and stand in need of expression. In love, in art, in avarice, in politics, in labor, in games, we study to utter our painful secret. The man is only half himself, the other half is his expression.

Notwithstanding this necessity to be published, adequate expression is rare. I know not how it is that we need an interpreter, but the great majority of men seem to be minors, who have not yet come into possession of their own, or mutes, who cannot report the conversation they have had with nature. There is no man who does not anticipate a supersensual utility in the sun and stars, earth and water. These stand and wait to render him a peculiar service. But there is some obstruction or some excess of phlegm in our constitution, which does not suffer them to yield the due effect. Too feeble fall the impressions of nature on us to make us artists. Every touch should thrill. Every man should be so much an artist that he could report in conversation what had befallen him. Yet, in our experience, the rays or appulses have sufficient force to arrive at the senses, but not enough to reach the quick and compel the reproduction of themselves in speech. The poet is the person in whom these powers are in balance, the man without impediment, who sees and handles that which others dream of, traverses the whole scale of experience, and is representative of man, in virtue of being the largest power to receive and to impart.

For the Universe has three children, born at one time, which reappear under different names in every system of thought, whether they be called cause, operation and effect; or more poetically, Jove, Pluto, Neptune; or theologically, the Father, the Spirit and the Son; but which we will call here the Knower, the Doer and the Sayer. These stand respectively for the love of truth, for the love of good, and for the love of beauty. These three are equal. Each is that which he is, essentially, so that he cannot be surmounted or analyzed, and each of these three has the power of the others latent in him and his own, patent.

The poet is the sayer, the namer, and represents beauty. He is a sovereign, and stands on the centre. For the world is not painted or adorned, but is from the beginning beautiful and God has not made some beautiful things, but Beauty is the creator of the universe. Therefore the poet is not any permissive potentate, but is emperor in his own right. Criticism is infested with a cant of materialism, which assumes that manual skill and activity is the first merit of all men, and disparages such as say and do not, overlooking the fact that some men, namely poets, are natural sayers, sent into the world to the end of expression, and confounds them with those whose province is action but who quit it to imitate the sayers. But Homer's words are as costly and admirable to Homer as Agamemnon's victories are to Agamemnon. The poet does not wait for the hero or the sage, but, as they act and think primarily, so he writes primarily what will and must be spoken, reckoning the others, though primaries also, yet, in respect to him, secondaries and servants; as sitters or models in the studio of a painter, or as assistants who bring building-materials to an architect.

For poetry was all written before time was, and whenever we are so finely organized that we can penetrate into that region where the air is music, we hear those primal warblings and attempt to write them down, but we lose ever and anon a word or a verse and substitute something of our own, and thus miswrite the poem. The men of more delicate ear write down these cadences more faithfully, and those transcripts, though imperfect, become the songs of the nations. For nature is as truly beautiful as it is good, or as it is reasonable, and must as much appear as it must be done, or be known. Words and deeds are quite indifferent modes of the divine energy. Words are also actions, and actions are a kind of words.

The sign and credentials of the poet are that he announces that which no man foretold. He is the true and only doctor; he knows and tells; he is the only teller of news, for he was present and privy to the appearance which he describes. He is a beholder of ideas and an utterer of the necessary and causal. For we do not speak now of men of poetical talents, or of industry and skill in metre, but of the true poet. I took part in a conversation the other day concerning a recent writer of lyrics, a man of subtle mind, whose head appeared to be a music-box of delicate tunes and rhythms, and whose skill and command of language we could not sufficiently praise. But when the question arose whether he was not only a lyrist but a poet, we were obliged to confess that he is plainly a contemporary, not an eternal man. He does not stand out of our low limitations, like a Chimborazo under the line, running up from a torrid base through all the climates of the globe, with belts of the herbage of every latitude on its high and mottled sides; but this genius is the landscape-garden of a modern house, adorned with fountains and statues, with well-bred men and women standing and sitting in the walks and terraces. We hear, through all the varied music, the groundtone of conventional life. Our poets are men of talents who sing, and not the children of music. The argument is secondary, the finish of the verses is primary.

For it is not metres, but a metre-making argument that makes a poem,—a thought so passionate and alive that like the spirit of a plant or an animal it has an architecture of its own, and adorns nature with a new thing. The thought and the form are equal in the order of time, but in the order of genesis the thought is prior to the form. The poet has a new thought; he has a whole new experience to unfold; he will tell us how it was with him, and all men will be the richer in his fortune. For the experience of each new age requires a new confession, and the world seems always waiting for its poet. I remember when I was young how much I was moved one morning by tidings that genius had appeared in a youth who sat near me at table. He had left his work and gone rambling none knew whither, and had written hundreds of lines, but could not tell whether that which was in him was therein told; he could tell nothing but that all was changed,—man, beast, heaven, earth and sea. How gladly we listened! how credulous! Society seemed to be compromised. We sat in the aurora of a sunrise which was to put out all the stars. Boston seemed to be at twice the distance it had the night before, or was much farther than that. Rome,—what was Rome? Plutarch and Shakspeare were in the yellow leaf, and Homer no more should be heard of. It is much to know that poetry has been written this very day, under this very roof, by your side. What! that wonderful spirit has not expired! These stony moments are still sparkling and animated! I had fancied that the oracles were all silent, and nature had spent her fires; and behold! all night, from every pore, these fine auroras have been streaming. Every one has some interest in the advent of the poet, and no one knows how much it may concern him. We know that the secret of the world is profound, but who or what shall be our interpreter, we know not. A mountain ramble, a new style of face, a new person, may put the key into our hands. Of course the value of genius to us is in the veracity of its report. Talent may frolic and juggle; genius realizes and adds. Mankind in good earnest have availed so far in understanding themselves and their work, that the foremost watchman on the peak announces his news. It is the truest word ever spoken, and the phrase will be the fittest, most musical, and the unerring voice of the world for that time.

All that we call sacred history attests that the birth of a poet is the principal event in chronology. Man, never so often deceived, still watches for the arrival of a brother who can hold him steady to a truth until he has made it his own. With what joy I begin to read a poem which I confide in as an inspiration! And now my chains are to be broken; I shall mount above these clouds and opaque airs in which I live,—opaque, though they seem transparent,—and from the heaven of truth I shall see and comprehend my relations. That will reconcile me to life and renovate nature, to see trifles animated by a tendency, and to know what I am doing. Life will no more be a noise; now I shall see men and women, and know the signs by which they may be discerned from fools and satans. This day shall be better than my birthday: then I became an animal; now I am invited into the science of the real. Such is the hope, but the fruition is postponed. Oftener it falls that this winged man, who will carry me into the heaven, whirls me into mists, then leaps and frisks about with me as it were from cloud to cloud, still affirming that he is bound heavenward; and I, being myself a novice, am slow in perceiving that he does not know the way into the heavens, and is merely bent that I should admire his skill to rise like a fowl or a flying fish, a little way from the ground or the water; but the all-piercing, all-feeding and ocular air of heaven that man shall never inhabit. I tumble down again soon into my old nooks, and lead the life of exaggerations as before, and have lost my faith in the possibility of any guide who can lead me thither where I would be.

But, leaving these victims of vanity, let us, with new hope, observe how nature, by worthier impulses, has insured the poet's fidelity to his office of announcement and affirming, namely by the beauty of things, which becomes a new and higher beauty when expressed. Nature offers all her creatures to him as a picture-language. Being used as a type, a second wonderful value appears in the object, far better than its old value; as the carpenter's stretched cord, if you hold your ear close enough, is musical in the breeze. "Things more excellent than every image," says Jamblichus, "are expressed through images." Things admit of being used as symbols because nature is a symbol, in the whole, and in every part. Every line we can draw in the sand has expression; and there is no body without its spirit or genius. All form is an effect of character; all condition, of the quality of the life; all harmony, of health; and for this reason a perception of beauty should be sympathetic, or proper only to the good. The beautiful rests on the foundations of the necessary. The soul makes the body, as the wise Spenser teaches:—

> "So every spirit, as it is more pure,
> And hath in it the more of heavenly light,
> So it the fairer body doth procure
> To habit in, and it more fairly dight,
> With cheerful grace and amiable sight.
> For, of the soul, the body form doth take,
> For soul is form, and doth the body make."

Here we find ourselves suddenly not in a critical speculation but in a holy place, and should go very warily and reverently. We stand before the secret of the world, there where Being passes into Appearance and Unity into Variety.

The Universe is the externization of the soul. Wherever the life is, that bursts into appearance around it. Our science is sensual, and therefore superficial. The earth and the heavenly bodies, physics and chemistry, we sensually treat, as if they were self-existent; but these are the retinue of that Being we have. "The mighty heaven," said Proclus, "exhibits, in its transfigurations, clear images of the splendor of intellectual perceptions;

being moved in conjunction with the unapparent periods of intellectual natures." Therefore science always goes abreast with the just elevation of the man, keeping step with religion and metaphysics; or the state of science is an index of our self-knowledge. Since every thing in nature answers to a moral power, if any phenomenon remains brute and dark it is because the corresponding faculty in the observer is not yet active.

No wonder then, if these waters be so deep, that we hover over them with a religious regard. The beauty of the fable proves the importance of the sense; to the poet, and to all others; or, if you please, every man is so far a poet as to be susceptible of these enchantments of nature; for all men have the thoughts whereof the universe is the celebration. I find that the fascination resides in the symbol. Who loves nature? Who does not? Is it only poets, and men of leisure and cultivation, who live with her? No; but also hunters, farmers, grooms and butchers, though they express their affection in their choice of life and not in their choice of words. The writer wonders what the coachman or the hunter values in riding, in horses and dogs. It is not superficial qualities. When you talk with him he holds these at as slight a rate as you. His worship is sympathetic; he has no definitions, but he is commanded in nature by the living power which he feels to be there present. No imitation or playing of these things would content him; he loves the earnest of the north wind, of rain, of stone and wood and iron. A beauty not explicable is dearer than a beauty which we can see to the end of. It is nature the symbol, nature certifying the supernatural, body overflowed by life which he worships with coarse but sincere rites.

The inwardness and mystery of this attachment drive men of every class to the use of emblems. The schools of poets and philosophers are not more intoxicated with their symbols than the populace with theirs. In our political parties, compute the power of badges and emblems. See the great ball which they roll from Baltimore to Bunker Hill! In the political processions, Lowell goes in a loom, and Lynn in a shoe, and Salem in a ship. Witness the cider-barrel, the log-cabin, the hickory-stick, the palmetto, and all the cognizances of party. See the power of national emblems. Some stars, lilies, leopards, a crescent, a lion, an eagle, or other figure which came into credit God knows how, on an old rag of bunting, blowing in the wind on a fort at the ends of the earth, shall make the blood tingle under the rudest or the most conventional exterior. The people fancy they hate poetry, and they are all poets and mystics!

Beyond this universality of the symbolic language, we are apprised of the divineness of this superior use of things, whereby the world is a temple whose walls are covered with emblems, pictures, and commandments of the Deity,—in this, that there is no fact in nature which does not carry the whole sense of nature; and the distinctions which we make in events and in affairs, of low and high, honest and base, disappear when nature is used as a symbol. Thought makes everything fit for use. The vocabulary of an omniscient man would embrace words and images excluded from polite conversation. What would be base, or even obscene, to the obscene, becomes illustrious, spoken in a new connection of thought. The piety of the Hebrew prophets purges their grossness. The circumcision is an example of the power of poetry to raise the low and offensive. Small and mean things serve as well as great symbols. The meaner the type by which a law is expressed, the more pungent it is, and the more lasting in the memories of men; just as we choose the smallest box or case in which any needful utensil can be carried. Bare lists of words are found suggestive to an imaginative and excited mind; as it is related of Lord Chatham that he was accustomed to read in Bailey's Dictionary when he was preparing to speak in Parliament. The poorest experience is rich enough for all the purposes of expressing thought. Why covet a knowledge of new facts? Day and night, house and garden, a few books, a few actions, serve us as well as would all trades and all spectacles. We are far from having exhausted the significance of the few symbols we use. We can come to use them yet with a terrible simplicity. It does not need that a poem should be long. Every word was once a poem. Every new relation is a new word. Also we use defects and deformities to a sacred purpose, so expressing our sense that the evils of the world are such only to the evil eye. In the old mythology, mythologists observe, defects are ascribed to divine natures, as lameness to Vulcan, blindness to Cupid, and the like,— to signify exuberances.

For as it is dislocation and detachment from the life of God that makes things ugly, the poet, who re-attaches things to nature and the Whole,— re-attaching even artificial things and violation of nature, to nature, by a deeper insight,—disposes very easily of the most disagreeable facts. Readers of poetry see the factory-village and the railway, and fancy that the poetry of the landscape is broken up by these; for these works of art are not yet consecrated in their reading; but the poet sees them fall within the great Order not less than the beehive or the spider's geometrical web. Nature adopts them very fast into her vital circles, and the gliding train of cars she loves like her own. Besides, in a centred mind, it signifies nothing how many mechanical inventions you exhibit. Though you add millions, and never so surprising, the fact of mechanics has not gained a grain's weight. The spiritual fact remains unalterable, by many or by few particulars; as no mountain is of any appreciable height to break the curve of the sphere. A shrewd country-boy goes to the city for the first time, and the complacent citizen is not satisfied with his little wonder. It is not that he does not see all the fine houses and know that he never saw such before, but he disposes of them as easily as the poet finds place for the railway. The chief value of the new fact is to enhance the great and constant fact of Life, which can dwarf any and every circumstance, and to which the belt of wampum and the commerce of America are alike.

The world being thus put under the mind for verb and noun, the poet is he who can articulate it. For though life is great, and fascinates and absorbs; and though all men are intelligent of the symbols through which it is named; yet they cannot originally use them. We are symbols and inhabit symbols; workmen, work, and tools, words and things, birth and death, all are emblems; but we sympathize with the symbols, and being infatuated with the economical uses of things, we do not know that they are thoughts. The poet, by an ulterior intellectual perception, gives them a power which makes their old use forgotten, and puts eyes and a tongue into every dumb and inanimate object. He perceives the independence of the thought on the symbol, the stability of the thought, the accidency and fugacity of the symbol. As the eyes of Lyncaeus were said to see through the earth, so the poet turns the world to glass, and shows us all things in their right series and procession. For through that better perception he stands one step nearer to things, and sees the flowing or metamorphosis; perceives that thought is multiform; that within the form of every creature is a force impelling it to ascend into a higher form; and following with his eyes the life, uses the forms which express that life, and so his speech flows with the flowing of nature. All the facts of the animal economy, sex, nutriment, gestation, birth, growth, are symbols of the passage of the world into the soul of man, to suffer there a change and reappear a new and higher fact. He uses forms according to the life, and not according to the form. This is true science. The poet alone knows astronomy, chemistry, vegetation and animation, for he does not stop at these facts, but employs them as signs. He knows why the plain or meadow of space was strown with these flowers we call suns and moons and stars; why the great deep is adorned with animals, with men and gods; for in every word he speaks he rides on them as the horses of thought.

By virtue of this science the poet is the Namer or Language-maker, naming things sometimes after their appearance, sometimes after their essence, and giving to every one its own name and not another's, thereby rejoicing the intellect, which delights in detachment or boundary. The poets made all the words, and therefore language is the archives of history, and, if we must say it, a sort of tomb of the muses. For though the origin of most of our words is forgotten, each word was at first a stroke of genius, and obtained currency because for the moment it symbolized the world to the first speaker and to the hearer. The etymologist finds the deadest word to have been once a brilliant picture. Language is fossil poetry. As the limestone of the continent consists of infinite masses of the shells of animalcules, so language is made up of images or tropes, which now, in their secondary use, have long ceased to remind us of their poetic origin. But the poet names the thing because he sees it, or comes one step nearer to it than any other. This expression or naming is not art, but a second nature, grown out of the first, as a leaf out of a tree. What we call nature is a certain self-regulated motion or change; and nature does all things by her own hands, and does not leave another to baptize her but baptizes herself; and this through the metamorphosis again. I remember that a certain poet described it to me thus:—

Genius is the activity which repairs the decays of things, whether wholly or partly of a material and finite kind. Nature, through all her kingdoms, insures herself. Nobody cares for planting the poor fungus; so she shakes down from the gills of one agaric countless spores, any one of which, being preserved, transmits new billions of spores tomorrow or next day. The new agaric of this hour has a chance which the old one had not. This atom of seed is thrown into a new place, not subject to the accidents which destroyed its parent two rods off. She makes a man; and having brought him to ripe age, she will no longer run the risk of losing this wonder at a blow, but she detaches from him a new self, that the kind may be safe from accidents to which the individual is exposed. So when the soul of the poet has come to ripeness of thought, she detaches and sends away from it its poems or songs,—a fearless, sleepless, deathless progeny, which is not exposed to the accidents of the weary kingdom of time; a fearless, vivacious offspring, clad with wings (such was the virtue of the soul out of which they came) which carry them fast and far, and infix them irrecoverably into the hearts of men. These wings are the beauty of the poet's soul. The songs, thus flying immortal from their mortal parent, are pursued by clamorous flights of censures, which swarm in far greater numbers and threaten to devour them; but these last are not winged. At the end of a very short leap they fall plump down and rot, having received from the souls out of which they came no beautiful wings. But the melodies of the poet ascend and leap and pierce into the deeps of infinite time.

❋

So far the bard taught me, using his freer speech. But nature has a higher end, in the production of new individuals, than security, namely *ascension,* or the passage of the soul into higher forms. I knew in my younger days the sculptor who made the statue of the youth which stands in the public garden. He was, as I remember, unable to tell directly what made him happy or unhappy, but by wonderful indirections he could tell. He rose one day, according to his habit, before the dawn, and saw the morning break, grand as the eternity out of which it came, and for many days after, he strove to express this tranquillity, and lo! his chisel had fashioned out of marble the form of a beautiful youth, Phosphorus, whose aspect is such that it is said all persons who look on it become silent. The poet also resigns himself to his mood, and that thought which agitated him is expressed, but *alter idem,* in a manner totally new. The expression is organic, or the new type which things themselves take when liberated. As, in the sun, objects paint their images on the retina of the eye, so they, sharing the aspiration of the whole universe, tend to paint a far more delicate copy of their essence in his mind. Like the metamorphosis of things into higher organic forms is their change into melodies. Over everything stands its daemon or soul, and, as the form of the thing is reflected by the eye, so the soul of the thing is reflected by a melody. The sea, the mountain-ridge, Niagara, and every flower-bed, pre-exist, or super-exist, in pre-cantations, which sail like odors in the air, and when any man goes by with an ear sufficiently fine, he overhears them and endeavors to write down the notes without diluting or depraving them. And herein is the legitimation of criticism, in the mind's faith that the poems are a corrupt version of some text in nature with which they ought to be made to tally. A rhyme in one of our sonnets should not be less pleasing than the iterated nodes of a seashell, or the resembling difference of a group of flowers. The pairing of the birds is an idyl, not tedious as our idyls are; a tempest is a rough ode, without falsehood or rant; a summer, with its harvest sow, reaped and stored, is an epic song, subordinating how many admirable executed parts. Why should not the symmetry and truth that modulate these, glide into our spirits, and we participate the invention of nature?

This insight, which expresses itself by what is called Imagination, is a very high sort of seeing, which does not come by study, but by the intellect being where and what it sees; by sharing the path or circuit of things through forms, and so making them translucid to others. The path of things is silent. Will they suffer a speaker to go with them? A spy they will not suffer; a lover, a poet, is the transcendency of their own nature,— him they will suffer. The condition of true naming, on the poet's part, is his resigning himself to the divine *aura* which breathes through forms, and accompanying that.

It is a secret which every intellectual man quickly learns, that beyond the energy of his possessed and conscious intellect he is capable of a new energy (as of an intellect doubled on itself), by abandonment to the nature of things; that beside his privacy of power as an individual man, there is a great public power on which he can draw, by unlocking, at all risks, his human doors, and suffering the ethereal tides to roll and circulate through him; then he is caught up into the life of the Universe, his speech is thunder, his thought is law, and his words are universally intelligible as the plants and animals. The poet knows that he speaks adequately then only when he speaks somewhat wildly, or "with the flower of the mind," not with the intellect used as an organ, but with the intellect released from all service and suffered to take its direction from its celestial life; or as the ancients were wont to express themselves, not with intellect alone but with the intellect inebriated by nectar. As the traveller who has lost his way throws his reins on his horse's neck and trusts to the instinct of the animal to find his road, so must we do with the divine animal who carries us through this world. For if in any manner we can stimulate this instinct, new passages are opened for us into nature; the mind flows into and through things hardest and highest, and the metamorphosis is possible.

This is the reason why bards love wine, mead, narcotics, coffee, tea, opium, the fumes of sandalwood and tobacco, or whatever other procurers of animal exhilaration. All men avail themselves of such means as they can, to add this extraordinary power to their normal powers; and to this end they prize conversation, music, pictures, sculpture, dancing, theatres, travelling, war, mobs, fires, gaming, politics, or love, or science, or animal intoxication,—which are several coarser or finer *quasi*-mechanical substitutes for the true nectar, which is the ravishment of the intellect by coming nearer to the fact. These are auxiliaries to the centrifugal tendency of a man, to his passage out into free space, and they help him to escape the custody of that body in which he is pent up, and of that jail-yard of individual relations in which he is enclosed. Hence a great number of such as were professionally expressers of Beauty, as painters, poets, musicians and actors, have been more than others wont to lead a life of pleasure and indulgence; all but the few who received the true nectar; and, as it was a spurious mode of attaining freedom, as it was an emancipation not into the heavens but into the freedom of baser places, they were punished for that advantage they won, by a dissipation and deterioration. But never can any advantage be taken of nature by a trick. The spirit of the world, the great calm presence of the Creator, comes not forth to the sorceries of opium or of wine. The sublime vision comes to the pure and simple soul in a clean and chaste body. That is not an inspiration, which we owe to narcotics, but some counterfeit excitement and fury. Milton says that the lyric poet may drink wine and live generously, but the epic poet, he who shall sing of the gods and their descent unto men, must drink water out of a wooden bowl. For poetry is not 'Devil's wine,' but God's wine. It is with this as it is with toys. We fill the hands and nurseries of our children with all manner of dolls, drums and horses; withdrawing their eyes from the plain face and sufficing objects of nature, the sun and moon, the animals, the water and stones, which should be their toys. So the poet's habit of living should be set on a key so low that the common influences should delight him. His cheerfulness should be the gift of the sunlight; the air should suffice for his inspiration, and he should be tipsy with water. That spirit which suffices quiet hearts, which seems to come forth to such from every dry knoll of sere grass, from every pine stump and half-imbedded stone on which the dull March sun shines, comes forth to the poor and hungry, and such as are of simple taste. If thou fill thy brain with Boston and New York, with fashion and covetousness, and wilt stimulate thy jaded senses with wine and French coffee, thou shalt find no radiance of wisdom in the lonely waste of the pine woods.

If the imagination intoxicates the poet, it is not inactive in other men. The metamorphosis excites in the beholder an emotion of joy. The use of symbols has a certain power of emancipation and exhilaration for all men. We seem to be touched by a wand which makes us dance and run about happily, like children. We are like persons who come out of a cave or cellar into the open air. This is the effect on us of tropes, fables, oracles and all poetic forms. Poets are thus liberating gods. Men have really got a new sense, and found within their world another world, or nest of worlds; for, the metamorphosis once seen, we divine that it does not stop. I will not now consider how much this makes the charm of algebra and the mathematics, which also have their tropes, but it is felt in every definition; as when Aristotle defines space to be an immovable vessel in which things are contained;—or when Plato defines a line to be a flowing point; or figure to be a bound of solid; and many the like. What a joyful sense of freedom we have when Vitruvius announces the old opinion of artists that no architect can build any house well who does not know something of anatomy. When Socrates, in Charmides, tells us that the soul is cured of its maladies by certain incantations, and that these incantations are beautiful reasons, from which temperence is generated in souls; when Plato calls the world an animal, and Timaeus affirms that the plants also are animals; or affirms a man to be a heavenly tree, growing with his root, which is his head, upward; and, as George Chapman, following him, writes,

"So in our tree of man, whose nervie root
"Springs in his top;"

when Orpheus speaks of hoariness as "that white flower which marks extreme old age;" when Proclus calls the universe the statue of the intellect; when Chaucer, in his praise of 'Gentilesse,' compares good blood in mean condition to fire, which, though carried to the darkest house betwixt this and the mount of Caucasus, will yet hold its natural office and burn as bright as if twenty thousand men did it behold; when John saw, in the Apocalypse, the ruin of the world through evil, and the stars fall from heaven as the fig tree casteth her untimely fruit; when Aesop reports the whole catalogue of common daily relations through the masquerade of birds and beasts;—we take the cheerful hint of the immortality of our essence and its versatile habit and escapes, as when the gypsies say of themselves "it is in vain to hang them, they cannot die."

The poets are thus liberating gods. The ancient British bards had for the title of their order, "Those who are free throughout the world." They are free, and they make free. An imaginative book renders us much more service at first, by stimulating us through its tropes, than afterward when we arrive at the precise sense of the author. I think nothing is of any value in books excepting the transcendental and extraordinary. If a man is inflamed and carried away by his thought, to that degree that he forgets the authors and the public and heeds only this one dream which holds him like an insanity, let me read his paper, and you may have all the arguments and histories and criticism. All the value which attaches to Pythagoras, Paracelsus, Cornelius Agrippa, Cardan, Kepler, Swedenborg, Schelling, Oken, or any other who introduces questionable facts into his cosmogony, as angels, devils, magic, astrology, palmistry, mesmerism, and so on, is the certificate we have of departure from routine, and that here is a new witness. That also is the best success in conversation, the magic of liberty, which puts the world like a ball in our hands. How cheap even the liberty then seems; how mean to study, when an emotion communicates to the intellect the power to sap and unheave nature; how great the perspective! nations, times, systems, enter and disappear like threads in tapestry of large figure and many colors; dream delivers us to dream, and while the drunkenness lasts we will sell our bed, our philosophy, our religion, in our opulence.

There is good reason why we should prize this liberation. The fate of the poor shepherd, who, blinded and lost in the snow-storm, perishes in a drift within a few feet of his cottage door, is an emblem of the state of man. On the brink of the waters of life and truth, we are miserably dying. The inaccessibleness of every thought but that we are in, is wonderful. What if you come near to it; you are as remote when you are nearest as when you are farthest. Every thought is also a prison; every heaven is also a prison. Therefore we love the poet, the inventor, who in any form, whether in an ode or in an action or in looks and behavior, has yielded us a new thought. He unlocks our chains and admits us to a new scene.

This emancipation is dear to all men, and the power to impart it, as it must come from greater depth and scope of thought, is a measure of intellect. Therefore all books of the imagination endure, all which ascend to that truth that the writer sees nature beneath him, and uses it as his exponent. Every verse or sentence possessing this virtue will take care of its own immortality. The religions of the world are the ejaculations of a few imaginative men.

But the quality of the imagination is to flow, and not to freeze. The poet did not stop at the color or the form, but read their meaning; neither may he rest in this meaning, but he makes the same objects exponents of his new thought. Here is the difference betwixt the poet and the mystic, that the last nails a symbol to one sense, which was a true sense for a moment, but soon becomes old and false. For all symbols are fluxional; all language is vehicular and transitive, and is good, as ferries and horses are, for conveyance, not as farms and houses are, for homestead. Mysticism consists in the mistake of an accidental and individual symbol for an universal one. The morning-redness happens to be the favorite meteor to the eyes of Jacob Behmen, and comes to stand to him for truth and faith; and, he believes, should stand for the same realities to every reader. But the first reader prefers as naturally the symbol of a mother and child, or a gardener and his bulb, or a jeweller polishing a gem. Either of these, or a myriad more, are equally good to the person to whom they are significant. Only they must be held lightly, and be very willingly translated into the equivalent terms which others use. And the mystic must be steadily told,—All that you say is just as true without the tedious use of that symbol as with it. Let us have a little algebra, instead of this trite rhetoric,— universal signs, instead of these village symbols,—and we shall both be gainers. The history of hierarchies seems to show that all religious error consisted in making the symbol too stark and solid, and was at last nothing but an excess of the organ of language.

Swedenborg, of all men in the recent ages, stands eminently for the translator of nature into thought. I do not know the man in history to whom things stood so uniformly for words. Before him the metamorphosis continually plays. Everything on which his eye rests, obeys the impulses of moral nature. The figs become grapes whilst he eats them. When some of his angels affirmed a truth, the laurel twig which they held blossomed in their hands. The noise which at a distance appeared like gnashing and thumping, on coming nearer was found to be the voice of disputants. The men in one of his visions, seen in heavenly light, appeared like dragons, and seemed in darkness; but to each other they appeared as men, and when the light from heaven shone into their cabin, they complained of the darkness, and were compelled to shut the window that they might see.

There was this perception in him which makes the poet or seer an object of awe and terror, namely that the same man or society of men may wear one aspect to themselves and their companions, and a different aspect to higher intelligences. Certain priests, whom he describes as conversing very learnedly together, appeared to the children who were at some distance, like dead horses; and many the like misappearances. And instantly the mind inquires whether these fishes under the bridge, yonder oxen in the pasture, those dogs in the yard, are immutably fishes, oxen and dogs, or only so appear to me, and perchance to themselves appear upright men; and whether I appear as a man to all eyes. The Brahmins and Pythagoras propounded the same question, and if any poet has witnessed the transformation he doubtless found it in harmony with various experiences. We have all seen changes as considerable in wheat and caterpillars. He is the poet and shall draw us with love and terror, who sees through the flowing vest the firm nature, and can declare it.

I look in vain for the poet whom I describe. We do not with sufficient plainness or sufficient profoundness address ourselves to life, nor dare we chaunt our own times and social circumstance. If we filled the day with bravery, we should not shrink from celebrating it. Time and nature yield us many gifts, but not yet the timely man, the new religion, the reconciler, whom all things await. Dante's praise is that he dared to write his autobiography in colossal cipher, or into universality. We have yet had no genius in America, with tyrannous eye, which knew the value of our incomparable materials, and saw, in the barbarism and materialism of the times, another carnival of the same gods whose picture he so much admires in Homer; then in the Middle Age; then in Calvinism. Banks and tariffs, the newspaper and caucus, Methodism and Unitarianism, are flat and dull to dull people, but rest on the same foundations of wonder as the town of Troy and the temple of Delphi, and are as swiftly passing away. Our logrolling, our stumps and their politics, our fisheries, our Negroes and Indians, our boasts and our repudiations, the wrath of rogues and the pusillanimity of honest men, the northern trade, the southern planting, the western clearing, Oregon and Texas, are yet unsung. Yet America is a poem in our eyes; its ample geography dazzles the imagination, and it will not wait long for metres. If I have not found that excellent combination of gifts in my countrymen which I seek, neither could I aid myself to fix the idea of the poet by reading now and then in Chalmers's collection of five centuries of English poets. These are wits more than poets, though there have been poets among them. But when we adhere to the ideal of the poet, we have our difficulties even with Milton and Homer. Milton is too literary, and Homer too literal and historical.

But I am not wise enough for a national criticism, and must use the old largeness a little longer, to discharge my errand from the muse to the poet concerning his art.

Art is the path of the creator to his work. The paths or methods are ideal and eternal, though few men ever see them; not the artist himself for years, or for a lifetime, unless he come into the conditions. The painter, the sculptor, the composer, the epic rhapsodist, the orator, all partake one desire, namely to express themselves symmetrically and abundantly, not dwarfishly and fragmentarily. They found or put themselves to certain conditions, as, the painter and sculptor before some impressive human figures; the orator into the assembly of the people; and the others in such scenes as each has found exciting to his intellect; and each presently feels the new desire. He hears a voice, he sees a beckoning. Then he is apprised, with wonder, what herds of daemons hem him in. He can no more rest; he says, with the old painter, "By God it is in me and must go forth of me." He pursues a beauty, half seen, which flies before him. The poet pours out verses in every solitude. Most of the things he says are conventional, no doubt; but by and by he says something which is original and beautiful. That charms him. He would say nothing else but such things. In our way of talking we say 'That is yours, this is mine;' but the poet knows well that it is not his; that it is as strange and beautiful to him as to you; he would fain hear the like eloquence at length. Once having tasted this immortal ichor, he cannot have enough of it, and as an admirable creative power exists in these intellections, it is of the last importance that these things get spoken. What a little of all we know is said! What drops of all the sea of our science are baled up! and by what accident it is that these are exposed, when so many secrets sleep in nature! Hence the necessity of speech and song; hence these throbs and heart-beatings in the orator, at the door of the assembly, to the end namely that thought may be ejaculated as Logos, or Word.

Doubt not, O poet, but persist. Say 'It is in me, and shall out.' Stand there, balked and dumb, stuttering and stammering, hissed and hooted, stand and strive, until at last rage draw out of thee that *dream*-power which every night shows thee is thine own; a power transcending all limit and privacy, and by virtue of which a man is the conductor of the whole river of electricity. Nothing walks, or creeps, or grows, or exists, which must not in turn arise and walk before him as exponent of his meaning. Comes he to that power, his genius is no longer exhaustible. All the creatures by pairs and by tribes pour into his mind as into a Noah's ark, to come forth again to people a new world. This is like the stock of air for our respiration or for the combustion of our fireplace; not a measure of gallons, but the entire atmosphere if wanted. And therefore the rich poets, as Homer, Chaucer, Shakspeare, and Raphael, have obviously no limits to their works except the limits of their lifetime, and resemble a mirror carried through the street, ready to render an image of every created thing.

O poet! a new nobility is conferred in groves and pastures, and not in castles or by the sword-blade any longer. The conditions are hard, but equal. Thou shalt leave the world, and know the muse only. Thou shalt not know any longer the times, customs, graces, politics, or opinions of men, but shalt take all from the muse. For the time of towns is tolled from the world by funereal chimes, but in nature the universal hours are counted by succeeding tribes of animals and plants, and by growth of joy on joy. God wills also that thou abdicate a manifold and duplex life, and that thou be content that others speak for thee. Others shall be thy gentlemen and shall represent all courtesy and worldly life for thee; others shall do the great and resounding actions also. Thou shalt lie close hid with nature, and canst not be afforded to the Capitol or the Exchange. The world is full of renunciations and apprenticeships, and this is thine; thou must pass for a fool and a churl for a long season. This is the screen and sheath in which Pan has protected his well-beloved flower, and thou shalt be known only to thine own, and they shall console thee with tenderest love. And thou shalt not be able to rehearse the names of thy friends in thy verse, for an old shame before the holy ideal. And this is the reward; that the ideal shall be real to thee, and the impressions of the actual world shall fall like summer rain, copious, but not troublesome to thy invulnerable essence. Thou shalt have the whole land for thy park and manor, the sea for thy bath and navigation, without tax and without envy; the woods and the rivers thou shalt own, and thou shalt possess that wherein others are only tenants and boarders. Thou true landlord! sealord! air-lord! Wherever snow falls or water flows or birds fly, wherever day and night meet in twilight, wherever the blue heaven is hung by clouds or sown with stars, wherever are forms with transparent bound-aries, wherever are outlets into celestial space, wherever is danger, and awe, and love,—there is Beauty, plenteous as rain, shed for thee, and though thou shoulds't walk the world over, thou shalt not be able to find a condition inopportune or ignoble.

Walt Whitman, "Preface" to the First Edition of *Leaves of Grass,* 1855

Walt Whitman clearly felt himself to be the poetic conduit for the energy in America that Emerson was seeking. The growth of the cities, U.S. expansion into the West, the vast new experiment in democracy inspired the democratic vistas of Whitman's first experiments in free verse. His long line alternating with the short, his evasion of end-rhyme and traditional meter, seem breathless and brazen next to Wordsworth.

Whitman read all of Emerson and read him seriously. ("I was simmering, simmering, simmering; Emerson brought me to a boil," he admitted later in his life.) In fact, he sent Emerson the first edition of *Leaves of Grass,* which included this prose preface, a work clearly influenced by "The Poet" and Emerson's ideas of self-reliance, correspondence, and organic form, as well as the romantic concerns with common language and common theme. There are few end-stops in this preface. Instead, the dashes and ellipses map a continuous unfolding of thought and theme and mirror Whitman's hyperbolically patriotic view of his country as proceeding and new and done with the past. Emerson was impressed. Indeed, he sent a letter of praise to Whitman in 1855, which Whitman duly printed as the preface to his next edition in 1856.

Subsequent published versions of this preface appeared shorter by one third due to Whitman's practice of lifting large sections for use in his new poems.

✳

Preface 1855—*Leaves of Grass,* First Edition

America does not repel the past or what it has produced under its forms or amid other politics or the idea of castes or the old religions . . . accepts the lesson with calmness . . . is not so impatient as has been supposed that the slough still sticks to opinions and manners and literature while the life which served its requirements has passed into the new life of the new forms . . . perceives that the corpse is slowly borne from the eating and sleeping rooms of the house . . . perceives that it waits a little while in the door . . . that it was fittest for its days . . . that its action has descended to the stalwart and wellshaped heir who approaches . . . and that he shall be fittest for his days.

The Americans of all nations at any time upon the earth have probably the fullest poetical nature. The United States themselves are essentially the greatest poem. In the history of the earth hitherto the largest and most stirring appear tame and orderly to their ampler largeness and stir. Here at last is something in the doings of man that corresponds with the broadcast doings of the day and night. Here is not merely a nation but a teeming nation of nations. Here is action untied from strings necessarily blind to particulars and details magnificently moving in vast masses. Here is the hospitality which forever indicates heroes. . . . Here are the roughs and beards and space and ruggedness and nonchalance that the soul loves. Here the performance disdaining the trivial unapproached in the tremendous audacity of its crowds and groupings and the push of its perspective spreads with crampless and flowing breadth and showers its prolific and splendid extravagance. One sees it must indeed own the riches of the summer and winter, and need never be bankrupt while corn grows from the ground or the orchards drop apples or the bays contain fish or men beget children upon women.

Other states indicate themselves in their deputies. . . . but the genius of the United States is not best or most in its executives or legislatures, nor in its ambassadors or authors or colleges or churches or parlors, nor even in its newspapers or inventors . . . but always most in the common people. Their manners speech dress friendships—the freshness and candor of their physiognomy—the picturesque looseness of their carriage . . . their deathless attachment to freedom—their aversion to anything indecorous or soft or mean—the practical acknowledgment of the citizens of one state by the citizens of all other states—the fierceness of their roused resentment—their curiosity and welcome of novelty—their self-esteem and wonderful sympathy—their susceptibility to a slight—the air they have of persons who never knew how it felt to stand in the presence of superiors—the fluency of their speech—their delight in music, the sure symptom of manly tenderness and native elegance of soul . . . their good temper and openhandedness—the terrible significance of their elections

—the President's taking off his hat to them not they to him—these too are unrhymed poetry. It awaits the gigantic and generous treatment worthy of it.

The largeness of nature or the nation were monstrous without a corresponding largeness and generosity of the spirit of the citizen. Not nature nor swarming states nor streets and steamships nor prosperous business nor farms nor capital nor learning may suffice for the ideal of man . . . nor suffice the poet. No reminiscences may suffice either. A live nation can always cut a deep mark and can have the best authority the cheapest . . . namely from its own soul. This is the sum of the profitable uses of individuals or states and of present action and grandeur and of the subjects of poets.—As if it were necessary to trot back generation after generation to the eastern records! As if the beauty and sacredness of the demonstrable must fall behind that of the mythical! As if men do not make their mark out of any times! As if the opening of the western continent by discovery and what has transpired since in North and South America were less than the small theatre of the antique or the aimless sleep-walking of the middle ages! The pride of the United States leaves the wealth and finesse of the cities and all returns of commerce and agriculture and all the magnitude of geography or shows of exterior victory to enjoy the breed of full-sized men or one fullsized man unconquerable and simple.

The American poets are to enclose old and new for America is the race of races. Of them a bard is to be commensurate with a people. To him the other continents arrive as contributions . . . he gives them reception for their sake and his own sake. His spirit responds to his country's spirit. . . . he incarnates its geography and natural life and rivers and lakes. Mississippi with annual freshets and changing chutes, Missouri and Columbia and Ohio and Saint Lawrence with the falls and beautiful masculine Hudson, do not embouchure where they spend themselves more than they embouchure into him. The blue breadth over the inland sea of Virginia and Maryland and the sea off Massachusetts and Maine and over Manhattan bay and over Champlain and Erie and over Ontario and Huron and Michigan and Superior, and over the Texan and Mexican and Floridian and Cuban seas and over the seas off California and Oregon, is not tallied by the blue breadth of the waters below more than the breadth of above and below is tallied by him. When the long Atlantic coast stretches longer and the Pacific coast stretches longer he easily stretches with them north and south. He spans between them also from east to west and reflects what is between them. On him rise solid growths that offset the growths of pine and cedar and hemlock and liveoak and locust and chestnut and cypress and hickory and limetree and cottonwood and tuliptree and cactus and wildvine and tamarind and persimmon. . . . and tangles as tangled as any canebrake or swamp. . . . and forests coated with transparent ice and icicles hanging from the boughs and crackling in the wind. . . . and sides and peaks of mountains. . . . and pasturage sweet and free as savannah or upland or prairie. . . . with flights and songs and screams that answer those of the wildpigeon and highhold and orchard oriole and coot and surf-duck and redshouldered-hawk and fish-hawk and white-ibis and indian-hen and cat-owl and waterpheasant and qua-bird and pied-sheldrake and blackbird and mockingbird and buzzard and condor and night-heron and eagle. To him the hereditary countenance descends both mother's and father's. To him enter the essences of the real things and past and present events—of the enormous diversity of temperature and agriculture and mines—the tribes of red aborigines—the weatherbeaten vessels entering new ports or making landings on rocky coasts—the first settlements north or south—the rapid stature and muscle—the haughty defiance of '76, and the war and peace and formation of the constitution. . . . the union always surrounded by blatherers and always calm and impregnable—the perpetual coming of immigrants—the wharf hem'd cities and superior marine—the unsurveyed interior—the loghouses and clearings and wild animals and hunters and trappers. . . . the free commerce—the fisheries and whaling and golddigging—the endless gestation of new states—the convening of Congress every December, the members duly coming up from all climates and the uttermost parts. . . . the noble character of the young mechanics and of all free American workmen and workwomen. . . . the general ardor and friendliness and enterprise—the perfect equality of the female with the male. . . . the large amativeness—the fluid movement of the population— the factories and mercantile life and laborsaving machinery—the Yankee swap—the New-York firemen and the target excursion—the southern plantation life—the character of the northeast and of the northwest and southwest—slavery and the tremulous spreading of hands to protect it, and the stern opposition to it which shall never cease till it ceases or the speaking of tongues and the moving of lips cease. For such the expression of the American poet is to be transcendent and new. It is to be indirect and not direct or descriptive or epic. Its quality goes through these to much more. Let the age and wars of other nations be chanted and their eras and characters be illustrated and that finish the verse. Not so the great psalm of the republic. Here the theme is creative and has vista. Here comes one among the wellbeloved stonecutters and plans with decision and science and sees the solid and beautiful forms of the future where there are now no solid forms.

Of all nations the United States with veins full of poetical stuff most need poets and will doubtless have the greatest and use them the greatest. Their Presidents shall not be their common referee so much as their poets shall. Of all mankind the great poet is the equable man. Not in him but off from him things are grotesque or eccentric or fail of their sanity. Nothing out of its place is good and nothing in its place is bad. He bestows on every object or quality its fit proportions neither more nor less. He is the arbiter of the diverse and he is the key. He is the equalizer of his age and land. . . . he supplies what wants supplying and checks what wants checking. If peace is the routine out of him speaks the spirit of peace, large, rich, thrifty, building vast and populous cities, encouraging agriculture and the arts and commerce—lighting the study of man, the soul, immortality—federal, state or municipal government, marriage, health, freetrade, intertravel by land and sea. . . . nothing too close, nothing too far off . . . the stars not too far off. In war he is the most deadly force of the war. Who recruits him recruits horse and foot . . . he fetches parks of artillery the best that engineer ever knew. If the time becomes slothful and heavy he knows how to arouse it . . . he can make every word he speaks draw blood. Whatever stagnates in the flat of custom or obedience or legislation he never stagnates. Obedience does not master him, he masters it. High up out of reach he stands turning a concentrated light . . . he turns the pivot with his finger . . . he baffles the swiftest runners as he stands and easily overtakes and envelops them. The time straying toward infidelity and confections and persiflage he withholds by his steady faith . . . he spreads out his dishes . . . he offers the sweet firmfibred meat that grows men and women. His brain is the ultimate brain. He is no arguer . . . he is judgment. He judges not as the judge judges but as the sun falling around a helpless thing. As he sees the farthest he has the most faith. His thoughts are the hymns of the praise of things. In the talk on the soul and eternity and God off of his equal plane he is silent. He sees eternity less like a play with a prologue and denouement. . . . he sees eternity in men and women . . . he does not see men and women as dreams or dots. Faith is the antiseptic of the soul . . . it pervades the common people and preserves them . . . they never give up believing and expecting and trusting. There is that indescribable freshness and unconsciousness about an illiterate person that humbles and mocks the power of the noblest expressive genius. The poet sees for a certainty how one not a great artist may be just as sacred and perfect as the greatest artist. . . . . . The power to destroy or remould is freely used by him but never the power of attack. What is past is past. If he does not expose superior models and prove himself by every step he takes he is not what is wanted. The presence of the greatest poet conquers . . . not parleying or struggling or any prepared attempts. Now he has passed that way see after him! there is not left any vestige of despair or misanthropy or cunning or exclusiveness or the ignominy of a nativity or color or delusion of hell or the necessity of hell. . . . . and no man thenceforward shall be degraded for ignorance or weakness or sin.

The greatest poet hardly knows pettiness or triviality. If he breathes into any thing that was before thought small it dilates with the grandeur and life of the universe. He is a seer. . . . he is individual . . . he is complete in himself. . . . the others are as good as he, only he sees it and they do not. He is not one of the chorus. . . . he does not stop for any regulation . . . he is the president of regulation. What the eyesight does to the rest he does to the rest. Who knows the curious mystery of the eyesight? The other senses corroborate themselves, but this is removed from any proof but its own and foreruns the identities of the spiritual world. A single glance of it mocks all the investigations of man and all the instruments and books of the earth and all reasoning. What is marvellous? what is unlikely? what is impossible or baseless or vague? after you have once just opened the space of a peachpit and given audience to far and near and to the sunset and had all things enter with electric swiftness softly and duly without confusion or jostling or jam.

The land and sea, the animals fishes and birds, the sky of heaven and the orbs, the forests mountains and rivers, are not small themes . . . but folks expect of the poet to indicate more than the beauty and dignity which always attach to dumb real objects. . . . they expect him to indicate the path between reality and their souls. Men and women perceive the beauty well enough . . probably as well as he. The passionate tenacity of hunters, woodmen, early risers, cultivators of gardens and orchards and fields, the love of healthy women for the manly form, seafaring persons, drivers of horses, the passion for light and the open air, all is an old varied sign of the unfailing perception of beauty and of a residence of the poetic in outdoor people. They can never be assisted by poets to perceive . . . some may but they never can. The poetic quality is not marshalled in rhyme or uniformity or abstract addresses to things nor in melancholy complaints or good precepts, but is the life of these and much else and is in the soul. The profit of rhyme is that it drops seeds of a sweeter and more luxuriant rhyme, and of uniformity that it conveys itself into its own roots in the ground out of sight. The rhyme and uniformity of perfect poems show the free growth of metrical laws and bud from them as unerringly and loosely as lilacs or roses on a bush, and take shapes as compact as the shapes of chestnuts and oranges and melons and pears, and shed the perfume impalpable to form. The fluency and ornaments of the finest poems or music or orations or recitations are not independent but dependent. All beauty comes from beautiful blood and a beautiful brain. If the greatnesses are in conjunction in a man or woman it is enough. . . . the fact will prevail through the universe. . . . but the gaggery and gilt of a million years will not prevail. Who troubles himself about his ornaments or fluency is lost. This is what you shall do: Love the earth and sun and the animals, despise riches, give alms to every one that asks, stand up for the stupid and crazy, devote your income and labor to others, hate tyrants, argue not concerning God, have patience and indulgence toward the people, take off your hat to nothing known or unknown or to any man or number of men, go freely with powerful uneducated persons and with the young and with the mothers of families, read these leaves in the open air every season of every year of your life, re-examine all you have been told at school or church or in any book, dismiss whatever insults your own soul, and your very flesh shall be a great poem and have the richest fluency not only in its words but in the silent lines of its lips and face and between the lashes of your eyes and in every motion and joint of your body. . . . . . . The poet shall not spend his time in unneeded work. He shall know that the ground is always ready ploughed and manured. . . . others may not know it but he shall. He shall go directly to the creation. His trust shall master the trust of everything he touches. . . . and shall master all attachment.

The known universe has one complete lover and that is the greatest poet. He consumes an eternal passion and is indifferent which chance happens and which possible contingency of fortune or misfortune and persuades daily and hourly his delicious pay. What balks or breaks others is fuel for his burning progress to contact and amorous joy. Other proportions of the reception of pleasure dwindle to nothing to his proportions. All expected from heaven or from the highest he is rapport with in the sight of the daybreak or a scene of the winter woods or the presence of children playing or with his arm round the neck of a man or woman. His love above all love has leisure and expanse. . . . he leaves room ahead of himself. He is no irresolute or suspicious lover . . . he is sure . . . he scorns intervals. His experience and the showers and thrills are not for nothing. Nothing can jar him. . . . suffering and darkness cannot—death and fear cannot. To him complaint and jealousy and envy are corpses buried and rotten in the earth. . . . he saw them buried. The sea is not surer of the shore or the shore of the sea than he is of the fruition of his love and of all perfection and beauty.

The fruition of beauty is no chance of hit or miss . . . it is inevitable as life. . . . it is exact and plumb as gravitation. From the eyesight proceeds another eyesight and from the hearing proceeds another hearing and from the voice proceeds another voice eternally curious of the harmony of things with man. To these respond perfections not only in the committees that were supposed to stand for the rest but in the rest themselves just the same. These understand the law of perfection in masses and floods . . . that its finish is to each for itself and onward from itself . . . that it is profuse and impartial . . . that there is not a minute of the light or dark nor an acre of the earth or sea without it—nor any direction of the sky nor any trade or employment nor any turn of events. This is the reason that about the proper expression of beauty there is precision and balance . . . one part does not need to be thrust above another. The best singer is not the one who has the most lithe and powerful organ . . . the pleasure of poems is not in them that take the handsomest measure and similes and sound.

Without effort and without exposing in the least how it is done the greatest poet brings the spirit of any or all events and passions and scenes and persons some more and some less to bear on your individual character as you hear or read. To do this well is to compete with the laws that pursue and follow time. What is the purpose must surely be there and the clue of it must be there. . . . and the faintest indication is the indication of the best and then becomes the clearest indication. Past and present and future are not disjoined but joined. The greatest poet forms the consistence of what is to be from what has been and is. He drags the dead out of their coffins and stands them again on their feet. . . . he says to the past, Rise and walk before me that I may realize you. He learns the lesson. . . . he places himself where the future becomes present. The greatest poet does not only dazzle his rays over character and scenes and passions . . . he finally ascends and finishes all . . . he exhibits the pinnacles that no man can tell what they are for or what is beyond. . . . he glows a moment on the extremest verge. He is most wonderful in his last half-hidden smile or frown . . . by that flash of the moment of parting the one that sees it shall be encouraged or terrified afterward for many years. The greatest poet does not moralize or make application of morals . . . he knows the soul. The soul has that measureless pride which consists in never acknowledging any lessons but its own. But it has sympathy as measureless as its pride and the one balances the other and neither can stretch too far while it stretches in company with the other. The inmost secrets of art sleep with the twain. The greatest poet has lain close betwixt both and they are vital in his style and thoughts.

The art of art, the glory of expression and the sunshine of the light of letters is simplicity. Nothing is better than simplicity. . . . nothing can make up for excess or for the lack of definiteness. To carry on the heave of impulse and pierce intellectual depths and give all subjects their articulations are powers neither common nor very uncommon. But to speak in literature with the perfect rectitude and insousiance of the movements of animals and the unimpeachableness of the sentiment of trees in the woods and grass by the roadside is the flawless triumph of art. If you have looked on him who has achieved it you have looked on one of the masters of the artists of all nations and times. You shall not contemplate the flight of the graygull over the bay or the mettlesome action of the blood horse or the tall leaning of sunflowers on their stalk or the appearance of the sun journeying through heaven or the appearance of the moon afterward with any more satisfaction than you shall contemplate him. The greatest poet has less a marked style and is more the channel of thoughts and things without increase or diminution, and is the free channel of himself. He swears to his art, I will not be meddlesome, I will not have in my writing any elegance or effect or originality to hang in the way between me and the rest like curtains. I will have nothing hang in the way, not the richest curtains. What I tell I tell for precisely what it is. Let who may exalt or startle or fascinate or sooth I will have purposes as health or heat or snow has and be as regardless of observation. What I experience or portray shall go from my composition without a shred of my composition. You shall stand by my side and look in the mirror with me.

The old red blood and stainless gentility of great poets will be proved by their unconstraint. A heroic person walks at his ease through and out of that custom or precedent or authority that suits him not. Of the traits of the brotherhood of writers savans musicians inventors and artists nothing is finer than silent defiance advancing from new free forms. In the need of poems philosophy politics mechanism science behaviour, the craft of art, an appropriate native grand-opera, shipcraft, or any craft, he is greatest forever and forever who contributes the greatest original practical example. The cleanest expression is that which finds no sphere worthy of itself and makes one.

The messages of great poets to each man and woman are, Come to us on equal terms, Only then can you understand us, We are no better than you, What we enclose you enclose, What we enjoy you may enjoy. Did you suppose there could be only one Supreme? We affirm there can be unnumbered Supremes, and that one does not countervail another any more than one eyesight countervails another . . . and that men can be good or grand only of the consciousness of their supremacy within them. What do you think is the grandeur of storms and dismemberments and the deadliest battles and wrecks and the wildest fury of the elements and the power of the sea and the motion of nature and of the throes of human desires and dignity and hate and love? It is that something in the soul which says, Rage on, Whirl on, I tread master here and everywhere, Master of the spasms of the sky and of the shatter of the sea, Master of nature and passion and death, And of all terror and all pain.

The American bards shall be marked for generosity and affection and for encouraging competitors . . They shall be kosmos . . without monopoly or secresy . . glad to pass any thing to any one . . hungry for equals night and day. They shall not be careful of riches and privilege. . . . they shall be riches and privilege. . . . they shall perceive who the most affluent man is. The most affluent man is he that confronts all the shows he sees by equivalents out of the stronger wealth of himself. The American bard shall delineate no class of persons nor one or two out of the strata of interests nor love most nor truth most nor the soul most nor the body most. . . . and not be for the eastern states more than the western or the northern states more than the southern.

Exact science and its practical movements are no checks on the greatest poet but always his encouragement and support. The outset and remembrance are there . . there the arms that lifted him first and brace him best. . . . there he returns after all his goings and comings. The sailor and traveler . . the anatomist, chemist, astronomer, geologist, phrenologist, spiritualist, mathematician, historian and lexicographer are not poets, but they are the lawgivers of poets and their construction underlies the structure of every perfect poem. No matter what rises or is uttered they sent the seed of the conception of it . . . of them and by them stand the visible proofs of souls. . . . . always of their fatherstuff must be begotten the sinewy races of bards. If there shall be love and content between the father and the son and if the greatness of the son is the exuding of the greatness of the father there shall be love between the poet and the man of demonstrable science. In the beauty of poems are the tuft and final applause of science.

Great is the faith of the flush of knowledge and of the investigation of the depths of qualities and things. Cleaving and circling here swells the soul of the poet yet it president of itself always. The depths are fathomless and therefore calm. The innocence and nakedness are resumed . . . they are neither modest nor immodest. The whole theory of the special and supernatural and all that was twined with it or educed out of it departs as a dream. What has ever happened. . . . what happens and whatever may or shall happen, the vital laws enclose all. . . . they are sufficient for any case and for all cases . . . none to be hurried or retarded. . . . any miracle of affairs or persons inadmissible in the vast clear scheme where every motion and every spear of grass and the frames and spirits of men and women and all that concerns them are unspeakably perfect miracles all referring to all and each distinct and in its place. It is also not consistent with the reality of the soul to admit that there is anything in the known universe more divine than men and women.

Men and women and the earth and all upon it are simply to be taken as they are, and the investigation of their past and present and future shall be unintermitted and shall be done with perfect candor. Upon this basis philosophy speculates ever looking toward the poet, ever regarding the eternal tendencies of all toward happiness never inconsistent with what is clear to the senses and to the soul. For the eternal tendencies of all toward happiness make the only point of sane philosophy. Whatever comprehends less than that . . . whatever is less than the laws of light and of astronomical motion . . . or less than the laws that follow the thief the liar the glutton and the drunkard through this life and doubtless afterward. . . . . . or less than vast stretches of time or the slow formation of density or the patient upheaving or strata—is of no account. Whatever would put God in a poem or system of philosophy as contending against some being or influence is also of no account. Sanity and ensemble characterise the great master . . . spoilt in one principle all is spoilt. The great master has nothing to do with miracles. He sees health for himself in being one of the mass. . . . he sees the hiatus in singular eminence. To the perfect shape comes common ground. To be under the general law is great for that is to correspond with it. The master knows that he is unspeakably great and that all are unspeakably great. . . . that nothing for instance is greater than to conceive children and bring them up well . . . that to be is just as great as to perceive or tell.

In the make of the great masters the idea of political liberty is indispensible. Liberty takes the adherence of heroes wherever men and women exist. . . . but never takes any adherence or welcome from the rest more than from poets. They are the voice and exposition of liberty. They out of ages are worthy the grand idea. . . . to them it is confided and they must sustain it. Nothing has precedence of it and nothing can warp or degrade it. The attitude of great poets is to cheer up slaves and horrify despots. The turn of their necks, the sound of their feet, the motions of their wrists, are full of hazard to the one and hope to the other. Come nigh them awhile and though they neither speak or advise you shall learn the faithful American lesson. Liberty is poorly served by men whose good intent is quelled from one failure or two failures or any number of failures, or from the casual indifference or ingratitude of the people, or from the sharp show of the tushes of power, or the bringing to bear soldiers and cannon or any penal statutes. Liberty relies upon itself, invites no one, promises nothing, sits in calmness and light, is positive and composed, and knows no discouragement. The battle rages with many a loud alarm and frequent advance and retreat. . . . the enemy triumphs. . . . the prison, the handcuffs, the iron necklace and anklet, the scaffold, garrote and leadballs do their work. . . . the cause is asleep. . . . the strong throats are choked with their own blood. . . . the young men drop their eyelashes toward the ground when they pass each other. . . . and is liberty gone out of that place? No never. When liberty goes it is not the first to go nor the second or third to go . . it waits for all the rest to go . . it is the last . . .

When the memories of the old martyrs are faded utterly away . . . when the large names of patriots are laughed at in the public halls from the lips of the orators. . . . when the boys are no more christened after the same but christened after tyrants and traitors instead. . . . when the laws of the free are grudgingly permitted and laws for informers and bloodmoney are sweet to the taste of the people. . . . when I and you walk abroad upon the earth stung with compassion at the sight of numberless brothers answering our equal friendship and calling no man master—and when we are elated with noble joy at the sight of slaves. . . . when the soul retires in the cool communion of the night and surveys its experience and has much extasy over the word and deed that put back a helpless innocent person into the gripe of the gripers or into any cruel inferiority. . . . when those in all parts of these states who could easier realize the true American character but do not yet—when the swarms of cringers, suckers, doughfaces, lice of politics, planners of sly involutions for their own preferment to city offices or state legislatures or the judiciary or congress or the presidency, obtain a response of love and natural deference from the people whether they get the offices or no. . . . when it is better to be a bound booby and rogue in office at a high salary than the poorest free mechanic or farmer with his hat unmoved from his head and firm eyes and a candid and generous heart. . . . and when servility by town or state or the federal government or any oppression on a large scale or small scale can be tried on without its own punishment following duly after in exact proportion against the smallest chance of escape. . . . or rather when all life and all the souls of men and women are discharged from any part of the earth—then only shall the instinct of liberty be discharged from that part of the earth.

As the attributes of the poets of the kosmos concentre in the real body and soul and in the pleasure of things they possess the superiority of genuineness over all fiction and romance. As they emit themselves facts are showered over with light. . . . the daylight is lit with more volatile light. . . . also the deep between the setting and rising sun goes deeper many fold. Each precise object or condition or combination or process exhibits a beauty. . . . the multiplication table its—old age its—the carpenter's trade its—the grand-opera its. . . . the hugehulled cleanshaped New-York clipper at sea under steam or full sail gleams with unmatched beauty. . . . the American circles and large harmonies of government gleam with theirs. . . . and the commonest definite intentions and actions with theirs. The poets of the kosmos advance through all interpositions and coverings and turmoils and stratagems to first principles. They are of use. . . . they dissolve poverty from its need and riches from its conceit. You large proprietor they say shall not realize or perceive more than any one else. The owner of the library is not he who holds a legal title to it having bought and paid for it. Any one and every one is owner of the library who can read the same through all the varieties of tongues and subjects and styles, and in whom they enter with ease and take residence and force toward paternity and maternity, and make supple and powerful and rich and large. . . . . These American states strong and healthy and accomplished shall receive no pleasure from violations of natural models and must not permit them. In paintings or mouldings or carvings in mineral or wood, or in the illustrations of books or newspapers, or in any comic or tragic prints, or in the patterns of woven stuffs or any thing to beautify rooms or furniture or costumes, or to put upon cornices or monuments or on the prows or sterns of ships, or to put anywhere before the human eye indoors or out, that which distorts honest shapes or which creates unearthly beings or places or contingencies is a nuisance and revolt. Of the human form especially it is so great it must never be made ridiculous. Of ornaments to a work nothing outre can be allowed . . but those ornaments can be allowed that conform to the perfect facts of the open air and that flow out of the nature of the work and come irrepressibly from it and are necessary to the completion of the work. Most works are most beautiful without ornament . . . Exaggerations will be revenged in human physiology. Clean and vigorous children are jetted and conceived only in those communities where the models of natural forms are public every day. . . . . . Great genius and the people of these states must never be demeaned to romances. As soon as histories are properly told there is no more need of romances.

The great poets are also to be known by the absence in them of tricks and by the justification of perfect personal candor. Then folks echo a new cheap joy and a divine voice leaping from their brains: How beautiful is candor! All faults may be forgiven of him who has perfect candor. Henceforth let no man of us lie, for we have seen that openness wins the inner and outer world and that there is no single exception, and that never since our earth gathered itself in a mass have deceit or subterfuge or prevarication attracted its smallest particle or the faintest tinge of a shade—and that through the enveloping wealth and rank of a state or the whole republic of states a sneak or sly person shall be discovered and despised. . . .

and that the soul has never been once fooled and never can be fooled. . . . and thrift without the loving nod of the soul is only a fœtid puff. . . . and there never grew up in any of the continents of the globe nor upon any planet or satellite or star, nor upon the asteroids, nor in any part of ethereal space, nor in the midst of density, nor under the fluid wet of the sea, nor in that condition which precedes the birth of babes, nor at any time during the changes of life, nor in that condition that follows what we term death, nor in any stretch of abeyance or action afterward of vitality, nor in any process of formation or reformation anywhere, a being whose instinct hated the truth.

Extreme caution or prudence, the soundest organic health, large hope and comparison and fondness for women and children, large alimentiveness and destructiveness and causality, with a perfect sense of the oneness of nature and the propriety of the same spirit applied to human affairs . . these are called up of the float of the brain of the world to be parts of the greatest poet from his birth out of his mother's womb and from her birth out of her mother's. Caution seldom goes far enough. It has been thought that the prudent citizen was the citizen who applied himself to solid gains and did well for himself and his family and completed a lawful life without debt or crime. The greatest poet sees and admits these economies as he sees the economies of food and sleep, but has higher notions of prudence than to think he gives much when he gives a few slight attentions at the latch of the gate. The premises of the prudence of life are not the hospitality of it or the ripeness and harvest of it. Beyond the independence of a little sum laid aside for burial-money, and of a few clapboards around and shingles overhead on a lot of American soil owned, and the easy dollars that supply the year's plain clothing and meals, the melancholy prudence of the abandonment of such a great being as a man is to the toss and pallor of years of moneymaking with all their scorching days and icy nights and all their stifling deceits and underhanded dodgings, or infinitessimals of parlors, or shameless stuffing while others starve . . and all the loss of the bloom and odor of the earth and of the flowers and atmosphere and of the sea and of the true taste of the women and men you pass or have to do with in youth or middle age, and the issuing sickness and desperate revolt at the close of a life without elevation or naivete, and the ghastly chatter of a death without serenity or majesty, is the great fraud upon modern civilization and forethought, blotching the surface and system which civilization undeniably drafts, and moistening with tears the immense features it spreads and spreads with such velocity before the reached kisses of the soul . . . Still the right explanation remains to be made about prudence. The prudence of the mere wealth and respectability of the most esteemed life appears too faint for the eye to observe at all when little and large alike drop quietly aside at the thought of the prudence suitable for immortality. What is wisdom that fills the thinness of a year or seventy or eighty years to wisdom spaced out by ages and coming back at a certain time with strong reinforcements and rich presents and the clear faces of wedding-guests as far as you can look in every direction running gaily toward you? Only the soul is of itself. . . . all else has reference to what ensues. All that a person does or thinks is of consequence. Not a move can a man or woman make that affects him or her in a day or a month or any part of the direct lifetime or the hour of death but the same affects him or her onward afterward through the indirect lifetime. The indirect is always as great and real as the direct. The spirit receives from the body just as much as it gives to the body. Not one name of word or deed . . not of venereal sores or discolorations . . not the privacy of the onanist . . not of the putrid veins of gluttons or rumdrinkers . . . not peculation or cunning or betrayal or murder . . no serpentine poison of those that seduce women . . not the foolish yielding of women . . not prostitution . . not of any depravity of young men . . not of the attainment of gain by discreditable means . . not any nastiness of appetite . . not any harshness of officers to men or judges to prisoners or fathers to sons or sons to fathers or of husbands to wives or bosses to their boys . . not of greedy looks or malignant wishes . . . nor any of the wiles practised by people upon themselves . . . ever is or ever can be stamped on the programme but it is duly realized and returned, and that returned in further performances . . . and they returned again. Nor can the push of charity or personal force ever be any thing else than the profoundest reason, whether it bring arguments to hand or no. No specification is necessary . . to add or subtract or divide is in vain. Little or big, learned or unlearned, white or black, legal or illegal, sick or well, from the first inspiration down the windpipe to the last expiration out of it, all that a male or female does that is vigorous and benevolent and clean is so much sure profit to him or her in the unshakable order of the universe and through the whole scope of it forever. If the savage or felon is wise it is well. . . . if the greatest poet or savan is wise it is simply the same . . if the President or chief justice is wise it is the same . . . if the young mechanic or farmer is wise it is no more or less . . if the prostitute is wise it is no more nor less. The interest will come round . . all will come round. All the best actions of war and peace . . . all help given to relatives and strangers and the poor and old and sorrowful and young children and widows and the sick, and to all shunned persons . . all furtherance of fugitives and of the escape of slaves . . all the self-denial that stood steady and aloof on wrecks and saw others take the seats of the boats . . . all offering of substance or life for the good old cause, or for a friend's sake or opinion's sake . . . all pains of enthusiasts scoffed at by their neighbors . . all the vast sweet love and precious suffering of mothers . . . all honest men baffled in strifes recorded or unrecorded. . . . all the grandeur and good of the few ancient nations whose fragments of annals we inherit . . and all the good of the hundreds of far mightier and more ancient nations unknown to us by name or date or location. . . . all that was ever manfully begun, whether it succeeded or no. . . . all that has at any time been well suggested out of the divine heart of man or by the divinity of his mouth or by the shaping of his great hands . . and all that is well thought or done this day on any part of the surface of the globe . . or on any of the wandering stars or fixed stars by those there as we are here . . or that is hence forth to be well thought or done by you whoever you are, or by any one—these singly and wholly inured at their time and inure now and will inure always to the identities from which they sprung or shall spring . . . Did you guess any of them lived only its moment? The world does not so exist . . no parts palpable or impalpable so exist . . . no result exists now without being from its long antecedent result, and that from its antecedent, and so backward without the farthest mentionable spot coming a bit nearer the beginning than any other spot. . . . . Whatever satisfies the soul is truth. The prudence of the greatest poets answers at last the craving and glut of the soul, is not contemptuous of less ways of prudence if they conform to its ways, puts off nothing, permits no let-up for its own case or any case, has no particular sabbath or judgment-day, divides not the living from the dead or the righteous from the unrighteous, is satisfied with the present, matches every thought or act by its correlative, knows no possible forgiveness or deputed atonement . . knows that the young man who composedly periled his life and lost it has done exceeding well for himself, while the man who has not periled his life and retains it to old age in riches and ease has perhaps achieved nothing for himself worth mentioning . . and that only that person has no great prudence to learn who has learnt to prefer real longlived things, and favors body and soul the same, and perceives the indirect assuredly following the direct, and what evil or good he does leaping onward and waiting to meet him again—and who in his spirit in any emergency whatever neither hurries or avoids death.

The direct trial of him who would be the greatest poet is today. If he does not flood himself with the immediate age as with vast oceanic tides. . . . . and if he does not attract his own land body and soul to himself and hang on its neck with incomparable love and plunge his semitic muscle into its merits and demerits . . . and if he be not himself the age transfigured. . . . and if to him is not opened the eternity which gives similitude to all periods and locations and processes and animate and inanimate forms, and which is the bond of time, and rises up from its inconceivable vagueness and infiniteness in the swimming shape of today, and is held by the ductile anchors of life, and makes the present spot the passage from what was to what shall be, and commits itself to the representation of this wave of an hour and this one of the sixty beautiful children of the wave—let him merge in the general run and wait his development. . . . . Still the final test of poems or any character or work remains. The prescient poet projects himself centuries ahead and judges performer or performance after the changes of time. Does it live through them? Does it still hold on untired? Will the same style and the direction of genius to similar points be satisfactory now? Has no new discovery in science or arrival at superior planes of thought and judgment and behaviour fixed him or his so that either can be looked down upon? Have the marches of tens and hundreds and thousands of years made willing detours to the right hand and the left hand for his sake? Is he beloved long and long after he is buried? Does the young man think often of him? and the young woman think often of him? and do the middleaged and the old think of him?

A great poem is for ages and ages in common and for all degrees and complexions and all departments and sects and for a woman as much as a man and a man as much as a woman. A great poem is no finish to a man or woman but rather a beginning. Has any one fancied he could sit at last under some due authority and rest satisfied with explanations and realize and be content and full? To no such terminus does the greatest poet bring . . . he brings neither cessation or sheltered fatness and ease. The touch of him tells in action. Whom he takes he takes with firm sure grasp into live regions previously unattainable. . . . thenceforward is no rest. . . . they see the space and ineffable sheen that turn the old spots and lights into dead vacuums. The companion of him beholds the birth and progress of stars and learns one of the meanings. Now there shall be a man cohered out of tumult and chaos. . . . the elder encourages the younger and shows him how . . . they two shall launch off fearlessly together till the new world fits an orbit for itself and looks unabashed on the lesser orbits of the stars and sweeps through the ceaseless rings and shall never be quiet again.

There will soon be no more priests. Their work is done. They may wait awhile . . perhaps a generation or two . . dropping off by degrees. A superior breed shall take their place. . . . the gangs of kosmos and prophets en masse shall take their place. A new order shall arise and they shall be the priests of man, and every man shall be his own priest. The churches built under their umbrage shall be the churches of man and women. Through the divinity of themselves shall the kosmos and the new breed of poets be interpreters of men and women and of all events and things. They shall find their inspiration in real objects today, symptoms of the past and future. . . . They shall not deign to defend immortality or God or the perfection of things or liberty or the exquisite beauty and reality of the soul. They shall arise in America and be responded to from the remainder of the earth.

The English language befriends the grand American expression. . . . it is brawny enough and limber and full enough. On the tough stock of a race who through all change of circumstance was never without the idea of political liberty, which is the animus of all liberty, it has attracted the terms of daintier and gayer and subtler and more elegant tongues. It is the powerful language of resistance . . . it is the dialect of common sense. It is the speech of the proud and melancholy races and of all who aspire. It is the chosen tongue to express growth faith self-esteem freedom justice equality friendliness amplitude prudence decision and courage. It is the medium that shall well nigh express the inexpressible.

No great literature nor any like style of behaviour or oratory or social intercourse or household arrangements or public institutions or the treatment by bosses of employed people, nor executive detail or detail of the army or navy, nor spirit of legislation or courts or police or tuition or architecture or songs or amusements or the costumes of young men, can long elude the jealous and passionate instinct of American standards. Whether or no the sign appears from the mouths of the people, it throbs a live interrogation in every freeman's and freewoman's heart after that which passes by, or this built to remain. Is it uniform with my country? Are its disposals without ignominious distinctions? Is it for the evergrowing communes of brothers and lovers, large, well-united, proud beyond the old models, generous beyond all models? Is it something grown fresh out of the fields or drawn from the sea for use to me today here? I know that what answers for me an American must answer for any individual or nation that serves for a part of my materials. Does this answer? or is it without reference to universal needs? or sprung of the needs of the less developed society of special ranks? or old needs of pleasure overlaid by modern science and forms? Does this acknowledge liberty with audible and absolute acknowledgment, and set slavery at nought for life and death? Will it help breed one goodshaped and wellhung man, and a woman to be his perfect and independent mate? Does it improve manners? Is it for the nursing of the young of the republic? Does it solve readily with the sweet milk of the nipples of the breasts of the mother of many children? Has it too the old ever-fresh forbearance and impartiality? Does it look with the same love on the last born and on those hardening toward stature, and on the errant, and on those who disdain all strength of assault outside of their own?

The poems distilled from other poems will probably pass away. The coward will surely pass away. The expectation of the vital and great can only be satisfied by the demeanor of the vital and great. The swarms of the polished deprecating and reflectors and the polite float off and leave no remembrance. America prepares with composure and goodwill for the visitors that have sent word. It is not intellect that is to be their warrant and welcome. The talented, the artist, the ingenious, the editor, the statesman, the erudite . . they are not unappreciated . . they fall in their place and do their work. The soul of the nation also does its work. No disguise can pass on it . . no disguise can conceal from it. It rejects none, it permits all. Only toward as good as itself and toward the like of itself will it advance half-way. An individual is as superb as a nation when he has the qualities which make a superb nation. The soul of the largest and wealthiest and proudest nation may well go half-way to meet that of its poets. The signs are effectual. There is no fear of mistake. If the one is true the other is true. The proof of a poet is that his country absorbs him as affectionately as he has absorbed it.

Emily Dickinson, Letters to Thomas Wentworth Higginson, 1862

"You think my gait 'spasmodic.' I am in danger, sir. You think me 'uncontrolled.' I have no tribunal." Emily Dickinson, born in 1830 in Amherst, Massachusetts, was familiar with and had read Emerson, Keats, and Browning (though she never read *Leaves of Grass*, for she "was told that it was disgraceful"). As has often been stated, Dickinson's hymnbook was her manual of prosody. Her poems are typically written in common ballad meter of alternating four and three stresses per line. Yet the liberties she took in end-rhyme violate all the rules, creating a wellspring of possibility for future poets. Her famous use of the dash for dramatic effect and her unsystematic use of capitalization were so original and dramatic that her first publishers—including her "Preceptor," Thomas Wentworth Higginson—changed them to conform to accepted usage.

Except for a few anonymous poems, Dickinson's work remained unpublished in her lifetime. Her sister, Lavinia, discovered the famous trunk of 1,775 carefully wrapped poems at Dickinson's death in 1886, and a slim volume was printed in 1890, followed by more. It was not until 1950, when Harvard bought all available manuscripts, that the complete—and original—poems were issued.

In 1862—the same year she wrote 356 poems!—Dickinson sent Higginson, a young writer at the *Atlantic Monthly*, 4 poems and a note, initiating a literary correspondence that would last until her death. Here are a few letters from that pivotal year.

❋

Selected Letters to Thomas Wentworth Higginson

15 April 1862
Mr Higginson,
Are you too deeply occupied to say if my Verse is alive?
The Mind is so near itself—it cannot see, distinctly—and I have none to ask—

Should you think it breathed—and had you the leisure to tell me, I should feel quick gratitude—

If I make the mistake—that you dared to tell me—would give me sincerer honor—toward you—

I enclose my name—asking you, if you please—Sir—to tell me what is true?

That you will not betray me—it is needless to ask—since Honor is it's own pawn—

❋

25 April 1862
Mr Higginson,

Your kindness claimed earlier gratitude—but I was ill—and write to-day, from my pillow.

Thank you for the surgery—it was not so painful as I supposed. I bring you others—as you ask—though they might not differ—

While my thought is undressed—I can make the distinction, but when I put them in the Gown—they look alike, and numb.

You asked how old I was? I made no verse—but one or two—until this winter—Sir—

I had a terror—since September—I could tell to none—and so I sing, as the Boy does by the Burying Ground—because I am afraid—You inquire my Books—For Poets—I have Keats—and Mr and Mrs Browning. For Prose—Mr Ruskin—Sir Thomas Browne—and the Revelations. I went to school—but in your manner of the phrase—had no education. When a little Girl, I had a friend, who taught me Immortality—but venturing too near, himself—he never returned—Soon after, my Tutor, died —and for several years, my Lexicon—was my only companion—Then I found one more—but he was not contented I be his scholar—so he left the Land.

You ask of my Companions Hills—Sir—and the Sundown—and a Dog—large as myself, that my Father bought me—They are better than Beings—because they know—but do not tell—and the noise in the Pool, at Noon—excels my Piano. I have a Brother and Sister—My Mother does not care for thought—and Father, too busy with his Briefs—to notice what we do—He buys me many Books—but begs me not to read them—because he fears they joggle the Mind. They are religious—except me—and address an Eclipse, every morning—whom they call their "Father." But I fear my story fatigues you—I would like to learn—Could you tell me how to grow—or is it unconveyed—like Melody—or Witchcraft?

You speak of Mr Whitman—I never read his Book—but was told that he was disgraceful—

I read Miss Prescott's "Circumstance," but it followed me, in the Dark—so I avoided her—

Two Editors of Journals came to my Father's House, this winter—and asked me for my Mind—and when I asked them "Why," they said I was penurious—and they, would use it for the World—

I could not weigh myself—Myself—

My size felt small—to me—I read your Chapters in the Atlantic—and experienced honor for you—I was sure you would not reject a confiding question—

Is this—Sir—what you asked me to tell you?
Your friend,
E—Dickinson.

❈

7 June 1862
Dear friend.

Your letter gave no Drunkenness, because I tasted Rum before—Domingo comes but once—yet I have had few pleasures so deep as your opinion, and if I tried to thank you, my tears would block my tongue—

My dying Tutor told me that he would like to live till I had been a poet, but Death was much of Mob as I could muster—then—And when far afterward—a sudden light on Orchards, or a new fashion in the wind troubled my attention—I felt a palsy, here—the Verses just relieve—

Your second letter surprised me, and for a moment, swung—I had not supposed it. Your first—gave no dishonor, because the True—are not ashamed—I thanked you for your justice—but could not drop the Bells whose jingling cooled my Tramp—Perhaps the Balm, seemed better, because you bled me, first.

I smile when you suggest that I delay "to publish"—that being foreign to my thought, as Firmament to Fin—

If fame belonged to me, I could not escape her—if she did not, the longest day would pass me on the chase—and the approbation of my Dog, would forsake me—then—My Barefoot-Rank is better—

You think my gait "spasmodic"—I am in danger—Sir—

You think me "uncontrolled"—I have no Tribunal.

Would you have time to be the "friend" you should think I need? I have a little shape—it would not crowd your Desk—nor make much Racket as the Mouse, that dents your Galleries—

If I might bring you what I do—not so frequent to trouble you—and ask you if I told it clear—'twould be control, to me—

The Sailor cannot see the North—but knows the Needle can—

The "hand you stretch me in the Dark," I put mine in, and turn away—I have no Saxon, now—

> As if I asked a common Alms,
> And in my wondering hand
> A Stranger pressed a Kingdom,
> And I, bewildered, stand—
> As if I asked the Orient
> Had it for me a Morn—
> And it should lift it's purple Dikes,
> And shatter me with Dawn!

But, will you be my Preceptor, Mr Higginson?
Your friend
E Dickinson—

❋

July 1862

Could you believe me—without? I had no portrait, now, but am small, like the Wren, and my Hair is bold, like the Chestnut Bur—and my eyes, like the Sherry in the Glass, that the Guest leaves—Would this do just as well?

It often alarms Father—He says Death might occur, and he has Molds of all the rest—but has no Mold of me, but I noticed the Quick wore off those things, in a few days, and forestall the dishonor—You will think no caprice of me—

You said "Dark." I know the Butterfly—and the Lizard—and the Orchis—

Are not those your Countrymen?

I am happy to be your scholar, and will deserve the kindness, I cannot repay.

If you truly consent, I recite, now—

Will you tell me my fault, frankly as to yourself, for I had rather wince, than die. Men do not call the surgeon, to commend—the Bone, but to set it, Sir, and fracture within, is more critical. And for this, Preceptor, I shall bring you—Obedience—the Blossom from my Garden, and every gratitude I know. Perhaps you smile at me. I could not stop for that—My Business is Circumference—An ignorance, not of Customs, but if caught with the Dawn—or the Sunset see me—Myself the only Kangaroo among the Beauty, Sir, if you please, it afflicts me, and I thought that instruction would take it away.

Because you have much business, beside the growth of me—you will appoint, yourself, how often I shall come—without your inconvenience. And if at any time—you regret you received me, or I prove a different fabric to that you supposed—you must banish me—

When I state myself, as the Representative of the Verse—it does not mean—me—but a supposed person. You are true, about the "perfection."

Today, makes Yesterday mean.

You spoke of Pippa Passes—I never heard anybody speak of Pippa Passes—before.

You see my posture is benighted.

To thank you, baffles me. Are you perfectly powerful? Had I a pleasure you had not, I could delight to bring it.

Your Scholar

❋

August 1862
Dear friend—

Are these more orderly? I thank you for the Truth—

I had no Monarch in my life, and cannot rule myself, and when I try to organize—my little Force explodes—and leaves me bare and charred—

I think you called me "Wayward." Will you help me improve?

I suppose the pride that stops the Breath, in the Core of Woods, is not of Ourself—

You say I confess the little mistake, and omit the large—Because I can see Orthography—but the Ignorance out of sight—is my Preceptor's charge—

Of "shunning Men and Women"—they talk of Hallowed things, aloud—and embarrass my Dog—He and I dont object to them, if they'll exist their side. I think Carlo would please you—He is dumb and brave—I think you would like the Chestnut Tree, I met in my walk. It hit my notice suddenly—and I thought the Skies were in Blossom—

Then there's a noiseless noise in the Orchard—that I let persons hear—You told me in one letter, you could not come to see me, "now," and I made no answer, not because I had none, but did not think myself the price that you should come so far—

I do not ask so large a pleasure, lest you might deny me—

You say "Beyond your knowledge." You would not jest with me, because I believe you—but Preceptor—you cannot mean it? All men say "What" to me, but I thought it a fashion—

When much in the Woods as a little Girl, I was told that the Snake would bite me, that I might pick a poisonous flower, or Goblins kidnap me, but I went along and met no one but Angels, who were far shyer of me, than I could be of them, so I hav'nt that confidence in fraud which many exercise.

I shall observe your precept—though I dont understand it, always.

I marked a line in One Verse—because I met it after I made it—and never consciously touch a paint, mixed by another person—

I do not let go it, because it is mine.

Have you the portrait of Mrs Browning? Persons sent me three—If you had none, will you have mine?

Your Scholar—

Gerard Manley Hopkins, "Author's Preface" to the First Edition of *Poems of Gerard Manley Hopkins*, 1883

Gerard Manley Hopkins, an ordained Jesuit priest, died in 1889 at the age of forty-five, virtually unpublished. Torn between his clerical duties and his passion for poetry, as well as by his intense inner religious struggles, Hopkins produced a small, but strenuous, and ultimately distinctive body of work, including poems such as "The Windhover," "God's Grandeur," and "Carrion Comfort." The first edition of his poems was published in 1918, edited by his friend and literary correspondent, the poet Robert Bridges, and included this preface, wherein he explains his theory of sprung rhythm.

Hopkins's invention of what he called sprung rhythm was a method, like Whitman's and Wordsworth's, of accessing the rhythms of common speech. A trained musician, as well as a scholar of ancient languages, Hopkins devised a system of scanning that attempted a musical analysis of speech and placed an uncommon emphasis on the stress and pitch of speech patterns. His breaking of tradition went in a different direction from Whitman's, back to the earlier accentual or "strong stress" verse of the Anglo-Saxons. Hopkins worked to eliminate many of the slack syllables in a poetic line, toward developing a rhythm sprung from expectation, that is, from the traditional rhythm of iambic pentameter.

❋

Author's Preface

The poems in this book are written some in Running Rhythm, the common rhythm in English use, some in Sprung Rhythm, and some in a mixture of the two. And those in the common rhythm are some counterpointed, some not.

Common English rhythm, called Running Rhythm above, is measured by feet of either two or three syllables and (putting aside the imperfect feet at the beginning and end of lines and also some unusual measures, in which feet seem to be paired together and double or composite feet to arise) never more or less.

Every foot has one principal stress or accent, and this or the syllable it falls on may be called the Stress of the foot and the other part, the one or two unaccented syllables, the Slack. Feet (and the rhythms made out of them) in which the stress comes first are called Falling Feet and Falling rhythms, feet and rhythm in which the slack comes first are called Rising Feet and Rhythms, and if the stress is between two slacks there will be Rocking Feet and Rhythms. These distinctions are real and true to nature; but for purposes of scanning it is a great convenience to follow the example of music and take the stress always first, as the accent or the chief accent always comes first in a musical bar. If this is done there will be in common English verse only two possible feet—the so-called accentual Trochee and Dactyl, and correspondingly only two possible uniform rhythms, the so-called Trochaic and Dactylic. But they may be mixed and then what the Greeks called a Logaoedic rhythm arises. These are the facts and according to these the scanning of ordinary regularly-written English verse is very simple indeed and to bring in other principles is here unnecessary.

But because verse written strictly in these feet and by these principles will become same and tame the poets have brought in licences and departures from rule to give variety, and especially when the natural rhythm is rising, as in the common ten-syllable or five-foot verse, rhymed or blank. These irregularities are chiefly Reversed Feet and Reversed or Counterpoint Rhythm, which two things are two steps or degrees of licence in the same kind. By a reversed foot I mean the putting the stress where, to judge by the rest of the measure, the slack should be and the slack where the stress, and this is done freely at the beginning of a line and, in the course of a line, after a pause; only scarcely ever in the second foot or place and never in the last, unless when the poet designs some extraordinary effect; for these places are characteristic and sensitive and cannot well be touched. But the reversal of the first foot and of some middle foot after a strong pause is a thing so natural that our poets have generally done it, from Chaucer down, without remark and it commonly passes unnoticed and cannot be said to amount to a formal change of rhythm, but rather is that irregularity which all natural growth and motion shews. If however the reversal is repeated in two feet running, especially so as to include the sensitive second foot, it must be due either to great want of ear or else is a calculated effect, the superinducing or mounting of a new rhythm upon the old; and since the new or mounted rhythm is actually heard and at the same time the mind naturally supplies the natural or standard foregoing rhythm, for we do not forget what the rhythm is that by rights we should be hearing, two rhythms are in some manner running at once and we have something answerable to counterpoint in music, which is two or more strains of tune going on together, and this is Counterpoint Rhythm. Of this kind of verse Milton is the great master and the choruses of Samson Agonistes are written throughout in it—but with the disadvantage that he does not let the reader clearly know what the ground-rhythm is meant to be and so they have struck most readers as merely irregular. And in fact if you counterpoint throughout, since one only of the counter rhythms is actually heard, the other is really destroyed or cannot come to exist, and what is written is one rhythm only and probably Sprung Rhythm, of which I now speak.

Sprung Rhythm, as used in this book, is measured by feet of from one to four syllables, regularly, and for particular effects any number of weak or slack syllables may be used. It has one stress, which falls on the only syllable, if there is only one, or, if there are more, then scanning as above, on the first, and so gives rise to four sorts of feet, a monosyllable and the so-called accentual Trochee, Dactyl, and the First Paeon. And there will be four corresponding natural rhythms; but nominally the feet are mixed and any one may follow any other. And hence Sprung Rhythm differs from Running Rhythm in having or being only one nominal rhythm, a mixed or 'logaoedic' one, instead of three, but on the other hand in having twice the flexibility of foot, so that any two stresses may either follow one another running or be divided by one, two, or three slack syllables. But strict Sprung Rhythm cannot be counterpointed. In Sprung Rhythm, as in logaoedic rhythm generally, the feet are assumed to be equally long or strong and their seeming inequality is made up by pause or stressing.

Remark also that it is natural in Sprung Rhythm for the lines to be rove over, that is for the scanning of each line immediately to take up that of the one before, so that if the first has one or more syllables at its end the other must have so many the less at its beginning; and in fact the scanning runs on without break from the beginning, say, of a stanza to the end and all the stanza is one long strain, though written in lines asunder.

Two licences are natural to Sprung Rhythm. The one is rests, as in music; but of this an example is scarcely to be found in this book, unless in the Echos, second line. The other is hangers or outrides, that is one, two, or three slack syllables added to a foot and not counting in the nominal scanning. They are so called because they seem to hang below the line or ride forward or backward from it in another dimension than the line itself, according to a principle needless to explain here. These outriding half feet or hangers are marked by a loop underneath them, and plenty of them will be found.

The other marks are easily understood, namely accents, where the reader might be in doubt which syllable should have the stress; slurs, that is loops over syllables, to tie them together into the time of one; little loops at the end of a line to shew that the rhyme goes on to the first letter of the next line; what in music are called pauses ⌢, to shew that the syllable should be dwelt on; and twirls ∿, to mark reversed or counterpointed rhythm.

Note on the nature and history of Sprung Rhythm—Sprung Rhythm is the most natural of things. For (1) it is the rhythm of common speech and of written prose, when rhythm is perceived in them. (2) It is the rhythm of all but the most monotonously regular music, so that in the words of choruses and refrains and in songs written closely to music it arises. (3) It is found in nursery rhymes, weather saws, and so on; because, however these may have been once made in running rhythm, the terminations having dropped off by the change of language, the stresses come together and so the rhythm is sprung. (4) It arises in common verse when reversed or counterpointed, for the same reason.

But nevertheless in spite of all this and though Greek and Latin lyric verse, which is well known, and the old English verse seen in Pierce Ploughman are in sprung rhythm, it has in fact ceased to be used since the Elizabethan age, Greene being the last writer who can be said to have recognized it. For perhaps there was not, down to our days, a single, even short, poem in English in which sprung rhythm is employed—not for single effects or in fixed places—but as the governing principle of the scansion. I say this because the contrary has been asserted: if it is otherwise the poem should be cited.

❋

Some of the sonnets in this book are in five-foot, some in six-foot or alexandrine lines.

Nos. 13 and 22 are Curtal-Sonnets, that is they are constructed in proportions resembling those of the sonnet proper, namely, 6 + 4 instead of 8 + 6, with however a halfline tailpiece (so that the equation is rather $^{12}/_2$ + $^9/_2$ = $^{21}/_2$ = 10 $^1/_2$).

II. Crise de Vers
1859–1945

Charles Baudelaire, translated by Norman Cameron: *The Painter of Modern Life*, Parts 1-4, 1859-1860

Many would agree that the beginnings of what we would come to call the modern poem emerged in mid-century France with the poems of Baudelaire. His *Fleurs du Mal* (Flowers of Evil), published in 1857, caused a scandal with its blasphemy, urban subject matter, and ironic tone. The metaphors in these poems express the disillusion and alienation of an artist confronted with a society he has only contempt for: a swan who tries to bathe in dried-up waters, an albatross whose great wings prevent him from walking on the ground. Baudelaire is also the originator of the first significant prose poems, publishing his *Le Spleen de Paris: Petits Poèmes en Prose* (Paris Spleen) in magazines in the early 1860s, paving the way for Rimbaud's *Illuminations,* as well as work by Stéphane Mallarmé, Max Jacob, and Gertrude Stein.

Extremely influential for his poetry, and for his translations of Edgar Allen Poe, Baudelaire is also called "the father of modern art criticism" and was one of the leading critics of his time. Ostensibly about artists, *The Painter of Modern Life* is a call, like Coleridge's and Emerson's before it, for a refiguring of the role of the artist /poet in his or her confrontation with modern life. Modeled on his friend, the artist Constantin Guys, Baudelaire's *flâneur* is a detached observer of urban life, not a participant.

Baudelaire, the first great poet of the modern city is also the first poet to insist on " l'art pour l'art", or art for art's sake, as a way to defend oneself against the crassness of what Stéphane Mallarmé would later call the mob. His beloved flaneurs, artists, dandies, and prostitutes make clear their disaffiliation from society through their total allegiance to artifice and aesthetics. That stance will be a precursor to the extremely individualist and impersonal forms of the later symbolists and the modernists—Yeats, Eliot, Pound—and establish irony as method, chief tool of the modern age.

✳

The Painter of Modern Life

I. BEAUTY, FASHION AND HAPPINESS

There are educated people, and even artists, who when visiting the Louvre Museum pass rapidly and without glance by rows of pictures that are highly interesting, although of the second rank, and station themselves in rapture before a Titian or Raphael—one of those pictures that have been especially popularised by the art of the engraver. Then they go away satisfied, many a one reflecting how well he knows the Louvre. Similarly there are people who, because they have in their time read Bossuet and Racine, believe themselves to be well-versed in the history of literature.

Fortunately there come on the scene from time to time the men to right such wrongs: critics, art-lovers and keen students, who point out that Raphael is not everything, nor Racine either; that lesser craftsmen have much that is good, solid and delightful; and finally that a love of universal beauty, as expressed by the classical poets and artists, is no excuse for ignoring particular beauty—the beauty of the occasion, and of day-to-day existence.

I should add that during the last few years society has slightly improved in this respect. The value attached by art-lovers nowadays to the charming colored reproductions of the eighteenth century shows that there has been a highly desirable public reaction. Debucourt, the Saint-Aubins and many others are now listed in the dictionaries as artists deserving study.

But these artists depict the past; and today I wish to concern myself with the depiction of contemporary life. The past is interesting not only for the beauty distilled from it by the artists to whom it was the present, but also because it is past—for its historical value. The same is true of the present. The pleasure we derive from the depiction of the present arises not only from the beauty in which it can be attired, but also from its essential quality of being the present.

I have before me a series of reproductions of fashion-drawings, starting at the Revolution and ending almost at the Consulate. The costumes here depicted, which seem ridiculous to thoughtless people—those people who are so serious because they lack true seriousness—have a double charm, both artistic and historical. They are very often attractive and intelligently drawn; but what to me is at least as important, and what I am happy to find in all or almost all of them, is an understanding of the spirit and the aesthetic values of their period. A man's idea of what is beautiful imprints itself upon all his attire and bearing; it crumples or smoothes his coat, rounds out or straightens his movements, and in time subtly penetrates even his features. A man ends by resembling what he would like to be.

These reproductions can be regarded either as handsome or as ugly; if the latter, they become caricatures; if the former, they are like antique statues.

The women who wore these costumes resembled one another more or less closely, in accordance with the various degrees of poetic sensibility or of vulgarity with which they were endowed. Their living substance puts movement into what to us seems too rigid. The spectator's imagination can still today see the stir and hear the rustle of this tunic or that shawl.

One of these days, perhaps, some theatre will show a play in which we shall behold a resurrection of those costumes in which our ancestors thought themselves just as fascinating as we think ourselves in *our* poor garments—which also have, it is true, their own grace, but more of a moral and spiritual description; and if these costumes are worn and lent animation by intelligent actresses and actors, we shall be astonished at ourselves for having been able to laugh so fatuously. The past, whilst retaining the fascination of a ghost, will regain the light and movement of life, and will become the present.

If an impartial person were to scan, one by one, *all* French fashions, from the nation's beginnings to the present day, he would find nothing shocking, or even surprising, about any of them. The transitions from one to another would be as elaborately detailed as in the world of biology. There would be no gaps, and therefore no surprises. And if, when contemplating the sketch depicting any particular period, he were also to recall the philosophy which especially influenced or disturbed that period, he would see what a profound harmony prevails between all the various branches of history; and that, even during the centuries which to us seem the maddest and most monstrous, the deathless appetite for beauty has always found its satisfaction.

This would, indeed, be an excellent opportunity to build a rational and historical theory of beauty, in opposition to the theory of a beauty that is single and absolute, to show that beauty, although it makes but a single impression, always and inevitably contains two elements; for the difficulty of discerning, behind the singleness of the impression, the separate elements that go to its making, does not at all invalidate the fact that more than a single element must be there. Beauty is composed of one element that is eternal, invariable and exceedingly difficult to assess, and of another element that is relative and a product of circumstance. This latter element may be described as being, either severally or jointly, the period, its fashions, its morals and its appetites. Without this second element, which is, so to speak the amusing, stimulating, appetizing icing on the divine cake, the first element would be indigestible and beyond our powers of appreciation; unadapted and unsuitable to human nature. I defy anyone to discover any particle of beauty that does not contain both these elements.

I can select if desired two examples from the extreme ends of the scale of history. In religious art the duality I have described can be seen at a glance: the element of eternal beauty discloses itself only by the permission and under the direction of the religion that the artist professes. And, likewise, even in the most frivolous productions of a sensitive artist belonging to one of these periods that we vaingloriously describe as civilized, the duality is equally apparent; the eternal element is both veiled and expressed, either by contemporary fashion or at least by the author's personal temperament.

The duality of art is an inevitable result of the duality of human nature. You may, if you wish, regard the eternally existing element as the soul of art, and the changeable element as its body. That is why Stendhal—an impertinent, teasing and even unpleasant writer, but one whose impertinences usefully stimulate reflection—came nearer to the truth than many other people when he observed that: "Beauty is only the promise of happiness." This definition certainly overshoots the mark: it places beauty too much in subjection to the infinitely variable concept of happiness, and too lightly robs beauty of its aristocratic quality. But it has the great merit of distinctly departing from the error of the academicians.

I have explained all this more than once before, and what I have written here is sufficient for those who enjoy playing with abstractions; but I know that most French readers are not very fond of this sport, and I myself am eager to pass on to the positive and particular part of my theme.

2. SKETCHES OF CONTEMPORARY SCENES

For sketches of contemporary scenes, for the depiction of the life of the citizen and the pageantry of fashion, obviously the best method is that which is quickest and least costly. The more beauty the artist puts into them, the more valuable his work will be; but there is in ordinary life, in the daily metamorphoses of outward appearances, a rapid movement that demands from the artist an equal speed of execution.

Eighteenth-century engravings in several colors have, as I was saying just now, come back into fashion. Pastels, etchings and aquatints have in turn contributed their quotas to the immense dictionary of modern life that is scattered through bookshops and art-lovers' portfolios, and behind the windows of the cheapest stores. As soon as lithography made its appearance, it at once proved to be highly suited for this enormous and seemingly frivolous task.

This class of work has provided us with real monuments. The works of Gavarni and Daumier have justly been described as complementary to the *Comédie humaine*. Balzac himself, I am convinced, would not have been disinclined to adopt this idea, which is all the more accurate in that the artist who paints contemporary scenes is a genius of mixed nature—that is to say, a genius with a considerable component of literary ability. Observer, idle looker-on, philosopher, call him what you will, you are certainly obliged, when describing such an artist, to use a term that you could not apply to the painter of eternal, or at any rate more lasting, subjects such as those of history or religion. Sometimes he is a poet; more often he has a kinship with the novelist or the moralist; he is the painter of the occasion, and also of all its suggestions of the eternal.

Every country, to its pleasure and glory, has possessed a few such men. At the present time, in addition to Daumier and Gavarni (the first names that one recalls) one may mention Devéria, Maurin, Numa, (recorders of the usurpatory graces of the Restoration), Eugène Lami (the last-named almost English in his love of the aristocratic elegances) and even Timolet and Travies, those chroniclers of poverty and restricted lives.

3. ARTIST, MAN OF THE WORLD, MAN OF THE MASSES, CHILD

I wish today to entertain my readers with an account of a remarkable man, of such powerful and distinct originality that it is sufficient unto itself and does not even seek applause. None of his drawings is signed—if by a signature one means those few alphabetical characters, so easy to counterfeit, that spell out a name and are solemnly appended by so many other artists to their most casual sketches. But all his works bear the signature of his brilliant soul; and art-lovers who have seen and appreciated them will easily recognize them by the description that I propose to give.

Deeply in love with the masses, and also with anonymity, Mr. C. G. pushes originality to the point of bashfulness, Mr. Thackeray, who, as is well known, is a keen student of artistic matters, and himself draws the illustrations for his novels, once referred to Mr. G. in a little-read London periodical. Mr. G. was vexed as if by an outrage upon his modesty. Again, more recently, when he learnt that I proposed to write an appreciation of his personality and talent, he besought me most imperiously to suppress his name, and to speak of his works only as those of an unknown artist.

I shall humbly fall in with this bizarre wish. We shall pretend to believe, the reader and I, that Mr. G. does not exist, and we shall concern ourselves with his drawings and watercolors, for which he professes a patrician contempt, as if we were scholars passing judgment on some valuable historic documents that have been found by chance and whose author must always be unknown. Nay, more, completely to ease my conscience, we shall suppose that all I have to say concerning his character, so curiously and mysteriously brilliant, has been suggested, with greater or less accuracy, by his work alone; that it is all poetical supposition, conjecture, a product of my imagination.

Mr. G. is elderly. Jean-Jacques began writing, it is said, at the age of forty-two. It was perhaps at about the same age that Mr. G., obsessed with all the images in his head, had the audacity to lay ink and colors on a white page. If the truth must be told, he drew like a barbarian or a child, struggling angrily against the clumsiness of his fingers and the disobedience of his instrument. I have seen a great number of these primitive daubs, and I confess that most of the people who know, or claim to know, about such matters could have failed, without disgrace to themselves, to recognize the genius latent in these murky scribbles. Today Mr. G., after discovering entirely by himself all the little tricks of the trade, has become a powerful master in his own style, and has retained of his first ingenuousness only what is required to lend to his rich gifts an unexpected extra flavor. When he comes across one of the first attempts of his "youth," he tears them up or burns them with a comical shamefacedness.

For ten years I wished to make the acquaintance of Mr. G., who is by nature very much a traveller and a cosmopolitan. I knew that for a long time he had worked for an English illustrated magazine, which had published reproductions of his travel sketches (Spain, Turkey, the Crimea.) Since then I have seen a considerable quantity of these drawings, hastily executed on the spot, and have thus been able to "read" a detailed and day-by-day account, much better than any other, of the Crimean campaign.

The same magazine had also published—always without a signature—numerous other compositions by the same author, taken from new ballets and operas. When at last I met him, the first thing I realized was that here was not exactly an *artist*, but rather a *man of the world*.

I beg you to understand here the word "artist" in a very narrow sense, and the words "man of the world" in their widest sense. Man of the world —that means a man of the world as a whole, a man who understands the world and the mysterious yet legitimate reasons for all its habits. Artist—that means a specialist, a man bound to his palette as a serf is bound to his glebe. Mr. G. does not like to be called an artist. Is he not to some extent right? He is interested in the world as a whole; he wants to know, understand and appreciate everything that happens on the surface of this globe of ours.

The artist lives very little, or not at all, in the world of morals or of politics. He who lives in the Quartier Bréda does not know what is happening in the Faubourg Saint-Germain. With two or three exceptions, which need not be named, most artists are, it must be confessed, simply very clever animals, pure artisans, with the intelligences and brains of the village or hamlet. Their conversation, which is necessarily restricted to a very small range of interests, quickly becomes intolerable to the "man of the world," that spiritual citizen of the universe.

To begin to understand Mr. G., therefore, you should first of all take note that what may be regarded as the mainspring of his genius is *a keen appreciation of life*.

Do you remember a picture (for indeed it is a picture!) composed by the most powerful writer of our time and entitled "l'Homme des foules" [The man of the masses.] From behind the window of a café a convalescent joyfully contemplates the crowd, and in imagination enters into all the thoughts that are going on around him. Recently returned from the shades of death, he delightedly breathes in all the germs and odors of life. Having been on the brink of entire forgetting, he now remembers, and eagerly wishes to remember, everything. Finally he rushes through the crowd in search of an unknown person, a glimpse of whose face has suddenly fascinated him. His keen appreciation of life has become a fatal and irresistible passion!

Imagine an artist whose spiritual condition is always that of this convalescent, and you will have the key to the character of Mr. G.

Now, convalescence is a sort of return to childhood. The convalescent enjoys, as the child does, the faculty of taking a lively interest in everything, even in the apparently most trivial things. Let us return, if we can, by a retrospective effort of the imagination, to our youngest, most matutinal impressions. We shall recognize that they had a remarkable affinity with the highly colored impressions that we received, later on, after a physical illness—provided that this illness did no damage to our mental or spiritual faculties. For the child everything is *new;* he is always *exhilarated.* Nothing more closely resembles what is called inspiration than the joy of a child absorbing form and color. I shall venture to go further, and assert that inspiration has something in common with cerebral congestion, and that every sublime thought is accompanied by a nervous shock, or greater or less violence, which reaches even the brain.

The nerves of the man of genius are strong; those of a child are weak. In the former reason plays a considerable role; in the latter almost the whole being is occupied by sensibility. Nevertheless, genius is simply *childhood rediscovered* by an act of will; childhood now endowed, for its self-expression, with the organs of a man and that analytical power that enables a man to put order into the automatically amassed sum of physical experiences.

This deep and joyful appreciation of life is the explanation of the fixed and animally ecstatic gaze of a child confronted by what is *new*—whatever it may be, a face or a landscape, light, gilding, colors, shot silks, the magic of a woman's beauty enhanced by her labors at the dressing-table.

A friend of mine once told me that when he was very small he used to watch his father dressing, and would gaze, in wonderment mixed with delight, at the muscles of the arms, the graduated shades of faint pink and yellow in the skin, and the bluish network of veins. The picture of life's outward appearances was already filling the child with deep respect, and laying hold of his very brain. Already he was obsessed and possessed by the contemplation of form. Predestination was precociously showing the tip of its nose. My friend's doom was sealed. Need I add that today this child is a well-known painter?

I was asking you just now to regard Mr. G. as a perpetual convalescent.

To complete your notion of him, think of him also as a child-man, as a man possessing at every moment the genius of childhood—a genius, that is to say, for which no aspect of life has become stalely familiar.

I have told you that I was disinclined to call him an artist pure and simple, and that he himself rejected this title with a modesty tinged with aristocratic disdain. I would like to call him a "dandy," and would have good reason to do so; for the word "dandy" implies a certain quintessence of character and a subtle understanding of the whole moral mechanism of human society. But, against this, the dandy aspires to indifference; and it is here that Mr. G., ruled as he is by an insatiable passion—the passion for seeing and feeling—violently breaks with dandyism. "*Amabam amare*," said St. Augustine. I am passionately in love with passion, Mr. G. would readily admit. The dandy is indifferent, or feigns to be so, for reasons of policy and caste. Mr. G. has a horror of indifferent people. He is a master of difficult art—people of sensibility will understand me—of *being sincere without being ridiculous*. I might well honor him with the title of philosopher, to which he has more than one claim, were it not that his excessive love of things visible, tangible and reduced to plastic form inspires him with a certain repugnance towards those things that constitute the impalpable realm of the metaphysician. So let us relegate him to the rank of a pure pictorial moralist, like La Bruyère.

The masses are his domain, as the air is the bird's and the sea the fish's. His passion is his profession—that of *wedding himself to the masses*. To the perfect spectator, the impassioned observer, it is an immense joy to make his domicile amongst numbers, amidst fluctuation and movement, amidst the fugitive and infinite. To be away from home, and yet to feel at home; to behold the world, to be in the midst of the world, and yet to remain hidden from the world—these are some of the minor pleasures of such independent, impassioned and impartial spirits, whom words can only clumsily describe.

The observer is a prince who always rejoices in his incognito. The lover of life makes the world his family, just as a lover of the fair sex enlists in his family all the beauties that he has captured, may capture or will never capture; or just as a lover of paintings lives in an enchanted society of dreams depicted on canvas. So the lover of the life of the universe enters into the masses as into a huge reservoir of electrical energy. He may also be compared to a mirror as huge as the masses themselves; to a kaleidoscope endowed with awareness, which at each of its movements reproduces the multiplicity of life and the restless grace of all life's elements. He is an *I* insatiably eager for the *not-I*, continually interpreting and expressing the latter in images more lovely than life itself, images always changing and fugitive.

"Any man," Mr. G. once said, in one of those conversations that he illuminates with his intense gaze and evocative gestures, "who is not stricken by an unrest so positive as to absorb all his faculties, and who *is capable of being bored in the bosom of a crowd*, any such man is a fool—a fool, and I despise him!"

When Mr. G. wakes in the morning, opens his eyes and sees the rollicking sunlight beating on the squares of his windows, he thinks to himself remorsefully and regretfully: "What an imperious command! What a fanfare of light! Already for hours, now, there has been light everywhere—light wasted by my sleep! How many things I might have seen *in a new light*—and I did not see them!"

So he leaves his house, and watches the running river of life's essence, so majestic and so bright. He admires the eternal beauty and astonishing harmony of life in capital cities—a harmony still providentially preserved amidst the turbulence of human freedom. He contemplates the landscape of stone caressed by the mist or smacked by the sunlight. He rejoices in fine carriages, in proud horses, in the dazzling smartness of grooms, in the dexterity of servants, in the undulous gait of women, in the handsome children who are happy to be alive and well-dressed. He rejoices in life as a whole.

If a fashion or the cut of a garment has been slightly altered; if buckles or bunches of ribbons have been dethroned by rosettes; if women's caps have been enlarged, or the chignon has descended by a quarter of an inch upon the nape; if the waist has been raised and the skirt amplified— be sure that, from an enormous distance, his eagle's eye has already perceived it.

A regiment passes, on its way, perhaps, to the ends of the earth, filling the air of the boulevards with its fanfares as seductive and as fickle as hope—and behold, the eye of Mr. G. has already seen, inspected and analyzed these troops' weapons, march-discipline and physique. Equipment, the glitter of metal, music, firm glances, heavy and serious mustaches—all these have entered pell-mell into him; and in a few minutes the resulting poem will virtually be already composed. And now his soul lives with the soul of the regiment, that proud image of delight in obedience.

But evening has come. It is the strange and suspect hour when the sky's curtains are drawn and the cities light up. The gas-light makes a stain upon the red of the sunset. Honest men and rogues, sane men and madmen, think to themselves: "At last the day is over." Worthy men and wicked men turn their thoughts to pleasure, and each of them hurries to the place of his choice, to drink the cup of forgetfulness. Mr. G. will be the last person remaining wherever light shines, poetry thunders, life teems, music throbs; wherever any human passion can "pose" for his inspection; wherever the natural man and the man of convention display themselves in a strange beauty; wherever the sun shines on the fleeting joys of that depraved animal, man.

"In sooth, a day well spent!" thinks a certain type of reader, whom we have all met. "Any of us has enough genius to fill his day in that fashion." No! Few men are gifted with the faculty of seeing, and still fewer have the power of expressing what they see. Now, at an hour when other men are asleep, Mr. G. is bent over his table, darting at a sheet of paper the same glance that shortly before was lingering upon all sorts of objects. He is at sword-play with his pencil, pen or brush; he makes the water in his glass spirtle to the ceiling; he wipes his pen on his shirt—eager, violent, busy, as if he feared that his images might escape him; cantankerous although alone, bullying himself onward.

And objects are reborn upon the paper, true to life and more than true to life, beautiful and more than beautiful, strange and endowed with an enthusiastic vitality, like the soul of the author. Out of nature has been distilled fantasy. All the stuffs with which memory is encumbered are classified and arranged in order, and harmonized and subjected to that compulsory formalization which results from a *childish* perceptiveness—that is to say, a perceptiveness acute and magical by reason of its simplicity!

4. MODERNITY

Thus he goes his way, hurrying and seeking. What does he seek? It is certain that this man, such a one as I have described, this solitary gifted with an active imagination, and always travelling across the great human desert, has a higher aim than any mere idle spectator—a more general aim, something else than the fleeting pleasures of the occasion.

This "something else" that he seeks is what we may be allowed to call "modernity"; for there is no better word to express the idea behind it. His business is to separate from contemporary fashion whatever it may contain of poetry within history; to extract the eternal from the ephemeral.

If we cast an eye over the usual exhibitions of modern paintings, we are struck by the artists' general tendency to clothe all their subjects in the costumes of antiquity. Almost all of them use the fashions and furnishings of the Renaissance, just as David used the modes and furnishings of ancient Rome. There is, however, this difference: that David, having selected specifically Greek or Roman themes, could do no otherwise than array them in ancient style; whereas the painters of the day, whilst selecting themes of a general nature, applicable to all periods, insist on rigging them out in costumes of the Middle Ages, the Renaissance or the East. This is clearly a sign of great laziness; for it is much more convenient to declare that the dress of a period is entirely ugly than to apply oneself to distilling from it whatever mysterious beauty it may contain, however minimal or fleeting.

Modernity is that which is ephemeral, fugitive, contingent upon the occasion; it is half of art, whose other half is the eternal and unchangeable.

Every old-time painter had his own modernity; most of the lovely portraits that have come down to us from bygone times are clad in the costumes of their various periods. They are perfectly harmonious, because the costume, the coiffure, and even the gesture, the glance and the smile (every period has its own deportment, glance and smile) compose a whole that has a complete truth to life.

This ephemeral and fugitive element, subject to so frequent metamorphoses, is not to be despised or ignored. By disregarding it, you necessarily fall into the void of a beauty abstract and indefinable, such beauty as that one woman must have had who lived before the first sin was committed. If, for the correct and inevitable costume of a given period, you substitute another, you are creating an anomaly such as could be excused only in some fashionable masquerade. (For example, the goddesses, nymphs and sultanas of the eighteenth century are portraits *morally* in keeping with their time.)

It is beyond doubt an excellent thing to study the Old Masters in order to learn how to paint; but this can only be a subsidiary exercise, if your purpose is to understand the nature of beauty in the present time. The draperies of Rubens or Veronese will not teach you to depict *moiré antique* or *satin à la reine* or any other stuff of modern manufacture that is designed to be supported and carried on a crinoline or on starched muslin petticoats. The weave and grain are not the same as in the stuffs of ancient Venice, or in those worn at the court of Catherine. Furthermore, the cut of the petticoat or bodice itself is completely different; the pleats are arranged in a new system; and lastly, the gestures and carriage of the woman herself give her gown a life and physical existence which are not those of the robe of the woman of antiquity.

In short, in order that any particular modernity may be worthy of eventually becoming antiquity, it is necessary that the mysterious beauty involuntarily lent to it by human life should be distilled from it. This is the task to which Mr. G. especially applies himself.

I have said that every period has its deportment, its glance and its gesture. This statement can be verified with especial ease in any vast portrait-gallery, such as that of Versailles. But it has a still wider application. In any of those unities known as nations, professions or classes, the passing centuries introduce a variety not only of gestures and manners, but also of actual facial features. Particular types of nose, mouth and forehead occupy given spaces of time which I shall not endeavor to determine here, but which could certainly be made a subject of exact calculation.

Portrait-painters are insufficiently aware of all this; and the great fault of Mr. Ingres, in particular, is that he tries to impose upon every type that comes before his easel a more or less despotic idea of perfection, borrowed from the classical repertory.

On such a question it would be easy, and indeed permissible, to argue *a priori*. The perpetual correlation between what is called "the soul" and what is called "the body" shows quite clearly how all that is material, or in other words a projection of the spiritual, reflects and always will reflect the spiritual from which it derives. If a painter who is patient and scrupulous, but of mediocre powers or imagination, has the task of painting a contemporary courtesan and "takes his inspiration" (this is the accepted phase) from a courtesan by Titian or Raphael, it is very highly probable that his work will be false, ambiguous and obscure. Studying a masterpiece dealing with a similar subject, but in bygone times, will not teach him the attitude, the facial expression, the grimaces or the living aspect of one of those creatures whom the dictionary of fashion has successively classified under the coarse or facetious titles of "fallen" or "kept" women, "gay girls" or "tarts."

The same criticism can be strictly applied to the depiction of the soldier or the dandy, or even of animals such as dogs or horses; indeed, of everything that goes to make up the outward appearances of an epoch. Woe on him who seeks in the study of antiquity anything but pure art, logic and general method! By immersing himself too long in the past he loses his memory of the present; he surrenders the values and privileges supplied by circumstance; for almost all our originality comes from the stamp that *time* imprints upon our perceptions.

The reader will understand, without my telling him, that I could easily support these statements in regard to the depiction of many other things besides women. What would you say, for example, (I offer an extreme case,) of a painter of naval subjects who, when called upon to depict the sober and elegant beauty of a modern ship-of-the-line, were to weary his eyes with studying the overloaded and convoluted outlines and monumental stern of an old galleon, or the complicated heads-of-sail of the sixteenth century? Or what would you think of an artist whom you had commissioned to portray a blood-horse famous in the solemn annals of the turf, if he were to confine his researches to the museums, and to content himself with studying the horses in the galleries of the pasts—in Van Dyck, Bourgignon, or Van der Meulen?

Mr. G., under a natural compulsion and the tyranny of circumstance, has followed a quite different path. He began by observing life, and only later did he set himself to learn methods of depicting it. The result has been an enthralling originality, in which any relic of barbarism or ingenuousness appears as a further proof of his faithfulness to the impressions he has received—as a compliment paid to truth.

For most of us, and especially for men of affairs, in whose eyes nature has no existence except in its utilitarian relations to their business, the fantastic reality of life has been remarkably staled by use. Mr. G., on the other hand, takes it in unceasingly; his memory and his eyes are full of it.

Arthur Rimbaud, translated by Oliver Bernard: The "Voyant" Letter to Paul Demeny, 1871

In the spring of 1871, Rimbaud wrote to his teacher Georges Izambard and to his friend Paul Demeny the two now famous "lettres du voyant" (the latter of which is printed here), each containing a poetic manifesto describing his search for a visionary language and lifestyle that would transport him out of the bourgeois culture that he, like Baudelaire, rejected, and into the future unknown. He was sixteen years old and living at home with his mother in Charleville, France. He would soon write to the established poet Paul Verlaine who lived in Paris with his wife and infant son: "I have formed the project of making a great poem, and I cannot work in Charleville."

Rimbaud's "voyant" or visionary letters did not become available until 1912, and the wildly imaginative, hallucinatory language of *Une Saison en enfer* (A Season in Hell) did not reach the general public until 1901 when copies of it were discovered gathering dust in a Belgian Publishing House. Verlaine published *Illuminations*, Rimbaud's book of prose poems, or "colored plates," in 1886. It contains two of the first instances of free verse in French: "Seascape" and "Movement." Rimbaud's poetry influenced the symbolists with its visionary strain, and the later surrealists with his professed method of bypassing the rational mind by employing what he called "le dereglement de tous les sens" (derangement of all the senses).

❋

The Voyant Letter

To Paul Demeny
Charleville, 15 May 1871
I've decided to give you an hour of modern literature. I begin at once with a topical psalm:

PARISIAN WAR SONG
Spring is evidently here; for . . .
[. . . . .]
A. RIMBAUD

—And now here is a discourse in prose on the future of poetry:

All ancient poetry culminated in Greek poetry, harmonious Life.—
From Greece to the romantic movement—in the Middle Ages—there
are men of letters, versifiers. From Ennius to Theroldus, from Theroldus
to Casimir Delavigne, it's all rhymed prose, a game, the enfeeblement and
glory of countless idiotic generations: Racine is the pure, strong, great
man—If his rhymes had been effaced, and his hemistiches got mixed up,
today the Divine Fool would be as unknown as any old author of *Origins.*
After Racine the game gets crumby. It has been going on for two thousand years!

Neither joke nor paradox. My reason inspires me with more certitude
on this subject than any *Young-France* was ever inspired with rage. Besides, *newcomers* are free to condemn their ancestors: one is at home, and
there's plenty of time.

Romanticism has never been properly judged. Who was there to judge
it? The Critics!! The Romantics? who prove so clearly that the song is
very seldom the work, that is to say, the idea sung and intended by the
singer.

For *I* is someone else. If brass wakes up a trumpet, it is not its fault. To
me this is obvious: I witness the unfolding of my own thought: I watch it,
I listen to it: I make a stroke of the bow: the symphony begins to stir in
the depths, or springs on to the stage.

If the old fools had not discovered only the *false* significance of the
Ego, we should not now be having to sweep away those millions of skele-
tons which, since time immemorial, have been piling up the fruits of their
one-eyed intellects, and claiming to be, themselves, the authors of them!

In Greece, I say, verses and lyres take their rhythm from Action. After
that, music and rhymes are a game, a pastime. The curious are charmed with
the study of this past: many of them delight in reviving these antiquities—
that's their affair. Universal mind has always thrown out its ideas naturally;
men would pick up a part of these fruits of the brain: they acted through
them, they wrote books through them: and so things went on, since man

did not work on himself, either not yet being awake, or not yet in the fullness of the great dream. Writers, civil servants: author, creator, poet, *that* man never existed!

The first study for a man who wants to be a poet is the knowledge of himself, complete. He looks for his soul, inspects it, puts it to the test, learns it. As soon as he knows it, he must cultivate it! It seems simple: in every brain a natural development takes place; so many *egoists* proclaim themselves authors; there are plenty of others who attribute their intellectual progress to themselves!—But the soul has to be made monstrous, that's the point: after the fashion of the *comprachicos,* if you like! Imagine a man planting and cultivating warts on his face.

I say that one must be a *seer,* make onself [*sic*] a *seer.*

The poet makes himself a *seer* by a long, prodigious, and rational *disordering* of *all the senses.* Every form of love, of suffering, of madness; he searches himself, he consumes all the poisons in him, and keeps only their quintessences. This is an unspeakable torture during which he needs all his faith and superhuman strength, and during which he becomes the great patient, the great criminal, the great accursed—and the great learned one!—among men.—For he arrives at the *unknown!* Because he has cultivated his own soul—which was rich to begin with—more than any other man! He reaches the unknown; and even if, crazed, he ends up by losing the understanding of his visions, at least he has seen them! Let him die charging through those unutterable, unnameable things: other horrible workers will come; they will begin from the horizons where he has succumbed!

—Continued in six minutes—

Here I shall interpolate a second psalm to decorate the text: be so good as to lend a friendly ear, and everyone will be delighted.—I take the bow in my hand, and begin:

MY LITTLE MISTRESSES
A tincture of tears washes . . .
[. . . . .]
A. R.

There. And take notice that if I were not afraid of making you spend more than sixty centimes on postage—I, poor urchin, without a copper to my name for the last seven months!—I would also give you my *Lovers of Paris,* one hundred hexameters, Sir, and my *Death of Paris,* two hundred hexameters!

—To continue:

So, then, the poet really is the thief of fire.

He is responsible for humanity, even for the *animals;* he must see to it that his inventions can be smelt, felt, heard. If what he brings back from *down there* has form, he brings forth form; if it is formless, he brings forth formlessness. A language has to be found—for that matter, every word being an idea, the time of the universal language will come! One has to be an academician—deader than a fossil—to finish a dictionary of any language. Weak-minded people, beginning by *thinking about* the first letter of the alphabet, would soon rush into madness!

This language would be of the soul, for the soul, containing everything, smells, sounds, colours; thought latching on to thought and pulling. The poet would define the amount of the unknown awakening in the universal soul in his own time: he would produce more than the formulation of his thought or the measurement of *his march towards Progress!* An enormity who has become normal, absorbed by everyone, he would really be a *multiplier of progress!*

This future will, as you see, be materialistic.—Always filled with *Number* and *Harmony,* these poems will be made to endure. Essentially, it will be Greek poetry again, in a way.

Eternal art will have its function, since poets are citizens. Poetry will no longer take its rhythm from action; *it will be ahead of it!*

Poets like this will exist! When the unending servitude of women is broken, when she lives by and for herself, when man—hitherto abominable—has given her her freedom, she too will be a poet! Woman will discover part of the unknown! Will her world of ideas be different from ours? She will discover things strange and unfathomable, repulsive and delicious. We shall take them unto ourselves, we shall understand them.

Meanwhile let us ask the *poet* for the *new*—in ideas and in forms. All the bright boys will imagine they can soon satisfy this demand:—it is not so!

The first romantics were *seers* without quite realizing it: the cultivation of their souls began accidentally: abandoned locomotives, but with their fires still alight, which the rails still carry along for a while.—Sometimes Lamartine is a *seer,* but strangled by the old form. Hugo, who is *too obsti-*

148 ❋ Arthur Rimbaud

nate, really has VISION in his last works: *Les Misérables* is a real poem. I have *Les Châtiments* with me; *Stella* shows the limit of Hugo's *vision*. Too many Belmontets and Lamennais, Jehovahs and columns, old cracked enormities.

Musset is fourteen times execrable to us suffering generations carried away by visions—to whom his angelic sloth is an insult! O! the insipid tales and proverbs! O the *Nuits!* O *Rolla*, O *Namouna*, O *the Chalice!* it is all French, that is, detestable to the highest degree; French, not Parisian! More work of the evil genius that inspired Rabelais, Voltaire, Jean La Fontaine, with M. Taine's commentary! Springlike, the wit of Musset! Charming, his love! There's enamel painting and solid poetry for you! *French* poetry will be enjoyed for a long time—but in France. Every grocer's boy can reel off a Rollaesque speech, every budding priest has the five hundred rhymes hidden away in the secrecy of a notebook. At fifteen, these outbursts of passion make boys lecherous, at sixteen they are already content to recite them with *feeling;* at eighteeen, even at seventeen, every schoolboy who has the ability does a Rolla, writes a Rolla! Perhaps some still die of it. Musset could not do anything: there were visions behind the gauze of the curtains: he closed his eyes. French, sloppy, dragged from barroom to schoolroom desk, the fine corpse is dead, and henceforth let us not even bother to awaken it with our execrations!

The second Romantics are very *seeing:* Théophile Gautier, Leconte de Lisle, Théodore de Banville. But because examining the invisible and hearing the unheard-of is quite different from recapturing the spirit of dead things, Baudelaire is the first *seer,* king of poets, *a real God!* Unluckily he lived in too artistic a circle; and the form which is so much praised in him is trivial. Inventions from the unknown demand new forms.

Broken-in to the old forms, among the simpletons, A. Renaud—has done his Rolla—L. Grandet—has done his Rolla; the Gauls and the Mussets, G. Lafenestre, Coran, Cl. Popelin, Soulary, L. Salles; the scholars, Marc, Aicard, Theuriet; the dead and the imbeciles, Autran, Barbier, L. Pichat, Lemoyne, the Deschamps, the Des Essarts; the journalists, L. Cladel, Robert Luzarches, X. de Ricard; the fantasists, C. Mendès; the bohemians; the women; the talents, Léon Dierx and Sully-Prudhomme, Coppée—the new school, called Parnassian, possesses two seers: Albert Mérat and Paul Verlaine, a real poet.—So there you are.

So, then, I am working to make myself into a *seer*—And now let us close with a pious hymn.

SQUATTINGS

Very late, when he feels his stomach churn . . .

[. . . . .]

You will be damnable if you don't answer this: quickly, because in a week I shall be in Paris, perhaps.

Goodbye,

A. RIMBAUD

Stéphane Mallarmé, translated by Bradford Cook: "Crisis in Poetry," 1896

"For I bring news, the most amazing and unprecedented news. We have been experimenting with verse," Mallarmé told an audience at Oxford in 1894, anticipating the profound impact his poetry—as well as that of Verlaine, Rimbaud, and LaForgue—would have on the English-speaking world. His news was from the French avant-garde, news of *vers libre,* the prose poem, departures from the traditional meter of the alexandrine (the French equivalent of the English pentameter), and adventures in typography such as in his own poems, especially in his collection, *Un Coup de Dés* (Throw of the Dice). Indeed, as he said, "On a touché au vers" (The poetic line has been touched).

Although the metamorphosis from romanticism to French symbolism began with the aestheticism of Baudelaire, it was Mallarmé's and Verlaine's poetry that would come to exemplify the extremes of this new "pure poetry." Symbolism called for a language that did not describe, but approached reality by the means of, as Mallarmé says in this essay, "evocation, allusion, suggestion." Symbolist poetics sought to evoke the essence of things by inventing a language without reference to external reality or individual perspective. According to Mallarmé, the poet's voice must be stilled (eliminating what Keats had much earlier termed Wordsworth's "egotistical sublime") and the primacy of the Word reinstated. Toward this end, Mallarmé theorized about a poetics that would aspire to the abstract quality, structure, and mystery of music.

❊

Crisis in Poetry

A fundamental and fascinating crisis in literature is now at hand.

Such is the plain and present truth in the eyes of all those for whom literature is of primary importance. What we are witnessing as the finale of our own century is not upheaval (as was the case a hundred years ago), but rather a fluttering in the temple's veil—meaningful folds and even a little tearing.

This is disconcerting for the French reading public, whose habits were interrupted by the death of Victor Hugo. Pursuing his mysterious task, Hugo reduced all prose—philosophy, oratory, history—to poetry; and since he was himself poetry personified, he nearly abolished the philosopher's, speaker's, or historian's right to self-expression. In that wasteland, with silence all around, he was a monument. Yet in a crypt of equal silence lay the divinity of this majestic, unconscious idea: namely, that the form we call verse is itself, quite simply, literature; that we have verse so long as we have diction, rhythm so long as we have style. Poetry, I think, waited patiently and respectfully until this giant (whose ever more grasping, ever firmer blacksmith's hand was coming to be the definition of verse) had disappeared; then it broke up. The entire language was fitted out for prosody, and therein it re-discovered its vital sense of pause. Now it could fly off, freely scattering its numberless and irreducible elements. Or we might well compare it to the multiple sounds issuing from a purely verbal orchestration.

That was the beginning of the change in poetry which Verlaine, with his fluid verse, had secretly and unexpectedly prepared when he returned to certain primitive resources in language.

I was witness to this adventure. And although my role in it was not so influential as has been claimed (for no single person was responsible), I did at least take great interest in it. It is time to discuss it, and it seems better to do so at a distance, or, so to speak, anonymously.

It will be agreed that because of the priority on magic power which is given to rhyme, French poetry has been intermittent ever since its evolution. It shines for a moment, dies out, and waits. There is extinction—or rather wear and tear which reveal the weft; there is repetition. After an almost century-long period of poetic orgy and excess which can be compared only to the Renaissance, the latest poetic urge (counteracting a number of different circumstances) is being fulfilled not by a darkening or cooling off process, but, on the contrary, by a variation in continuing brilliance. The retempering of verse, ordinarily a secret affair, is now being done openly: poets are resorting to delightful approximations.

The kind of treatment that has been given to the hieratic canon of verse can, I think, be divided into three graduated parts.

Official prosody has cut and dried rules; there lies its obstinacy. It gives its official approval to such "wise" procedures as the observance of the hemistich, and pronounces judgment on the slightest effort to simulate versification. It is like the law which states, for example, that abstinence from theft is the essence of honesty. But this is precisely what we need least to learn; for if we have not understood it by ourselves from the first, it is useless to obey it.

Those who are still faithful to the alexandrine, i.e., to the modern hexameter, have gone inside it and loosened this rigid, childish metrical mechanism; and so, now that such artificial metronomes have been abolished, there is joy for our ears alone in perceiving all possible combinations and interrelationships of twelve tones.

Consider the most recent literary taste.

Here is a rather typical and interesting example of it.

Henri de Régnier, a poet of great tact, still considers the alexandrine to be *the* gem—a gem, however, which (like sword or flower) he discloses but rarely, and even then only with some well-considered pattern in mind. He disturbs this verse form only with the greatest circumspection; he hovers and plays around it, yields to its related harmonics, and finally shows it forth in all its pride and purity. His fingering may fail at the eleventh syllable, or often linger on to a thirteenth. He excels in such accompaniments, which are, of course, the delicate, proud invention of his own original talent; they point up the temporary uneasiness of those who play the traditional poetic instrument. We discover a quite different example of knowing disobedience in the case of Jules Laforgue, who, in the beginning, abandoned the old worn-out form and initiated us in the secret and unfailing charm of defective verse.

Up to now, therefore (as shown in the two examples just mentioned), there has been either the delicacy of a Régnier or the self-indulgence of a Laforgue in metrical treatment, as a result of the fatigue brought on by the abuse of our national rhythm. That rhythm, like the national flag, must be used sparingly. There has, however, been one interesting exception: an occasional and wilful disobedience in the form of beautifully executed dissonances for the sensitive ear. And to think that, scarcely fifteen years ago, pedants that we are, we would have been outraged by this phenomenon—as if it were an illiterate's sacrilege! Let me say, finally, that the official alexandrine, like a memory, haunts about these rhythmic variations and thus adds to their luster.

Modern free verse—unlike the seventeenth-century free verse, which we find in fables or operas, and which was simply an arrangement of various well-known meters ungoverned by strophes—derives its entire originality from what we may properly call its "polymorphic" character. And the breaking up of official verse should now be what the poets will, should even be endless, provided there is pleasure to be had in it. For example, there might be a certain euphony which the reader's own poetic instinct could fragmentize with a sort of native and unerring accuracy (such has been the recent verse of Moréas). Or perhaps a rhythmical gesture of languor and revery, or of startled passion (as in the work of Vielé-Griffin). Prior to these, there was Kahn's very skillful notation of the tonal value of words. But these are only a few of the names; there are others equally typical; Charles Morice, Verhaeren, Dujardin, Mockel, etc., whose works should be consulted; they will bear out what I have said.

But the truly remarkable fact is this: for the first time in the literary history of any nation, along with the general and traditional great organ of orthodox verse which finds its ecstasy on an ever-ready keyboard, any poet with an individual technique and ear can build his own instrument, so long as his fluting, bowing, or drumming are accomplished—play that instrument and dedicate it, along with others, to Language.

Thus we have won a great new freedom; and it is my firm belief that no beauty of the past has been destroyed as a result. I am convinced that the solemn poetic tradition which was mainly established by our classical genius will continue to be observed on all important occasions. But whenever it shall seem unfitting to disturb the echoes of that venerable past for sentimental or narrative purposes, we shall be careful to avoid such disturbance. Each soul is a melody; its strands must be bound up. Each poet has his flute or viol, with which to do so.

In my opinion, we have been late in finding the true condition and possibility not only of poetic self-expression, but of free and individual modulation.

Languages are imperfect because multiple; the supreme language is missing. Inasmuch as thought consists of writing without pen and paper, without whispering even, without the sound of the immortal Word, the diversity of languages on earth means that no one can utter words which would bear the miraculous stamp of Truth Herself Incarnate. This is clearly nature's law—we stumble on it with a smile of resignation—to the effect that we have no sufficient reason for equating ourselves with God. But then, esthetically, I am disappointed when I consider how impossible it is for language to express things by means of certain keys which would reproduce their brilliance and aura—keys which do exist as a part of the instrument of the human voice, or among languages, or sometimes even in one language. When compared to the opacity of the word *ombre*, the word *ténèbres* does not seem very dark; and how frustrating the perverseness and contradiction which lend dark tones to *jour*, bright tones to *nuit!* We dream of words brilliant at once in meaning and sound, or darkening in meaning and so in sound, luminously and elementally self-succeeding. *But*, let us remember that if our dream were fulfilled, *verse would not exist*—verse which, in all its wisdom, atones for the sins of languages, comes nobly to their aid.

Strange mystery—and so, equally mysterious and meaningful, prosody sprang forth in primitive times.

The ideal would be a reasonable number of words stretched beneath our mastering glance, arranged in enduring figures, and followed by silence.

Granted that individual inventiveness, in the case of a French poet, need not outweigh the influence of his poetic heritage; still it would be highly annoying if he were not able to follow his own paths, walk through their numberless little flowers, and gather up whatever notes his voice might find. The attempt to do so has been made just recently, and poets are still conducting learned research in the direction of syllable stressing, for example. But apart from that, there is the fascinating pastime of breaking the old alexandrine into still recognizable fragments, alternately elusive or revealing. This is preferable to total and sudden novelty. It was good to relax the rules, but the ardor which got the new school too far out of tune should now be cooled. Most delightfully out of tune, yes; but to go further, as a result of that liberation, and to suppose that every poet henceforth should invent his own prosody and base it on his own special musical gift—to say nothing of his own spelling system—is simply ridiculous. That kind of thing is cannon fodder for the newspaper boys. Verses will always be similar, and the old proportions and regularity will be observed, because the poetic act consists of our sudden realization that an idea is naturally fractionized into several motifs of equal value which must be assembled. They rhyme; and their outward stamp of authenticity is that common meter which the final stress establishes.

But the crisis in poetry lies less in the very interesting interregnum or rest treatment undergone by versification, than in certain new states of our poetic mind.

We now *hear* undeniable rays of light, like arrows gilding and piercing the meanderings of song. I mean that, since Wagner appeared, Music and Verse have combined to form Poetry.

Either one of these two elements, of course, may profitably stand apart in triumph and integrity, in a quiet concert of its own if it chooses not to speak distinctly. Or else the poem can tell of their reassociation and restrengthening: the instrumentation is brightened to the point of perfect clarity beneath the orchestral veil, while verse flies down into the evening darkness of the sounds. That modern meteor—the symphony—approaches thought with the consent or ignorance of the musician. And thought itself is no longer expressed merely in common language.

Thus Mystery bursts forth ineffably throughout the heavens of Its own impersonal magnificence, wherein it was ordained that the orchestra should complement our age-old effort to make the spoken word our only form of music.

Twin symbols interrelated.

The Decadent or Mystic Schools (as they call themselves or as they were hastily labeled by the public press) find their common meeting-ground in an Idealism which (as in the case of fugues and sonatas) shuns the materials in nature, avoids any thought that might tend to arrange them too directly or precisely, and retains only the suggestiveness of things. The poet must establish a careful relationship between two images, from which a third element, clear and fusible, will be distilled and caught by our imagination. We renounce that erroneous esthetic (even though it has been responsible for certain masterpieces) which would have the poet fill the delicate pages of his book with the actual and palpable wood of trees, rather than with the forest's shuddering or the silent scattering of thunder through the foliage. A few well-chosen sounds blown heavenward on the trumpet of true majesty will suffice to conjure up the architecture of the ideal and only habitable palace—palace of no palpable stone, else the book could not be properly closed.

It is not *description* which can unveil the efficacy and beauty of monuments, seas, or the human face in all their maturity and native state, but rather evocation, *allusion, suggestion*. These somewhat arbitrary terms reveal what may well be a very decisive tendency in modern literature, a tendency which limits literature and yet sets it free. For what is the magic charm of art, if not this: that, beyond the confines of a fistful of dust or of all other reality, beyond the book itself, beyond the very text, it delivers up that volatile scattering which we call the Spirit, Who cares for nothing save universal musicality.

Speech is no more than a commercial approach to reality. In literature, allusion is sufficient: essences are distilled and then embodied in Idea.

Song, when it becomes impalpable joy, will rise to heaven.

This is the ideal I would call Transposition; Structure is something else.

If the poem is to be pure, the poet's voice must be stilled and the initiative taken by the words themselves, which will be set in motion as they meet unequally in collision. And in an exchange of gleams they will flame out like some glittering swath of fire sweeping over precious stones, and thus replace the audible breathing in lyric poetry of old—replace the poet's own personal and passionate control of verse.

The inner structures of a book of verse must be inborn; in this way, chance will be totally eliminated and the poet will be absent. From each theme, itself predestined, a given harmony will be born somewhere in the parts of the total poem and take its proper place within the volume; because, for every sound, there is an echo. Motifs of like pattern will move in balance from point to point. There will be none of the sublime incoherence found in the page-settings of the Romantics, none of the artificial unity that used to be based on the square measurements of the book. Everything will be hesitation, disposition of parts, their alternations and relationships—all this contributing to the rhythmic totality, which will be the very silence of the poem, in its blank spaces, as that silence is translated by each structural element in its own way. (Certain recent publications have heralded this sort of book; and if we may admit their ideals as complements to our own, it must then be granted that young poets have seen what an overwhelming and harmonious totality a poem must be, and have stammered out the magic concept of the Great Work.) Then again, the perfect symmetry of verses within the poem, of poems within the volume, will extend even beyond the volume itself; and this will be the creation of many poets who will inscribe, on spiritual space, the expanded signature of genius—as anonymous and perfect as a work of art.

Chimaera, yes! And yet the mere thought of it is proof (reflected from Her scales) that during the last twenty-five years poetry has been visited by some nameless and absolute flash of lightning—like the muddied, dripping gleams on my windowpane which are washed away and brightened by streaming showers of rain—revealing that, in general, all books contain the amalgamation of a certain number of age-old truths; that actually there is only one book on earth, that it is the law of the earth, the earth's true Bible. The difference between individual works is simply the difference between individual interpretations of one true and established text, which are proposed in a mighty gathering of those ages we call civilized or literary.

Certainly, whenever I sit at concerts, amid the obscurity and ecstasy of sound, I always perceive the nascent form of some one of those poems which have their origin and dwelling in human life—a poem more understandable because unheard, because the composer, in his desire to portray its majestic lines, was not even *tempted* to "explain everything." My feeling—or my doubtlessly ineradicable prejudice as a writer—is that nothing will endure if it remains unspoken; that our present task, precisely (now that the great literary rhythms I spoke of are being broken up and scattered in a series of distinct and almost orchestrated shiverings), is to find a way of transposing the symphony to the Book: in short, to regain our rightful due. For, undeniably, the true source of Music must not be the elemental sound of brasses, strings, or wood winds, but the intellectual and written word in all its glory—Music of perfect fulness and clarity, the totality of universal relationships.

One of the undeniable ideals of our time is to divide words into two different categories: first, for vulgar or immediate, second, for essential purposes.

The first is for narrative, instruction, or description (even though an adequate exchange of human thoughts might well be achieved through the silent exchange of money). The elementary use of language involves that universal *journalistic style* which characterizes all kinds of contemporary writing, with the exception of literature

Why should we perform the miracle by which a natural object is almost made to disappear beneath the magic waving wand of the written word, if not to divorce that object from the direct and the palpable, and so conjure up its *essence* in all purity?

When I say: "a flower!" then from that forgetfulness to which my voice consigns all floral form, something different from the usual calyces arises, something all music, essence, and softness: the flower which is absent from all bouquets.

Language, in the hands of the mob, leads to the same facility and directness as does money. But, in the Poet's hands, it is turned, above all, to dream and song; and, by the constituent virtue and necessity of an art which lives on fiction, it achieves its full efficacy.

Out of a number of words, poetry fashions a single new word which is total in itself and foreign to the language—a kind of incantation. Thus the desired isolation of language is effected; and chance (which might still have governed these elements, despite their artful and alternating renewal through meaning and sound) is thereby instantly and thoroughly abolished. Then we realize, to our amazement, that we had never truly heard this or that ordinary poetic fragment; and, at the same time, our recollection of the object thus conjured up bathes in a totally new atmosphere.

André Breton, translated by Richard Seaver and Helen R. Lane: *Manifesto of Surrealism,* 1924

By 1922, the poet André Breton had announced the death of Dada in favor of surrealism—a term first coined by Guillaume Apollinaire to describe the work of Italian painter Giorgio de Chirico and meant to refer to "a new spirit" that was emerging in France that would transform not only art but life. Taking Rimbaud's "Alchemy of the Word" literally, surrealism's aim, as Breton would state in his *Second Manifesto,* was "total recovery of our psychic force" through language. Its primary methods—automatic writing and the dream—were ways to "short circuit" the rational mind, thereby allowing the unconscious mind to merge with the conscious and produce a *surreality.* Surrealism's initial efforts focused on the production of poems, such as Breton's 1920 collaboration with Phillipe Soupault of automatic writings, *Les Champs magnétiques* (The Magnetic Fields) and his 1928 novel, *Nadja.* Yet *La Révolution surréaliste* was meant to be a revolution in consciousness as well, expanding its methods to politics and social relations, to, as Breton wrote, "the problem of human expression in all its forms."

Breton was the spokesperson for the movement, one which included both poets and painters such as René Char, Antonin Artaud, Robert Desnos, Salvador Dali, Paul Éluard, Max Ernst, Louis Aragon, and Joan Miro, with Baudelaire, Lautrémont, and Rimbaud as presiding spirits. Over thirty years, Breton issued a series of decrees, condemnations, and manifestos which defined the movement, beginning with this essay, *Manifesto of Surrealism. The Second Manifesto* of 1930 was largely a diatribe against his enemies, one in which he ceremoniously and in print disowns those artists and poets he feels have betrayed the uncompromising, demanding nature of surrealism. A *Third Manifesto* appeared in 1942. Each manifesto was, in turn, followed by the publishing of a preface a few years later.

❋

Manifesto of Surrealism

So strong is the belief in life, in what is most fragile in life—*real* life, I mean—that in the end this belief is lost. Man, that inveterate dreamer, daily more discontent with his destiny, has trouble assessing the objects he has been led to use, objects that his nonchalance has brought his way, or that he has earned through his own efforts, almost always through his own efforts, for he has agreed to work, at least he has not refused to try his luck (or what he calls his luck!). At this point he feels extremely modest: he knows what women he has had, what silly affairs he has been involved in; he is unimpressed by his wealth or poverty, in this respect he is still a newborn babe and, as for the approval of his conscience, I confess that he does very nicely without it. If he still retains a certain lucidity, all he can do is turn back toward his childhood which, however his guides and mentors may have botched it, still strikes him as somehow charming. There, the absence of any known restrictions allows him the perspective of several lives lived at once; this illusion becomes firmly rooted within him; now he is only interested in the fleeting, the extreme facility of everything. Children set off each day without a worry in the world. Everything is near at hand, the worst material conditions are fine. The woods are white or black, one will never sleep.

But it is true that we would not dare venture so far, it is not merely a question of distance. Threat is piled upon threat, one yields, abandons a portion of the terrain to be conquered. This imagination which knows no bounds is henceforth allowed to be exercised only in strict accordance with the laws of an arbitrary utility; it is incapable of assuming this inferior role for very long and, in the vicinity of the twentieth year, generally prefers to abandon man to his lusterless fate.

Though he may later try to pull himself together upon occasion, having felt that he is losing by slow degrees all reason for living, incapable as he has become of being able to rise to some exceptional situation such as love, he will hardly succeed. This is because he henceforth belongs body and soul to an imperative practical necessity which demands his constant attention. None of his gestures will be expansive, none of his ideas generous or far-reaching. In his mind's eye, events real or imagined will be seen only as they relate to a welter of similar events, events in which he has not participated, *abortive* events. What am I saying: he will judge them in relationship to one of these events whose consequences are more reassuring than the others. On no account will he view them as his salvation.

Beloved imagination, what I most like in you is your unsparing quality.

The mere word "freedom" is the only one that still excites me. I deem it capable of indefinitely sustaining the old human fanaticism. It doubtless satisfies my only legitimate aspiration. Among all the many misfortunes to which we are heir, it is only fair to admit that we are allowed the greatest degree of freedom of thought. It is up to us not to misuse it. To reduce the imagination to a state of slavery—even though it would mean the elimination of what is commonly called happiness—is to betray all sense of absolute justice within oneself. Imagination alone offers me some intimation of what *can be*, and this is enough to remove to some slight degree the terrible injunction; enough, too, to allow me to devote myself to it without fear of making a mistake (as though it were possible to make a bigger mistake). Where does it begin to turn bad, and where does the mind's stability cease? For the mind, is the possibility of erring not rather the contingency of good?

There remains madness, "the madness that one locks up," as it has aptly been described. That madness or another. . . . We all know, in fact, that the insane owe their incarceration to a tiny number of legally reprehensible acts and that, were it not for these acts their freedom (or what we see as their freedom) would not be threatened. I am willing to admit that they are, to some degree, victims of their imagination, in that it induces them not to pay attention to certain rules—outside of which the species feels itself threatened—which we are all supposed to know and respect. But their profound indifference to the way in which we judge them, and even to the various punishments meted out to them, allows us to suppose that they derive a great deal of comfort and consolation from their imagination, that they enjoy their madness sufficiently to endure the thought that its validity does not extend beyond themselves. And, indeed, hallucinations, illusions, etc., are not a source of trifling pleasure. The best controlled sensuality partakes of it, and I know that there are many evenings when I would gladly tame that pretty hand which, during the last pages of Taine's *L'Intelligence,* indulges in some curious misdeeds. I could spend my whole life prying loose the secrets of the insane. These people are honest to a fault, and their naiveté has no peer but my own. Christopher Columbus should have set out to discover America with a boatload of madmen. And note how this madness has taken shape, and endured.

❈

It is not the fear of madness which will oblige us to leave the flag of imagination furled.

The case against the realistic attitude demands to be examined, following the case against the materialistic attitude. The latter, more poetic in fact than the former, admittedly implies on the part of man a kind of monstrous pride which, admittedly, is monstrous, but not a new and more complete decay. It should above all be viewed as a welcome reaction against certain ridiculous tendencies of spiritualism. Finally, it is not incompatible with a certain nobility of thought.

By contrast, the realistic attitude, inspired by positivism, from Saint Thomas Aquinas to Anatole France, clearly seems to me to be hostile to any intellectual or moral advancement. I loathe it, for it is made up of mediocrity, hate, and dull conceit. It is this attitude which today gives birth to these ridiculous books, these insulting plays. It constantly feeds on and derives strength from the newspapers and stultifies both science and art by assiduously flattering the lowest of tastes; clarity bordering on stupidity, a dog's life. The activity of the best minds feels the effects of it; the law of the lowest common denominator finally prevails upon them as it does upon the others. An amusing result of this state of affairs, in literature for example, is the generous supply of novels. Each person adds his personal little "observation" to the whole. As a cleansing antidote to all this, M. Paul Valéry recently suggested that an anthology be compiled in which the largest possible number of opening passages from novels be offered; the resulting insanity, he predicted, would be a source of considerable edification. The most famous authors would be included. Such a thought reflects great credit on Paul Valéry who, some time ago, speaking of novels, assured me that, so far as he was concerned, he would continue to refrain from writing: "The Marquise went out at five." But has he kept his word?

If the purely informative style, of which the sentence just quoted is a prime example, is virtually the rule rather than the exception in the novel form, it is because, in all fairness, the author's ambition is severely circumscribed. The circumstantial, needlessly specific nature of each of their notations leads me to believe that they are perpetrating a joke at my expense. I am spared not even one of the character's slightest vacillations: will he be fairhaired? what will his name be? will we first meet him during the summer? So many questions resolved once and for all, as chance directs; the only discretionary power left me is to close the book, which I am careful to do somewhere in the vicinity of the first page. And the descriptions! There is nothing to which their vacuity can be compared; they are nothing but so many superimposed images taken from some stock catalogue, which the author utilizes more and more whenever he chooses; he seizes the opportunity to slip me his postcards, he tries to make me agree with him about the clichés:

The small room into which the young man was shown was covered with yellow wallpaper: there were geraniums in the windows, which were covered with muslin curtains; the setting sun cast a harsh light over the entire setting. . . . There was nothing special about the room. The furniture, of yellow wood, was all very old. A sofa with a tall back turned down, an oval table opposite the sofa, a dressing table and a mirror set against the pierglass, some chairs along the walls, two or three etchings of no value portraying some German girls with birds in their hands—such were the furnishings.*

I am in no mood to admit that the mind is interested in occupying itself with such matters, even fleetingly. It may be argued that this school-boy description has its place, and that at this juncture of the book the author has his reasons for burdening me. Nevertheless he is wasting his time, for I refuse to go into his room. Others' laziness or fatigue does not interest me. I have too unstable a notion of the continuity of life to equate or compare my moments of depression or weakness with my best moments. When one ceases to feel, I am of the opinion one should keep quiet. And I would like it understood that I am not accusing or condemning lack of originality *as such*. I am only saying that I do not take particular note of the empty moments of my life, that it may be unworthy for any man to crystallize those which seem to him to be so. I shall, with your permission, *ignore* the description of that room, and many more like it.

Not so fast, there; I'm getting into the area of psychology, a subject about which I shall be careful not to joke.

The author attacks a character and, this being settled upon, parades his hero to and fro across the world. No matter what happens, this hero, whose actions and reactions are admirably predictable, is compelled not to thwart or upset—even though he looks as though he is—the calculations of which he is the object. The currents of life can appear to lift him up,

---

*Dostoevski, *Crime and Punishment.*

roll him over, cast him down, he will still belong to this *readymade* human type. A simple game of chess which doesn't interest me in the least—man, whoever he may be, being for me a mediocre opponent. What I cannot bear are those wretched discussions relative to such and such a move, since winning or losing is not in question. And if the game is not worth the candle, if objective reason does a frightful job—as indeed it does—of serving him who calls upon it, is it not fitting and proper to avoid all contact with these categories? "Diversity is so vast that every different tone of voice, every step, cough, every wipe of the nose, every sneeze. . . ."* If in a cluster of grapes there are no two alike, why do you want me to describe this grape by the other, by all the others, why do you want me to make a palatable grape? Our brains are dulled by the incurable mania of wanting to make the unknown known, classifiable. The desire for analysis wins out over the sentiments.** The result is statements of undue length whose persuasive power is attributable solely to their strangeness and which impress the reader only by the abstract quality of their vocabulary, which moreover is ill-defined. If the general ideas that philosophy has thus far come up with as topics of discussion revealed by their very nature their definitive incursion into a broader or more general area, I would be the first to greet the news with joy. But up till now it has been nothing but idle repartee; the flashes of wit and other niceties vie in concealing from us the true thought in search of itself, instead of concentrating on obtaining successes. It seems to me that every act is its own justification, at least for the person who has been capable of committing it, that it is endowed with a radiant power which the slightest gloss is certain to diminish. Because of this gloss, it even in a sense ceases to happen. It gains nothing to be thus distinguished. Stendhal's heroes are subject to the comments and appraisals—appraisals which are more or less successful—made by that author, which add not one whit to their glory. Where we really find them again is at the point at which Stendhal has lost them.

❁

We are still living under the reign of logic: this, of course, is what I have been driving at. But in this day and age logical methods are applicable

---

*Pascal.
**Barrès, *Proust*.

only to solving problems of secondary interest. The absolute rationalism that is still in vogue allows us to consider only facts relating directly to our experience. Logical ends, on the contrary, escape us. It is pointless to add that experience itself has found itself increasingly circumscribed. It paces back and forth in a cage from which it is more and more difficult to make it emerge. It too leans for support on what is most immediately expedient, and it is protected by the sentinels of common sense. Under the pretense of civilization and progress, we have managed to banish from the mind everything that may rightly or wrongly be termed superstition, or fancy; forbidden is any kind of search for truth which is not in conformance with accepted practices. It was, apparently, by pure chance that a part of our mental world which we pretended not to be concerned with any longer—and, in my opinion by far the most important part—has been brought back to light. For this we must give thanks to the discoveries of Sigmund Freud. On the basis of these discoveries a current of opinion is finally forming by means of which the human explorer will be able to carry his investigations much further, authorized as he will henceforth be not to confine himself solely to the most summary realities. The imagination is perhaps on the point of reasserting itself, of reclaiming its rights. If the depths of our mind contain within it strange forces capable of augmenting those on the surface, or of waging a victorious battle against them, there is every reason to seize them—first to seize them, then, if need be, to submit them to the control of our reason. The analysts themselves have everything to gain by it. But it is worth noting that no means has been designated a priori for carrying out this undertaking, that until further notice it can be construed to be the province of poets as well as scholars, and that its success is not dependent upon the more or less capricious paths that will be followed.

❋

Freud very rightly brought his critical faculties to bear upon the dream. It is, in fact, inadmissible that this considerable portion of psychic activity (since, at least from man's birth until his death, thought offers no solution of continuity, the sum of the moments of dream, from the point of view of time, and taking into consideration only the time of pure dreaming, that is the dreams of sleep, is not inferior to the sum of the moments of reality, or, to be more precisely limiting, the moments of waking) has still today been so grossly neglected. I have always been amazed at the way an ordinary observer lends so much more credence and attaches so much more importance to waking events than to those occurring in dreams. It is because man, when he ceases to sleep, is above all the plaything of his memory, and in its normal state memory takes pleasure in weakly retracing for him the circumstances of the dream, in stripping it of any real importance, and in dismissing the only *determinant* from the point where he thinks he has left it a few hours before: this firm hope, this concern. He is under the impression of continuing something that is worthwhile. Thus the dream finds itself reduced to a mere parenthesis, as is the night. And, like the night, dreams generally contribute little to furthering our understanding. This curious state of affairs seems to me to call for certain reflections:

1) Within the limits where they operate (or are thought to operate) dreams give every evidence of being continuous and show signs of organization. Memory alone arrogates to itself the right to excerpt from dreams, to ignore the transitions, and to depict for us rather a series of dreams than the *dream itself.* By the same token, at any given moment we have only a distinct notion of realities, the coordination of which is a question of will.* What is worth noting is that nothing allows us to presuppose a greater dissipation of the elements of which the dream is constituted. I am sorry to have to speak about it according to a formula which in principle excludes the dream. When will we have sleeping logicians, sleeping philosophers? I would like to sleep, in order to surrender myself to the dreamers, the way I surrender myself to those who read me with eyes wide open; in order to stop imposing, in this realm, the conscious rhythm of my thought. Perhaps my dream last night follows that of the night before, and will be continued the next night, with an exemplary strictness. *It's quite possible,* as the saying goes. And since it has not been proved in the slightest that, in doing so, the "reality" with which I am kept busy continues to exist in the state of dream, that it does not sink back down into the immemorial, why should I

---

*Account must be taken of the *depth* of the dream. For the most part I retain only what I can glean from its most superficial layers. What I most enjoy contemplating about a dream is everything that sinks back below the surface in a waking state, everything I have forgotten about my activities in the course of the preceding day, dark foliage, stupid branches. In "reality," likewise, I prefer to *fall.*

not grant to dreams what I occasionally refuse reality, that is, this value of certainty in itself which, in its own time, is not open to my repudiation? Why should I not expect from the sign of the dream more than I expect from a degree of consciousness which is daily more acute? Can't the dream also be used in solving the fundamental questions of life? Are these questions the same in one case as in the other and, in the dream, do these questions already exist? Is the dream any less restrictive or punitive than the rest? I am growing old and, more than that reality to which I believe I subject myself, it is perhaps the dream, the difference with which I treat the dream, which makes me grow old.

2) Let me come back again to the waking state. I have no choice but to consider it a phenomenon of interference. Not only does the mind display, in this state, a strange tendency to lose its bearings (as evidenced by the slips and mistakes the secrets of which are just beginning to be revealed to us), but, what is more, it does not appear that, when the mind is functioning normally, it really responds to anything but the suggestions which come to it from the depths of that dark night to which I commend it. However conditioned it may be, its balance is relative. It scarcely dares express itself and, if it does, it confines itself to verifying that such and such an idea, or such and such a woman, has made an impression on it. What impression it would be hard pressed to say, by which it reveals the degree of its subjectivity, and nothing more. This idea, this woman, disturb it, they tend to make it less severe. What they do is isolate the mind for a second from its solvent and spirit it to heaven, as the beautiful precipitate it can be, that it is. When all else fails, it then calls upon chance, a divinity even more obscure than the others to whom it ascribes all its aberrations. Who can say to me that the angle by which that idea which affects it is offered, that what it likes in the eye of that woman is not precisely what links it to its dream, binds it to those fundamental facts which, through its own fault, it has lost? And if things were different, what might it be capable of? I would like to provide it with the key to this corridor.

3) The mind of the man who dreams is fully satisfied by what happens to him. The agonizing question of possibility is no longer pertinent. Kill, fly faster, love to your heart's content. And if you should die, are you not certain of reawaking among the dead? Let yourself be carried along, events

will not tolerate your interference. You are nameless. The ease of everything is priceless.

What reason, I ask, a reason so much vaster than the other, makes dreams seem so natural and allows me to welcome unreservedly a welter of episodes so strange that they would confound me now as I write? And yet I can believe my eyes, my ears: this great day has arrived, this beast has spoken.

If man's awaking is harder, if it breaks the spell too abruptly, it is because he has been led to make for himself too impoverished a notion of atonement.

4) From the moment when it is subjected to a methodical examination, when, by means yet to be determined, we succeed in recording the contents of dreams in their entirety (and that presupposes a discipline of memory spanning generations; but let us nonetheless begin by noting the most salient facts), when its graph will expand with unparalleled volume and regularity, we may hope that the mysteries which really are not will give way to the great Mystery. I believe in the future resolution of these two states, dream and reality, which are seemingly so contradictory, into a kind of absolute reality, a *surreality*, if one may so speak. It is in quest of this surreality that I am going, certain not to find it but too unmindful of my death not to calculate to some slight degree the joys of its possession.

A story is told according to which Saint-Pol-Roux, in times gone by, used to have a notice posted on the door of his manor house in Camaret, every evening before he went to sleep, which read: THE POET IS WORKING.

A great deal more could be said, but in passing I merely wanted to touch upon a subject which in itself would require a very long and much more detailed discussion; I shall come back to it. At this juncture, my intention was merely to mark a point by noting the *hate of the marvelous* which rages in certain men, this absurdity beneath which they try to bury it. Let us not mince words: the marvelous is always beautiful, anything marvelous is beautiful, in fact only the marvelous is beautiful.

❊

In the realm of literature, only the marvelous is capable of fecundating works which belong to an inferior category such as the novel, and generally speaking, anything that involves storytelling. Lewis' *The Monk* is an admirable proof of this. It is infused throughout with the presence of the marvelous. Long before the author has freed his main characters from all temporal constraints, one feels them ready to act with an unprecedented pride. This passion for eternity with which they are constantly stirred lends an unforgettable intensity to their torments, and to mine. I mean that this book, from beginning to end, and in the purest way imaginable, exercises an exalting effect only upon that part of the mind which aspires to leave the earth and that, stripped of an insignificant part of its plot, which belongs to the period in which it was written, it constitutes a paragon of precision and innocent grandeur.* It seems to me none better has been done, and that the character of Mathilda in particular is the most moving creation that one can credit to this *figurative* fashion in literature. She is less a character than a continual temptation. And if a character is not a temptation, what is he? An extreme temptation, she. In *The Monk,* the "nothing is impossible for him who dares try" gives it its full, convincing measure. Ghosts play a logical role in the book, since the critical mind does not seize them in order to dispute them. Ambrosio's punishment is likewise treated in a legitimate manner, since it is finally accepted by the critical faculty as a natural denouement.

It may seem arbitrary on my part, when discussing the marvelous, to choose this model, from which both the Nordic literatures and Oriental literatures have borrowed time and time again, not to mention the religious literatures of every country. This is because most of the examples which these literatures could have furnished me with are tainted by puerility, for the simple reason that they are addressed to children. At an early age children are weaned on the marvelous, and later on they fail to retain a sufficient virginity of mind to thoroughly enjoy fairy tales. No matter how charming they may be, a grown man would think he were reverting to childhood by nourishing himself on fairy tales, and I am the first to admit that all such tales are not suitable for him. The fabric of adorable improbabilities must be made a trifle more subtle the older we grow, and we are still at the stage of waiting for this kind of spider. . . . But the faculties do not change radically. Fear, the attraction of the un-

---

*What is admirable about the fantastic is that there is no longer anything fantastic: only the real.

usual, chance, the taste for things extravagant are all devices which we can always call upon without fear of deception. There are fairy tales to be written for adults, fairy tales still almost blue.

❀

The marvelous is not the same in every period of history: it partakes in some obscure way of a sort of general revelation only the fragments of which come down to us: they are the romantic *ruins*, the modern *mannequin*, or any other symbol capable of affecting the human sensibility for a period of time. In these areas which make us smile, there is still portrayed the incurable human restlessness, and this is why I take them into consideration and why I judge them inseparable from certain productions of genius which are, more than the others, painfully afflicted by them. They are Villon's gibbets, Racine's Greeks, Baudelaire's couches. They coincide with an eclipse of the taste I am made to endure, I whose notion of taste is the image of a big spot. Amid the bad taste of my time I strive to go further than anyone else. It would have been I, had I lived in 1820, I "the bleeding nun," I who would not have spared this cunning and banal "let us conceal" whereof the parodical Cuisin speaks, it would have been I, I who would have reveled in the enormous metaphors, as he says, all phases of the "silver disk." For today I think of a *castle*, half of which is not necessarily in ruins; this castle belongs to me, I picture it in a rustic setting, not far from Paris. The outbuildings are too numerous to mention, and, as for the interior, it has been frightfully restored, in such a manner as to leave nothing to be desired from the viewpoint of comfort. Automobiles are parked before the door, concealed by the shade of the trees. A few of my friends are living here as permanent guests: there is Louis Aragon leaving; he only has time enough to say hello; Philippe Soupault gets up with the stars, and Paul Eluard, our great Eluard, has not yet come home. There are Robert Desnos and Roger Vitrac out on the grounds poring over an ancient edict on dueling; Georges Auric, Jean Paulhan; Max Morise, who rows so well, and Benjamin Péret, busy with his equations with birds; and Joseph Delteil; and Jean Carrive; and Georges Limbour, and Georges Limbours (there is a whole hedge of Georges Limbours); and Marcel Noll; there is T. Fraenkel waving to us from his captive balloon, Georges Malkine, Antonin Artaud, Francis Gérard, Pierre Naville, J.-A. Boiffard, and after them Jacques Baron and his brother, handsome and cordial, and so many others besides, and gorgeous women, I might add. Nothing is too good for these young men, their wishes are, as to wealth, so many commands. Francis Picabia comes to pay us a call, and last week, in the hall of mirrors, we received a certain Marcel Duchamp whom we had not hitherto known. Picasso goes hunting in the neighborhood. The spirit of *demoralization* has elected domicile in the castle, and it is with it we have to deal every time it is a question of contact with our fellowmen, but the doors are always open, and one does not begin by "thanking" everyone, you know. Moreover, the solitude is vast, we don't often run into one another. And anyway, isn't what matters that we be the masters of ourselves, the masters of women, and of love too?

I shall be proved guilty of poetic dishonesty: everyone will go parading about saying that I live on the rue Fontaine and that he will have none of the water that flows therefrom. To be sure! But is he certain that this castle into which I cordially invite him is an image? What if this castle really existed! My guests are there to prove it does; their whim is the luminous road that leads to it. We really live by our fantasies when we *give free rein to them*. And how could what one might do bother the other, there, safely sheltered from the sentimental pursuit and at the trysting place of opportunities?

※

Man proposes and disposes. He and he alone can determine whether he is completely master of himself, that is, whether he maintains the body of his desires, daily more formidable, in a state of anarchy. Poetry teaches him to. It bears within itself the perfect compensation for the miseries we endure. It can also be an organizer, if ever, as the result of a less intimate disappointment, we contemplate taking it seriously. The time is coming when it decrees the end of money and by itself will break the bread of heaven for the earth! There will still be gatherings on the public squares, and *movements* you never dared hope participate in. Farewell to absurd choices, the dreams of dark abyss, rivalries, the prolonged patience, the flight of the seasons, the artificial order of ideas, the ramp of danger, time for everything! May you only take the trouble to *practice* poetry. Is it not incumbent upon us, who are already living off it, to try and impose what we hold to be our case for further inquiry?

It matters not whether there is a certain disproportion between this defense and the illustration that will follow it. It was a question of going back to the sources of poetic imagination and, what is more, of remaining there. Not that I pretend to have done so. It requires a great deal of fortitude to try to set up one's abode in these distant regions where everything seems at first to be so awkward and difficult, all the more so if one wants to try to take someone there. Besides, one is never sure of really being there. If one is going to all that trouble, one might just as well stop off somewhere else. Be that as it may, the fact is that the way to these regions is clearly marked, and that to attain the true goal is now merely a matter of the travelers' ability to endure.

❋

We are all more or less aware of the road traveled. I was careful to relate, in the course of a study of the case of Robert Desnos entitled ENTRÉE DES MÉDIUMS,* that I had been led to "concentrate my attention on the more or less partial sentences which, when one is quite alone and on the verge of falling asleep, become perceptible for the mind without its being possible to discover what provoked them." I had then just attempted the poetic adventure with the minimum of risks, that is, my aspirations were the same as they are today but I trusted in the slowness of formulation to keep me from useless contacts, contacts of which I completely disapproved. This attitude involved a modesty of thought certain vestiges of which I still retain. At the end of my life, I shall doubtless manage to speak with great effort the way people speak, to apologize for my voice and my few remaining gestures. The virtue of the spoken word (and the written word all the more so) seemed to me to derive from the faculty of foreshortening in a striking manner the exposition (since there was exposition) of a small number of facts, poetic or other, of which I made myself the substance. I had come to the conclusion that Rimbaud had not proceeded any differently. I was composing, with a concern for variety that deserved better, the final poems of *Mont de piété,* that is, I managed to extract from the blank lines of this book an incredible advantage. These

---

*See *Les Pas Perdus,* published by N. R. F.

lines were the closed eye to the operations of thought that I believed I was obliged to keep hidden from the reader. It was not deceit on my part, but my love of shocking the reader. I had the illusion of a possible complicity, which I had more and more difficulty giving up. I had begun to cherish words excessively for the space they allow around them, for their tangencies with countless other words that I did not utter. The poem BLACK FOREST derives precisely from this state of mind. It took me six months to write it, and you may take my word for it that I did not rest a single day. But this stemmed from the opinion I had of myself in those days, which was high, please don't judge me too harshly. I enjoy these stupid confessions. At that point cubist pseudo-poetry was trying to get a foothold, but it had emerged defenseless from Picasso's brain, and I was thought to be as dull as dishwater (and still am). I had a sneaking suspicion, moreover, that from the viewpoint of poetry I was off on the wrong road, but I hedged my bet as best I could, defying lyricism with salvos of definitions and formulas (the Dada phenomena were waiting in the wings, ready to come on stage) and pretending to search for an application of poetry to advertising (I went so far as to claim that the world would end, not with a good book but with a beautiful advertisement for heaven or for hell).

In those days, a man at least as boring as I, Pierre Reverdy, was writing:

The image is a pure creation of the mind.
It cannot be born from a comparison but from a juxtaposition of two more or less distant realities.
The more the relationship between the two juxtaposed realities is distant and true, the stronger the image will be—the greater its emotional power and poetic reality . . .*

These words, however sibylline for the uninitiated, were extremely revealing, and I pondered them for a long time. But the image eluded me. Reverdy's aesthetic, a completely a posteriori aesthetic, led me to mistake the effects for the causes. It was in the midst of all this that I renounced irrevocably my point of view.

---

*Nord-Sud, March 1918.

*

One evening, therefore, before I fell asleep, I perceived, so clearly articulated that it was impossible to change a word, but nonetheless removed from the sound of any voice, a rather strange phrase which came to me without any apparent relationship to the events in which, my consciousness agrees, I was then involved, a phrase which seemed to me insistent, a phrase, if I may be so bold, *which was knocking at the window*. I took cursory note of it and prepared to move on when its organic character caught my attention. Actually, this phrase astonished me: unfortunately I cannot remember it exactly, but it was something like: "There is a man cut in two by the window," but there could be no question of ambiguity, accompanied as it was by the faint visual image* of a man walking cut half way up by a window perpendicular to the axis of his body. Beyond the slightest shadow of a doubt, what I saw was the simple reconstruction in space of a man leaning out a window. But this window having shifted with the man, I realized that I was dealing with an image of a fairly rare sort, and all I could think of was to incorporate it into my material for poetic construction. No sooner had I granted it this capacity than it was in fact succeeded by a whole series of phrases, with only brief pauses between them, which surprised me only slightly less and left me with the impression of their being so gratuitous that the control I had then exercised upon myself

---

*Were I a painter, this visual depiction would doubtless have become more important for me than the other. It was most certainly my previous predispositions which decided the matter. Since that day, I have had occasion to concentrate my attention voluntarily on similar apparitions, and I know that they are fully as clear as auditory phenomena. With a pencil and white sheet of paper to hand, I could easily trace their outlines. Here again it is not a matter of drawing, *but simply of tracing*. I could thus depict a tree, a wave, a musical instrument, all manner of things of which I am presently incapable of providing even the roughest sketch. I would plunge into it, convinced that I would find my way again, in a maze of lines which at first glance would seem to be going nowhere. And, upon opening my eyes, I would get the very strong impression of something "never seen." The proof of what I am saying has been provided many times by Robert Desnos: to be convinced, one has only to leaf through the pages of issue number 36 of *Feuilles libres* which contains several of his drawings (*Romeo and Juliet, A Man Died This Morning*, etc.) which were taken by this magazine as the drawings of a madman and published as such.

seemed to me illusory and all I could think of was putting an end to the interminable quarrel raging within me.*

❋

Completely occupied as I still was with Freud at that time, and familiar as I was with his methods of examination which I had had some slight occasion to use on some patients during the war, I resolved to obtain from myself what we were trying to obtain from them, namely, a monologue spoken as rapidly as possible without any intervention on the part of the critical faculties, a monologue consequently unencumbered by the slightest inhibition and which was, as closely as possible, akin to *spoken thought*. It had seemed to me, and still does—the way in which the phrase about the man cut in two had come to me is an indication of it—that the speed of thought is no greater than the speed of speech, and that thought does not necessarily defy language, nor even the fast-moving pen. It was in this frame of mind that Philippe Soupault—to whom I had confided these initial conclusions—and I decided to blacken some paper, with a praiseworthy disdain for what might result from a literary point of view. The ease of execution did the rest. By the end of the first day we were able to read to ourselves some fifty or so pages obtained in this manner, and begin to compare our results. All in all, Soupault's pages and mine proved to be remarkably similar: the same overconstruction, shortcomings of a similar nature, but also, on both our parts, the illusion of an extraordinary verve, a great deal of emotion, a considerable choice of images of a quality such that we would not have been capable of preparing a single one in longhand, a very special picturesque quality and, here and there, a strong comical effect. The only difference between our two texts seemed to me to derive essentially from our respective tempers, Soupault's being less static

---

*Knut Hamsum ascribes this sort of revelation to which I had been subjected as deriving from *hunger*, and he may not be wrong. (The fact is I did not eat every day during that period of my life). Most certainly the manifestations that he describes in these terms are clearly the same:

"The following day I awoke at any early hour. It was still dark. My eyes had been open for a long time when I heard the clock in the apartment above strike five. I wanted to go back to sleep, but I couldn't; I was wide awake and a thousand thoughts were crowding through my mind.

than mine, and, if he does not mind my offering this one slight criticism, from the fact that he had made the error of putting a few words by way of titles at the top of certain pages, I suppose in a spirit of mystification. On the other hand, I must give credit where credit is due and say that he constantly and vigorously opposed any effort to retouch or correct, however slightly, any passage of this kind which seemed to me unfortunate. In this he was, to be sure, absolutely right.* It is, in fact, difficult to appreciate fairly the various elements present; one may even go so far as to say that it is impossible to appreciate them at a first reading. To you who write, these elements are, on the surface, *as strange to you as they are to anyone else,* and naturally you are wary of them. Poetically speaking, what strikes you about them above all is their *extreme degree of immediate absurdity,* the quality of this absurdity, upon closer scrutiny, being to give way to everything admissible, everything legitimate in the world: the disclosure of a certain number of properties and of facts no less objective, in the final analysis, than the others.

❋

In homage to Guillaume Apollinaire, who had just died and who, on several occasions, seemed to us to have followed a discipline of this kind, without however having sacrificed to it any mediocre literary means, Soupault and I baptized the new mode of pure expression which we had at our disposal and which we wished to pass on to our friends, by the name of SURREALISM. I believe that there is no point today in dwelling any further on this word and that the meaning we gave it initially has generally prevailed over its Apollinarian sense. To be even fairer, we could probably have taken over the world SUPERNATURALISM employed by Gérard de Nerval in his dedication to the *Filles de feu.*** It appears, in fact, that Nerval possessed to a tee the spirit with which we claim a kinship,

---

*I believe more and more in the infallibility of my thought with respect to myself, and this is too fair. Nonetheless, with this *thought-writing,* where one is at the mercy of the first outside distraction, "ebullutions" can occur. It would be inexcusable for us to pretend otherwise. By definition, thought is strong, and incapable of catching itself in error. The blame for these obvious weaknesses must be placed on suggestions that come to it from without.

**And also by Thomas Carlyle in *Sartor Resartus* ([Book III] Chapter VIII, "Natural Supernaturalism"), 1833–34.

Apollinaire having possessed, on the contrary, naught but *the letter,* still imperfect, of Surrealism, having shown himself powerless to give a valid theoretical idea of it. Here are two passages by Nerval which seem to me to be extremely significant in this respect:

> I am going to explain to you, my dear Dumas, the phenomenon of which you have spoken a short while ago. There are, as you know, certain storytellers who cannot invent without identifying with the characters their imagination has dreamt up. You may recall how convincingly our old friend Nodier used to tell how it had been his misfortune during the Revolution to be guillotined; one became so completely convinced of what he was saying that one began to wonder how he had managed to have his head glued back on.
>
> . . . And since you have been indiscreet enough to quote one of the sonnets composed in this SUPERNATURALISTIC dream-state, as the Germans would call it, you will have to hear them all. You will find them at the end of the volume. They are hardly any more obscure than Hegel's metaphysics or Swedenborg's MEMORABILIA, and would lose their charm if they were explained, if such were possible; at least admit the worth of the expression. . . .*

Those who might dispute our right to employ the term SURREALISM in the very special sense that we understand it are being extremely dishonest, for there can be no doubt that this word had no currency before we came along. Therefore, I am defining it once and for all:

SURREALISM, *n.* Psychic automatism in its pure state, by which one proposes to express—verbally, by means of the written word, or in any other manner—the actual functioning of thought. Dictated by thought, in the absence of any control exercised by reason, exempt from any aesthetic or moral concern.

ENCYCLOPEDIA. *Philosophy.* Surrealism is based on the belief in the superior reality of certain forms of previously neglected associations, in the omnipotence of dream, in the disinterested play of thought. It tends to ruin once and for all all other psychic mechanisms and to substitute itself for them in solving all the principal problems of life. The follow-

---

*See also *L'Idéoréalisme* by Saint-Pol-Roux.

ing have performed acts of ABSOLUTE SURREALISM: Messrs. Aragon, Baron, Boiffard, Breton, Carrive, Crevel, Delteil, Desnos, Eluard, Gérard, Limbour, Malkine, Morise, Naville, Noll, Péret, Picon, Soupault, Vitrac.

❋

They seem to be, up to the present time, the only ones, and there would be no ambiguity about it were it not for the case of Isidore Ducasse, about whom I lack information. And, of course, if one is to judge them only superficially by their results, a good number of poets could pass for Surrealists, beginning with Dante and, in his finer moments, Shakespeare. *In the course of the various attempts I have made to reduce what is, by breach of trust, called genius, I have found nothing which in the final analysis can be attributed to any other method than that.*

❋

Young's *Nights* are Surrealist from one end to the other; unfortunately it is a priest who is speaking, a bad priest no doubt, but a priest nonetheless.

Swift is Surrealist in malice,
Sade is Surrealist in sadism.
Chateaubriand is Surrealist in exoticism.
Constant is Surrealist in politics.
Hugo is Surrealist when he isn't stupid.
Desbordes-Valmore is Surrealist in love.
Bertrand is Surrealist in the past.
Rabbe is Surrealist in death.
Poe is Surrealist in adventure.
Baudelaire is Surrealist in morality.
Rimbaud is Surrealist in the way he lived, and elsewhere.
Mallarmé is Surrealist when he is confiding.
Jarry is Surrealist in absinthe.
Nouveau is Surrealist in the kiss.
Saint-Pol-Roux is Surrealist in his use of symbols.
Fargue is Surrealist in the atmosphere.

Vaché is Surrealist in me.
Reverdy is Surrealist at home.
Saint-Jean-Perse is Surrealist at a distance.
Roussel is Surrealist as a storyteller.
Etc.

I would like to stress this point: they are not always Surrealists, in that I discern in each of them a certain number of preconceived ideas to which—very naively!—they hold. They hold to them because they had not *heard the Surrealist voice,* the one that continues to preach on the eve of death and above the storms, because they did not want to serve simply to orchestrate the marvelous score. They were instruments too full of pride, and this is why they have not always produced a harmonious sound.*

But we, who have made no effort whatsoever to filter, who in our works have made ourselves into simple receptacles of so many echoes, modest *recording instruments* who are not mesmerized by the drawings we are making, perhaps we serve an even nobler cause. Thus do we render with integrity the "talent" which has been lent to us. You might as well speak of the talent of this platinum ruler, this mirror, this door, and of the sky, if you like.

We do not have any talent; ask Philippe Soupault:

> *"Anatomical products of manufacture and low-income dwellings will destroy the tallest cities."*

Ask Roger Vitrac:

> *"No sooner had I called forth the marble-admiral than he turned on his heel like a horse which rears at the sight of the North star and showed me, in the plane of his two-pointed cocked hat, a region where I was to spend my life."*

Ask Paul Eluard:

---

*I could say the same of a number of philosophers and painters, including, among these latter, Uccello, from painters of the past, and, in the modern era, Seurat, Gustave Moreau, Matisse (in "La Musique," for example), Derain, Picasso, (by far the most pure), Braque, Duchamp, Picabia, Chirico (so admirable for so long), Klee, Man Ray, Max Ernst, and, one so close to us, André Masson.

"This is an oft-told tale that I tell, a famous poem that I reread: I am leaning against a wall, with my verdant ears and my lips burned to a crisp."

Ask Max Morise:

"The bear of the caves and his friend the bittern, the vol-au-vent and his valet the wind, the Lord Chancellor with his Lady, the scarecrow for sparrows and his accomplice the sparrow, the test tube and his daughter the needle, this carnivore and his brother the carnival, the sweeper and his monocle, the Mississippi and its little dog, the coral and its jug of milk, the Miracle and its Good Lord, might just as well go and disappear from the surface of the sea."

Ask Joseph Delteil:

"Alas! I believe in the virtue of birds. And a feather is all it takes to make me die laughing."

Ask Louis Aragon:

"During a short break in the party, as the players were gathering around a bowl of flaming punch, I asked the tree if it still had its red ribbon."

And ask me, who was unable to keep myself from writing the serpentine, distracting lines of this preface.

Ask Robert Desnos, he who, more than any of us, has perhaps got closest to the Surrealist truth, he who, in his still unpublished works* and in the course of the numerous experiments he has been a party to, has fully justified the hope I placed in Surrealism and leads me to believe that a great deal more will still come of it. Desnos *speaks* Surrealist at will. His extraordinary agility in orally following his thought is worth as much to us as any number of splendid speeches which are lost, Desnos having better things to do than record them. He reads himself like an open book, and does nothing to retain the pages, which fly away in the windy wake of his life.

---

*NOUVELLES HÉBRIDES, DÉSORDE FORMEL, DEUIL POUR DEUIL.

✿✿✿✿✿✿✿✿✿✿✿✿✿✿✿✿✿✿✿✿✿✿✿✿

SECRETS OF THE MAGICAL
SURREALIST ART

Written Surrealist composition
or
first and last draft

After you have settled yourself in a place as favorable as possible to the concentration of your mind upon itself, have writing materials brought to you. Put yourself in as passive, or receptive, a state of mind as you can. Forget about your genius, your talents, and the talents of everyone else. Keep reminding yourself that literature is one of the saddest roads that leads to everything. Write quickly, without any preconceived subject, fast enough so that you will not remember what you're writing and be tempted to reread what you have written. The first sentence will come spontaneously, so compelling is the truth that with every passing second there is a sentence unknown to our consciousness which is only crying out to be heard. It is somewhat of a problem to form an opinion about the next sentence; it doubtless partakes both of our conscious activity and of the other, if one agrees that the fact of having written the first entails a minimum of perception. This should be of no importance to you, however; to a large extent, this is what is most interesting and intriguing about the Surrealist game. The fact still remains that punctuation no doubt resists the absolute continuity of the flow with which we are concerned, although it may seem as necessary as the arrangement of knots in a vibrating cord. Go on as long as you like. Put your trust in the inexhaustible nature of the murmur. If silence threatens to settle in if you should ever happen to make a mistake—a mistake, perhaps due to carelessness—break off without hesitation with an overly clear line. Following a word the origin of which seems suspicious to you, place any letter whatsoever, the letter "l" for example, always the letter "l," and bring the arbitrary back by making this letter the first of the following word.

How not to be bored any longer when with others

This is very difficult. Don't be at home for anyone, and occasionally, when no one has forced his way in, interrupting you in the midst of your

Surrealist activity, and you, crossing your arms, say: "It doesn't matter, there are doubtless better things to do or not do. Interest in life is indefensible. Simplicity, what is going on inside me, is still tiresome to me!" or any other revolting banality.

To make speeches

Just prior to the elections, in the first country which deems it worthwhile to proceed in this kind of public expression of opinion, have yourself put on the ballot. Each of us has within himself the potential of an orator: multicolored loin cloths, glass trinkets of words. Through Surrealism he will take despair unawares in its poverty. One night, on a stage, he will, by himself, carve up the eternal heaven, that *Peau de l'ours*. He will promise so much that any promises he keeps will be a source of wonder and dismay. In answer to the claims of an entire people he will give a partial and ludicrous vote. He will make the bitterest enemies partake of a secret desire which will blow up the countries. And in this he will succeed simply by allowing himself to be moved by the immense word which dissolves into pity and revolves in hate. Incapable of failure, he will play on the velvet of all failures. He will be truly elected, and women will love him with an all-consuming passion.

To write false novels

Whoever you may be, if the spirit moves you burn a few laurel leaves and, without wishing to tend this meager fire, you will begin to write a novel. Surrealism will allow you to: all you have to do is set the needle marked "fair" at "action," and the rest will follow naturally. Here are some characters rather different in appearance; their names in your handwriting are a question of capital letters, and they will conduct themselves with the same ease with respect to active verbs as does the impersonal pronoun "it" with respect towards such as "is raining," "is," "must," etc. They will command them, so to speak, and wherever observation, reflection, and the faculty of generalization prove to be of no help to you, you may rest assured that they will credit you with a thousand intentions you never had. Thus endowed with a tiny number of physical and moral characteristics, these beings who in truth owe you so little will thereafter deviate not one iota from a certain line of conduct about which you need not concern yourself any further. Out of this will result a plot more or less clever in appearance, justifying point by point this moving or comforting denouement about which you couldn't care less. Your false novel will simulate to a marvelous degree a real novel; you will be rich, and everyone will agree that "you've really got a lot of guts," since it's also in this region that this something is located.

Of course, by an analogous method, and provided you ignore what you are reviewing, you can successfully devote yourself to false literary criticism.

*How to catch the eye of a woman
you pass in the street*

. . . .
. . . .
. . . .
. . . .
. . . .

Against death

Surrealism will usher you into death, which is a secret society. It will glove your hand, burying therein the profound M with which the word Memory begins. Do not forget to make proper arrangements for your last will and testament: speaking personally, I ask that I be taken to the cemetery in a moving van. May my friends destroy every last copy of the printing of the *Speech concerning the Modicum of Reality.*

Language has been given to man so that he may make Surrealist use of it. To the extent that he is required to make himself understood, he manages more or less to express himself, and by so doing to fulfill certain functions culled from among the most vulgar. Speaking, reading a letter, present no real problem for him, provided that, in so doing, he does not set himself a goal above the mean, that is, provided he confines himself to carrying on a conversation (for the pleasure of conversing) with someone. He is not worried about the words that are going to come, nor about the sentence which will follow after the sentence he is just completing. To a very simple question, he will be capable of making a lightning-like reply. In the absence of minor tics acquired through contact with others, he can without any ado offer an opinion on a limited number of subjects; for that he does not need to "count up to ten" before speaking or to formulate anything whatever ahead of time. Who has been able to convince him that this faculty of the first draft will only do him a disservice when he makes up his mind to establish more delicate relationships? There is no subject about which he should refuse to talk, to write about prolifically. All that results from listening to oneself, from reading what one has written, is the suspension of the occult, that admirable help. I am in no hurry to understand myself (basta! I shall always understand myself). If such and such a sentence of mine turns out to be somewhat disappointing, at least momentarily, I place my trust in the following sentence to redeem its sins: I carefully refrain from starting it over again or polishing it. The only thing that might prove fatal to me would be the slightest loss of impetus. Words, groups of words *which follow one another,* manifest among themselves the greatest solidarity. It is not up to me to favor one group over the other. It is up to a miraculous equivalent to intervene—and intervene it does.

Not only does this unrestricted language, which I am trying to render forever valid, which seems to me to adapt itself to all of life's circumstances, not only does this language not deprive me of any of my means, on the contrary it lends me an extraordinary lucidity, and it does so in an area where I least expected it. I shall even go so far as to maintain that it instructs me and, indeed, I have had occasion to use *surreally* words whose meaning I have forgotten. I was subsequently able to verify that the way in which I had used them corresponded perfectly with their definition. This would lead one to believe that we do not "learn," that all we ever do is "relearn." There are felicitous turns of speech that I have thus familiarized myself with. And I am not talking about the *poetic consciousness of objects* which I have been able to acquire only after a spiritual contact with them repeated a thousand times over.

The forms of Surrealist language adapt themselves best to dialogue. Here, two thoughts confront each other; while one is being delivered, the other is busy with it; but how is it busy with it? To assume that it incorporates it within itself would be tantamount to admitting that there is a time during which it is possible for it to live completely off that other thought, which is highly unlikely. And, in fact, the attention it pays is completely exterior; it has only time enough to approve or reject—generally reject—with all the consideration of which man is capable. This mode of language, more-over, does not allow the heart of the matter to be plumbed. My attention, prey to an entreaty which it cannot in all decency reject, treats the oppos-ing thought as an enemy; in ordinary conversation, it "takes it up" almost always on the words, the figures of speech, it employs; it puts me in a po-sition to turn it to good advantage in my reply by distorting them. This is true to such a degree that in certain pathological states of mind, where the sensorial disorders occupy the patient's complete attention, he limits him-self, while continuing to answer the questions, to seizing the last word spoken in his presence or the last portion of the Surrealist sentence some trace of which he finds in his mind.

> Q. "How old are you?" A. "You." *(Echolalia.)*
> Q. "What is your name?" A. "Forty-five houses." *(Ganser syndrome, or beside-the-point replies.)*

There is no conversation in which some trace of this disorder does not occur. The effort to be social which dictates it and the considerable prac-tice we have at it are the only things which enable us to conceal it tem-porarily. It is also the great weakness of the book that it is in constant conflict with its best, by which I mean the most demanding, readers. In the very short dialogue that I concocted above between the doctor and the madman, it was in fact the madman who got the better of the exchange. Because, through his replies, he obtrudes upon the attention of the doctor examining him—and because he is not the person asking the questions. Does this mean that his thought at this point is the stronger? Perhaps. He is free not to care any longer about his age or name.

Poetic Surrealism, which is the subject of this study, has focused its efforts up to this point on reestablishing dialogue in its absolute truth, by freeing both interlocutors from any obligations of politeness. Each of them simply pursues his soliloquy without trying to derive any special di-alectical pleasure from it and without trying to impose anything whatso-ever upon his neighbor. The remarks exchanged are not, as is generally the case, meant to develop some thesis, however unimportant it may be; they are as disaffected as possible. As for the reply that they elicit, it is, in principle, totally indifferent to the personal pride of the person speaking. The words, the images are only so many springboards for the mind of the listener. In *Les Champs magnétiques*, the first purely Surrealist work, this is the way in which the pages grouped together under the title *Barrières* must be conceived of—pages wherein Soupault and I show ourselves to be impartial interlocutors.

❋

Surrealism does not allow those who devote themselves to it to forsake it whenever they like. There is every reason to believe that it acts on the mind very much as drugs do; like drugs, it creates a certain state of need and can push man to frightful revolts. It also is, if you like, an artificial paradise, and the taste one has for it derives from Baudelaire's criticism for the same reason as the others. Thus the analysis of the mysterious effects and special pleasures it can produce—in many respects Surrealism occurs as a *new vice* which does not necessarily seem to be restricted to the happy few; like hashish, it has the ability to satisfy all manner of tastes— such an analysis has to be included in the present study.

1. It is true of Surrealist images as it is of opium images that man does not evoke them; rather they "come to him spontaneously, despotically. He cannot chase them away; for the will is powerless now and no longer controls the faculties."* It remains to be seen whether images have ever been "evoked." If one accepts, as I do, Reverdy's definition it does not seem possible to bring together, voluntarily, what he calls "two distant realities." The juxtaposition is made or not made, and that is the long and the short of it. Personally, I absolutely refuse to believe that, in Reverdy's work, images such as

> In the brook, there is a song that flows

or:

> Day unfolded like a white tablecloth

or:

> The world goes back into a sack

reveal the slightest degree of premeditation. In my opinion, it is erroneous to claim that "the mind has grasped the relationship" of two realities in the

---

*Baudelaire.

presence of each other. First of all, it has seized nothing consciously. It is, as it were, from the fortuitous juxtaposition of the two terms that a particular light has sprung, *the light of the image,* to which we are infinitely sensitive. The value of the image depends upon the beauty of the spark obtained; it is, consequently, a function of the difference of potential between the two conductors. When the difference exists only slightly, as in a comparison,* the spark is lacking. Now, it is not within man's power, so far as I can tell, to effect the juxtaposition of two realities so far apart. The principle of the association of ideas, such as we conceive of it, militates against it. Or else we would have to revert to an elliptical art, which Reverdy deplores as much as I. We are therefore obliged to admit that the two terms of the image are not deduced one from the other by the mind for the specific purpose of producing the spark, that they are the simultaneous products of the activity I call Surrealist, reason's role being limited to taking note of, and appreciating, the luminous phenomenon.

And just as the length of the spark increases to the extent that it occurs in rarefied gases, the Surrealist atmosphere created by automatic writing, which I have wanted to put within the reach of everyone, is especially conducive to the production of the most beautiful images. One can even go so far as to say that in this dizzying race the images appear like the only guideposts of the mind. By slow degrees the mind becomes convinced of the supreme reality of these images. At first limiting itself to submitting to them, it soon realizes that they flatter its reason, and increase its knowledge accordingly. The mind becomes aware of the limitless expanses wherein its desires are made manifest, where the pros and cons are constantly consumed, where its obscurity does not betray it. It goes forward, borne by these images which enrapture it, which scarcely leave it any time to blow upon the fire in its fingers. This is the most beautiful night of all, the *lightning-filled night:* day, compared to it, is night.

The countless kinds of Surrealist images would require a classification which I do not intend to make today. To group them according to their particular affinities would lead me far afield; what I basically want to mention is their common virtue. For me, their greatest virtue, I must con-

---

*Compare the image in the work of Jules Renard.

fess, is the one that is arbitrary to the highest degree, the one that takes the longest time to translate into practical language, either because it contains an immense amount of seeming contradiction or because one of its terms is strangely concealed; or because, presenting itself as something sensational, it seems to end weakly (because it suddenly closes the angle of its compass), or because it derives from itself a ridiculous *formal* justification, or because it is of a hallucinatory kind, or because it very naturally gives to the abstract the mask of the concrete, or the opposite, or because it implies the negation of some elementary physical property, or because it provokes laughter. Here, in order, are a few examples of it:

The ruby of champagne. (LAUTRÉAMONT)

Beautiful as the law of arrested development of the breast in adults, whose propensity to growth is not in proportion to the quantity of molecules that their organism assimilates. (LAUTRÉAMONT)

A church stood dazzling as a bell. (PHILIPPE SOUPAULT)

In Rrose Sélavy's sleep there is a dwarf issued from a well who comes to eat her bread at night. (ROBERT DESNOS)

On the bridge the dew with the head of a tabby cat lulls itself to sleep. (ANDRÉ BRETON)

A little to the left, in my firmament foretold, I see—but it's doubtless but a mist of blood and murder—the gleaming glass of liberty's disturbances. (LOUIS ARAGON)

In the forest aflame
The lions were fresh. (ROBERT VITRAC)

The color of a woman's stockings is not necessarily in the likeness of her eyes, which led a philosopher who it is pointless to mention, to say: "Cephalopods have more reasons to hate progress than do quadrupeds." (MAX MORISE)

1st. Whether we like it or not, there is enough there to satisfy several demands of the mind. All these images seem to attest to the fact that the mind is ripe for something more than the benign joys it allows itself in general. This is the only way it has of turning to its own advantage the ideal quantity of events with which it is entrusted.* These images show it the extent of its ordinary dissipation and the drawbacks that it offers for it. In the final analysis, it's not such a bad thing for these images to upset the mind, for to upset the mind is to put it in the wrong. The sentences I quote make ample provision for this. But the mind which relishes them draws therefrom the conviction that it is on the *right track;* on its own, the mind is incapable of finding itself guilty of cavil; it has nothing to fear, since, moreover, it attempts to embrace everything.

2nd. The mind which plunges into Surrealism relives with glowing excitement the best part of its childhood. For such a mind, it is similar to the certainty with which a person who is drowning reviews once more, in the space of less than a second, all the insurmountable moments of his life. Some may say to me that the parallel is not very encouraging. But I have no intention of encouraging those who tell me that. From childhood memories, and from a few others, there emanates a sentiment of being unintegrated, and then later of *having gone astray,* which I hold to be the most fertile that exists. It is perhaps childhood that comes closest to one's "real life"; childhood beyond which man has at his disposal, aside from his laissez-passer, only a few complimentary tickets; childhood where everything nevertheless conspires to bring about the effective, risk-free possession of oneself. Thanks to Surrealism, it seems that opportunity knocks a second time. It is as though we were still running toward our salvation, or our perdition. In the shadow we again see a precious terror. Thank God, it's still only Purgatory. With a shudder, we cross what the occultists call *dangerous territory.* In my wake I raise up monsters that are lying in wait; they are not yet too ill-disposed toward me, and I am not lost, since I fear them. Here are "the elephants with the heads of women and the flying lions" which used to make Soupault and me tremble in our boots to meet, here is the "soluble fish" which still frightens me slightly. SOLUBLE FISH, am I not the soluble fish, I was born under the sign of Pisces, and man is soluble in his thought! The flora and fauna of Surrealism are inadmissible.

---

*Let us not forget that, according to Novalis' formula, "there are series of events which run parallel to real events. Men and circumstances generally modify the ideal train of circumstances, so that it seems imperfect; and their consequences are also equally imperfect. Thus it was with the Reformation; instead of Protestantism, we got Lutheranism."

3rd. I do not believe in the establishment of a conventional Surrealist pattern any time in the near future. The characteristics common to all the texts of this kind, including those I have just cited and many others which alone could offer us a logical analysis and a careful grammatical analysis, do not preclude a certain evolution of Surrealist prose in time. Coming on the heels of a large number of essays I have written in this vein over the past five years, most of which I am indulgent enough to think are extremely disordered, the short anecdotes which comprise the balance of this volume offer me a glaring proof of what I am saying. I do not judge them to be any more worthless, because of that, in portraying for the reader the benefits which the Surrealist contribution is liable to make to his consciousness.

Surrealist methods would, moreover, demand to be heard. Everything is valid when it comes to obtaining the desired suddenness from certain associations. The pieces of paper that Picasso and Braque insert into their work have the same value as the introduction of a platitude into a literary analysis of the most rigorous sort. It is even permissible to entitle POEM what we get from the most random assemblage possible (observe, if you will, the syntax) of headlines and scraps of headlines cut out of the newspapers:

POEM

A burst of laughter
of sapphire in the island of Ceylon

The most beautiful straws
HAVE A FADED COLOR
UNDER THE LOCKS

on an isolated farm

FROM DAY TO DAY

the pleasant

grows worse

A carriage road

takes you to the edge of the unknown

coffee

preaches for its saint

THE DAILY ARTISAN OF YOUR BEAUTY

Madam,

a pair

of silk stockings

is not

A leap into space

A STAG

Love above all

Everything could be worked out so well

PARIS IS A BIG VILLAGE

192 ✳ André Breton

Watch out for
the fire that covers
THE PRAYER
of fair weather

Know that
The ultraviolet rays
have finished their task
short and sweet

THE FIRST WHITE PAPER
OF CHANCE
Red will be

The wandering singer
WHERE IS HE?
in memory
in his house
AT THE SUITORS' BALL

I do
as I dance
What people did, what they're going to do

And we could offer many many more examples. The theater, philosophy, science, criticism would all succeed in finding their bearings there. I
hasten to add that future Surrealist techniques do not interest me.

Far more serious, in my opinion*—I have intimated it often enough—
are the applications of Surrealism to action. To be sure, I do not believe in
the prophetic nature of the Surrealist word. "It is the oracle, the things I
say."** Yes, *as much as I like,* but what of the oracle itself?*** Men's piety
does not fool me. The Surrealist voice that shook Cumae, Dodona, and
Delphi is nothing more than the voice which dictates my less irascible
speeches to me. My *time* must not be its time, why should this voice help
me resolve the childish problem of my destiny? I pretend, unfortunately,
to act in a world where, in order to take into account its suggestions, I
would be obliged to resort to two kinds of interpreters, one to translate its
judgments for me, the other, impossible to find, to transmit to my fellow
men whatever sense I could make out of them. This world, in which I en-

---

*Whatever reservations I may be allowed to make concerning responsibility in gen-
eral and the medico-legal considerations which determine an individual's degree
of responsibility—complete responsibility, irresponsibility, limited responsibility
(sic)—however difficult it may be for me to accept the principle of any kind of responsibility, I would like to know how the first punishable offenses, the Surrealist
character of which will be clearly apparent, will be judged. Will the accused be ac-
quitted, or will he merely be given the benefit of the doubt because of extenuating
circumstances? It's a shame that the violation of the laws governing the Press is today scarcely repressed, for if it were not we would soon see a trial of this sort: the
accused has published a book which is an outrage to public decency. Several of his
"most respected and honorable" fellow citizens have lodged a complaint against
him, and he is also charged with slander and libel. There are also all sorts of other
charges against him, such as insulting and defaming the army, inciting to murder,
rape, etc. The accused, moreover, wastes no time in agreeing with the accusers in
"stigmatizing" most of the ideas expressed. His only defense is claiming that he
does not consider himself to be the author of his book, said book being no more
and no less than a Surrealist concoction which precludes any question of merit or
lack of merit on the part of the person who signs it; further, that all he has done is
copy a document without offering any opinion thereon, and that he is at least as
foreign to the accused text as is the presiding judge himself.

What is true for the publication of a book will also hold true for a whole host of
other acts as soon as Surrealist methods begin to enjoy widespread favor. When
that happens, a new morality must be substituted for the prevailing morality, the
source of all our trials and tribulations.
**Rimbaud.

dure what I endure (don't go see) this modern world, I mean, what the devil do you want me to do with it? Perhaps the Surrealist voice will be stilled, I have given up trying to keep track of those who have disappeared. I shall no longer enter into, however briefly, the marvelous detailed description of my years and my days. I shall be like Nijinski who was taken last year to the Russian ballet and did not realize what spectacle it was he was seeing. I shall be alone, very alone within myself, indifferent to all the world's ballets. What I have done, what I have left undone, I give it to you.

❋

And ever since I have had a great desire to show forbearance to scientific musing, however unbecoming, in the final analysis, from every point of view. Radios? Fine. Syphilis? If you like. Photography? I don't see any reason why not. The cinema? Three cheers for darkened rooms. War? Gave us a good laugh. The telephone? Hello. Youth? Charming white hair. Try to make me say thank you: "Thank you." Thank you. If the common man has a high opinion of things which properly speaking belong to the realm of the laboratory, it is because such research has resulted in the manufacture of a machine or the discovery of some serum which the man in the street views as affecting him directly. He is quite sure that they have been trying to improve his lot. I am not quite sure to what extent scholars are motivated by humanitarian aims, but it does not seem to me that this factor constitutes a

---

***Still, STILL. . . . We must absolutely get to the bottom of this. Today, June 8, 1924, about one o'clock, the voice whispered to me: "Béthune, Bethune." What did it mean? I have never been to Béthune, and have only the vaguest notion to where it is located on the map of France. Béthune evokes nothing for me, not even a scene from *The Three Musketeers*. I should have left for Béthune, where perhaps there was something awaiting me; that would have been too simple, really. Someone told me they had read in a book by Chesterton about a detective who, in order to find someone he is looking for in a certain city, simply scoured from roof to cellar the houses which, from the outside, seemed somehow abnormal to him, were it only in some slight detail. This system is as good as any other.

Similarly, in 1919, Soupault went into any number of impossible buildings to ask the concierge whether Philippe Soupault did in fact live there. He would not have been surprised, I suspect, by an affirmative reply. He would have gone and knocked on his door.

very marked degree of goodness. I am, of course, referring to true scholars and not to the vulgarizers and popularizers of all sorts who take out patents. In this realm as in any other, I believe in the pure Surrealist joy of the man who, forewarned that all others before him have failed, refuses to admit defeat, sets off from whatever point he chooses, along any other path save a reasonable one, and arrives wherever he can. Such and such an image, by which he deems it opportune to indicate his progress and which may result, perhaps, in his receiving public acclaim, is to me, I must confess, a matter of complete indifference. Nor is the material with which he must perforce encumber himself; his glass tubes or my metallic feathers . . . As for his method, I am willing to give it as much credit as I do mine. I have seen the inventor of the cutaneous plantar reflex at work; he manipulated his subjects without respite, it was much more than an "examination" he was employing; *it was obvious that he was following no set plan.* Here and there he formulated a remark, distantly, without nonetheless setting down his needle, while his hammer was never still. He left to others the futile task of curing patients. He was wholly consumed by and devoted to that sacred fever.

❋

Surrealism, such as I conceive of it, asserts our complete *nonconformism* clearly enough so that there can be no question of translating it, at the trial of the real world, as evidence for the defense. It could, on the contrary, only serve to justify the complete state of distraction which we hope to achieve here below. Kant's absentmindedness regarding women, Pasteur's absentmindedness about "grapes," Curie's absentmindedness with respect to vehicles, are in this regard profoundly symptomatic. This world is only very relatively in tune with thought, and incidents of this kind are only the most obvious episodes of a war in which I am proud to be participating. Surrealism is the "invisible ray" which will one day enable us to win out over our opponents. "You are no longer trembling, carcass." This summer the roses are blue; the wood is of glass. The earth, draped in its verdant cloak, makes as little impression upon me as a ghost. It is living and ceasing to live that are imaginary solutions. Existence is elsewhere.

Federico García Lorca, translated by J. L. Gilli: "Theory and Function of the *Duende*," 1933

In 1933, three years before he was ambushed and murdered by the fascists in the Spanish Civil War, Federico García Lorca delivered his lecture "Juego y teoría del duende" to audiences in Burenos Aires and then Havana. Like Mallarmé before him, Lorca was striving for a poetry that, as Walter Pater said, "aspires to the condition of music." For Lorca, though, the music he was thinking of was not classical; it was the "cante jondo" or deep song of his native Granada, the ancient Andalusian music influenced by Gypsies, Hebrews, and Arabs. His first book, *Poema del Cante Jondo* (Poem of the Deep Song), written when he was twenty-three years old, sought to capture the dark tones, passion and pain of this ancestor of flamenco.

Lorca was also deeply influenced by the surrealists—he was a close friend of Salvador Dali—and his later work, especially *Poeta en Nueva York* (Poet in New York), evidenced the wild juxtaposition and randomness of images and quest for an escape from the rational that characterized the poetry of that movement. Lorca's conception of the *duende*—an Andalusian word used to describe the particular quality of deep song—is at the heart of his poetics. Part surrealist, part negative capability, *duende* combines folkloric and dreamlike images with dark tones of death and passion.

❋

Theory and Function of the *Duende*

Anyone traveling in that stretched bull-hide between the Júcar, the Guadalete, the Sil, or the Pisuerga rivers, would sooner or later hear the expression: "This has much *duende*." Manuel Torres, a great Andalusian artist, on one occasion said to a singer: "You have voice, you have style, but you will never be a success because you have no *duende*."

All through Andalusia, from the rock of Jaén to the shell of Cádiz, people constantly speak of the *duende,* and recognize it with unfailing instinct when it appears. The wonderful flamenco singer *El Lebrijano,* creator of the *Debla,* said: "When I sing with *duende* nobody can equal me." The old gipsy dancer *La Malena* exclaimed once on hearing Brailowsky play Bach: "Olé! This has *duende!,*" yet she was bored by Gluck, Brahms, and Darius Milhaud. And Manuel Torres, a man with more culture in his veins than anybody I have known, when listening to Fala playing his own "Nocturno del Generalife," made this splendid pronouncement: "All that has dark sounds has *duende.*" And there is no greater truth.

These "dark sounds" are the mystery, the roots thrusting into the fertile loam known to all of us, ignored by all of us, but from which we get what is real in art. Torres here agrees with Goethe who defined the *duende* when he attributed to Paganini "a mysterious power that everyone feels but that no philosopher has explained."

Thus the *duende* is a power and not a behaviour, it is a struggle and not a concept. I have heard an old guitarist master say: "The *duende* is not in the throat; the *duende* surges up from the soles of the feet." Which means that it is not a matter of ability, but of real live form; of blood; of ancient culture; of creative action.

This "mysterious power that everyone feels but that no philosopher has explained" is in fact the spirit of the earth. It is the same *duende* that gripped the heart of Nietzsche, who had been seeking its external forms on the Rialto Bridge or in the music of Bizet without ever finding it or being aware that the *duende* he pursued had jumped from the mysterious Greeks to the dancers of Cádiz or the broken Dionysiac cry of Silverio's *seguiriya.*

I do not want anybody to confuse the *duende* with Luther's theological daemon of doubt, at whom with a Bacchic touch he flung an inkpot in Nuremberg; nor with the Catholic daemon, destructive and not very intelligent, who disguises himself as a bitch in order to enter convents.

No. The dark and quivering *duende* that I am talking about is a descendant of the merry daemon of Socrates, all marble and salt, who angrily scratched his master on the day he drank hemlock; a descendant also of Descartes' melancholy daemon, small as a green almond, who, tired of lines and circles, went out along the canals to hear the drunken sailors sing.

Every step that a man, or as Neitzsche would say an artist, takes towards the tower of his perfection is at the cost of the struggle he maintains with a *duende*, not with an angel, as has been said, and not with a muse. It is necessary to draw this fundamental distinction in order to arrive at the root of any work.

The angel guides and endows with gifts like St. Raphael, or defends and wards off like St. Michael, or warns like St. Gabriel.

The angel may dazzle, but he merely hovers over the head of man; he bestows his graces, and man quite effortlessly achieves his work, his sympathy, or his dance. The angel on the road to Damascus and the one who entered through the lattice of the little window at Assisi, or the one who followed the steps of Heinrich Suso, is an angel that *commands*, and no one can resist his radiance because he moves his steel wings in the ambit of the elect.

The muse dictates and, occasionally, inspires. There is relatively little she can do, for she is by now distant and so weary—I have seen her twice—that I had to strengthen her with half a heart of marble. The muse-inspired poets hear voices without knowing where they come from; they come from the muse, who encourages them and sometimes swallows them up. Such was the case of Apollinaire, a great poet destroyed by the horrible muse with whom the magnificent and angelic Rousseau painted him. The muse arouses the intellect, and brings colonnaded landscapes and a false taste of laurel. Very often intellect is poetry's enemy because it is too much given to imitation, because it lifts the poet to a throne of sharp edges and makes him oblivious of the fact that he may suddenly be devoured by ants, or a great arsenic lobster may fall on his head. Against all this the muses who appear in monocles or among the faintly warm lacquer-roses of a little salon are powerless.

Angel and muse come from without; the angel gives radiance, the muse gives precepts (Hesiod learned from them). Gold leaf or fold of tunics, the poet receives his norms in his coppice of laurels. On the other hand, the *duende* has to be roused in the very cells of the blood.

We must repel the angel, and kick out the muse, and lose our fear of the violet fragrance irradiating from eighteenth-century poetry, and of the great telescope in whose lenses sleeps the confining, ailing muse.

The real struggle is with the *duende*.

One knows how to seek God, whether it be by the rough ways of the hermit or by the subtlety of the mystic; with a tower like St. Theresa's, or with the three pathways of St. John of the Cross. And even if we have to exclaim with Isaiah's voice: "Truly thou art the hidden God," ultimately God sends his first thorns of fire to whoever seeks him.

To help us seek the *duende* there is neither map nor discipline. All one knows is that it burns the blood like powdered glass, that it exhausts, that it rejects all the sweet geometry one has learned, that it breaks with all styles, that it compels Goya, master of greys, silvers, and of those pinks in the best English paintings, to paint with his knees and with his fists horrible bitumen blacks; or that it leaves Mossen Cinto Verdaguer naked in the cold air of the Pyrenees; or that it takes Jorge Manrique to wait for death in the wilderness of Ocaña; or that it dresses the delicate body of Rimbaud in an acrobat's green suit; or that it puts the eyes of a dead fish on Count Lautréamont in the early morning Boulevard.

The great artists of Southern Spain, gipsy or flamenco, whether they sing or dance or play, know that no real emotion is possible unless there is *duende*. They may even deceive an audience by giving the impression of possessing *duende*, in the same manner as one is deceived every day by writers, painters, or literary fashions without *duende*; but if one looks closely and is not misled by being inattentive, the fraud will soon be discovered and the *duende*-artifice put to flight.

On one occasion, the Andalusian flamenco singer Pastora Pavón, *La Niña de los Peines* (The Girl with the Combs), a sombre Hispanic genius with an imagination matching that of Goya or Rafael *El Gallo*, was singing in a small tavern at Cádiz. She sang with her voice of shadow, with her voice of liquid metal, with her moss-covered voice, and with her voice entangled in her long hair. She would soak her voice in *manzanilla*, or lose it in dark and distant thickets. Yet she failed completely; it was all to no purpose. The audience remained silent.

Among the audience was Ignacio Espeleta, handsome as a Roman tortoise, who was once asked: "How is it that you never work?," and with a smile worthy of Argantonio, he replied: "Why should I work if I come from Cádiz?"

Also present was Eloísa, the fiery aristocratic whore of Seville, direct descendant of Soledad Vargas, who in the year 1930 refused to marry a Rothschild because he was not her equal in blood. There were also the Floridas, believed by many to be butchers, while in reality they were ancient priests still sacrificing bulls to Geryon; and in a corner sat that imposing breeder of bulls Don Pablo Murube, looking like a Cretan mask.

Pastora Pavón finished singing in the midst of silence. Only a little man, one of those emasculated dancers who suddenly spring up from behind bottles of white brandy, said sarcastically in a very low voice: "Viva Paris!" as if to say: "Here we do not care for ability, technique, or mastery. Here we care for something else."

At that moment *La Niña de los Peines* got up like a woman possessed, broken as a medieval mourner, drank without pause a large glass of *cazalla*, a fire-water brandy, and sat down to sing without voice, breathless, without subtlety, her throat burning, but . . . with *duende*. She succeeded in getting rid of the scaffolding of the song, to make way for a furious and fiery *duende*, companion of sand-laden winds, that made those who were listening tear their clothes rhythmically, like Caribbean Negroes clustered before the image of St. Barbara.

La Niña de los Peines had to tear her voice, because she knew that she was being listened to by an élite not asking for forms but for the marrow of forms, for music exalted into purest essence. She had to impoverish her skills and aids; that is, she had to drive away her muse and remain alone so that the *duende* might come and join in a hand-to-hand fight. And how she sang! Now she was in earnest, her voice was a jet of blood, admirable because of its pain and its sincerity, and it opened like a ten-fingered hand in the nailed but tempestuous feet of a Christ by Juan de Juni.

The appearance of the *duende* always presupposes a radical change of all forms based on old structures. It gives a sensation of freshness wholly unknown, having the quality of a newly created rose, of miracle, and produces in the end an almost religious enthusiasm.

In all Arabic music, dance, or song, the appearance of the *duende* is greeted with vociferous shouts of "Alá! Alá!," "God! God!" which are not far from the *olé* of bullfighting. And in the singing of Southern Spain, the presence of the *duende* is followed by shouts of "Viva Dios!," a profound, human, and tender cry of communion with God through the five senses, by virtue of the *duende* which stirs the voice and body of the dancer, a real and poetical abstraction from this world, as pure as that obtained through seven gardens by the rare seventeenth-century poet Pedro Soto de Rojas, or by St. John Climacus on his trembling ladder of lament.

It follows that when this abstraction is reached, its effects are felt by everyone; by the initiated, who have seen how style can conquer poor matter, and by the ignorant in an indefinable but authentic emotion. A few years ago, in a dancing contest at Jerez de la Frontera, an old woman of eighty carried off the prize against beautiful women and girls with waists like water, merely by raising her arms, throwing back her head, and stamping her foot on the platform; in that gathering of muses and angels, beauties of shape and beauties of smile, the moribund *duende,* dragging her wings of rusty knives along the ground, was bound to win and did in fact win.

All the Arts are capable of possessing *duende,* but naturally the field is widest in music, in dance, and in spoken poetry, because they require a living body as interpreter—they are forms that arise and die ceaselessly, and are defined by an exact present.

Often the composer's *duende* passes to the interpreter. It is also worth noting that even if the composer or poet is false, the interpreter's *duende* can create a new marvel bearing little resemblance to the original work. Such was the case of the *duende*-possessed Eleonora Duse, who unearthed failures in order to turn them into successes, by virtue of what she put into them; or of Paganini, who, according to Goethe, could produce profound melodies out of quite commonplace music; or of a delightful girl in Puerto de Santa María whom I once saw sing and dance that frightful Italian song *O Mari!,* with such rhythm, such pauses, and such meaning that she transformed the cheap Italian song into a firm snake of solid gold. In every instance it was indeed a case of the interpreter re-creating the original work: living blood and artistic genius were put into bodies void of expression.

All the Arts, and all countries too, are capable of *duende,* angel, or muse. While Germany has, with some exceptions, a muse, and Italy has permanently an angel, Spain is always moved by the *duende,* being a country of ancient music and dance, where the *duende* squeezes lemons of daybreak, as well as being a nation of death, a nation open to death.

In every country death has finality. It arrives and the blinds are drawn. Not in Spain. In Spain they are lifted. Many Spaniards live between walls until the day they die, when they are taken out to the sun. A dead person in Spain is more alive when dead than is the case anywhere else—his profile cuts like the edge of a barber's razor. The jest about death and the silent contemplation of it is familiar to Spaniards. From Quevedo's "Dream of the skulls" to the "Putrescent bishop" of Valdés Leal, and from the Marbella of the seventeenth century, who died in childbirth on the highway, saying:

La sangre de mis entrañas
cubriendo el caballa está.
Las patas de tu caballo
echan fuego de alquitrán . . .[1]

to the recent youth of Salamanca, killed by a bull, who exclaimed:

Amigos, que yo me muero;
amigos, yo estoy muy malo.
Tres pañuelos tengo dentro
y este que meto son cuatro . . .[2]

there is a fence of saltpetre flowers, over which rises a people contemplating death, a people who at their most austere are inspired by the verses of Jeremiah, or at their most lyrical by fragrant cypresses. But also a country where what matters most has the ultimate metallic quality of death.

The knife and the cart-wheel, the razor and the prickly beards of shepherds, the bare moon, the fly, damp cupboards, rubble, religious images covered with lacework, quick-lime, and the wounding outline of eaves and watch-towers, in Spain all these have minute grass-blades of death, as well as allusions and voices perceptible to the alert mind, exciting our memory with the inert air of our own passing. The link of Spanish art with the soil is not entirely fortuitous, it is an art abounding in thistles and tangible stones; the lamentation of Pleberio or the dances of the master Josef María de Valdivielso are not isolated examples; it is no accident that from all European balladry this Spanish love-song stands out:

«Si tú eres mi linda amiga,
cómo no me miras, di?»
«Ojos con que te miraba
a la sombra se los di.»
«Si tú eres mi linda amiga,
cómo no me besas, di?»
«Labios con que te besaba

---

[1] The blood from my womb now covers the horse. The hooves of your horse spark tarry fire . . .
[2] Friends, I am dying; friends, I am in a bad way. Three handkerchiefs I have inside, and now this is the fourth . . .

a la tierra se los di.»
«Si tú eres mi linda amiga,
cómo no me abrazas, di?»
«Brazos con que te abrazaba,
de gusanos los cubrí.»[3]

Neither is it unexpected to find this song among the earliest Spanish lyric poetry:

Dentro del vergel
moriré,
entro del rosal
matar me han.
Yo me iba, mi madre,
las rosas coger,
hallara la muerte
dentro del vergel.
Yo me iba, mi madre,
las rosas cortar,
hallara la muerte
dentro del rosal.
Dentro del vergel
moriré,
dentro del rosal
matar me han.[4]

The moon-frozen heads which Zurbarán painted, the butter-yellow and the lightning yellow of El Greco, the prose of Fr Sigüenza, the whole of Goya's work, the apse of the church at El Escorial, all our polychrome

---

[3] "If you are my sweetheart, why won't you look at me, pray?"
"Eyes I had to look at thee, to the shadow I gave them."
"If you are my sweetheart, why won't you kiss me, pray?"
"Lips I had to kiss thee, to the earth I gave them."
"If you are my sweetheart, why won't you embrace me, pray?"
"Arms I had to embrace thee, with worms I covered them."
[4] In the garden I shall die, in the rosebush I shall be killed. I was going, dear mother, to pick some roses, I found death in the garden. I was going, dear mother, to cut some roses, I found death in the rosebush. In the garden I shall die, in the rosebush I shall be killed.

sculpture, the crypt of the ducal house of Osuna, "Death with the guitar" in the chapel of the Benaventes at Medina de Rioseco, all these are the cultured counterpart of the pilgrimages to St. Andrés de Teixido, where the dead have a place in the procession; of the dirges sung by the women of Asturias by lantern-light on the November night; of the dance of the Sibyl in the cathedrals of Majorca and Toledo; of the obscure *In recort* from Tortosa; and of the innumerable Good Friday ceremonies which, together with the most civilized spectacle of bullfighting, constitute the popular triumph of death in Spain. Of all the countries in the world, only Mexico can match Spain in this.

As soon as the muse is aware of death, she shuts her door, or raises a plinth, or parades an urn, or writes an epitaph with waxen hand. And she immediately tears her wreath in a silence that wavers between two breezes. Beneath the truncated arch of the ode, she binds with a mournful touch the precise flowers that the Italians painted in the fifteenth century, and summons the dependable cockerel of Lucretius to frighten away unsuspected shadows.

When the angel is aware of death, he slowly circles round, and weaves with icy tears and narcissi the elegy we have seen trembling in the hands of Keats, or Villasandino, or Herrera, or Bécquer, or Juan Ramón Jiménez. But, what a flutter if the angel feels a spider, however minute, on his tender rosy feet!

The *duende*, on the other hand, does not appear if it sees no possibility of death, if it does not know that it will haunt death's house, if it is not certain that it can move those branches we all carry, which neither enjoy nor ever will enjoy any solace.

In idea, in sound, or in gesture, the *duende* likes a straight fight with the creator on the edge of the well. While angel and muse are content with violin or measured rhythm, the *duende* wounds, and in the healing of this wound which never closes is the prodigious, the original in the work of man.

The magical quality of a poem consists in its being always possessed by the *duende*, so that whoever beholds it is baptized with dark water. Because with *duende* it is easier to love and to understand, and also one is *certain* to be loved and understood; and this struggle for expression and for the communication of expression reaches at times, in poetry, the character of a fight to the death.

Let us remember the case of the very flamenca- and *duende*-possessed

St. Theresa, flamenca not for having stopped a fierce bull with three magnificent passes, which she did; not for having boasted of her good looks in front of Fr. Juan de la Miseria, nor for having slapped the Papal Nuncio, but for being one of the few creatures whose *duende* (not whose angel, for the angel never attacks) transfixed her with a dart, wishing her dead for having stolen its last secret—the delicate bridge uniting the five senses with that core made living flesh, living cloud, living sea, of Love freed from Time.

She was a brave vanquisher of the *duende,* in contrast with Philip of Austria, who, hankering after the muse and the angel of Theology, found himself imprisoned by the *duende* of bleak fervours in that edifice of El Escorial, where geometry borders on dream, and where the *duende* wears a muse's mask for the eternal punishment of the great king.

We have said that the *duende* likes the edge of things, the wound, and that it is drawn to where forms fuse themselves in a longing greater than their visible expressions.

In Spain (as in the East, where dance is a religious expression) the *duende* has a boundless field in the bodies of the girl dancers of Cádiz, praised by Martial, in the breasts of singers, praised by Juvenal, and in the whole liturgy of bullfighting, a true religious drama where, as in the Mass, there is adoration and a God is sacrificed.

It is as though the whole *duende* of the classical world converged into this perfect spectacle, symbol of the culture and great sensibility of a people who have discovered man's finest anger, his finest melancholy, and his finest grief. Neither in Spanish dancing nor in bullfighting does anybody have any enjoyment; the *duende* takes care to make one suffer through the drama, in living forms, and prepares the steps for an escape from the surrounding reality.

The *duende* works on the body of a dancer like a breeze on the sand. With magic powers it transforms a girl into a paralytic of the moon, or fills with adolescent blushes an old broken man begging round the taverns, or conveys in tresses of long hair the scent of a harbour at night, and at every moment it works the arms into movements which have generated the dances of all times.

But, it is worth emphasizing, the *duende* can never repeat itself, as the shapes of the sea do not repeat themselves in the storm.

It is in bullfighting that the *duende* attains its most impressive character, because, on the one hand, it has to fight with death, which may bring destruction, and on the other, with geometry, the fundamental basic measure of the spectacle.

The bull has its orbit, the bullfighter his, and between orbit and orbit there exists a point of danger where lies the apex of the terrible game.

It is possible to have muse with the *muleta* and angel with the *banderillas,* and to be considered a good bullfighter; but in the work with the cape when the bull is still free of wounds, and again at the final killing, the help of the *duende* is required to hit the nail of artistic truth.

The bullfighter scaring the spectators by his temerity is not bullfighting, he is on the absurd plane of one playing with his life, which anyone can do; on the other hand, the bullfighter who is bitten by the *duende* gives a lesson of Pythagorian music, and we forget that he is constantly throwing his heart at the horns.

Lagartijo with his Roman *duende,* Joselito with his Jewish *duende,* Belmonte with his baroque *duende,* and Cagancho with his gipsy *duende,* from the twilight of the bull-ring they show poets, painters, and musicians, the four great pathways of Spanish tradition.

Spain is the only country where death is a natural spectacle, where death blows long fanfares at the arrival of each spring, and its art is always governed by a shrewd *duende* which has given it its distinctive character and its inventive quality.

The *duende* that for the first time in sculpture fills the cheeks of the master Mateo of Compostela's saints with red blood, is the same that makes St. John of the Cross moan, or burns naked nymphs in the religious sonnets of Lope de Vega.

The *duende* that raised the tower of Sahagún or worked warm bricks in Calatayud or Teruel, is the same *duende* that breaks the clouds of El Greco and sends Quevedo's bailiffs rolling with a kick, and kindles Goya's visions.

When it rains, it brings out a *duende*-possessed Velázquez, secretly, behind the greys of his monarchs; in the snow it brings out Herrera naked to prove that coldness does not kill; when the *duende* burns, it draws Berruguete into its blaze, and makes him discover a new dimension in sculpture.

The muse of Góngora and the angel of Garcilaso have to relinquish the laurel wreath when the *duende* of St. John of the Cross appears, when

El ciervo vulnerado
por el otero asoma.[5]

The muse of Gonzalo de Berceo and the angel of the Archpriest of Hita draw aside to let Jorge Manrique pass when he comes to the gates of Belmonte castle mortally wounded. The muse of Gregorio Hernández and the angel of José de Mora have to withdraw to allow the *duende* to pass, weeping Mena's tears of blood. Similarly, the melancholy muse of Catalonia, and the rain-drenched angel of Galicia, have to look with loving wonder at the *duende* of Castille, so remote from the warm bread and the placid cow grazing outside a compass of wind-swept skies and dry earth.

The *duende* of Quevedo and the *duende* of Cervantes, the one with phosphorescent green anemones, and the other with anemones of plaster of Ruidera, crown the altar-piece of the *duende* in Spain.

It is clear that each art has a *duende* of a different kind and form, but they all join their roots at a point where the "dark sounds" of Manuel Torres emerge, ultimate matter, uncontrollable and quivering common foundation of wood, of sound, of canvas, and of words.

"Dark sounds" behind which we discover in tender intimacy volcanoes, ants, gentle breezes, and the Milky Way clasping the great night to her waist.

Ladies and gentlemen: I have raised three arches and with clumsy hand I have placed in them the muse, the angel, and the *duende*.

The muse remains quiet; she can assume the closely pleated tunic, or the staring cow's eyes of Pompeii, or the large nose with four faces which her friend Picasso gave her. The angel may stir in the tresses painted by Antonello of Messina, or in Lippi's tunic or in the violin of Masolino and of Rousseau.

The *duende*—where is the *duende*? Through the empty arch comes an air of the mind that blows insistently over the heads of the dead, in search of new landscapes and unsuspected accents; an air smelling of a child's saliva, of pounded grass, and medusal veil announcing the constant baptism of newly created things.

---

[5] The wounded deer over the hill appears.

Paul Valéry, translated by Denise Folliet: "Poetry and Abstract Thought," 1939

Like Flaubert with the novel, and Mallarmé with verse, Paul Valéry dreamt of a pure language, untainted by personal emotion or external social or political realities, a language abstracted from nature and referential only to itself. "We yearn for a profound geometry," he writes in another essay, "Man and the Sea Shell," "a very exact knowledge of what is revealed by dissection and microscopic examination, and an exquisite artistic feeling which, taken together, might enable us to isolate some simple basic principle of natural morphology." How does thought move? How does the poem grow?

The French symbolists were searching for a new form which would demonstrate the essential laws of language, just as science demonstrated the essence of the physical universe. The poem—precise, objective, pure as mathematics or architecture, stripped of the personal voice—is postulated as a made thing, a construct, as illustrated by Valéry's anecdote about Mallarmé and Degas. In "Poetry and Abstract Thought," we can see the determined turn which the French symbolists made from the egocentrism of romanticism toward the impersonal Truth of the word itself. With this new aesthetic comes, again, a redefinition of the poet. No longer the divinely inspired channeler of inspiration, high priest of the imagination as Keats would have it—or the madman of surrealism—he or she is a craftsman, an artificer—or a scientist in a lab coat, as T. S. Eliot famously described Valéry.

❋

Poetry and Abstract Thought

The idea of Poetry is often contrasted with that of Thought, and particularly "Abstract Thought." People say "Poetry and Abstract Thought" as they say Good and Evil, Vice and Virtue, Hot and Cold. Most people, without thinking any further, believe that the analytical work of the intellect, the efforts of will and precision in which it implicates the mind, are incompatible with that freshness of inspiration, that flow of expression, that grace and fancy which are the signs of poetry and which reveal it at its very first words. If a poet's work is judged profound, its profundity seems to be of a quite different order from that of a philosopher or a scientist. Some people go so far as to think that even meditation on his art, the kind of exact reasoning applied to the cultivation of roses, can only harm a poet, since the principal and most charming object of his desire must be to communicate the impression of a newly and happily born state of creative emotion which, through surprise and pleasure, has the power to remove the poem once and for all from any further criticism.

This opinion may possibly contain a grain of truth, though its simplicity makes me suspect it to be of scholarly origin. I feel we have learned and adopted this antithesis without reflection, and that we now find it firmly fixed in our mind, as a verbal contrast, as though it represented a clear and real relationship between two well-defined notions. It must be admitted that that character always in a hurry to have done, whom we call *our mind,* has a weakness for this kind of simplification, which freely enables him to form all kinds of combinations and judgments, to display his logic, and to develop his rhetorical resources—in short, to carry out as brilliantly as possible his business of being a mind.

At all events, this classic contrast, crystallized, as it were, by language, has always seemed to me too abrupt, and at the same time too facile, not to provoke me to examine the things themselves more closely.

Poetry, Abstract Thought. That is soon said, and we immediately assume that we have said something sufficiently clear and sufficiently precise for us to proceed, without having to go back over our experiences; and to build a theory or begin a discussion using this contrast (so attractive in its simplicity) as pretext, argument, and substance. One could even fashion a whole metaphysics—or at the least a "psychology"—on this basis, and evolve for oneself a system of mental life, of knowledge, and of the invention and production of the works of the mind, whose consequence would inevitably be the same terminological dissonance that had served as its starting point. . . .

For my part I have the strange and dangerous habit, in every subject, of wanting to begin at the beginning (that is, at my *own* beginning), which entails beginning again, going back over the whole road, just as though many others had not already mapped and traveled it. . . .

This is the road offered to us, or imposed on us, by *language.*

With every question, before making any deep examination of the content, I take a look at the language; I generally proceed like a surgeon who sterilizes his hands and prepares the area to be operated on. This is what I call *cleaning up the verbal situation.* You must excuse this expression equating the words and forms of speech with the hands and instruments of a surgeon.

I maintain that we must be careful of a problem's first contact with our minds. We should be careful of the first words a question utters in our mind. A new question arising in us is in a state of infancy; it stammers; it finds only strange terms, loaded with adventitious values and associations; it is forced to borrow these. But it thereby insensibly deflects our true need. Without realizing it we desert our original problem, and in the end we shall come to believe that we have chosen an opinion wholly our own, forgetting that our choice was exercised only on a mass of opinions that are the more or less blind work of other men and of chance. This is what happens with the programs of political parties, no one of which is (or can be) the one that would exactly match our temperament and our interests. If we choose one among them, we gradually become the man suited to that party and to that program.

Philosophical and aesthetic questions are so richly obscured by the quantity, diversity, and antiquity of researches, arguments, and solutions, all produced within the orbit of a very restricted vocabulary, of which each author uses the words according to his own inclinations, that taken as a whole such works give me the impression of a district in the classical Underworld especially reserved for deep thinkers. Here, are the Danaïdes, Ixions, and Sisyphuses, eternally laboring to fill bottomless casks and to push back the falling rock, that is, to redefine the same dozen words whose combinations form the treasure of Speculative Knowledge.

Allow me to add to these preliminary considerations one last remark and one illustration. Here is the remark: you have surely noticed the curious fact that a certain *word,* which is perfectly clear when you hear or use it in *everyday* speech, and which presents no difficulty when caught up in the rapidity of an ordinary sentence, becomes mysteriously cumbersome, offers a strange resistance, defeats all efforts at definition, the moment you withdraw it from circulation for separate study and try to find its meaning after taking away its temporary function. It is almost comic to inquire the exact meaning of a term that one uses constantly with complete satisfaction. For example: I stop the word *Time* in its flight. This word was utterly limpid, precise, honest, and faithful in its service as long as it was part of a remark and was uttered by someone who wished to say something. But here it is, isolated, caught on the wing. It takes its revenge. It makes us believe that it has more meanings than uses. It was only a *means,* and it has become an *end,* the object of a terrible philosophical desire. It turns into an enigma, an abyss, a torment of thought . . . .

It is the same with the word *Life* and all the rest.

This readily observed phenomenon has taken on great critical value for me. Moreover, I have drawn from it an illustration that, for me, nicely conveys this strange property of our verbal material.

Each and every word that enables us to leap so rapidly across the chasm of thought, and to follow the prompting of an idea that constructs its own expression, appears to me like one of those light planks which one throws across a ditch or a mountain crevasse and which will bear a man crossing it rapidly. But he must pass without weighing on it, without stopping—above all, he must not take it into his head to dance on the slender plank to test its resistance! . . . Otherwise the fragile bridge tips or breaks immediately, and all is hurled into the depths. Consult your own experience; and you will find that we understand each other, and ourselves, only thanks to our *rapid passage over words.* We must not lay stress upon them, or we shall see the clearest discourse dissolve into enigmas and more or less learned illusions.

But how are we to think—I should say *rethink,* study deeply whatever seems to merit deep study—if we hold language to be something essentially provisional, as a banknote or a check is provisional, what we call its "value" requiring us to forget its true nature, which is that of a piece of paper, generally dirty? The paper has passed through so many hands. . . . But words have passed through so many mouths, so many phrases, so many uses and abuses, that the most delicate precautions must be taken to avoid too much confusion in our minds between what we think and are trying to think, and what dictionaries, authors, and, for that matter, the whole human race since the beginning of language, want us to think. . . .

I shall therefore take care not to accept what the words *Poetry* and *Abstract Thought* suggest to me the moment they are pronounced. But I shall look into myself. There I shall seek my real difficulties and my actual observations of my real states; there I shall find my own sense of the rational and the irrational; I shall see whether the alleged antithesis exists and how it exists in a living condition. I confess that it is my habit, when dealing with problems of the mind, to distinguish between those which I might have invented and which represent a need truly felt by my mind, and the rest, which are other people's problems. Of the latter, more than one (say forty per cent) seem to me to be nonexistent, to be no more than apparent problems: *I do not feel them.* And as for the rest, more than one seem to me to be badly stated. . . . I do not say I am right. I say that I observe what occurs within myself when I attempt to replace the verbal formulas by values and meanings that are nonverbal, that are independent of the language used. I discover naïve impulses and images, raw products of my needs and of my personal experiences. *It is my life itself that is surprised,* and my life must, if it can, provide my answers, for it is only in the reactions of our life that the full force, and as it were the necessity, of our truth can reside. The thought proceeding from that life never uses for its own account certain words which seem to it fit only for external consumption; nor certain others whose depths are obscure and which may only deceive thought as to its real strength and value.

I have, then, noticed in myself certain states which I may well call *poetic,* since some of them were finally realized in poems. They came about from no apparent cause, arising from some accident or other; they developed according to their own nature, and consequently I found myself for a time jolted out of my habitual state of mind. Then, the cycle completed, I returned to the rule of ordinary exchanges between my life and my thought. But meanwhile *a poem had been made,* and in completing itself the cycle left something behind. This closed cycle is the cycle of an act which has, as it were, aroused and given external form to a poetic power. . . .

On other occasions I have noticed that some no less insignificant incident caused—or seemed to cause—a quite different excursion, a digression of another nature and with another result. For example, a sudden concatenation of ideas, an analogy, would strike me in much the way the sound of a horn in the heart of a forest makes one prick up one's ears, and virtually directs the co-ordinated attention of all one's muscles toward some point in the distance, among the leafy depths. But this time, instead of a poem, it was an analysis of the sudden intellectual sensation that was taking hold of me. It was not verses that were being formed more or less easily during this phase, but some proposition or other that was destined to be incorporated among my habits of thought, some formula that would henceforward serve as an instrument for further researches. . . .

I apologize for thus revealing myself to you; but in my opinion it is more useful to speak of what one has experienced than to pretend to a knowledge that is entirely impersonal, an observation with no observer. In fact there is no theory that is not a fragment, carefully prepared, of some autobiography.

I do not pretend to be teaching you anything at all. I will say nothing you do not already know; but I will, perhaps, say it in a different order. You do not need to be told that a poet is not always incapable of solving a *rule of three;* or that a logician is not always incapable of seeing in words something other than concepts, categories, and mere pretexts for syllogisms.

On this point I would add this paradoxical remark: if the logician could never be other than a logician, he would not, and could not, be a logician; and if the poet were never anything but a poet, without the slightest hope of being able to reason abstractly, he would leave no poetic traces behind him. I believe in all sincerity that if each man were not able to live a number of other lives besides his own, he would not be able to live his own life.

My experience has thus shown me that the same *self* can take very different forms, can become an abstract thinker or a poet, by successive specializations, each of which is a deviation from that entirely unattached state which is superficially in accord with exterior surroundings and which is the average state of our existence, the state of undifferentiated exchanges.

Let us first see in what may consist that initial and *invariably accidental* shock which will construct the poetic instrument within us, and above all, what are its effects. The problem can be put in this way: Poetry is an art of Language; certain combinations of words can produce an emotion that others do not produce, and which we shall call *poetic*. What kind of emotion is this?

I recognize it in myself by this: that all possible objects of the ordinary world, external or internal, beings, events, feelings, and actions, while keeping their usual appearance, are suddenly placed in an indefinable but wonderfully fitting relationship with the modes of our general sensibility. That is to say that these well-known things and beings—or rather the ideas that represent them—somehow change in value. They attract one another, they are connected in ways quite different from the ordinary; they become (if you will permit the expression) *musicalized*, resonant, and, as it were, harmonically related. The poetic universe, thus defined, offers extensive analogies with what we can postulate of the dream world.

Since the word *dream* has found its way into this talk, I shall say in passing that in modern times, beginning with Romanticism, there has arisen a fairly understandable confusion between the notion of the dream and that of poetry. Neither the dream nor the daydream is necessarily poetic; it may be so: but figures formed *by chance* are only *by chance* harmonious figures.

In any case, our memories of dreams teach us, by frequent and common experience, that our consciousness can be invaded, filled, entirely absorbed by the production of an *existence* in which objects and beings seem the same as those in the waking state; but their meanings, relationships, modes of variation and of substitution are quite different and doubtless represent, like symbols or allegories, the immediate fluctuations of our *general* sensibility uncontrolled by the sensitivities of our *specialized* senses. In very much the same way the *poetic state* takes hold of us, develops and finally disintegrates.

This is to say that the *state of poetry* is completely irregular, inconstant, involuntary, and fragile, and that we lose it, as we find it, *by accident.* But this state is not enough to make a poet, any more than it is enough to see a treasure in a dream to find it, on waking, sparkling at the foot of one's bed.

A poet's function—do not be startled by this remark—is not to experience the poetic state: that is a private affair. His function is to create it in others. The poet is recognized—or at least everyone recognizes his own poet—by the simple fact that he causes his reader to become "inspired." Positively speaking, inspiration is a graceful attribute with which the reader endows his poet: the reader sees in us the transcendent merits of virtues and graces that develop in him. He seeks and finds in us the wondrous cause of his own wonder.

But poetic feeling and the artificial synthesis of this state in some work are two quite distinct things, as different as sensation and action. A sustained action is much more complex than any spontaneous production, particularly when it has to be carried out in a sphere as conventional as that of language. Here you see emerging through my explanations the famous ABSTRACT THOUGHT which custom opposes to POETRY. We shall come back to that in a moment. Meanwhile I should like to tell you a true story, so that you may feel as I felt, and in a curiously clear way, the whole difference that exists between the poetic state or emotion, even creative and original, and the production of a work. It is a rather remarkable observation of myself that I made about a year ago.

I had left my house to relax from some tedious piece of work by walking and by a consequent change of scene. As I went along the street where I live, I was suddenly *gripped* by a rhythm which took possession of me and soon gave me the impression of some force outside myself. It was as though someone else were making use of my *living-machine*. Then another rhythm overtook and combined with the first, and certain strange *transverse* relations were set up between these two principles (I am explaining myself as best I can). They combined the movement of my walking legs and some kind of song I was murmuring, or rather which was being murmured *through me*. This composition became more and more complicated and soon in its complexity went far beyond anything I could reasonably produce with my ordinary, usable rhythmic faculties. The sense of strangeness that I mentioned became almost painful, almost disquieting. I am no musician; I am completely ignorant of musical technique; yet here I was, prey to a development in several parts more complicated than any poet could dream. I argued that there had been an error of person, that this grace had descended on the wrong head, since I could make no use of a gift which for a musician would doubtless have assumed value, form, and duration, while these parts that mingled and separated offered me in vain a composition whose cunningly organized sequence amazed my ignorance and reduced it to despair.

After about twenty minutes the magic suddenly vanished, leaving me on the bank of the Seine, as perplexed as the duck in the fable, that saw a swan emerge from the egg she had hatched. As the swan flew away, my surprise changed to reflection. I knew that walking often induces in me a quickened flow of ideas and that there is a certain reciprocity between my pace and my thoughts—my thoughts modify my pace; my pace provokes my thoughts—which after all is remarkable enough, but is fairly understandable. Our various "reaction periods" are doubtless synchronized, and it is interesting to have to admit that a reciprocal modification is possible between a form of action which is purely muscular and a varied production of images, judgments, and reasonings.

But in the case I am speaking of, my movement in walking became in my consciousness a very subtle system of rhythms, instead of instigating those images, interior words, and potential actions which one calls *ideas*. As for ideas, they are things of a species familiar to me; they are things that I can note, provoke, and handle. . . . *But I cannot say the same of my unexpected rhythms.*

What was I to think? I supposed that mental activity while walking must correspond with a general excitement exerting itself in the region of my brain; this excitement satisfied and relieved itself as best it could, and so long as its energy was expended, it mattered little whether this was on ideas, memories, or rhythms unconsciously hummed. On that day, the energy was expended in a rhythmical intuition that developed before the awakening in my consciousness of *the person who knows that he does not know music.* I imagine it is the same as when *the person who knows he cannot fly* has not yet become active in the man who dreams he is flying.

I apologize for this long and true story—as true, that is, as a story of this kind can be. Notice that everything I have said, or tried to say, happened in relation to what we call the *External World,* what we call *Our Body,* and what we call *Our Mind,* and requires a kind of vague collaboration between these three great powers.

Why have I told you this? In order to bring out the profound difference existing between spontaneous production by the mind—or rather by our *sensibility as a whole*—and the fabrication of works. In my story, the substance of a musical composition was freely given to me, but the organization which would have seized, fixed, and reshaped it was lacking. The great painter Degas often repeated to me a very true and simple remark by Mallarmé. Degas occasionally wrote verses, and some of those he left were delightful. But he often found great difficulty in this work accessory to his painting. (He was, by the way, the kind of man who would bring all possible difficulty to any art whatever.) One day he said to Mallarmé: "Yours is a hellish craft. I can't manage to say what I want, and yet I'm full of ideas. . . ." And Mallarmé answered: "My dear Degas, one does not make poetry with ideas, but with *words.*"

Mallarmé was right. But when Degas spoke of ideas, he was, after all, thinking of inner speech or of images, which might have been expressed in *words.* But these words, these secret phrases which he called ideas, all these intentions and perceptions of the mind, do not make verses. There is something else, then, a modification, or a transformation, sudden or not, spontaneous or not, laborious or not, which must necessarily intervene between the thought that produces ideas—that activity and multiplicity of inner questions and solutions—and, on the other hand, that discourse, so different from ordinary speech, which is verse, which is so curiously ordered, which answers no need *unless it be the need it must itself create,* which never speaks but of absent things or of things profoundly and secretly felt: strange discourse, as though made by someone *other* than the speaker and addressed to someone *other* than the listener. In short, it is a *language within a language.*

Let us look into these mysteries.

Poetry is an art of language. But language is a practical creation. It may be observed that in all communication between men, certainty comes only from practical acts and from the verification which practical acts give us. *I ask you for a light. You give me a light:* you have understood me.

But in asking me for a light, you were able to speak those few unimportant words with a certain intonation, a certain tone of voice, a certain inflection, a certain languor or briskness perceptible to me. I have understood your words, since without even thinking I handed you what you asked for—a light. But the matter does not end there. The strange thing: the sound and as it were the features of your little sentence come back to me, echo within me, as though they were pleased to be there; I, too, like to hear myself repeat this little phrase, which has almost lost its meaning, which has stopped being of use, and which can yet go on living, though with quite another life. It has acquired a value; and has acquired it *at the expense of its finite significance.* It has created the need to be heard again. . . . . Here we are on the very threshold of the poetic state. This tiny experience will help us to the discovery of more than one truth.

It has shown us that language can produce effects of two quite different kinds. One of them tends to bring about the complete negation of language itself. I speak to you, and if you have understood my words, those very words are abolished. If you have understood, it means that the words have vanished from your minds and are replaced by their counterpart, by images, relationships, impulses; so that you have within you the means to retransmit these ideas and images in a language that may be very different from the one you received. *Understanding* consists in the more or less rapid replacement of a system of sounds, intervals, and signs by something quite different, which is, in short, a modification or interior reorganization of the person to whom one is speaking. And here is the counterproof of this proposition: the person who does not understand *repeats* the *words,* or *has them repeated* to him.

Consequently, the perfection of a discourse whose sole aim is comprehension obviously consists in the ease with which the words forming it are transformed into something quite different: the *language* is transformed first into *non-language* and then, if we wish, into a form of language differing from the original form.

In other terms, in practical or abstract uses of language, the form—that is the physical, the concrete part, the very act of speech—does not last; it does not outlive understanding; it dissolves in the light; it has acted; it has done its work; it has brought about understanding; it has lived.

But on the other hand, the moment this concrete form takes on, by an effect of its own, such importance that it asserts itself and makes itself, as it were, respected; and not only remarked and respected, but desired and therefore repeated—then something new happens: we are insensibly transformed and ready to live, breathe, and think in accordance with a rule and under laws which are no longer of the practical order—that is, nothing that may occur in this state will be resolved, finished, or abolished by a specific act. We are entering the poetic universe.

Permit me to support this notion of a *poetic universe* by referring to a similar notion that, being much simpler, is easier to explain: the notion of a *musical universe*. I would ask you to make a small sacrifice: limit yourselves for a moment to your faculty of hearing. One simple sense, like that of hearing, will offer us all we need for our definition and will absolve us from entering into all the difficulties and subtleties to which the conventional structure and historical complexities of ordinary language would lead us. We live by ear in the world of noises. Taken as a whole, it is generally incoherent and irregularly supplied by all the mechanical incidents which the ear may interpret as it can. But the same ear isolates from this chaos a group of noises particularly remarkable and simple—that is, easily recognizable by our sense of hearing and furnishing it with points of reference. These elements have relations with one another which we sense as we do the elements themselves. The interval between two of these privileged noises is as clear to us as each of them. These are the *sounds*, and these units of sonority tend to form clear combinations, successive or simultaneous implications, series, and intersections which one may term *intelligible:* this is why abstract possibilities exist in music. But I must return to my subject.

I will confine myself to saying that the contrast between noise and sound is the contrast between pure and impure, order and disorder; that this differentiation between pure sensations and others has permitted the constitution of music; that it has been possible to control, unify, and codify this constitution, thanks to the intervention of physical science, which knows how to adjust measure to sensation so as to obtain the important result of teaching us to produce this sonorous sensation consistently, and in a continuous and identical fashion, by instruments that are, in reality, *measuring instruments.*

The musician is thus in possession of a perfect system of well-defined means which exactly match sensations with acts. From this it results that music has formed a domain absolutely its own. The world of the art of music, a world of sounds, is distinct from the world of noises. Whereas a *noise* merely rouses in us some isolated event—a dog, a door, a motor car—*a sound evokes, of itself, the musical universe.* If, in this hall where I am speaking to you and where you hear the noise of my voice, a tuning fork or a well-tempered instrument began to vibrate, you would at once, as soon as you were affected by this pure and exceptional noise that cannot be confused with others, have the feeling of a beginning, the beginning of a world; a quite different atmosphere would immediately be created, a new order would arise, and you yourselves would unconsciously *organize* yourselves to receive it. The musical universe, therefore, was within you, with all its associations and proportions—as in a saturated salt solution a crystalline universe awaits the molecular shock of a minute crystal in order *to declare itself.* I dare not say: the crystalline idea of such a system awaits. . . .

And here is the counter proof of our little experiment: if, in a concert hall dominated by a resounding symphony, a chair happens to fall, someone coughs, or a door shuts, we immediately have the impression of a kind of rupture. Something indefinable, something like a spell or a Venetian glass, has been broken or cracked. . . .

The poetic universe is not created so powerfully or so easily. It exists, but the poet is deprived of the immense advantages possessed by the musician. He does not have before him, ready for the uses of beauty, a body of resources expressly made for his art. He has to borrow *language*—the voice of the public, that collection of traditional and irrational terms and rules, oddly created and transformed, oddly codified, and very variedly understood and pronounced. Here there is no physicist who has determined the relations between these elements; no tuning forks, no metronomes, no inventors of scales or theoreticians of harmony. Rather, on the contrary, the phonetic and semantic fluctuations of vocabulary. Nothing pure; but a mixture of completely incoherent auditive and psychic stimuli. Each word is an instantaneous coupling of a *sound* and a *sense* that have no connection with each other. Each sentence is an act so complex that I doubt whether anyone has yet been able to provide a tolerable definition of it. As for the use of the resources of language and the modes of this action, you know what diversity there is, and what confusion sometimes results. A discourse can be logical, packed with sense, but devoid of rhythm and measure. It can be pleasing to the ear, yet completely absurd or insignificant; it can be clear, yet useless; vague, yet delightful. But to grasp its strange multiplicity, which is no more than the multiplicity of life itself, it suffices to name all the sciences which have been created to deal with this diversity, each to study one of its aspects. One can analyze a text in many different ways, for it falls successively under the jurisdiction of phonetics, semantics, syntax, logic, rhetoric, philology, not to mention metrics, prosody, and etymology. . . .

So the poet is at grips with this verbal matter, obliged to speculate on sound and sense at once, and to satisfy not only harmony and musical timing but all the various intellectual and aesthetic conditions, not to mention the conventional rules. . . .

You can see what an effort the poet's undertaking would require if he had *consciously* to solve all these problems. . . .

It is always interesting to try to reconstruct one of our complex activities, one of those complete actions which demand a specialization at once mental, sensuous, and motor, supposing that in order to accomplish this act we were obliged to understand and organize all the functions that we know play their part in it. Even if this attempt, at once imaginative and analytical, is clumsy, it will always teach us something. As for myself, who am, I admit, much more attentive to the formation or fabrication of works than to the works themselves, I have a habit, or obsession, of appreciating works only as actions. In my eyes a poet is a man who, as a result of a certain incident, undergoes a hidden transformation. He leaves his ordinary condition of general disposability, and I see taking shape in him an agent, a living system for producing verses. As among animals one suddenly sees emerging a capable hunter, a nest maker, a bridge builder, a digger of tunnels and galleries, so in a man one sees a composite organization declare itself, bending its functions to a specific piece of work. Think of a very small child: the child we have all been bore many possibilities within him.

After a few months of life he has learned, at the same or almost the same time, to speak and to walk. He has acquired two types of action. That is to say that he now possesses two kinds of potentiality from which the accidental circumstances of each moment will draw what they can, in answer to his varying needs and imaginings.

Having learned to use his legs, he will discover that he can not only walk, but run; and not only walk and run, but dance. This is a great event. He has at that moment both invented and discovered a kind of *secondary use* for his limbs, a generalization of his formula of movement. In fact, whereas walking is after all a rather dull and not easily perfectible action, this new form of action, the Dance, admits of an infinite number of creations and variations or *figures*.

But will he not find an analogous development in speech? He will explore the possibilities of his faculty of speech; he will discover that more can be done with it than to ask for jam and deny his little sins. He will grasp the power of reasoning; he will invent stories to amuse himself when he is alone; he will repeat to himself words that he loves for their strangeness and mystery.

So, parallel with *Walking* and *Dancing*, he will acquire and distinguish the divergent types, *Prose* and *Poetry*.

This parallel has long struck and attracted me; but someone saw it before I did. According to Racan, Malherbe made use of it. In my opinion it is more than a simple comparison. I see in it an analogy as substantial and pregnant as those found in physics when one observes the identity of formulas that represent the measurement of seemingly very different phenomena. Here is how our comparison develops.

Walking, like prose, has a definite aim. It is an act directed at something we wish to reach. Actual circumstances, such as the need for some object, the impulse of my desire, the state of my body, my sight, the terrain, etc., which order the manner of walking, prescribe its direction and its speed, and give it a *definite end*. All the characteristics of walking derive from these instantaneous conditions, which combine *in a novel way* each time. There are no movements in walking that are not special adaptations, but, each time, they are abolished and, as it were, absorbed by the accomplishment of the act, by the attainment of the goal.

The dance is quite another matter. It is, of course, a system of actions; but of actions whose end is in themselves. It goes nowhere. If it pursues an object, it is only an ideal object, a state, an enchantment, the phantom of a flower, an extreme of life, a smile—which forms at last on the face of the one who summoned it from empty space.

It is therefore not a question of carrying out a limited operation whose end is situated somewhere in our surroundings, but rather of creating, maintaining, and exalting a certain *state*, by a periodic movement that can be executed on the spot; a movement which is almost entirely dissociated from sight, but which is stimulated and regulated by auditive rhythms.

But please note this very simple observation, that however different the dance may be from walking and utilitarian movement, it uses the same organs, the same bones, the same muscles, only differently co-ordinated and aroused.

Here we come again to the contrast between prose and poetry. Prose and poetry use the same words, the same syntax, the same forms, and the same sounds or tones, but differently co-ordinated and differently aroused. Prose and poetry are therefore distinguished by the difference between certain links and associations which form and dissolve in our psychic and nervous organism, whereas the components of these modes of functioning are identical. This is why one should guard against reasoning about poetry as one does about prose. What is true of one very often has no meaning when it is sought in the other. But here is the great and decisive difference. When the man who is walking has reaching his goal—as I said—when he has reached the place, book, fruit, the object of his desire (which desire drew him from his repose), this possession at once entirely annuls his whole act; the effect swallows up the cause, the end absorbs the means; and, whatever the act, only the result remains. It is the same with utilitarian language: the language I use to express my design, my desire, my command, my opinion; this language, when it has served its purpose, evaporates almost as it is heard. I have given it forth to perish, to be radically transformed into something else in your mind; and I shall know that I was *understood* by the remarkable fact that my speech no longer exists: it has been completely replaced by its *meaning*—that is, by images, impulses, reactions, or acts that belong to you: in short, by an interior modification in you.

As a result the perfection of this kind of language, whose sole end is to be understood, obviously consists in the ease with which it is transformed into something altogether different.

The poem, on the other hand, does not die for having lived: it is expressly designed to be born again from its ashes and to become endlessly what it has just been. Poetry can be recognized by this property, that it tends to get itself reproduced in its own form: it stimulates us to reconstruct it identically.

That is an admirable and uniquely characteristic property.

I should like to give you a simple illustration. Think of a pendulum oscillating between two symmetrical points. Suppose that one of these extremes represents *form:* the concrete characteristics of the language, sound, rhythm, accent, tone, movement—in a word, the *Voice* in action. Then associate with the other point, the acnode of the first, all significant values, images and ideas, stimuli of feeling and memory, virtual impulses, and structures of understanding—in short, everything that makes the *content,* the meaning of a discourse. Now observe the effect of poetry on yourselves. You will find that at each line the meaning produced within you, far from destroying the musical form communicated to you, recalls it. The living pendulum that has swung from *sound* to *sense* swings back to its felt point of departure, as though the very sense which is present to your mind can find no other outlet or expression, no other answer, than the very music which gave it birth.

So between the form and the content, between the sound and the sense, between the poem and the state of poetry, a symmetry is revealed, an equality between importance, value, and power, which does not exist in prose; which is contrary to the law of prose—the law which ordains the inequality of the two constituents of language. The essential principle of the mechanics of poetry—that is, of the conditions for producing the poetic state by words—seems to me to be this harmonious exchange between expression and impression.

I introduce here a slight observation which I shall call "philosophical," meaning simply that we could do without it.

Our poetic pendulum travels from our sensation toward some idea or some sentiment, and returns toward some memory of the sensation and toward the potential act which could reproduce the sensation. Now, whatever is sensation is essentially *present.* There is no other definition of the present except sensation itself, which includes, perhaps the impulse to action that would modify that sensation. On the other hand, whatever is properly thought, image, sentiment, is always, in some way, *a production of absent things.* Memory is the substance of all thought. Anticipation and its gropings, desire, planning, the projection of our hopes, of our fears, are the main interior activity of our being.

Thought is, in short, the activity which causes what does not exist to come alive in us, lending to it, whether we will or no, our present powers, making us take the part for the whole, the image for reality, and giving us the illusion of seeing, acting, suffering, and possessing independently of our dear old body, which we leave with its cigarette in an armchair until we suddenly retrieve it when the telephone rings or, no less strangely, when our stomach demands provender. . . .

Between Voice and Thought, between Thought and Voice, between Presence and Absence, oscillates the poetic pendulum.

The result of this analysis is to show that the value of a poem resides in the indissolubility of sound and sense. Now this is a condition that seems to demand the impossible. There is no relation between the sound and the meaning of a word. The same thing is called HORSE in English, HIPPOS in Greek, EQUUS in Latin, and CHEVAL in French; but no manipulation of any of these terms will give me an idea of the animal in question; and no manipulation of the idea will yield me any of these words—otherwise, we should easily know all languages, beginning with our own.

Yet it is the poet's business to give us the feeling of an intimate union between the word and the mind.

This must be considered, strictly speaking, a marvelous result. I say *marvelous*, although it is not exceptionally rare. I use *marvelous* in the sense we give that word when we think of the miracles and prodigies of ancient magic. It must not be forgotten that for centuries poetry was used for purposes of enchantment. Those who took part in these strange operations had to believe in the power of the word, and far more in the efficacy of its sound than in its significance. Magic formulas are often without meaning; but it was never thought that their power depended on their intellectual content.

Let us listen to lines like these:

> *Mère des souvenirs, maîtresse des maîtresses . . .*

or

> *Sois sage, ô ma Douleur, et tiens-toi plus tranquille. . . .*

These words work on us (or at least on some of us) without telling us very much. They tell us, perhaps, that they have nothing to tell us; that, by the very means which usually tell us something, they are exercising a quite different function. They act on us like a chord of music. The impression produced depends largely on resonance, rhythm, and the number of syllables; but it is also the result of the simple bringing together of meanings. In the second of these lines the accord between the vague ideas of Wisdom and Grief, and the tender solemnity of the tone produce the inestimable value of a spell: the *momentary being* who made that line could not have done so had he been in a state where the form and the content occurred separately to this mind. On the contrary, he was in a special phase in the domain of his psychic existence, a phase in which the sound and the meaning of the word acquire or keep an equal importance— which is excluded from the habits of practical language, as from the needs of abstract language. The state in which the inseparability of sound and sense, in which the desire, the expectation, the possibility of their intimate and indissoluble fusion are required and sought or given, and sometimes anxiously awaited, is a comparatively rare state. It is rare, firstly because all the exigencies of life are against it; secondly because it is opposed to the crude simplifying and specializing of verbal notations.

But this state of inner modification, in which all the properties of our language are indistinctly but harmoniously summoned, is not enough to produce that complete object, that compound of beauties, that collection of happy chances for the mind which a noble poem offers us.

From this state we obtain only fragments. All the precious things that are found in the earth, gold, diamonds, uncut stones, are there scattered, strewn, grudgingly hidden in a quantity of rock or sand, where chance may sometimes uncover them. These riches would be nothing without the human labor that draws them from the massive night where they were sleeping, assembles them, alters and organizes them into ornaments. These fragments of metal embedded in formless matter, these oddly shaped crystals, must owe all their luster to intelligent labor. It is a labor of this kind that the true poet accomplishes. Faced with a beautiful poem, one can indeed feel that it is most unlikely that any man, however gifted, could have improvised without a backward glance, with no other effort than that of writing or dictating, such a simultaneous and complete system of lucky finds. Since the traces of effort, the second thoughts, the changes, the amount of time, the bad days, and the distaste have now vanished, effaced by the supreme return of a mind over its work, some people, seeing only the perfection of the result, will look on it as due to a sort of magic that they call INSPIRATION. They thus make of the poet a kind of temporary *medium*. If one were strictly to develop this doctrine of pure inspiration, one would arrive at some very strange results. For example, one would conclude that the poet, since he merely transmits what he receives, merely delivers to unknown people what he has taken from the unknown, has no need to understand what he writes, which is dictated by a mysterious voice. He could write poems in a language he did not know. . . .

In fact, the poet has indeed a kind of spiritual energy of a special nature: it is manifested in him and reveals him to himself in certain moments of infinite worth. Infinite for him. . . . I say, *infinite for him*, for, alas, experience shows us that these moments which seem to us to have a universal value are sometimes without a future, and in the end, make us ponder on this maxim: *what is of value for one person only has no value.* This is the iron law of Literature.

But every true poet is necessarily a first-rate critic. If one doubts this, one can have no idea of what the work of the mind is: that struggle with the inequality of moments, with chance associations, lapses of attention, external distractions. The mind is terribly variable, deceptive and self-deceiving, fertile in insoluble problems and illusory solutions. How could a remarkable work emerge from this chaos if this chaos that contains everything did not also contain some serious chances to know oneself and to choose within oneself whatever is worth taking from each moment and using carefully?

That is not all. Every true poet is much more capable than is generally known of right reasoning and abstract thought.

But one must not look for his real philosophy in his more or less philosophical utterances. In my opinion, the most authentic philosophy lies not so much in the objects of our reflection as in the very act of thought and in its handling. Take from metaphysics all its pet or special terms, all its traditional vocabulary, and you may realize that you have not impoverished the thought. Indeed, you may perhaps have eased and freshened it, and you will have got rid of other people's problems, so as to deal only with your own difficulties, your surprises that owe nothing to anyone, and whose intellectual spur you feel actually and directly.

It has often happened, however, as literary history tells us, that poetry has been made to enunciate theses or hypotheses and that the *complete* language which is its own—the language whose *form*, that is to say the action and sensation of the *Voice*, is of the same power as the *content*, that is to say the eventual modification of a *mind*—has been used to communicate "abstract" ideas, which are on the contrary independent of their form, or so we believe. Some very great poets have occasionally attempted this. But whatever may be the talent which exerts itself in this very noble undertaking, it cannot prevent the attention given to following the ideas from competing with the attention that follows the song. The DE RERUM NATURA is here in conflict with the nature of things. The state of mind of the reader of poems is not the state of mind of the reader of pure thought. The state of mind of a man dancing is not that of a man advancing through difficult country of which he is making a topographical survey or a geological prospectus.

I have said, nevertheless, that the poet has his abstract thought and, if you like, his philosophy; and I have said that it is at work in his very activity as a poet. I said this because I have observed it, in myself and in several others. Here, as elsewhere, I have no other reference, no other claim or excuse, than recourse to my own experience or to the most common observation.

Well, every time I have worked as a poet, I have noticed that my work exacted of me not only that presence of the poetic universe I have spoken of, but many reflections, decisions, choices, and combinations, without which all possible gifts of the Muses, or of Chance, would have remained like precious materials in a workshop without an architect. Now an architect is not himself necessarily built of precious materials. In so far as he is an architect of poems, a poet is quite different from what he is as a producer of those precious elements of which all poetry should be composed, but whose composition is separate and requires an entirely different mental effort.

One day someone told me that lyricism is enthusiam, and that the odes of the great lyricists were written at a single stroke, at the speed of the voice of delirium, and with the wind of inspiration blowing a gale. . . .

I replied that he was quite right; but that this was not a privilege of poetry alone, and that everyone knew that in building a locomotive it is indispensable for the builder to work at eighty miles an hour in order to do his job.

A poem is really a kind of machine for producing the poetic state of mind by means of words. The effect of this machine is uncertain, for nothing is certain about action on other minds. But whatever may be the result, in its uncertainty, the construction of the machine demands the solution of many problems. If the term *machine* shocks you, if my mechanical comparison seems crude, please notice that while the composition of even a very short poem may absorb years, the action of the poem on the reader will take only a few minutes. In a few minutes the reader will receive his shock from discoveries, connections, glimmers of expression that have been accumulated during months of research, waiting, patience, and impatience. He may attribute much more to inspiration than it can give. He will imagine the kind of person it would take to create, without pause, hesitation, or revision, this powerful and perfect work which transports him into a world where things and people, passions and thoughts, sonorities and meanings proceed from the same energy, are transformed one into another, and correspond according to exceptional laws of harmony, for it can only be an exceptional form of stimulus that simultaneously produces the exaltation of our sensibility, our intellect, our memory, and our powers of verbal action, so rarely granted to us in the ordinary course of life.

Perhaps I should remark here that the execution of a poetic work—if one considers it as the engineer just mentioned would consider the conception and construction of his locomotive, that is, making explicit the problems to be solved—would appear impossible. In no other art is the number of conditions and independent functions to be co-ordinated so large. I will not inflict on you a detailed demonstration of this proposition. It is enough for me to remind you of what I said regarding sound and sense, which are linked only by pure convention, but which must be made to collaborate as effectively as possible. From their double nature words often make me think of those complex quantities which geometricians take such pleasure in manipulating.

Fortunately, some strange virtue resides in certain moments in certain people's lives which simplifies things and reduces the insurmountable difficulties I spoke of to the scale of human energies.

The poet awakes within man at an unexpected event, an outward or inward incident: a tree, a face, a "subject," an emotion, a word. Sometimes it is the will to expression that starts the game, a need to translate what one feels; another time, on the contrary, it is an element of form, the outline of an expression which seeks its origin, seeks a meaning within the space of my mind. . . . Note this possible duality in ways of getting started: either something wants to express itself, or some means of expression wants to be used.

My poem Le Cimetière marin began in me by a rhythm, that of a French line . . . of ten syllables, divided into four and six. I had as yet no idea with which to fill out this form. Gradually a few hovering words settled in it, little by little determining the subject, and my labor (a very long labor) was before me. Another poem, *La Pythie*, first appeared as an eight-syllable line whose sound came of its own accord. But this line implied a sentence, of which it was part, and this sentence, if it existed, implied many other sentences. A problem of this kind has an infinite number of solutions. But with poetry the musical and metrical conditions greatly restrict the indefiniteness. Here is what happened: my fragment acted like a living fragment, since, plunged in the (no doubt nourishing) surroundings of my desire and waiting thought, it proliferated, and engendered all that was lacking: several lines before and a great many lines after.

I apologize for having chosen my examples from my own little story: but I could hardly have taken them elsewhere.

Perhaps you think my conception of the poet and the poem rather singular. Try to imagine, however, what the least of our acts implies. Think of everything that must go on inside a man who utters the smallest intelligible sentence, and then calculate all that is needed for a poem by Keats or Baudelaire to be formed on an empty page in front of the poet.

Think, too, that of all the arts, ours is perhaps that which co-ordinates the greatest number of independent parts or factors: sound, sense, the real and the imaginary, logic, syntax, and the double invention of content and form . . . and all this by means of a medium essentially practical, perpetually changing, soiled, a maid of all work, *everyday language,* from which we must draw a pure, ideal Voice, capable of communicating without weakness, without apparent effort, without offense to the ear, and without breaking the ephemeral sphere of the poetic universe, an idea of some *self* miraculously superior to Myself.

Aimé Césaire, translated by A. James Arnold: "Poetry and Knowledge," 1944–1945

Aimé Césaire was born in the French colony of Martinique in 1913. As a young man, he went to Paris to study where he met other students of African descent, including the poets Léopold Sédar Senghor from Senegal and Léon Damas from Guyana. Césaire and Senghor would become known as the cofounders of negritude, a term Césaire coined in his long poem *Cahier d'un retour au pays natal* (Notebook of a Return to My Native Land) in 1939. Negritude was an international anticolonialist movement both political and cultural, a movement which combined elements of the European surrealism that the poets encountered in Paris with a pride in and investigation into African history and culture. It drew strength, as well, from the writings coming out of the Harlem Renaissance, particularly those of Langston Hughes and Claude McKay.

Césaire returned to his native land in 1939, where, with his wife, Suzanne, and the philosopher René Ménil, he edited *Tropiques,* an international journal of surrealist poetry and anticolonialist philosophy. Originally delivered as a lecture at a conference on philosophy in Haiti in 1944, "Poetry and Knowledge" was first published in *Tropiques* in 1945.

❋

Poetry and Knowledge

Poetic knowledge is born in the great silence of scientific knowledge.

Mankind, once bewildered by sheer data, finally dominated them through reflection, observation, and experiment. Henceforth mankind knows how to make its way through the forest of phenomena. It knows how to utilize the world.

But it is not the lord of the world on that account.

A view of the world, yes; science affords a view of the world, but a summary and superficial view.

Physics classifies and explains, but the essence of things eludes it. The natural sciences classify, but the *quid proprium* of things eludes them.

As for mathematics, what eludes its abstract and logical activity is reality itself.

In short, scientific knowledge enumerates, measures, classifies and kills.

But it is not sufficient to state that scientific knowledge is succinct. It is necessary to add that it is *poor and half-starved.*

To acquire it mankind has sacrificed everything: desires, fears, feelings, psychological complexes.

To acquire the impersonality of scientific knowledge mankind *depersonalized* itself, *deindividualized* itself.

An impoverished knowledge, I submit, for at its inception—whatever other wealth it may have—there stands an impoverished humanity.

In Aldous Huxley's *Do What You Will* there is a very amusing page. "We all think we know what a lion is. A lion is a desert-colored animal with a mane and claws and an expression like Garibaldi's. But it is also, in Africa, all the neighboring antelopes and zebras, and therefore, indirectly, all the neighboring grass . . . If there were no antelopes and zebras there would be no lion. When the supply of game runs low, the king of beasts grows thin and mangy; it ceases altogether, and he dies."

It is just the same with knowledge. Scientific knowledge is a lion without antelopes and without zebras. It is gnawed from within. Gnawed by hunger, the hunger of feeling, the hunger of life.

Then dissatisfied mankind sought salvation elsewhere, in the fullness of here and now.

And mankind has gradually become aware that side by side with this half-starved scientific knowledge there is another kind of knowledge. A fulfilling knowledge.

The Ariadne's thread of this discovery: some very simple observations on the faculty that permitted the human whom one must call the primitive scientist to discover the most solid truths without benefit of induction or deduction, as if by flair.

And here we are taken back to the first days of humanity. It is an error to believe that knowledge, to be born, had to await the methodical exercise of thought or the scruples of experimentation. I even believe that mankind has never been closer to certain truths than in the first days of the species. At the time when mankind discovered with emotion the first sun, the first rain, the first breath, the first moon. At the time when mankind discovered in fear and rapture the throbbing newness of the world.

Attraction and terror. Trembling and wonderment. Strangeness and intimacy. Only the sacred phenomenon of love can still give us an idea of what that solemn encounter can have been . . .

It is in this state of fear and love, in this climate of emotion and imagination that mankind made its first, most fundamental and most decisive discoveries.

It was both desirable and inevitable that humanity should accede to greater precision.

It was both desirable and inevitable that humanity should experience nostalgia for greater feeling.

It is that mild autumnal nostalgia that threw mankind back from the clear light of scientific day to the nocturnal forces of poetry.

Poets have always known. All the legends of antiquity attest to it. But in modern times it is only in the nineteenth century, as the Apollonian era draws to a close, that poets dared to claim that they knew.

1850.—The revenge of Dionysus upon Apollo.

1850.—The great leap into the poetic void.

An extraordinary phenomenon . . . Until then the French attitude had been one of caution, circumspection, and suspicion. France was dying of prose. Then suddenly there was the great nervous spasm at the prospect of adventure. The prosiest nation, in its most eminent representatives— by the most mountainous routes, the hardest, haughtiest, and most breathtaking, by the only routes I am willing to call sacred and royal— with all weapons and equipment went over to the enemy. I mean to the death's-head army of freedom and imagination.

Prosy France went over to poetry. And everything changed.

Poetry ceased to be a game, even a serious one. Poetry ceased to be an occupation, even an honorable one.

Poetry became an adventure. The most beautiful human adventure. At the end of the road: clairvoyance and knowledge.

And so Baudelaire . . .

It is significant that much of his poetry relates to the idea of a penetration of the universe.

> Happy the man who can with vigorous wings
> Mount to those luminous fields serene!

The man whose thoughts, like larks,
Fly liberated to the skies at morning,
—Who hovers over life and effortlessly harks
To the language of flowers and voiceless things!

And in "Obsession":

But the shadows are themselves canvases
Wherein live, welling up in my eye by thousands,
Beings invisible to the familiar gaze . . .

And in "Gypsies on the Road":

Cybele, who loves them, increases her green glades,

Makes rock flow and desert bloom
Before these travelers, for whom
Lies open the familiar empire of future shades.

As for Rimbaud, literature is still registering the aftershocks of the incredible seismic tremor of his famous *lettre du voyant:*

I say that one has to be clairvoyant, to make oneself
clairvoyant.

Memorable words, words of distress and of victory . . .
Henceforth, the field is clear for humanity's most momentous dreams.
There is no longer any possibility of doubt about Mallarmé's enterprise. The clear-eyed boldness of what he wrote to Verlaine makes of Mallarmé rather more than the poet whose shadow is Paul Valéry: an engineer of the mind of special importance.

Apart from the prose pieces and the poetry of my youth and the
aftermath that echoed them . . . I have always dreamed of and attempted something else . . . A book, very simply, a book that
would be premeditated and architectonic, and not a collection of
chance inspirations, even wondrous ones. I shall go farther; I shall
say The Book, persuaded that at bottom there is only one, that
anyone, even a genius, who has written was working at unconsciously. The Orphic explanation of the Earth, which is the poet's
only duty. And the literary game par excellence . . . There you have
my vice revealed.

To pass from Mallarmé to Apollinaire is to go from the cold calculator, the strategist of poetry, to the enthusiastic adventurer and ringleader.

Apollinaire, great because he knew how to stake out his territory, fundamentally, between popular ballad and the war poem, was one of the awesome workmen whose advent Rimbaud had predicted.

> You whose mouth is made in the image of God
> A mouth that is order itself
> Be indulgent when you compare us
> To those who were the perfection of order
> We who seek adventure everywhere
>
> We are not your enemies
> We want to give you vast and strange domains
> Where mystery in bloom is offered to whoever would
>   pluck it
> New fires are found there colors yet unseen
> A thousand imponderable fantasms
> That await the conferral of reality
> We want to explore goodness an enormous country
>   where all is silence
> Then there is time that you can banish or call back
> Pity for us who fight always on the frontiers
> Of the limitless and of the future
> Pity our errors pity our sins

I come now, having skipped a few stops, I confess, to André Breton . . . Surrealism's glory will be in having aligned against it the whole block of admitted and unprofessed enemies of poetry. In having decanted several centuries of poetic experience. In having purged the past, oriented the present, prepared the future.

It was André Breton who wrote:

> After all, it is the poets over the centuries who have made it possible to receive, and who have enabled us to expect, the impulses that may once again place humankind at the heart of the universe, abstracting us for a second from our dissolving adventure, reminding us of an indefinitely perfectible place of resolution and echo for every pain and joy exterior to ourselves.

And still more significantly:

> Everything leads us to believe that there exists a certain mental
> point from which life and death, the real and the imaginary, the
> past and the future, the communicable and the incommunicable,
> high and low, cease to be perceived contradictorily. And one would
> search in vain for a motive in surrealist activity other than the de-
> termination of that point.

Never in the course of centuries has higher ambition been expressed
with greater tranquility.

This highest ambition is the ambition of poetry itself.

We have only to examine the conditions necessary to satisfy it, and
their precise mode.

The ground of poetic knowledge, an astonishing mobilization of all
human and cosmic forces.

It is not merely with his whole soul, it is with his entire being that
the poet approaches the poem. What presides over the poem is not the
most lucid intelligence, or the most acute sensibility, but an entire experience: all the women loved, all the desires experienced, all the dreams
dreamed, all the images received or grasped, the whole weight of the
body, the whole weight of the mind. All lived experience. All the possibility. Around the poem about to be made, the precious vortex: the ego,
the id, the world. And the most extraordinary contacts: all the pasts,
all the futures (the anticyclone builds its plateaux, the amoeba loses its
pseudopods, vanished vegetations meet). All the flux, all the rays. The
body is no longer deaf or blind. Everything has a right to live. Everything
is summoned. Everything awaits. Everything, I say. The individual whole
churned up by poetic inspiration. And, in a more disturbing way, the cosmic whole as well.

This is the right occasion to recall that the unconscious that all true
poetry calls upon is the receptacle of original relationships that bind us to
nature.

Within us, all the ages of mankind. Within us, all humankind. Within
us, animal, vegetable, mineral. Mankind is not only mankind. It is *universe*.

Everything happens as though prior to the secondary scattering of life,
there was a knotty primal unity whose gleam poets have homed in on.

Mankind, distracted by its activities, delighted by what is useful, has lost the sense of that fraternity. Here is the superiority of the animal. And of the tree still more than of the animal, because the tree is fixed, attachment and perseverance to essential nature . . .

And because the tree is stability, it is also surrender.

Surrender to the vital movement, to the creative élan. Joyous surrender.

And the flower is the sign of that recognition.

The superiority of the tree over mankind, of the tree that says "yes" over mankind who says "no." Superiority of the tree that is consent over mankind who is evasiveness; superiority of the tree, which is rootedness and deepening, over mankind who is agitation and malfeasance.

And that is why mankind does not blossom at all.

Mankind is no tree. Its arms imitate branches, but they are withered branches which, for having misunderstood their true function (to embrace life), have fallen down along the trunk, have dried up: mankind does not blossom at all.

But one man is the salvation of humanity, one man puts humanity back in the universal concert, one man unites the human flowering with universal flowering; that man is the poet.

But what has he done for that?

Very little, but that little he alone could do. Like the tree, like the animal, he has surrendered to primal life, he has said yes, he has consented to that immense life that transcends him. He has rooted himself in the earth, he has stretched out his arms, he has played with the sun, he has become a tree: he has blossomed, he has sung.

In other words poetry is in full bloom.

The blossoming of mankind to the dimensions of the world; giddy dilation. And it can be said that all true poetry, without ever abandoning its humanity, at the moment of greatest mystery ceases to be strictly human so as to begin to be truly cosmic.

There we see resolved, and by the poetic state, two of the most anguishing antinomies that exist: the antinomy of one and other, the antinomy of Self and World.

"Finally, oh happiness, oh reason, I listened to the azure sky, which is blackness, and I lived, a golden spark in nature's light."

So, pregnant with the world, the poet speaks.

In the beginning was the word . . .

. . . Never did a man believe it more powerfully than the poet.

And it is on the word, a chip off the world, secret and chaste slice of the world, that he gambles all our possibilities. Our first and last chance.

More and more the word promises to be an algebraic equation that makes the world intelligible. Just as the new Cartesian algebra permitted the construction of theoretical physics, so too an original handling of the word can make possible at any moment a new (theoretical and heedless) science that poetry could already give an approximate notion of. Then the time will come again when the study of the word will condition the study of nature. But at this juncture we are still in the shadows. . . .

Let's come back to the poet. Pregnant with the world, the poet speaks.

He speaks and his speech returns language to its purity.

By purity I mean not subject to habit or thought but only to the cosmic thrust. The poet's word, the primal word: rupestral design in the stuff of sound.

The poet's utterance: primal utterance, the universe played with and copied.

And because in every true poem, the poet plays the game of the world, the true poet hopes to surrender the word to its free associations, certain that in the final analysis that is to surrender it to the will of the universe.

Everything I have just said runs the risk of implying that the poet is defenseless. But that isn't at all correct. If I further specify that in poetic emotion nothing is ever closer to anything than to its opposite, it will be understood that no peacemaker, no plumber of the deep was ever more rebellious or pugnacious.

Take the old idea of the irritable poet and transfer it to poetry itself. In this sense it is appropriate to speak of poetic violence, of poetic aggressivity, of poetic instability. In this climate of flame and fury that is the climate of poetry money has no currency, courts pass no judgments, judges do not convict, juries do not acquit. Only the firing squads still know how to ply their trade. The farther one proceeds the more obvious the signs of the disaster become. Police functions are strangulated. Conventions wear out. The Grammont laws for the protection of mankind, the Locarno agreements for the protection of animals suddenly and marvelously give up their virtues. A wind of confusion.

. . . .

An agitation that shakes the most solid foundations. At the bloodied far end of mortal avenues an immense disloyal sun sneers. It is the sun of humor. And in the dust of the clouds crows write one name over and over:

ISIDORE DUCASSE COUNT OF LAUTRÉAMONT

Lautréamont, the very first in fact, integrated poetry and humor. He was the first to discover the functional role of humor. The first to make us feel that what love has begun, humor has the power to continue.

Sweeping clean the fields of the mind is not the least important role of humor. To dissolve with its blowtorch the fleeting connections that threaten to build up in our gray matter and harden it. It is humor, first and foremost, that assures Lautréamont—in opposition to Pascal, La Rouchefoucauld and so many other moralists—that had Cleopatra's nose been shorter the face of the world would not have been changed; that death and the sun can look one another in the face; that mankind is a subject empty of errors . . . that nothing is less strange than the contradictoriness one discovers in mankind. It is humor first and foremost that assures me it is as true to say the thief makes the opportunity as: "opportunity makes the thief . . ."

Humor alone assures me that the most prodigious turnabouts are legitimate. Humor alone alerts me to the other side of things.

We are now arriving in the crackling fields of metaphor.

One cannot think of the richness of the image without the repercussion suggesting the poverty of judgment.

> Judgment is poor from all the reason in the world.
> The image is rich with all the absurdity in the world.
> Judgement is rich with all the "thought" in the world.
> The image is rich with all the life in the universe.
> Judgment is poor from all the rationality in existence.
> The image is rich with all the irrational in life.
> Judgment is poor from all immanence.
> The image is rich with all transcendence.

Let me explain . . .

However much one may strain to reduce analytical judgment to synthetic judgment; or to say that judgment supposes the connecting of two different concepts; or to insist on the idea that there is no judgment without X; that all judgment is a surpassing toward the unknown; that all judgment is transcendence, it is nonetheless true that in all valid judgment the field of transcendence is limited.

The barriers are in place; the law of identity, the law of non-contradiction, the logical principle of the excluded middle.

Precious barriers. But remarkable limitations as well.

It is by means of the image, the revolutionary image, the distant image, the image that overthrows all the laws of thought that mankind finally breaks down the barrier.

In the image A is no longer A.

> You whose many raspberried laughs
> Are a flock of tame lambs.

In the image A can be A':

> The black focus plate, real strand suns, ah! wells of magic.
> In the image every object of thought is not necessarily A or A.'
> The image maintains the possibility of the happy medium.

Another by Rimbaud:

> The carts of silver and copper
> The prows of steel and silver
> Strike the foam
> Raise the bramble roots.

Without taking into consideration the encouraging complicity of the world as it is either *found* or *invented,* which permit us to say *motor* for *sun, dynamo* for *mountain, carburator* for *Carib,* etc . . . and to celebrate lyrically the shiny connecting rod of the moons and the tired piston of the stars . . .

Because the image extends inordinately the field of transcendence and the right of transcendence, poetry is always on the road to truth. And because the image is forever surpassing that which is perceived because the dialectic of the image transcends antinomies, on the whole modern science is perhaps only the pedantic verification of some mad images spewed out by poets . . .

When the sun of image reaches its zenith, everything becomes possible again . . . Accursed complexes dissolve, it's the instant of emergence . . .

What emerges is the individual foundation. The intimate conflicts, the obsessions, the phobias, the fixations. All the codes of the personal message.

It isn't a matter, as in the earlier lyric, of immortalizing an hour of pain or joy. Here we are well beyond anecdote, at the very heart of mankind, in the babbling hollow of destiny. My past is there to designate and to hide its face from me. My future is there to hold out its hand to me. Rockets flare. It is my childhood in flames. It is my childhood talking and looking for me. And within the person I am now the person I will be stands on tiptoe.

And what emerges as well is the old ancestral foundation.

Hereditary images that only the poetic atmosphere can bring to light again for ultimate decoding. The buried knowledge of the ages. The legendary cities of knowledge.

In this sense all the mythologies that the poet tumbles about, all the symbols he collects and regilds are true. And poetry alone takes them seriously. Which goes to make poetry a serious business.

The German philosopher Jung discovers the idea of energy and its conservation in Heraclitus's metaphor of the eternally living fire, in medieval legends related to saintly auras, in theories of metempsychosis. And for his part, Pierre Mabille regrets that the biologist should believe it "dishonorable to describe the evolution of blood corpuscles in terms of the story of the phoenix, or the functions of the spleen through the myth of Saturn engendering children only to devour them."

In other words, myth is repugnant to science whereas poetry is in accord with it. Which does not mean that science is superior to poetry. To tell the truth, myth is both inferior and superior to *law*. The inferiority of myth is in the degree of precision. The superiority of myth is in richness and sincerity. Only myth satisfies mankind completely; heart, reason, taste for detail and wholeness, taste for the false and the true, since myth is all that at once, a misty and emotional apprehension, rather than a means of poetic expression . . .

Thus, love and humor.

Thus, the word, image, and myth . . .

With the aid of these great powers of synthesis we can at last understand André Breton's words:

> Columbus had to sail with madmen to discover America.
> And look at how that madness has been embodied, and lasted . . .

It's not fear of madness that will oblige us to furl the flag of
   imagination.

It's not fear of madness that will oblige us to furl the flag of imagination.

And the poet Lucretius divines the indestructibility of matter, the plu-
rality of worlds, the existence of the infinitely small.

And the poet Seneca in *Medea* sends forth ships on the trail of new
worlds:

> In centuries to come the Ocean will burst the bonds within which it
> contains us. A land of infinity shall open before us. The pilot shall
> discover new countries and Thule will no longer be the ultimate
> land.

"It's not fear of madness that will oblige us to furl the flag of imagination . . ." And the painter Rousseau *invented* the vegetation of the tropics.
And the painter De Chirico unknowingly painted Apollinaire's future
wound on his forehead. And in the year 1924 the poet André Breton associated the number 1939 with the word *war.*

"It's not fear of madness that will oblige us to furl the flag of imagination." And the poet Rimbaud wrote *Illuminations.*

And the result is known to you: strange cities, extraordinary country-
sides, worlds twisted, crushed, torn apart, the cosmos given back to chaos,
order given back to disorder, being given over to becoming, everywhere
the absurd, everywhere the incoherent, the demential. And at the end of
all that! What is there? Failure! No, the flashing vision of his own destiny.
And the most authentic vision of the world if, as I stubbornly continue to
believe, Rimbaud is the first man to have experienced as feeling, as anguish, the modern idea of energetic forces in matter that cunningly wait
to ambush our quietude . . .

No: "It's not fear of madness that will oblige us to furl the flag of imagination . . ."

And now for a few proposals by way of summation and clarification:

FIRST PROPOSAL

Poetry is that process which through word, image, myth, love and humor establishes me at the living heart of myself and of the world.

SECOND PROPOSAL

The poetic process is a naturalizing process operating under the demential impulse of imagination.

THIRD PROPOSAL

Poetic knowledge splatters its object with all its mobilized richness.

FOURTH PROPOSAL

If affective energy can be endowed with causal power as Freud indicated, it is paradoxical to refuse it power and penetration. It is conceivable that nothing can resist the unheard of mobilization of force that poetry necessitates, or the multiplied élan of those forces.

FIFTH PROPOSAL

Marvelous discoveries occur at the equally marvelous contact of inner and outer totality perceived imaginatively and conjointly by, or more precisely within, the poet.

SIXTH PROPOSAL

Scientific truth has as its sign coherence and efficacy. Poetic truth has as its sign beauty.

SEVENTH AND FINAL PROPOSAL

The poetically beautiful is not merely beauty of expression or muscular euphoria. A too Apollonian or gymnastic idea of beauty paradoxically runs the risk of skinning, stuffing and hardening it.

COROLLARY

The music of poetry cannot be external or formal. The only *acceptable* poetic music comes from a greater distance than sound. To seek to musicalize poetry is the crime against poetic music, which can only be the striking of the mental wave against the rock of the world.

The poet is that very ancient yet new being, at once very complex and very simple who at the limit of dream and reality, of day and night, between absence and presence, searches for and receives in the sudden triggering of inner cataclysms the password of connivance and power.

III. The Poem as a
Field of Action
1918–1950

Ezra Pound, "A Retrospect," 1918

American expatriate poet, critic, editor of the London journal *Blast* and foreign correspondent for the journals *Poetry* and *The Little Review,* founder of vorticism—the British version of Italian futurism—and imagism, the latter being what T. S. Eliot would call "the *point de repère* usually and conveniently taken as the starting point of modern poetry"—in 1918, Ezra Pound was in a central position to write a "retrospective" on poetics. The "new fashion" he speaks of in this essay is no longer, however, defined by the French avant-garde, but by those influenced by it, the new English-speaking writers of high modernism, many of them his discoveries—T. S. Eliot, James Joyce, Wyndham Lewis, Richard Aldington, and H.D.

Originally printed in *Poetry* in 1913 as an imagist manifesto, the principles delineated in the section "A Few Don'ts"—precision, avoidance of excess, a musicality not tied to traditional meter—would come to define the qualities of subsequent modernisms. In addition, Pound's emphasis on the image as the thing itself, hard-edged and concrete, free from "emotional slither," signaled a marked break from important currents in French symbolism. Pound wrote his first imagist poem in Paris: it is a well-known story that he proceeded over a year to cut his initial thirty lines down to two:

> *In a Station of the Metro*
> The apparition of these faces in the crowd;
> Petals on a wet black bough.

Although his masterpiece, *The Cantos,* would stretch to epic length and take the rest of his life to complete, Pound maintained his original belief in the poet as craftsman, and his conception of the poem as an ideogrammatic field.

❋

A Retrospect

There has been so much scribbling about a new fashion in poetry, that I may perhaps be pardoned this brief recapitulation and retrospect.

In the spring or early summer of 1912, "H. D.," Richard Aldington and myself decided that we were agreed upon the three principles following:

1. Direct treatment of the "thing" whether subjective or objective.

2. To use absolutely no word that does not contribute to the presentation.

3. As regarding rhythm: to compose in the sequence of the musical phrase, not in sequence of a metronome.

Upon many points of taste and of predilection we differed, but agreeing upon these three positions we thought we had as much right to a group name, at least as much right, as a number of French "schools" proclaimed by Mr Flint in the August number of Harold Monro's magazine for 1911.

This school has since been "joined" or "followed" by numerous people who, whatever their merits, do not show any signs of agreement with the second specification. Indeed *vers libre* has become as prolix and as verbose as any of the flaccid varieties that preceded it. It has brought faults of its own. The actual language and phrasing is often as bad as that of our elders without even the excuse that the words are shoveled in to fill a metric pattern or to complete the noise of a rhyme-sound. Whether or no the phrases followed by the followers are musical must be left to the reader's decision. At times I can find a marked metre in "vers libres," as stale and hackneyed as any pseudo-Swinburnian, at times the writers seem to follow no musical structure whatever. But it is, on the whole, good that the field should be ploughed. Perhaps a few good poems have come from the new method, and if so it is justified.

Criticism is not a circumscription or a set of prohibitions. It provides fixed points of departure. It may startle a dull reader into alertness. That little of it which is good is mostly in stray phrases; or if it be an older artist helping a younger it is in great measure but rules of thumb, cautions gained by experience.

I set together a few phrases on practical working about the time the first remarks on imagisme were published. The first use of the word "Imagiste" was in my note to T.E. Hulme's five poems, printed at the end of my "Ripostes" in the autumn of 1912. I reprint my cautions from *Poetry* for March, 1913.

A FEW DON'TS

An "Image" is that which presents an intellectual and emotional complex in an instant of time. I use the term "complex" rather in the technical sense employed by the newer psychologists, such as Hart, though we might not agree absolutely in our application.

It is the presentation of such a "complex" instantaneously which gives that sense of sudden liberation; that sense of freedom from time limits and space limits; that sense of sudden growth, which we experience in the presence of the greatest works of art.

It is better to present one Image in a lifetime than to produce voluminous works.

All this, however, some may consider open to debate. The immediate necessity is to tabulate A LIST OF DON'TS for those beginning to write verses. I can not put all of them into Mosaic negative.

To begin with, consider the three propositions (demanding direct treatment, economy of words, and the sequence of the musical phrase), not as dogma—never consider anything as dogma—but as the result of long contemplation, which, even if it is some one else's contemplation, may be worth consideration.

Pay no attention to the criticism of men who have never themselves written a notable work. Consider the discrepancies between the actual writing of the Greek poets and dramatists, and the theories of the Graeco-Roman grammarians, concocted to explain their metres.

LANGUAGE

Use no superfluous word, no adjective which does not reveal something.

Don't use such an expression as "dim lands *of peace.*" It dulls the image. It mixes an abstraction with the concrete. It comes from the writer's not realizing that the natural object is always the *adequate* symbol.

Go in fear of abstractions. Do not retell in mediocre verse what has already been done in good prose. Don't think any intelligent person is going to be deceived when you try to shirk all the difficulties of the unspeakably difficult art of good prose by chopping your composition into line lengths.

What the expert is tired of today the public will be tired of tomorrow.

Don't imagine that the art of poetry is any simpler than the art of music, or that you can please the expert before you have spent at least as much effort on the art of verse as the average piano teacher spends on the art of music.

Be influenced by as many great artists as you can, but have the decency either to acknowledge the debt outright, or to try to conceal it.

Don't allow "influence" to mean merely that you mop up the particular decorative vocabulary of some one or two poets whom you happen to admire. A Turkish war correspondent was recently caught red-handed babbling in his dispatches of "dove-grey" hills, or else it was "pearl-pale," I can not remember.

Use either no ornament or good ornament.

RHYTHM AND RHYME

Let the candidate fill his mind with the finest cadences he can discover, preferably in a foreign language,[1] so that the meaning of the words may be less likely to divert his attention from the movement; e.g. Saxon charms, Hebridean Folk Songs, the verse of Dante, and the lyrics of Shakespeare—if he can dissociate the vocabulary from the cadence. Let him dissect the lyrics of Goethe coldly into their component sound values, syllables long and short, stressed and unstressed, into vowels and consonants.

It is not necessary that a poem should rely on its music, but if it does rely on its music that music must be such as will delight the expert.

Let the neophyte know assonance and alliteration, rhyme immediate and delayed, simple and polyphonic, as a musician would expect to know harmony and counterpoint and all the minutiae of his craft. No time is too great to give to these matters or to any one of them, even if the artist seldom have need of them.

Don't imagine that a thing will "go" in verse just because it's too dull to go in prose.

Don't be "viewy"—leave that to the writers of pretty little philosophic essays. Don't be descriptive; remember that the painter can describe a landscape much better than you can, and that he has to know a deal more about it.

When Shakespeare talks of the "Dawn in russet mantle clad" he presents something which the painter does not present. There is in this line of his nothing that one can call description; he presents.

Consider the way of the scientists rather than the way of an advertising agent for a new soap.

The scientist does not expect to be acclaimed as a great scientist until

---

1. This is for rhythm, his vocabulary must of course be found in his native tongue.

he has *discovered* something. He begins by learning what has been discovered already. He goes from that point onward. He does not bank on being a charming fellow personally. He does not expect his friends to applaud the results of his freshman class work. Freshmen in poetry are unfortunately not confined to a definite and recognizable class room. They are "all over the shop." Is it any wonder "the public is indifferent to poetry?"

Don't chop your stuff into separate *iambs*. Don't make each line stop dead at the end, and then begin every next line with a heave. Let the beginning of the next line catch the rise of the rhythm wave, unless you want a definite longish pause.

In short, behave as a musician, a good musician, when dealing with that phase of your art which has exact parallels in music. The same laws govern, and you are bound by no others.

Naturally, your rhythmic structure should not destroy the shape of your words, or their natural sound, or their meaning. It is improbable that, at the start, you will be able to get a rhythm-structure strong enough to affect them very much, though you may fall a victim to all sorts of false stopping due to line ends and cæsurae.

The Musician can rely on pitch and the volume of the orchestra. You can not. The term harmony is misapplied in poetry; it refers to simultaneous sounds of different pitch. There is, however, in the best verse a sort of residue of sound which remains in the ear of the hearer and acts more or less as an organ-base.

A rhyme must have in it some slight element of surprise if it is to give pleasure; it need not be bizarre or curious, but it must be well used if used at all.

Vide further Vidrac and Duhamel's notes on rhyme in *"Technique Poétique."*

That part of your poetry which strikes upon the imaginative *eye* of the reader will lose nothing by translation into a foreign tongue; that which appeals to the ear can reach only those who take it in the original.

Consider the definiteness of Dante's presentation, as compared with Milton's rhetoric. Read as much of Wordsworth as does not seem too un-utterably dull.[2]

If you want the gist of the matter go to Sappho, Catullus, Villon, Heine

---

2. Vide infra.

when he is in the vein, Gautier when he is not too frigid; or, if you have not the tongues, seek out the leisurely Chaucer. Good prose will do you no harm, and there is good discipline to be had by trying to write it.

Translation is likewise good training, if you find that your original matter "wobbles" when you try to rewrite it. The meaning of the poem to be translated can not "wobble."

If you are using a symmetrical form, don't put in what you want to say and then fill up the remaining vacuums with slush.

Don't mess up the perception of one sense by trying to define it in terms of another. This is usually only the result of being too lazy to find the exact word. To this clause there are possibly exceptions.

The first three simple prescriptions will throw out nine-tenths of all the bad poetry now accepted as standard and classic; and will prevent you from many a crime of production.

" . . . *Mais d'abord il faut être un poète*," as MM. Duhamel and Vildrac have said at the end of their little book, "*Notes sur la Technique Poétique*."

✳

Since March 1913, Ford Madox Hueffer has pointed out that Wordsworth was so intent on the ordinary or plain word that he never thought of hunting for *le mot juste*.

John Butler Yeats has handled or man-handled Wordsworth and the Victorians, and his criticism, contained in letters to his son, is now printed and available.

I do not like writing *about* art, my first, at least I think it was my first essay on the subject, was a protest against it.

PROLEGOMENA

Time was when the poet lay in a green field with his head against a tree and played his diversion on a ha'penny whistle, and Caesar's predecessors conquered the earth, and the predecessors of golden Crassus embezzled, and fashions had their say, and let him alone. And presumably he was fairly content in this circumstance, for I have small doubt that the occasional passerby, being attracted by curiosity to know why any one should lie under a tree and blow diversion on a ha'penny whistle, came and conversed with him, and that among these passers-by there was on occasion a person of charm or a young lady who had not read *Man and Superman;* and looking back upon this naïve state of affairs we call it the age of gold.

Metastasio, and he should know if any one, assures us that this age endures—even though the modern poet is expected to holloa his verses down a speaking tube to the editors of cheap magazines—S. S. McClure, or some one of that sort—even though hordes of authors meet in dreariness and drink healths to the "Copyright Bill"; even though these things be, the age of gold pertains. Imperceivably, if you like, but pertains. You meet unkempt Amyclas in a Soho restaurant and chant together of dead and forgotten things—it is a manner of speech among poets to chant of dead, half-forgotten things, there seems no special harm in it; it has always been done—and it's rather better to be a clerk in the Post Office than to look after a lot of stinking, verminous sheep—and at another hour of the day one substitutes the drawing-room for the restaurant and tea is probably more palatable than mead and mare's milk, and little cakes than honey. And in this fashion one survives the resignation of Mr Balfour, and the iniquities of the American customs-house, *e quel bufera infernal,* the periodical press. And then in the middle of it, there being apparently no other person at once capable and available one is stopped and asked to explain oneself.

I begin on the chord thus querulous, for I would much rather lie on what is left of Catullus' parlour floor and speculate the azure beneath it and the hills off to Salo and Riva with their forgotten gods moving unhindered amongst them, than discuss any processes and theories of art whatsoever. I would rather play tennis. I shall not argue.

CREDO

Rhythm.—I believe in an "absolute rhythm," a rhythm, that is, in poetry which corresponds exactly to the emotion or shade of emotion to be expressed. A man's rhythm must be interpretative, it will be, therefore, in the end, his own, uncounterfeiting, uncounterfeitable.

Symbols.—I believe that the proper and perfect symbol is the natural object, that if a man use "symbols" he must so use them that their symbolic function does not obtrude; so that *a* sense, and the poetic quality of the passage, is not lost to those who do not understand the symbol as such, to whom, for instance, a hawk is a hawk.

Technique.—I believe in technique as the test of a man's sincerity; in law when it is ascertainable; in the trampling down of every convention that impedes or obscures the determination of the law, or the precise rendering of the impulse.

Form.—I think there is a "fluid" as well as a "solid" content, that some poems may have form as a tree has form, some as water poured into a vase. That most symmetrical forms have certain uses. That a vast number of subjects cannot be precisely, and therefore not properly rendered in symmetrical forms.

"Thinking that alone worthy wherein the whole art is employed."[3] I think the artist should master all known forms and systems of metric, and I have with some persistence set about doing this, searching particularly into those periods wherein the systems came to birth or attained their maturity. It has been complained, with some justice, that I dump my note-books on the public. I think that only after a long struggle will poetry attain such a degree of development, or, if you will, modernity, that it will vitally concern people who are accustomed, in prose, to Henry James and Anatole France, in music to Debussy. I am constantly contending that it took two centuries of Provence and one of Tuscany to develop the media of Dante's masterwork, that it took the latinists of the Renaissance, and the Pleiade, and his own age of painted speech to prepare Shakespeare his tools. It is tremendously important that great poetry be written, it makes no jot of difference who writes it. The experimental demonstrations of one man may save the time of many—hence my furore over Arnaut Daniel—if a man's experiments try out one new rime, or dispense conclusively with one iota of currently accepted nonsense, he is merely playing fair with his colleagues when he chalks up his result.

No man ever writes very much poetry that "matters." In bulk, that is, no one produces much that is final, and when a man is not doing this highest thing, this saying the thing once for all and perfectly; when he is not matching Ποικιλόθρον᾽, ἀθάνατ᾽ ᾽ Αφρόδιτα or "Hist—said Kate the Queen," he had much better be making the sorts of experiment which may be of use to him in his later work, or to his successors.

"The lyf so short, the craft so long to lerne." It is a foolish thing for a man to begin his work on a too narrow foundation, it is a disgraceful

---

3. Dante, *De Volgari Eloquio.*

thing for a man's work not to show steady growth and increasing fineness from first to last.

As for "adaptations"; one finds that all the old masters of painting recommend to their pupils that they begin by copying masterwork, and proceed to their own composition.

As for "Every man his own poet," the more every man knows about poetry the better. I believe in every one writing poetry who wants to; most do. I believe in every man knowing enough of music to play "God bless our home" on the harmonium, but I do not believe in every man giving concerts and printing his sin.

The mastery of any art is the work of a lifetime. I should not discriminate between the "amateur" and the "professional." Or rather I should discriminate quite often in favour of the amateur, but I should discriminate between the amateur and the expert. It is certain that the present chaos will endure until the Art of poetry has been preached down the amateur gullet, until there is such a general understanding of the fact that poetry is an art and not a pastime; such a knowledge of technique; of technique of surface and technique of content, that the amateurs will cease to try to drown out the masters.

If a certain thing was said once for all in Atlantis or Arcadia, in 450 Before Christ or in 1290 after, it is not for us moderns to go saying it over, or to go obscuring the memory of the dead by saying the same thing with less skill and less conviction.

My pawing over the ancients and semi-ancients has been one struggle to find out what has been done, once for all, better than it can ever be done again, and to find out what remains for us to do, and plenty does remain, for if we still feel the same emotions as those which launched the thousand ships, it is quite certain that we come on these feelings differently, through different nuances, by different intellectual gradations. Each age has its own abounding gifts yet only some ages transmute them into matter of duration. No good poetry is ever written in a manner twenty years old, for to write in such a manner shows conclusively that the writer thinks from books, convention and *cliché*, and not from life, yet a man feeling the divorce of life and his art may naturally try to resurrect a forgotten mode if he finds in that mode some leaven, or if he think he sees in it some element lacking in contemporary art which might unite that art again to its sustenance, life.

In the art of Daniel and Cavalcanti, I have seen that precision which I miss in the Victorians, that explicit rendering, be it of external nature, or of emotion. Their testimony is of the eyewitness, their symptoms are first hand.

As for the nineteenth century, with all respect to its achievements, I think we shall look back upon it as a rather blurry, messy sort of a period, a rather sentimentalistic mannerish sort of a period. I say this without any self-righteousness, with no self-satisfaction.

As for there being a "movement" or my being of it, the conception of poetry as a "pure art" in the sense in which I use the term, revived with Swinburne. From the puritanical revolt to Swinburne, poetry had been merely the vehicle—yes, definitely, Arthur Symon's scruples and feelings about the word not withholding—the ox-cart and post-chaise for transmitting thoughts poetic or otherwise. And perhaps the "great Victorians," though it is doubtful, and assuredly the "nineties" continued the development of the art, confining their improvements, however, chiefly to sound and to refinements of manner.

Mr Yeats has once and for all stripped English poetry of its perdamnable rhetoric. He has boiled away all that is not poetic—and a good deal that is. He has become a classic in his own lifetime and *nel mezzo del cammin*. He has made our poetic idiom a thing pliable, a speech without inversions.

Robert Bridges, Maurice Hewlett and Frederic Manning are in their different ways seriously concerned with overhauling the metric, in testing the language and its adaptability to certain modes. Ford Hueffer is making some sort of experiments in modernity. The Provost of Oriel continues his translation of the *Divina Commedia*.

As to Twentieth century poetry, and the poetry which I expect to see written during the next decade or so, it will, I think, move against poppycock, it will be harder and saner, it will be what Mr Hewlett calls "nearer the bone." It will be as much like granite as it can be, its force will lie in its truth, its interpretative power (of course, poetic force does always rest there); I mean it will not try to seem forcible by rhetorical din, and luxurious riot. We will have fewer painted adjectives impeding the shock and stroke of it. At least for myself, I want it so, austere, direct, free from emotional slither.

✻

What is there now, in 1917, to be added?

I think the desire for vers libre is due to the sense of quantity reasserting itself after years of starvation. But I doubt if we can take over, for English, the rules of quantity laid down for Greek and Latin, mostly by Latin grammarians.

I think one should write vers libre only when one "must," that is to say, only when the "thing" builds up a rhythm more beautiful than that of set metres, or more real, more a part of the emotion of the "thing," more germane, intimate, interpretative than the measure of regular accentual verse; a rhythm which discontents one with set iambic or set anapaestic.

Eliot has said the thing very well when he said, "No *vers* is *libre* for the man who wants to do a good job."

As a matter of detail, there is vers libre with accent heavily marked as a drum-beat (as par example my "Dance Figure"), and on the other hand I think I have gone as far as can profitably be gone in the other direction (and perhaps too far). I mean I do not think one can use to any advantage rhythms much more tenuous and imperceptible than some I have used. I think progress lies rather in an attempt to approximate classical quantitative metres (NOT to copy them) than in a carelessness regarding such things.

❉

I agree with John Yeats on the relation of beauty to certitude. I prefer satire, which is due to emotion, to any sham of emotion.

I have had to write, or at least I have written a good deal about art, sculpture, painting and poetry. I have seen what seemed to me the best of contemporary work reviled and obstructed. Can any one write prose of permanent or durable interest when he is merely saying for one year what nearly every one will say at the end of three or four years? I have been battistrada for a sculptor, a painter, a novelist, several poets. I wrote also of certain French writers in *The New Age* in nineteen twelve or eleven.

I would much rather that people would look at Brzeska's sculpture and Lewis's drawings, and that they would read Joyce, Jules Romains, Eliot, than that they should read what I have said of these men, or that I should be asked to republish argumentative essays and reviews.

All that the critic can do for the reader or audience or spectator is to focus his gaze or audition. Rightly or wrongly I think my blasts and essays have done their work, and that more people are now likely to go to the sources than are likely to read this book.

Jammes's "Existences" in *"La Triomphe de la Vie"* is available. So are his early poems. I think we need a convenient anthology rather than descriptive criticism. Carl Sanburg wrote me from Chicago, "It's hell when poets can't afford to buy each other's books." Half the people who care, only borrow. In America so few people know each other that the difficulty lies more than half in distribution. Perhaps one should make an anthology: Romain's "Un Etre en Marche" and "Prières," Vildrac's "Visite." Retrospectively the fine wrought work of Laforgue, the flashes of Rimbaud, the hard-bit lines of Tristan Corbière, Tailhade's sketches in "Poèmes Aristophanesques," the "Litanies" of De Gourmont.

*

It is difficult at all times to write of the fine arts, it is almost impossible unless one can accompany one's prose with many reproductions. Still I would seize this chance or any chance to reaffirm my belief in Wyndham Lewis's genius, both in his drawings and his writings. And I would name an out of the way prose book, the "Scenes and Portraits" of Frederic Manning, as well as James Joyce's short stories and novel, "Dubliners" and the now well known "Portrait of the Artist" as well as Lewis's "Tarr," if, that is, I may treat my strange reader as if he were a new friend come into the room, intent on ransacking my bookshelf.

ONLY EMOTION ENDURES

"ONLY emotion endures." Surely it is better for me to name over the few beautiful poems that still ring in my head than for me to search my flat for back numbers of periodicals and rearrange all that I have said about friendly and hostile writers.

The first twelve lines of Padraic Colum's "Drover"; his "O woman shapely as a swan, on your account I shall not die"; Joyce's "I hear an army"; the lines of Yeats that ring in my head and in the heads of all young men of my time who care for poetry: Braseal and the Fisherman, "The fire that stirs about her when she stirs"; the later lines of "The Scholars," the faces of the Magi; William Carlos Williams's "Postlude,"

Aldington's version of "Atthis," and "H. D.'s" waves like pine tops, and her verse in "Des Imagistes" the first anthology; Hueffler's "How red your lips are" in his translation from Von der Vogelweide, his "Three Ten," the general effect of his "On Heaven"; his sense of the prose values or prose qualities in poetry; his ability to write poems that half-chant and are spoiled by a musician's additions; beyond these a poem by Alice Corbin, "One City Only," and another ending "But sliding water over a stone." These things have worn smooth in my head and I am not through with them, nor with Aldington's "In Via Sestina" nor his other poems in "Des Imagistes," though people have told me their flaws. It may be that their content is too much embedded in me for me to look back at the words.

I am almost a different person when I come to take up the argument for Eliot's poems.

T. S. Eliot, "Tradition and the Individual Talent," 1919

T. S. Eliot was thirty-one years old and living in London when this most famous of his essays was published in *The Egoist*. An expatriate American like Pound, he had already published a collection of poetry, *Prufrock and Other Observations,* whose ironic tone and sense of ennui was greatly influenced by his readings of the French symbolists, in particular Paul Verlaine, Jules LaForgue, and Tristan Corbière. With significant editing from Ezra Pound, *The Wasteland* would appear three years later, pioneering a new form, which, along with Pound's periodically appearing *Cantos,* would come to define the modernist aesthetic, one in which fragmentation, disjunction, and experimentation with multiple voices would shift attention from the poet to the poem.

One of the most influential critics of the last century, Eliot developed an aesthetic that, like Valéry's, was an argument for objectivity and craft, a further disavowal of the solipsism of the romantics. His argument for a knowledge of tradition, for a poet's erudition in both literary and political history—of his or her place in time—is not so much an argument against experimentation in form as it is a plea for the abandonment of the "wordsworthian or egotistical sublime" (as Keats called it) in the name of a "historical sense." Drawing on his debt to the Victorian poets who worked in the mode of the dramatic monologue, Browning and Tennyson in particular, Eliot takes the symbolist goal of impersonality a step further—to depersonalization. The role of the poet, thus, is one not of individual talent, but of catalyst, the poem the place where the poet disappears.

❋

Tradition and the Individual Talent

In English writing we seldom speak of tradition, though we occasionally apply its name in deploring its absence. We cannot refer to "the tradition" or to "a tradition"; at most, we employ the adjective in saying that the poetry of So-and-so is "traditional" or even "too traditional." Seldom, perhaps, does the word appear except in a phrase of censure. If otherwise, it is vaguely approbative, with the implication, as to the work approved, of some pleasing archaeological reconstruction. You can hardly make the word agreeable to English ears without this comfortable reference to the reassuring science of archaeology.

Certainly the word is not likely to appear in our appreciations of living or dead writers. Every nation, every race, has not only its own creative, but its own critical turn of mind; and is even more oblivious of the short-comings and limitations of its critical habits than of those of its creative genius. We know, or think we know, from the enormous mass of critical writing that has appeared in the French language the critical method or habit of the French; we only conclude (we are such unconscious people) that the French are "more critical" than we, and sometimes even plume ourselves a little with the fact, as if the French were the less spontaneous. Perhaps they are; but we might remind ourselves that criticism is as in-evitable as breathing, and that we should be none the worse for articulat-ing what passes in our minds when we read a book and feel an emotion about it, for criticizing our own minds in their work of criticism. One of the facts that might come to light in this process is our tendency to insist, when we praise a poet, upon those aspects of his work in which he least resembles any one else. In these aspects or parts of his work we pretend to find what is individual, what is the peculiar essence of the man. We dwell with satisfaction upon the poet's difference from his predecessors, especially his immediate predecessors; we endeavour to find something that can be isolated in order to be enjoyed. Whereas if we approach a poet without this prejudice we shall often find that not only the best, but the most individual parts of his work may be those in which the dead po-ets, his ancestors, assert their immortality most vigorously. And I do not mean the impressionable period of adolescence, but the period of full maturity.

Yet if the only form of tradition, of handing down, consisted in follow-ing the ways of the immediate generation before us in a blind or timid ad-herence to its successes, "tradition" should positively be discouraged. We have seen many such simple currents soon lost in the sand; and novelty is better than repetition. Tradition is a matter of much wider significance. It cannot be inherited, and if you want it you must obtain it by great labour. It involves, in the first place, the historical sense, which we may call nearly indispensable to any one who would continue to be a poet beyond his twenty-fifth year; and the historical sense involves a perception, not only of the pastness of the past, but of its presence; the historical sense compels a man to write not merely with his own generation in his bones, but with a feeling that the whole of literature of Europe from Homer and within it the whole of the literature of his own country has a simultaneous existence and composes a simultaneous order. This historical sense, which is a sense of the timeless as well as of the temporal and of the temporal together, is what makes a writer traditional. And it is at the same time what makes a writer most acutely conscious of his place in time, of his own contemporaneity.

No poet, no artist of any art, has his complete meaning alone. His significance, his appreciation is the appreciation of his relation to the dead poets and artists. You cannot value him alone; you must set him, for contrast and comparison, among the dead. I mean this as a principle of aesthetic, not merely historical, criticism. The necessity that he shall conform, that he shall cohere, is not onesided; what happens when a new work of art is created is something that happens simultaneously to all the works of art which preceded it. The existing monuments form an ideal order among themselves, which is modified by the introduction of the new (the really new) work of art among them. The existing order is complete before the new work arrives; for order to persist after the supervention of novelty, the *whole* existing order must be, if ever so slightly, altered; and so the relations, proportions, values of each work of art toward the whole are readjusted; and this is conformity between the old and the new. Whoever has approved this idea of order, of the form of European, of English literature will not find it preposterous that the past should be altered by the present as much as the present is directed by the past. And the poet who is aware of this will be aware of great difficulties and responsibilities.

In a peculiar sense he will be aware also that he must inevitably be judged by the standards of the past. I say judged, not amputated, by them; not judged to be as good as, or worse or better than, the dead; and certainly not judged by the canons of dead critics. It is a judgment, a comparison, in which two things are measured by each other. To conform merely would be for the new work not really to conform at all; it would not be new, and would therefore not be a work of art. And we do not quite say that the new is more valuable because it fits in; but its fitting in is a test of its value—a test, it is true, which can only be slowly and cautiously applied, for we are none of us infallible judges of conformity. We say: it appears to conform, and is perhaps individual, or it appears individual, and may conform; but we are hardly likely to find that it is one and not the other.

To proceed to a more intelligible exposition of the relation of the poet to the past: he can neither take the past as a lump, an indiscriminate bolus, nor can he form himself wholly on one or two private admirations, nor can he form himself wholly upon one preferred period. The first course is inadmissible, the second is an important experience of youth, and the third is a pleasant and highly desirable supplement. The poet must be very conscious of the main current, which does not at all flow invariably through the most distinguished reputations. He must be quite aware of the obvious fact that art never improves, but that the material of art is never quite the same. He must be aware that the mind of Europe—the mind of his own country—a mind which he learns in time to be much more important than his own private mind—is a mind which changes, and that this change is a development which abandons nothing *en route,* which does not superannuate either Shakespeare, or Homer, or the rock drawing of the Magdalenian draughtsmen. That this development, refinement perhaps, complication certainly, is not, from the point of view of the artist, any improvement. Perhaps not even an improvement from the point of view of the psychologist or not to the extent which we imagine; perhaps only in the end based upon a complication in economics and machinery. But the difference between the present and the past is that the conscious present is an awareness of the past in a way and to an extent which the past's awareness of itself cannot show.

Some one said: "The dead writers are remote from us because we *know* so much more than they did." Precisely, and they are that which we know.

I am alive to a usual objection to what is clearly part of my programme for the *métier* of poetry. The objection is that the doctrine requires a ridiculous amount of erudition (pedantry), a claim which can be rejected by appeal to the lives of poets in any pantheon. It will even be affirmed that much learning deadens or perverts poetic sensibility. While, however, we persist in believing that a poet ought to know as much as will not encroach upon his necessary receptivity and necessary laziness, it is not desirable to confine knowledge to whatever can be put into a useful shape for examinations, drawing-rooms, or the still more pretentious modes of publicity. Some can absorb knowledge, the more tardy must sweat for it. Shakespeare acquired more essential history from Plutarch than most men could from the whole British Museum. What is to be insisted upon is that the poet must develop or procure the consciousness of the past and that he should continue to develop this consciousness throughout his career.

What happens is a continual surrender of himself as he is at the moment to something which is more valuable. The progress of an artist is a continual self-sacrifice, a continual extinction of personality.

There remains to define this process of depersonalization and its relation to the sense of tradition. It is in this depersonalization that art may be said to approach the condition of science. I, therefore, invite you to consider, as a suggestive analogy, the action which takes place when a bit of finely filiated platinum is introduced into a chamber containing oxygen and sulphur dioxide.

II

Honest criticism and sensitive appreciation are directed not upon the poet but upon the poetry. If we attend to the confused cries of the newspaper critics and the *susurrus* of popular repetition that follows, we shall hear the names of poets in great numbers; if we seek not Blue-book knowledge but the enjoyment of poetry, and ask for a poem, we shall seldom find it. I have tried to point out the importance of the relation of the poem to other poems by other authors, and suggested the conception of poetry as a living whole of all the poetry that has ever been written. The other aspect of this Impersonal theory of poetry is the relation of the poem to its author. And I hinted, by an analogy, that the mind of the mature poet differs from that of the immature one not precisely in any valuation of "personality," not being necessarily more interesting, or having "more to say," but rather by being a more finely perfected medium in which special, or very varied, feelings are at liberty to enter into new combination.

The analogy was that of the catalyst. When the two gases previously mentioned are mixed in the presence of a filament of platinum, they form sulphurous acid. This combination takes place only if the platinum is present; nevertheless the newly formed acid contains no trace of platinum, and the platinum itself is apparently unaffected; has remained inert, neutral, and unchanged. The mind of the poet is the shred of platinum. It may partly or exclusively operate upon the experience of the man himself;

but, the more perfect the artist, the more completely separate in him will be the man who suffers and the mind which creates; the more perfectly will the mind digest and transmute the passions which are its material.

The experience, you will notice, the elements which enter the presence of the transforming catalyst, are of two kinds: emotions and feelings. The effect of a work of art upon the person who enjoys it is an experience different in kind from any experience not of art. It may be formed out of one emotion, or may be a combination of several; and various feelings, inhering for the writer in particular words or phrases or images, may be added to compose the final result. Or great poetry may be made without the direct use of any emotion whatever: composed out of feelings solely. Canto XV of the *Inferno* (Brunetto Latini) is a working up of the emotion evident in the situation; but the effect, though single as that of any work of art, is obtained by considerable complexity of detail. The last quatrain gives an image, a feeling attaching to an image, which "came," which did not develop simply out of what precedes, but which was probably in suspension in the poet's mind until the proper combination arrived for it to add itself to. The poet's mind is in fact a receptacle for seizing and storing up numberless feelings, phrases, images, which remain there until all the particles which can unite to form a new compound are present together.

If you compare several representative passages of the greatest poetry you see how great is the variety of types of combination, and also how completely any semi-ethical criterion of "sublimity" misses the mark. For it is not the "greatness," the intensity, of the emotions, the components, but the intensity of the artistic process, the pressure, so to speak, under which the fusion takes place, that counts. The episode of Paolo and Francesca employs a definite emotion, but the intensity of the poetry is something quite different from whatever intensity in the supposed experience it may give the impression of. It is no more intense, furthermore, than Canto XXVI, the voyage of Ulysses, which has not the direct dependence upon an emotion. Great variety is possible in the process of transmutation of emotion: the murder of Agamemnon, or the agony of Othello, gives an artistic effect apparently closer to a possible original than the scenes from Dante. In the *Agamemnon,* the artistic emotion approximates to the emotion of an actual spectator; in *Othello* to the emotion of the protagonist himself. But the difference between art and the event is always absolute; the combination which is the murder of Agamemnon is probably as complex as that which is the voyage of Ulysses. In either case there has been a fusion of elements.

The ode of Keats contains a number of feelings which have nothing particular to do with the nightingale, but which the nightingale, partly, perhaps, because of its attractive name, and partly because of its reputation, served to bring together.

The point of view which I am struggling to attack is perhaps related to the metaphysical theory of the substantial unity of the soul: for my meaning is, that the poet has, not a "personality" to express, but a particular medium, which is only a medium and not a personality, in which impressions and experiences combine in peculiar and unexpected ways. Impressions and experiences which are important for the man may take no place in the poetry, and those which become important in the poetry may play quite a negligible part in the man, the personality.

I will quote a passage which is unfamiliar enough to be regarded with fresh attention in the light—or darkness—of these observations:

> *And now methinks I could e'en chide myself*
> *For doating on her beauty, though her death*
> *Shall be revenged after no common action.*
> *Does the silkworm expend her yellow labours*
> *For thee? For thee does she undo herself?*
> *Are lordships sold to maintain ladyships*
> *For the poor benefit of a bewildering minute?*
> *Why does yon fellow falsify highways,*
> *And put his life between the judge's lips,*
> *To refine such a thing—keeps horse and men*
> *To beat their valours for her? . . .*

In this passage (as is evident if it is taken in its context) there is a combination of positive and negative emotions: an intensely strong attraction toward beauty and an equally intense fascination by the ugliness which is contrasted with it and which destroys it. This balance of contrasted emotion is in the dramatic situation to which the speech is pertinent, but that situation alone is inadequate to it. This is, so to speak, the structural emotion, provided by the drama. But the whole effect, the dominant tone, is due to the fact that a number of floating feelings, having an affinity to this emotion by no means superficially evident, have combined with it to give us a new art emotion.

It is not in his personal emotions, the emotions provoked by particular events in his life, that the poet is in any way remarkable or interesting.

His particular emotions may be simple, or crude, or flat. The emotion in his poetry will be a very complex thing, but not with the complexity of the emotions of people who have very complex or unusual emotions in life. One error, in fact, of eccentricity in poetry is to seek for new human emotions to express; and in this search for novelty in the wrong place it discovers the perverse. The business of the poet is not to find new emotions, but to use the ordinary ones and, in working them up into poetry, to express feelings which are not in actual emotions at all. And emotions which he has never experienced will serve his turn as well as those familiar to him. Consequently, we must believe that "emotion recollected in tranquillity" is an inexact formula. For it is neither emotion, nor recollection, nor, without distortion of meaning, tranquillity. It is a concentration, and a new thing resulting from the concentration, of a very great number of experiences which to the practical and active person would not seem to be experiences at all; it is a concentration which does not happen consciously or of deliberation. These experiences are not "recollected," and they finally unite in an atmosphere which is "tranquil" only in that it is a passive attending upon the event. Of course this is not quite the whole story. There is a great deal, in the writing of poetry, which must be conscious and deliberate. In fact, the bad poet is usually unconscious where he ought to be conscious, and conscious where he ought to be unconscious. Both errors tend to make him "personal." Poetry is not a turning loose of emotion, but an escape from emotion; it is not the expression of personality, but an escape from personality. But, of course, only those who have personality and emotions know what it means to want to escape from these things.

III

σ δε νοῦζ ἴσωζ Θειότεριόν τι χαὶ ἀπαθέζ ἐστιν

This essay proposes to halt at the frontier of metaphysics or mysticism, and confine itself to such practical conclusions as can be applied by the responsible person interested in poetry. To divert interest from the poet to the poetry is a laudable aim: for it would conduce to a juster estimation of actual poetry, good and bad. There are many people who appreciate the expression of sincere emotion in verse, and there is a smaller number of people who can appreciate technical excellence. But very few know when there is an expression of *significant* emotion, emotion which has its life in the poem and not in the history of the poet. The emotion of art is impersonal. And the poet cannot reach this impersonality without surrendering himself wholly to the work to be done. And he is not likely to know what is to be done unless he lives in what is not merely the present, but the present moment of the past, unless he is conscious, not of what is dead, but of what is already living.

Mina Loy, "Modern Poetry," 1925

"Prose bewitched" is what, in a letter to Robert Bridges, Gerard Manley Hopkins called unmetered poetry, and that is exactly what, a little over fifty years later, Mina Loy wrote: unmetered, unrhymed, most often unpunctuated verse which, even more scandalously, was often about sex. It was 1925. The New York Armory Show—and New York Dada—had come and gone with Marcell Duchamp's notorious toilet seat. William Carlos Williams had published his major experimentations *Kora in Hell* (1920) and *Spring and All* (1923). James Joyce's *Ulysses* had appeared three years earlier. And Myrna Loy, born in England, having lived in Florence with Tommaso Marinetti while he was proselytizing and publishing his manifestos of futurism, was now living in New York.

Loy—promoter of futurism, feminism,, and modernism—did not publish much criticism. Yet this essay, which appeared in *Charm*, a women's fashion magazine, conveys the sense of literary life in New York in the middle of a revolution. Widely published in magazines of the day such as *Little Review, Others, Transatlantic Review, Blind Man,* and Steiglitz's *Camera Work*, where her "Aphorisms of Futurism" appeared, Loy only published two books in her lifetime: *Lunar Baedecker* and *Lunar Baedeker & Time-Tables*. They are only recently back in print.

✳

Modern Poetry

Poetry is prose bewitched, a music made of visual thoughts, the sound of an idea.

The new poetry of the English language has proceeded out of America. Of things American it attains the aristocratic situation of vitality. This unexpectedly realized valuation of American jazz and American poetry is endorsed by two publics; the one universal, the other infinitesimal in comparison.

And why has the collective spirit of the modern world, of which both are the reflection, recognized itself unanimously in the new music of unprecedented instruments, and so rarely in the new poetry of unprecedented verse? It is because the sound of music capturing our involuntary attention is so easy to get in touch with, while the silent sound of poetry requires our voluntary attention to obliterate the cold barrier of print with the whole "intelligence of our senses." And many of us who have no habit of reading not alone with the eye but also with the ear, have—especially at a superficial first reading—overlooked the beauty of it.

More than to read poetry we must listen to poetry. All reading is the evocation of speech; the difference in our approach, then, in reading a poem or a newspaper is that our attitude in reading a poem must be rather that of listening to and looking at a pictured song. Modern poetry, like music, has received a fresh impetus from contemporary life; they have both gained in precipitance of movement. The structure of all poetry is the movement that an active individuality makes in expressing itself. Poetic rhythm, of which we have all spoken so much, is the chart of a temperament.

The variety and felicity of these structural movements in modern verse has more than vindicated the rebellion against tradition. It will be found that one can recognize each of the modern poets' work by the gait of their mentality. Or rather that the formation of their verses is determined by the spontaneous tempo of their response to life. And if at first it appears irksome to adjust pleasure to unaccustomed meters, let us reflect in time that hexameters and alexandrines, before they became poetic laws, originated as the spontaneous structure of a poet's inspiration.

Imagine a tennis champion who became inspired to write poetry, would not his verse be likely to embody the rhythmic transit of skimming balls? Would not his meter depend on his way of life, would it not form itself, without having recourse to traditional, remembered, or accepted forms? This, then, is the secret of the new poetry. It is the direct response of the poet's mind to the modern world of varieties in which he finds himself. In each one we can discover his particular inheritance of that world's beauty.

Close as this relationship of poetry to music is, I think only once has the logical transition from verse to music, on which I had so often speculated, been made, and that by the American, Ezra Pound. To speak of the modern movement is to speak of him; the masterly impresario of modern poets, for without the discoveries he made with his poet's instinct for poetry, this modern movement would still be rather a nebula than the constellation it has become. Not only a famous poet, but a man of action, he gave the public the required push on to modern poetry at the psychological moment. Pound, the purveyor of geniuses to such journals as the "Little Review," on which he conferred immortality by procuring for its pages the manuscripts of Joyce's "Ulysses." Almost together with the publication of his magnificent Cantos, his music was played in Paris; it utters the communings of a poet's mind with itself making decisions on harmony.

It was inevitable that the renaissance of poetry should proceed out of America, where latterly a thousand languages have been born, and each one, for purposes of communication at least, English—English enriched and variegated with the grammatical structure and voice-inflection of many races, in novel alloy with the fundamental time-is-money idiom of the United States, discovered by the newspaper cartoonists.

This composite language is a very living language, it grows as you speak. For the true American appears to be ashamed to say anything in the way it has been said before. Every moment he ingeniously coins new words for old ideas, to keep good humor warm. And on the baser avenues of Manhattan every voice swings to the triple rhythm of its race, its citizenship and its personality.

Out of the welter of this unclassifiable speech, while professors of Harvard and Oxford labored to preserve "God's English," the muse of modern literature arose, and her tongue had been loosened in the melting-pot.

You may think it impossible to conjure up the relationship of expression between the high browest modern poets and an adolescent Slav who has speculated in a wholesale job-lot of mandarines and is trying to sell them in a retail market on First Avenue. But it lies simply in this: both have had to become adapted to a country where the mind has to put on its verbal clothes at terrific speed if it would speak in time; where no one will listen if you attack him twice with the same missile of argument. And, that the ear that has listened to the greatest number of sounds will have the most to choose from when it comes to self-expression, each has been liberally educated in the flexibility of phrases.

So in the American poet wherever he may wander, however he may engage himself with an older culture, there has occurred no Europeanization of his fundamental advantage, the acuter shock of the New World consciousness upon life. His is still poetry that has proceeded out of America.

The harvest from this recent fertiliser is the poetry of E. E. Cummings. Where other poets have failed for being too modern he is more modern still, and altogether successful; where others were entirely anti-human in their fear of sentimentality, he keeps that rich compassion that poets having for common things leads them to deck them with their own conception; for surely if there were a heaven it would be where this horrible ugliness of human life would arise self-consciously as that which the poet has made of it.

Cummings has united free verse and rhyme which so urgently needed to be married. His rhymes are quite fresh—"radish-red" and "hazarded," and the freeness of his verse gives them a totally new metric relationship.

But fundamentally he is a great poet because his verse wells up abundantly from the foundations of his soul; a sonorous dynamo. And as I believe that the quality of genius must be largely unconscious, I can understand how Cummings can turn out such gabble when he is not being sublime. He is very often sublime.

In reading modern poetry one should beware of allowing mere technical eccentricities or grammatical disturbances to turn us from the main issue which is to get at the poem's reality. We should remember that this seeming strangeness is inevitable when any writer has come into an independent contact with nature: to each she must show herself in a new manner, for each has a different organic personality for perceiving her.

When the little controversies over what is permissible in art evaporate, we will always find that the seeming strangeness has disappeared with them in the larger aspect of the work which has the eternal quality that is common to all true art.

Out of the past most poets, after all, call to us with one or two perfect poems. And we have not complained of being too poor. You will find that the moderns have already done as much.

H. D., who is an interesting example of my claims for an American poet who engages with an older culture, has written at least two perfect poems: one about a swan.

Marianne Moore, whose writing so often amusingly suggests the soliloquies of a library clock, has written at least one perfect poem, "The Fish."

Lawrence Vail has written one perfect poem, the second "Cannibalistic Love Song," a snatch of primitive ideation with a rhythm as essential as daylight. Maxwell Bodenheim, I think, had one among his early work, and perfect also is a poem of Carlos Williams about the wind on a window-pane.

Williams brings me to a distinction that it is necessary to make in speaking of modern poets. Those I have spoken of are poets according to the old as well as the new reckoning; there are others who are poets only according to the new reckoning. They are headed by the doctor, Carlos Williams. Here is the poet whose expression derives from his life. He is a doctor. He loves bare facts. He is also a poet, he must recreate everything to suit himself. How can he reconcile these two selves?

Williams will make a poem of a bare fact—just show you something he noticed. The doctor wishes you to know just how uncompromisingly itself that fact is. But the poet would like you to realize all that it means to him, and he throws that bare fact onto paper in such a way that it becomes a part of Williams' own nature as well as the thing itself. That is the new rhythm.

Langston Hughes, "The Negro Artist and the Racial Mountain," 1926

Contemporary with New York Dada, the Harlem Renaissance was waging its own revolt from the status quo, which meant, for African American writers and poets such as Langston Hughes, Countee Cullen, Claude McKay, Jean Toomer, Sterling Brown, and Zora Neal Hurston, the white literary establishment. Not only a renaissance in literature, but also in theater, visual arts, and especially music, the Harlem Renaissance that began in the 1920s and 1930s proclaimed a new spirit for the arts and, consequently—as in Apollinaire's Paris—the creation of a new role for the poets.

Hughes was twenty-four years old when his essay "The Negro Artist and the Racial Mountain" appeared in *The Nation*. In part an aesthetic statement, speaking as it does for the use in poetry of common subjects and the capturing of the everyday speech and rhythms of black people in America, it is also a declaration of aesthetic freedom from white tradition.

The essay is also a defense, as Wordsworth's "Preface" to the *Lyrical Ballads* is, in anticipation of criticism leveled at his own work, in particular his second book of poems, *Fine Clothes to the Jew,* which, like the *Lyrical Ballads,* provoked harsh criticism from black and white critics alike, often for the same reasons: use of the vernacular and treatment of common people and common themes. "The poet lowrate from Harlem," declared Chicago's black newspaper, *The Whip.* In his own poems, Hughes searched for a rhythm which would adequately express the new age and found it in blues and jazz forms.

※

The Negro Artist and the Racial Mountain

One of the most promising of the young Negro poets said to me once, "I want to be a poet—not a Negro poet," meaning, I believe, "I want to write like a white poet"; meaning subconsciously, "I would like to be a white poet"; meaning behind that, "I would like to be white." And I was sorry the young man said that, for no great poet has ever been afraid of being himself. And I doubted then that, with his desire to run away spiritually from his race, this boy would ever be a great poet. But this is the mountain standing in the way of any true Negro art in America—this urge within the race toward whiteness, the desire to pour racial individuality into the mold of American standardization, and to be as little Negro and as much American as possible.

But let us look at the immediate background of this young poet. His family is of what I suppose one would call the Negro middle class: people who are by no means rich yet never uncomfortable nor hungry—smug, contented, respectable folk, members of the Baptist church. The father goes to work every morning. He is the chief steward at a large white club. The mother sometimes does fancy sewing or supervises parties for the rich families of the town. The children go to a mixed school. In the home they read white papers and magazines. And the mother often says, "Don't be like niggers," when the children are bad. A frequent phrase from the father is, "Look how well a white man does things." And so the word white comes to be unconsciously a symbol of all the virtues. It holds for the children beauty, morality, and money. The whisper of "I want to be white" runs silently through their minds. This young poet's home is, I believe, a fairly typical home of the colored middle class. One sees immediately how difficult it would be for an artist born in such a home to interest himself in interpreting the beauty of his own people. He is never taught to see that beauty. He is taught rather not to see it, or if he does, to be ashamed of it when it is not according to Caucasian patterns.

For racial culture the home of a self-styled "high-class" Negro has nothing better to offer. Instead there will be perhaps more aping of things white than in a less cultured or less wealthy home. The father is perhaps a doctor, lawyer, landowner, or politician. The mother may be a social worker, or a teacher, or she may do nothing and have a maid. Father is often dark but he has usually married the lightest woman he could find. The family attend a fashionable church where few really colored faces are to be found. And they themselves draw a color line. In the North they go to white theaters and white movies. And in the South they have at least two cars and a house "like white folks." Nordic manners, Nordic faces, Nordic hair, Nordic art (if any), and an Episcopal heaven. A very high mountain indeed for the would-be racial artist to climb in order to discover himself and his people.

But then there are the low-down folks, the so-called common element, and they are the majority—may the Lord be praised! The people who have their nip of gin on Saturday nights and are not too important to themselves or the community, or too well fed, or too learned to watch the lazy world go round. They live on Seventh Street in Washington or State Street in Chicago and they do not particularly care whether they are like white folks or anybody else. Their joy runs, bang! into ecstasy. Their religion soars to a shout. Work maybe a little today, rest a little tomorrow. Play awhile. Sing awhile. O, let's dance! These common people are not afraid of spirituals, as for a long time their more intellectual brethren were, and jazz is their child. They furnish a wealth of colorful, distinctive material for any artist because they still hold their own individuality in the face of American standardization. And perhaps these common people will give to the world its truly great Negro artist, the one who is not afraid to be himself. Whereas the better-class Negro would tell the artist what to do, the people at least let him alone when he does appear. And they are not ashamed of him—if they know he exists at all. And they accept what beauty is their own without question.

Certainly there is, for the American Negro artist who can escape the restrictions the more advanced among his own group would put upon him, a great field of unused material ready for his art. Without going outside his race, and even among the better classes with their "white" culture and conscious American manners, but still Negro enough to be different, there is sufficient material to furnish a black artist with a lifetime of creative work. And when he chooses to touch on the relations between Negroes and whites in this country with their innumerable overtones and undertones, surely, and especially for literature and the drama, there is an inexhaustible supply of themes at hand. To these the Negro artist can give his racial individuality, his heritage of rhythm and warmth, and his incongruous humor that so often, as in the Blues, becomes ironic laughter mixed with tears. But let us look again at the mountain.

A prominent Negro clubwoman in Philadelphia paid eleven dollars to hear Raquel Meller sing Andalusian popular songs. But she told me a few weeks before she would not think of going to hear "that woman," Clara Smith, a great black artist, sing Negro folk songs. And many an upper-class Negro church, even now, would not dream of employing a spiritual in its services. The drab melodies in white folks' hymnbooks are much to be preferred. "We want to worship the Lord correctly and quietly. We don't believe in 'shouting.' Let's be dull like the Nordics," they say, in effect.

The road for the serious black artist, then, who would produce a racial art is most certainly rocky and the mountain is high. Until recently, he received almost no encouragement for his work from either white or colored people. The fine novels of Chestnutt go out of print with neither race noticing their passing. The quaint charm and humor of Dunbar's dialect verse brought to him, in his day, largely the same kind of encouragement one would give a sideshow freak (A colored man writing poetry! How odd!) or a clown (How amusing!).

The present vogue in things Negro, although it may do as much harm as good for the budding colored artist, has at least done this: it has brought him forcibly to the attention of his own people among whom for so long, unless the other race had noticed him beforehand, he was a prophet with little honor. I understand that Charles Gilpin acted for years in Negro theaters without any special acclaim from his own, but when Broadway gave him eight curtain calls, Negroes, too, began to beat a tin pan in his honor. I know a young colored writer, a manual worker by day, who had been writing well for the colored magazines for some years, but it was not until he recently broke into the white publications and his first book was accepted by a prominent New York publisher that the "best" Negroes in his city took the trouble to discover that he lived there. Then almost immediately they decided to give a grand dinner for him. But the society ladies were careful to whisper to his mother that perhaps she'd better not come. They were not sure she would have an evening gown.

The Negro artist works against an undertow of sharp criticism and misunderstanding from his own group and unintentional bribes from the whites. "O, be respectable, write about nice people, show how good we are," say the Negroes. "Be stereotyped, don't go too far, don't shatter our illusions about you, don't amuse us too seriously. We will pay you," say the whites. Both would have told Jean Toomer not to write "Cane." The colored people did not praise it. The white people did not buy it. Most of the colored people who did read "Cane" hated it. They are afraid of it. Although the critics gave it good reviews the public remained indifferent. Yet (excepting the work of Du Bois) "Cane" contains the finest prose written by a Negro in America. And like the singing of Robeson, it is truly racial.

But in spite of the Nordicized Negro intelligentsia and the desires of some white editors we have an honest American Negro literature already with us. Now I await the rise of the Negro theater. Our folk music, having achieved world-wide fame, offers itself to the genius of the great individual American Negro composer who is to come. And within the next decade I expect to see the work of a growing school of colored artists who paint and model the beauty of dark faces and create with new technique the expressions of their own soul-world. And the Negro dancers who will dance like flame and the singers who will continue to carry our songs to all who listen—they will be with us in even greater numbers tomorrow.

Most of my own poems are racial in theme and treatment, derived from the life I know. In many of them I try to grasp and hold some of the meanings and rhythms of jazz. I am sincere as I know how to be in these poems and yet after every reading I answer questions like these from my own people: Do you think Negroes should always write about Negroes? I wish you wouldn't read some of your poems to white folks. How do you find any thing interesting in a place like a cabaret? Why do you write about black people? You aren't black. What makes you do so many jazz poems?

But jazz to me is one of the inherent expressions of Negro life in America: the eternal tom-tom beating in the Negro soul—the tom-tom of revolt against weariness in a white world, a world of subway trains, and work, work, work; the tom-tom of joy and laughter, and pain swallowed in a smile. Yet the Philadelphia clubwoman is ashamed to say that her race created it and she does not like me to write about it. The old subconscious "white is best" runs through her mind. Years of study under white teachers, a lifetime of white books, pictures, and papers, and white manners, morals, and Puritan standards made her dislike the spirituals. And now she turns up her nose at jazz and all its manifestations—likewise almost everything else distinctly racial. She doesn't care for the Winold Reiss portraits of Negroes because they are "too Negro." She does not want a true picture of herself from anybody. She wants the artist to flatter her, to make the white world believe that all Negroes are as smug and as near white in soul as she wants to be. But, to my mind, it is the duty of the younger Negro artist, if he accepts any duties at all from outsiders, to change through the force of his art that old whispering "I want to be white," hidden in the aspirations of his people, to "Why should I want to be white? I am Negro—and beautiful!"

So I am ashamed for the black poet who says, "I want to be a poet, not a Negro poet," as though his own racial world were not as interesting as any other world. I am ashamed, too, for the colored artist who runs from the painting of Negro faces to the painting of sunsets after the manner of the academicians because he fears the strange un-whiteness of his own features. An artist must be free to choose what he does, certainly, but he must also never be afraid to do what he might choose.

Let the blare of Negro jazz bands and the bellowing voice of Bessie Smith singing Blues penetrate the closed ears of the colored near-intellectuals until they listen and perhaps understand. Let Paul Robeson singing "Water Boy," and Rudolph Fisher writing about the streets of Harlem, and Jean Toomer holding the heart of Georgia in his hands, and Aaron Douglas drawing strange black fantasies cause the smug Negro middle class to turn from their white, respectable, ordinary books and papers to catch a glimmer of their own beauty. We younger Negro artists who create now intend to express our individual dark-skinned selves without fear of shame. If white people are pleased we are glad. If they are not, it doesn't matter. We know we are beautiful. And ugly too. The tom-tom cries and the tom-tom laughs. If colored people are pleased we are glad. If they are not, their displeasure doesn't matter either. We build our temples for tomorrow, strong as we know how, and we stand on top of the mountain, free within ourselves.

Louis Zukofsky, "An Objective," 1930–1931

"An Objective," republished here in the elided and concise form that
Louis Zukofsky wished for it when he revised it in 1967, was originally
three essays he wrote in 1930 and 1931: "Program: 'Objectivists'" and
"Sincerity and Objectification" appeared in the objectivist issue of *Poetry*
for which he was guest editor, and "Recencies," as the preface to his *An
"Objectivists" Anthology*. The objectivists—a term Zukofsky later argued
was never the name of a movement but meant as an adjective describing
the work of certain poets—included such poets as George Oppen,
Lorine Niedecker, Charles Reznikoff, and William Carlos Williams,
as well as Zukofsky himself.

Born in New York City in 1904, author of the book-length experimental poem, "A," Zukofsky was greatly influenced by Pound and
Williams. His poetics is akin to imagism in its belief in directness of
presentation (the original version of "Recencies" included part of Pound's
imagist manifesto) and avoidance of excess. What he says about Pound
could easily be said of him: "He has treated the arts as a science so that
their morality and immorality become a matter of accuracy and inaccu-
racy." His is a poetics based on what he calls "sincerity" and "objectification," a kind of machinist language calling for detail and precision
and concreteness. Where Paul Valéry says, "A poem is really a kind of
machine for producing the poetic state of mind by means of words," and
Williams calls it "a little (or big) machine made of words," with Zukofsky the poem moves even further toward its existence as an object constructed, and constructed with utmost attention paid to the language itself. The poet, thus, becomes a machinist or master craftsman/woman,
or, as Zukofsky says in another essay, one of "all who achieve construc-
tions apart from themselves."

❋

An Objective

I

An Objective: (Optics)—The lens bringing the rays from an object to a focus. That which is aimed at. (Use extended to poetry)—Desire for what is objectively perfect, inextricably the direction of historic and contemporary particulars.

It is understood that historic and contemporary particulars may mean a thing or things as well as an event or a chain of events: i.e. an Egyptian pulled-glass bottle in the shape of a fish or oak leaves, as well as the performance of Bach's *Matthew Passion* in Leipzig, and the rise of metallurgical plants in Siberia.

Omission of names is prompted by the historical method of the Chinese sage who wrote, "Then for nine reigns there was no literary production."

None at all; because there was neither consciousness of the "objectively perfect" nor an interest in clear or vital "particulars." Nothing—neither a new object nor the stripping of an old to the light—was "aimed at." Strabismus may be a topic of interest between two strabismics; those who see straight look away.

II

In sincerity shapes appear concomitants of word combinations, precursors of (if there is continuance) completed sound or structure, melody or form. Writing occurs which is the detail, not mirage, of seeing, of thinking with the things as they exist, and of directing them along a line of melody. Shapes suggest themselves, and the mind senses and receives awareness. Parallels sought for in the other arts call up the perfect line of occasional drawing, the clear beginnings of sculpture not proceeded with.

Presented with sincerity, the mind even tends to supply, in further suggestion, which does not attain rested totality, the totality not always found in sincerity and necessary only for perfect rest, complete appreciation. This rested totality may be called objectification—the apprehension satisfied completely as to the appearance of the art form as an object. That is: distinct from print which records action and existence and incites the mind to further suggestion, there exists, though it may not be harbored as solidity in the crook of an elbow, writing (audibility in two-dimensional print) which is an object or affects the mind as such. The codifications of the rhetoric books may have something to do with an explanation of this attainment, but its character may be simply described as the arrangement, into one apprehended unit, of minor units of sincerity—in other words, the resolving of words and their ideation into structure. Granted that the word combination "minor unit of sincerity" is an ironic index of the degradation of the power of the individual word in a culture which seems hardly to know that each word in itself is an arrangement, it may be said that each word possesses objectification to a powerful degree; but that the facts carried by one word are, in view of the preponderance of facts carried by combinations of words, not sufficiently explicit to warrant a realization of rested totality such as might be designated an art form. Yet the objectification which is a poem, or a unit of structural prose, may exist in a line or very few lines. The mind may conceivably prefer one object to another—the energy of the heat which is Aten to the benignness of the light which is Athena. But this is a matter of preference rather than the invalidation of the object not preferred. It is assumed that epistemological problems do not affect existence, that a personal structure of relations might be a definite object, or *vice versa*.

At any time, objectification in writing is rare. The poems or the prose structures of a generation are few. Properly no verse should be called a poem if it does not convey the totality of perfect rest.

It is questionable, however, whether the state of rest achieved by objectification is more pertinent to the mind than presentation in detail: the isolation of each noun so that in itself it is an image, the grouping of nouns so that they partake of the quality of things being together without violence to their individual intact natures, simple sensory adjectives as necessary as the nouns.

The disadvantage of strained metaphor is not that it is necessarily sentimental (the sentimental may at times have its positive personal qualities) but that it carries the mind to a diffuse everywhere and leaves it nowhere. One is brought back to the entirety of the single word which is in itself a relation, an implied metaphor, an arrangement, a harmony or a dissonance.

The economy of presentation in writing is a reassertion of faith that the combined letters—the words—are absolute symbols for objects, states, acts, interrelations, thoughts about them. If not, why use words—new or old?

III

The several definitions of *An Objective* and the use of this term extended to poetry are from the sixth movement of "A." The lines referred to read:

> The melody, the rest are accessory—
> ... my one voice; my other ...
> An objective—rays of the object brought to a focus,
> An objective—nature as creator—desire for what is objectively perfect,
> Inextricably the direction of historic and contemporary particulars.

Assuming the intention of these lines to be poetry, the implications are that a critic began as a poet, and that as a poet he had implicitly to be a critic.

A poet finds the continuously present analysis of his work preferable to criticism so-called. Yet what other criticism exclusive of his poem seems permissible? In preference to the brands of circumlocution requisite to ponderous journals, a "prose" criticism whose analysis follows without undue length of misinterpretation the more concise analysis of a considered poem seems permissible, if the general good demands such a prose. The direction of this prose, though it will be definition, will also be poetry, arising from the same source or what to a third reader might seem the same source as the poetry—a poetically charged mentality. Though perhaps gratifying to the poet whose poem is under observation—this prose, with all its poetic direction and right impetus, should, to the critic himself with his merely poetically charged mentality, seem secondary even tertiary and less; i.e. compared with that act which is a poem.

The graceless error of writing down to those who consciously want a something else from poetry—not poetry—as some stay for their own vanity; to "sometimes" think that minds elaborately equipped with specific information, like science, must always confuse it with other specific information, like poetry. That may be the case with unfortunates. The point, however, would be not to proffer solemnly or whiningly confusions to the confused, but to indicate by energetic mental behavior how certain information may be useful to other information, and when the divisions which signalize them are necessary.

Such a process does not need to be accurately painful; rather it should be painlessly complete—as certain people are complete and ready to go anywhere but to the doctor.

Certainly the more precise the writing, the purer the poetry—and going back to the critic, he should know what pure poetry is. Or we shall never know how to dispose of our sensations before we begin to read poetry, or how to raise them to honesty and intelligence—as well as—those of us who are precisely afflicted—to that precision of style, we should do well to cultivate.

A poem. A poem as object—And yet certainly it arose in the veins and capillaries, if only in the intelligence—Experienced—(every word can't be overdefined) experienced as an object—Perfect rest—Or nature as creator, existing perfect, experience perfecting activity of existence, making it—theologically, perhaps—like the Ineffable—

A poem. Also the materials which are outside (?) the veins and capillaries—The context—The context necessarily dealing with a world outside of it—The desire for what is objectively perfect, inextricably the direction of historic and contemporary particulars—A desire to place everything—everything aptly, perfectly, belonging within, one with, a context—

A poem. The context based on a world—Idle metaphor—a lime base— a fibre—not merely a charged vacuum tube—an aerie of personation—the desire for inclusiveness—The desire for an inclusive object.

A poem. This object in process—The poem as a job—A classic—

Homer's *the wet waves* not our *the wet waves* but enough association in the three words to make a context capable of extension from its time into the present. Because, there is, though meanings change, a linguistic etiquette, a record possibly clear to us as the usage of a past context—The context as it first meant—or if this may not be believed—an arrived-at equilibrium—or at least the past not even guessed by us arrived at an equilibrium of meaning determined by new meanings of word against word contemporarily read.

A poem: a context associated with "musical" shape, musical with quotation marks since it is not of notes as music, but of words more variable than variables, and used outside as well as within the context with communicative reference.

Impossible to communicate anything but particulars—historic and contemporary—things, human beings as things their instrumentalities of capillaries and veins binding up and bound up with events and contingencies. The revolutionary word if it must revolve cannot escape having a reference. It is not infinite. Even the infinite is a term.

Only good poetry—good an unnecessary adjective—is contemporary or classical. A standard of taste can be characterized only by acceptance of particular communication and concerned, so to speak, whenever the intelligence is in danger of being cluttered, with exclusions—not with books but with poetic invention. The nothing, not pure nothing, left over is not a matter of "recencies," but a matter of *pasts*, maybe *pasties.*

It would be just as well then dealing with "recencies" to deal with Donne or Shakespeare, if one knew them as well as a linguistic usage not their own can know them. And yet contexts and inventions seem to have been derived from them.

One can go further, try to dissect capillaries or intelligent nerves—and speak of the image felt as duration or perhaps of the image as the existence of the shape and movement of the poetic object. The poet's image is not dissociable from the movement or the cadenced shape of the poem.

An idea—not an empty concept. An idea—its value including its meaning. The desk, i.e. as object including its value—The object unrelated to palpable or predatory intent—Also the meaning, or what should be the meaning of science in modern civilization as pointed out in Thorstein Veblen.

No predatory manifestation—Yet a manifestation making the mind more temperate because the poem exists and has perhaps recorded both state and individual.

The components of the poetic object continued: the sound and pitch emphasis of a word are never apart from its meaning.

In this sense each poem has its own laws, since no criticism can take care of all the differences which each new composition in words is. Yet criticism would hardly be different if musical notations or signs were used instead of words. Example: any piece of original music and the special criticism it produces.

The components of the poetic object continued:

Typography—certainly—if print and the arrangement of it will help tell how the voice should sound. It is questionable on the other hand whether the letters of the alphabet can be felt as the Chinese feel their written characters. Yet most western poets of consequence seem constantly to communicate the letters of their alphabets as graphic representations of thought—no doubt the thought of the word influences the letters but the letters are there and seem to exude thought.

Add—the core that covers the work of poets who see with their ears, hear with their eyes, move with their noses and speak and breathe with their feet. And yet lunatics are sometimes profitably observed: the core that is covered, the valuable skeptic knows, may in itself be the intense vision of a fact.

Intention must, however, be distinguished from accomplishment which resolves the complexity of detail into a single object. Emphasize detail 130 times over—or there will be no poetic object.

Or put the job of explanation up to cabinet-making: certain joints show the carpentry not to advantage, certain joints are a fine evidence; some are with necessary craftsmanship in the object. The first type—showing the carpentry not to advantage—is always present in a great deal of unnecessary writing; the second and third are rare; the second—which is a fine evidence—is rare to this time; the third—which with necessary craftsmanship is hid in the object—is, whenever craftsmanship is present, characteristic of this time.

"Recencies?" No more modern than a Shakespearean conceit which manages to carry at least two ideas at a time. Or Dante's literal, anagogical and theological threefold meaning referred to in a letter to Can Grande.

In contemporary poetry three types of complexity are discernible: 1—the swift concatenation of multiple references usually lyrical in movement—almost any poem by Donne, for example; 2—the conceit—Shakespeare's "when to the sessions," his working out of love as bookkeeping, or Donne's "Valediction," his "two twin compasses"; 3—the complexity of the epic—Byron's *Don Juan*, or most of it.

The word *complexity* is perhaps misleading. Ultimately, the matter of poetic object and its simple entirety most not be forgotten.

I.e. order and the facts as order. The order of all poetry is to approach a state of music wherein the ideas present themselves sensuously and intelligently and are of no predatory intention. A hard job, as poets have found reconciling contrasting principles of facts. In poetry the poet is continually encountering the facts which in the making seem to want to disturb the music and yet the music or the movement cannot exist without the facts, without its facts. The base matter, to speak hurriedly, which must receive the signet of the form. Poems are only acts upon particulars.

Only through such activity do they become particulars themselves—i.e. poems.

The mind may construct its world—this is hardly philosophy—if the mind does construct its world there is always that world immanent or imminently outside which at least as a term has become an entity. Linguistic usage has somehow preserved these acts which were poems in other times and have transferred structures now. The good poems of today are not far from the good poems of yesterday.

Gertrude Stein, "Poetry and Grammar," 1935

In 1934 in Chicago, after Gertrude Stein had given the most popular of her lectures in America "Poetry and Grammar"—a student in the audience asked her what she meant by her poem "a rose is a rose is a rose is a rose." She replied: "Now you have seen hundreds of poems about roses and you know in your bones that the rose is not there. . . . I'm no fool. I know that in daily life we don't go around saying "is a. . . . is . . . is." . . . but I think that in that line the rose is red for the first time in English poetry for a hundred years."

A life-long expatriate, by the time Stein finally paid a visit to the country she had left in 1903, she was famous due to the popularity of *The Autobiography of Alice B. Toklas,* her chronicle of life in Paris with writers and painters. Her prose portraits of Matisse and Picasso had caught the eye of many, including William Carlos Williams, when they appeared in Alfred Steiglitz's *Camera Work.* Her play *Four Saints in Three Acts* had appeared on Broadway, and she had published the novel *The Making of Americans* and the prose poems of *TenderButtons.*

Stein felt she had important new discoveries to share. Her aim in her stylistic experiments was not only to free words from their conventional meaning, but to focus increased and scientific attention on the means of language itself—syntax and punctuation—in order to develop a literature that would not be based on memory and description but would sound the act of thinking and writing as it occurred. In this, one of the six lectures she wrote for her tour, Stein attempts an explanation of the distinction between poetry and prose through an examination of the structures of grammar.

✳

Poetry and Grammar

What is poetry and if you know what poetry is what is prose.

There is no use in telling more than you know, no not even if you do not know it.

But do you do you know what prose is and do you know what poetry is.

I have said that the words in plays written in poetry are more lively than the same words written by the same poet in other kinds of poetry. It undoubtedly was true of Shakespeare, is it inevitably true of everybody. That is one thing to think about. I said that the words in a play written in prose are not as lively words as the words written in other prose by the same writer. This is true of Goldsmith and I imagine it is true of almost any writer.

There again there is something to know.

One of the things that is a very interesting thing to know is how you are feeling inside you to the words that are coming out to be outside of you.

Do you always have the same kind of feeling in relation to the sounds as the words come out of you or do you not. All this has so much to do with grammar and with poetry and with prose.

Words have to do everything in poetry and prose and some writers write more in articles and prepositions and some say you should write in nouns, and of course one has to think of everything.

A noun is a name of anything, why after a thing is named write about it. A name is adequate or it is not. If it is adequate then why go on calling it, if it is not then calling it by its name does no good.

People if you like to believe it can be made by their names. Call anybody Paul and they get to be a Paul call anybody Alice and they get to be an Alice perhaps yes perhaps no, there is something in that, but generally speaking, things once they are named the name does not go on doing anything to them and so why write in nouns. Nouns are the name of anything and just naming names is alright when you want to call a roll but is it any good for anything else. To be sure in many places in Europe as in America they do like to call rolls.

As I say a noun is a name of a thing, and therefore slowly if you feel what is inside that thing you do not call it by the name by which it is known. Everybody knows that by the way they do when they are in love and a writer should always have that intensity of emotion about whatever is the object about which he writes. And therefore and I say it again more and more one does not use nouns.

Now what other things are there besides nouns, there are a lot of other things besides nouns.

When you are at school and learn grammar grammar is very exciting. I really do not know that anything has ever been more exciting than diagraming sentences. I suppose other things may be more exciting to others when they are at school but to me undoubtedly when I was at school the really completely exciting thing was diagraming sentences and that has been to me ever since the one thing that has been completely exciting and completely completing. I like the feeling the everlasting feeling of sentences as they diagram themselves.

In that way one is completely possessing something and incidentally one's self. Now in that diagraming of the sentences of course there are articles and prepositions and as I say there are nouns but nouns as I say even by definition are completely not interesting, the same thing is true of adjectives. Adjectives are not really and truly interesting. In a way anybody can know always has known that, because after all adjectives effect nouns and as nouns are not really interesting the thing that effects a not too interesting thing is of necessity not interesting. In a way as I say anybody knows that because the first thing that anybody takes out of anybody's writing are the adjectives. You see of yourself how true it is that which I have just said.

Beside the nouns and the adjectives there are verbs and adverbs. Verbs and adverbs are more interesting. In the first place they have one very nice quality and that is that they can be so mistaken. It is wonderful the number of mistakes a verb can make and that is equally true of its adverb. Nouns and adjectives never can make mistakes can never be mistaken but verbs can be so endlessly, both as to what they do and how they agree or disagree with whatever they do. The same is true of adverbs.

In that way any one can see that verbs and adverbs are more interesting than nouns and adjectives.

Beside being able to be mistaken and to make mistakes verbs can change to look like themselves or to look like something else, they are, so to speak on the move and adverbs move with them and each of them find themselves not at all annoying but very often very much mistaken. That is the reason any one can like what verbs can do. Then comes the thing that can of all things be most mistaken and they are prepositions. Prepositions can live one long life being really being nothing but absolutely nothing but mistaken and that makes them irritating if you feel that way about mistakes but certainly something that you can be continuously using and everlastingly enjoying. I like prepositions the best of all, and pretty soon we will go more completely into that.

Then there are articles. Articles are interesting just as nouns and adjectives are not. And why are they interesting just as nouns and adjectives are not. They are interesting because they do what a noun might do if a noun was not so unfortunately so completely unfortunately the name of something. Articles please, a and an and the please as the name that follows cannot please. They the names that is the nouns cannot please, because after all you know well after all that is what Shakespeare meant when he talked about a rose by any other name.

I hope now no one can have any illusion about a noun or about the adjective that goes with the noun.

But an article an article remains as a delicate and a varied something and any one who wants to write with articles and knows how to use them will always have the pleasure that using something that is varied and alive can give. That is what articles are.

Beside that there are conjunctions, and a conjunction is not varied but it has a force that need not make any one feel that they are dull. Conjunctions have made themselves live by their work. They work and as they work they live and even when they do not work and in these days they do not always live by work still nevertheless they do live.

So you see why I like to write with prepositions and conjunctions and articles and verbs and adverbs but not with nouns and adjectives. If you read my writing you will you do see what I mean.

Of course then there are pronouns. Pronouns are not as bad as nouns because in the first place practically they cannot have adjectives go with them. That already makes them better than nouns.

Then beside not being able to have adjectives go with them, they of course are not really the name of anything. They represent some one but they are not its or his name. In not being his or its or her name they already have a greater possibility of being something than if they were as a noun is the name of anything. Now actual given names of people are more lively than nouns which are the name of anything and I suppose that this is because after all the name is only given to that person when they are born, there is at least the element of choice even the element of change and anybody can be pretty well able to do what they like, they may be born Walter and become Hub, in such a way they are not like a noun. A noun has been the name of something for such a very long time.

That is the reason that slang exists it is to change the nouns which have been names for so long. I say again. Verbs and adverbs and articles and conjunctions and prepositions are lively because they all do something and as long as anything does something it keeps alive.

One might have in one's list added interjections but really interjections have nothing to do with anything not even with themselves. There so much for that. And now to go into the question of punctuation.

There are some punctuations that are interesting and there are some punctuations that are not. Let us begin with the punctuations that are not. Of these the one but the first and the most the completely most uninteresting is the question mark. The question mark is alright when it is all alone when it is used as a brand on cattle or when it could be used in decoration but connected with writing it is completely entirely completely uninteresting. It is evident that if you ask a question you ask a question but anybody who can read at all knows when a question is a question as it is written in writing. Therefore I ask you therefore wherefore should one use it the question mark. Beside it does not in its form go with ordinary printing and so it pleases neither the eye nor the ear and it is therefore like a noun, just an unnecessary name of something. A question is a question, anybody can know that a question is a question and so why add to it the question mark when it is already there when the question is already there in the writing. Therefore I never could bring myself to use the question mark, I always found it positively revolting, and now very few do use it. Exclamation marks have the same difficulty and also quotation marks, they are unnecessary, they are ugly, they spoil the line of the writing or the printing and anyway what is the use, if you do not know that a question is a question what is the use of its being a question. The same thing is true of an exclamation. And the same thing is true of a quotation. When I first began writing I found it simply impossible to use question marks and quotation marks and exclamation points and now anybody sees it that way. Perhaps some day they will see it some other way but now at any rate anybody can and does see it that way.

So there are the uninteresting things in punctuation uninteresting in a way that is perfectly obvious, and so we do not have to go any farther into that. There are besides dashes and dots, and these might be interesting spaces might be interesting. They might if one felt that way about them.

One other little punctuation mark one can have feelings about and that is the apostrophe for possession. Well feel as you like about that, I can see and I do see that for many that for some the possessive case apostrophe has a gentle tender insinuation that makes it very difficult to definitely decide to do without it. One does do without it, I do, I mostly always do, but I cannot deny that from time to time I feel myself having regrets and from time to time I put it in to make the possessive case. I absolutely do not like it all alone when it is outside the word when the word is a plural, no then positively and definitely no, I do not like it and in leaving it out I feel no regret, there it is unnecessary and not ornamental but inside a word and its s well perhaps, perhaps it does appeal by its weakness to your weakness. At least at any rate from time to time I do find myself letting it alone if it has come in and sometimes it has come in. I cannot positively deny but that I do from time to time let it come in.

So now to come to the real question of punctuation, periods, commas, colons, semi-colons and capitals and small letters.

I have had a long and complicated life with all these.

Let us begin with these I use the least first and these are colons and semi-colons, one might add to these commas.

When I first began writing, I felt that writing should go on, I still do feel that it should go on but when I first began writing I was completely possessed by the necessity that writing should go on and if writing should go on what had colons and semi-colons to do with it, what had commas to do with it, what had periods to do with it what had small letters and capitals to do with it to do with writing going on which was at that time the most profound need I had in connection with writing. What had colons and semi-colons to do with it what had commas to do with it what had periods to do with it.

What had periods to do with it. Inevitably no matter how completely I had to have writing go on, physically one had to again and again stop sometime and if one had to again and again stop some time then periods had to exist. Beside I had always liked the look of periods and I liked what they did. Stopping sometime did not really keep one from going on, it was nothing that interfered, it was only something that happened, and as it happened as a perfectly natural happening, I did believe in periods and I used them. I really never stopped using them.

Beside that periods might later come to have a life of their own to commence breaking up things in arbitrary ways, that has happened lately with me in a poem I have written called Winning His Way, later I will read you a little of it. By the time I had written this poem about three years ago periods had come to have for me completely a life of their own. They could begin to act as they thought best and one might interrupt one's writing with them that is not really interrupt one's writing with them but one could come to stop arbitrarily stop at times in one's writing and so they could be used and you could use them. Periods could come to exist in this way and they could come in this way to have a life of their own. They did not serve you in any servile way as commas and colons and semi-colons do. Yes you do feel what I mean.

Periods have a life of their own a necessity of their own a feeling of their own a time of their own. And that feeling that life that necessity that time can express itself in an infinite variety that is the reason that I have always remained true to periods so much so that as I say recently I have felt that one could need them more than one had ever needed them.

You can see what an entirely different thing a period is from a comma, a colon or a semi-colon.

There are two different ways of thinking about colons and semi-colons you can think of them as commas and as such they are purely servile or you can think of them as periods and then using them can make you feel adventurous. I can see that one might feel about them as periods but I myself never have, I began unfortunately to feel them as a comma and commas are servile they have no life of their own they are dependent upon use and convenience and they are put there just for practical purposes. Semi-colons and colons had for me from the first completely this character the character that a comma has and not the character that a period has and therefore and definitely I have never used them. But now dimly and definitely I do see that they might well possibly they might have in them something of the character of the period and so it might have been an adventure to use them. I really do not think so. I think however lively they are or disguised they are they are definitely more comma than period and so really I cannot regret not having used them. They are more powerful more imposing more pretentious than a comma but they are a comma all the same. They really have within them deeply within them fundamentally within them the comma nature. And now what does a comma do and what has it to do and why do I feel as I do about them.

What does a comma do.

I have refused them so often and left them out so much and did without them so continually that I have come finally to be indifferent to them. I do not now care whether you put them in or not but for a long time I felt very definitely about them and would have nothing to do with them.

As I say commas are servile and they have no life of their own, and their use is not a use, it is a way of replacing one's own interest and I do decidedly like to like my own interest my own interest in what I am doing. A comma by helping you along holding your coat for you and putting on your shoes keeps you from living your life as actively as you should lead it and to me for many years and I still do feel that way about it only now I do not pay as much attention to them, the use of them was positively degrading. Let me tell you what I feel and what I mean and what I felt and what I meant.

When I was writing those long sentences of The Making of Americans, verbs active present verbs with long dependent adverbial clauses became a passion with me. I have told you that I recognize verbs and adverbs aided by prepositions and conjunctions with pronouns as possessing the whole of the active life of writing.

Complications make eventually for simplicity and therefore I have always liked dependent adverbial clauses. I have liked dependent adverbial clauses because of their variety of dependence and independence. You can see how loving the intensity of complication of these things that commas would be degrading. Why if you want the pleasure of concentrating on the final simplicity of excessive complication would you want any artificial aid to bring about that simplicity. Do you see now why I feel about the comma as I did and as I do.

Think about anything you really like to do and you will see what I mean.

When it gets really difficult you want to disentangle rather than to cut the knot, at least so anybody feels who is working with any thread, so anybody feels who is working with any tool so anybody feels who is writing any sentence or reading it after it has been written. And what does a comma do, a comma does nothing but make easy a thing that if you like it enough is easy enough without the comma. A long complicated sentence should force itself upon you, make you know yourself knowing it and the comma, well at the most a comma is a poor period that it lets you stop and take a breath but if you want to take a breath you ought to know yourself that you want to take a breath. It is not like stopping altogether which is what a period does stopping altogether has something to do with going on, but taking a breath well you are always taking a breath and why emphasize one breath rather than another breath. Anyway that is the way I felt about it and I felt that about it very very strongly. And so I almost never used a comma. The longer, the more complicated the sentence the greater the number of the same kinds of words I had following one after another, the more the very many more I had of them the more I felt the passionate need of their taking care of themselves by themselves and not helping them, and thereby enfeebling them by putting in a comma.

So that is the way I felt punctuation in prose, in poetry it is a little different but more so and later I will go into that. But that is the way I felt about punctuation in prose.

Another part of punctuation is capital letters and small letters. Anybody can really do as they please about that and in English printing one may say that they always have.

If you read older books you will see that they do pretty well what they please with capitals and small letters and I have always felt that one does do pretty well what one pleases with capitals and small letters. Sometimes one feels that Italians should be with a capital and sometimes with a small letter, one can feel like that about almost anything. I myself do not feel like that about proper names, I rather like to look at them with a capital on them but I can perfectly understand that a great many do not feel that way about it. In short in prose capitals and small letters have really nothing to do with the inner life of sentences and paragraphs as the other punctuation marks have as I have just been saying.

We still have capitals and small letters and probably for some time we will go on having them but actually the tendency is always toward diminishing capitals and quite rightly because the feeling that goes with them is less and less of a feeling and so slowly and inevitably just as with horses capitals will have gone away. They will come back from time to time but perhaps never really come back to stay.

Perhaps yes perhaps not but really and inevitably really it really does not really make any difference.

But and they will be with us as long as human beings continue to exist and have a vocabulary, sentences and paragraphs will be with us and therefore inevitably and really periods will be with us and it is of these things that will be always inevitably with us in prose and in poetry because prose and also poetry will also always always be with us that I will go on telling to you all I know.

Sentences and paragraphs. Sentences are not emotional but paragraphs are. I can say that as often as I like and it always remains as it is, something that is.

I said I found this out first in listening to Basket my dog drinking. And anybody listening to any dog's drinking will see what I mean.

When I wrote The Making of Americans I tried to break down this essential combination by making enormously long sentences that would be as long as the longest paragraph and so to see if there was really and truly this essential difference between paragraphs and sentences, if one went far enough with this thing with making the sentences long enough to be as long as any paragraph and so producing in them the balance of a paragraph not a balance of a sentence, because of course the balance of a paragraph is not the same balance as the balance of a sentence.

It is only necessary to read anything in order to know that. I say if I succeeded in making my sentences so long that they held within themselves the balance of both both sentences and paragraphs, what was the result.

I did in some sentences in The Making of Americans succeed in doing this thing in creating a balance that was neither the balance of a sentence nor the balance of a paragraph and in doing so I felt dimly that I had done something that was not leading to anything because after all you should not lose two things in order to have one thing because in doing so you make writing just that much less varied.

That is one thing about what I did. There is also another thing and that was a very important thing, in doing this in achieving something that had neither the balance of a sentence nor the balance of a paragraph but a balance a new balance that had to do with a sense of movement of time included in a given space which as I have already said is a definitely American thing.

An American can fill up a space in having his movement of time by adding unexpectedly anything and yet getting within the included space everything he had intended getting.

A young french boy he is a red-haired descendant of the niece of Madame Recamier went to America for two weeks most unexpectedly and I said to him what did you notice most over there. Well he said at first they were not as different from us frenchmen as I expected them to be and then I did see that they were that they were different. And what, said I, well he said, when a train was going by at a terrific pace and we waved a hat the engine driver could make a bell quite carelessly go ting ting ting, the way anybody playing at a thing could do, it was not if you know what I mean professional he said. Perhaps you do see the connection with that and my sentences that had no longer the balance of sentences because they were not the parts of a paragraph nor were they a paragraph but they had made in so far as they had come to be so long and with the balance of their own that they had they had become something that was a whole thing and in so being they had a balance which was the balance of a space completely not filled but created by something moving as moving is not as moving should be. As I said Henry James in his later writing had had a dim feeling that this was what he knew he should do.

And so though as I say there must always be sentences and paragraphs the question can really be asked must there always be sentences and paragraphs is it not possible to achieve in itself and not by sentences and paragraphs the combination that sentences are not emotional and paragraphs are.

In a book called How to Write I worked a lot at this thing trying to find out just exactly what the balance the unemotional balance of a sentence is and what the emotional balance of a paragraph is and if it were possible to make even in a short sentence the two things come to be one. I think I did a few times succeed. Will you listen to one or two sentences where I did think I had done this thing.

He looks like a young man grown old.

HOW TO WRITE. (PLAIN EDITION) RANDOM HOUSE. PAGE 25.

It looks like a garden but he had hurt himself by accident.

HOW TO WRITE. PAGE 26.

A dog which you have never had before has sighed.

HOW TO WRITE. PAGE 27.

Once when they were nearly ready they had ordered it to close.

HOW TO WRITE. PAGE 29.

If a sound is made which grows louder and then stops how many times may it be repeated.

Battles are named because there have been hills which have made a hill in a battle.

A bay and hills hills are surrounded by their having their distance very near.

Poplars indeed will be and may be indeed will be cut down and will be sawn up and indeed will be used as wood and may be used for wood.

The thing to remember is that if it is not if it is not what having left it to them makes it be very likely as likely as they would be after all after all choosing choosing to be here on time.

❊

In spite of my intending to write about grammar and poetry I am still writing about grammar and prose, but and of course it may or may not be true if you find out essentially what prose is and essentially what poetry is may you not have an exciting thing happening as I had it happen with sentences and paragraphs.

After all the natural way to count is not that one and one make two but to go on counting by one and one as chinamen do as anybody does as Spaniards do as my little aunts did. One and one and one and one and one. That is the natural way to go on counting.

Now what has this to do with poetry. It has a lot to do with poetry.

Everything has a lot to do with poetry everything has a lot to do with prose.

And has prose anything to do with poetry and has poetry anything to do with prose.

And what have nouns to do with poetry and periods and capital letters. The other punctuation marks we never have to mention again. People may do as they like with them but we never have to mention them. But nouns still have to be mentioned because in coming to avoid nouns a great deal happens and has happened. It was one of the things that happened in a book I called Tender Buttons.

In The Making of Americans a long a very long prose book made up of sentences and paragraphs and the new thing that was something neither the sentence or the paragraph each one alone or in combination had ever done, I said I had gotten rid of nouns and adjectives as much as possible by the method of living in adverbs in verbs in pronouns, in adverbial clauses written or implied and in conjunctions.

But and after I had gone as far as I could in these long sentences and paragraphs that had come to do something else I then began very short things and in doing very short things I resolutely realized nouns and decided not to get around them but to meet them, to handle in short to refuse them by using them and in that way my real acquaintance with poetry was begun.

I will try to tell a little more clearly and in more detail just what happened and why it was if it was like natural counting, that is counting by one one one one one.

Nouns as you all know are the names of anything and as the names of anything of course one has had to use them. And what have they done. And what has any one done with them. That is something to know. It is as you may say as I may say a great deal to know.

Nouns are the name of anything and anything is named, that is what Adam and Eve did and if you like it is what anybody does, but do they go on just using the name until perhaps they do not know what the name is or if they do know what the name is they do not care about what the name is. This may happen of course it may. And what has poetry got to do with this and what has prose and if everything like a noun which is a name of anything is to be avoided what takes place. And what has that to do with poetry. A great deal I think and all this too has to do with other things with short and long lines and rhymes.

But first what is poetry and what is prose. I wonder if I can tell you.

We do know a little now what prose is. Prose is the balance the emotional balance that makes the reality of paragraphs and the unemotional balance that makes the reality of sentences and having realized completely realized that sentences are not emotional while paragraphs are, prose can be the essential balance that is made inside something that combines the sentence and the paragraph, examples of this I have been reading to you.

Now if that is what prose is and that undoubtedly is what prose is you can see that prose real prose really great written prose is bound to be made up more of verbs adverbs prepositions prepositional clauses and conjunctions than nouns. The vocabulary in prose of course is important if you like vocabulary is always important, in fact one of the things that you can find out and that I experimented with a great deal in How to Write vocabulary in itself and by itself can be interesting and can make sense. Anybody can know that by thinking of words. It is extraordinary how it is impossible that a vocabulary does not make sense. But that is natural indeed inevitable because a vocabulary is that by definition, and so because this is so the vocabulary in respect to prose is less important than the parts of speech, and the internal balance and the movement within a given space.

So then we understand we do know what prose is.

But what is poetry.

Is it more or is it less difficult to know what poetry is. I have sometimes thought it more difficult to know what poetry is but now that I do know what poetry is and if I do know what poetry is then it is not more difficult to know what it is than to know what prose is.

What is poetry.

Poetry has to do with vocabulary just as prose has not.

So you see prose and poetry are not at all alike. They are completely different.

Poetry is I say essentially a vocabulary just as prose is essentially not.

And what is the vocabulary of which poetry absolutely is. It is a vocabulary entirely based on the noun as prose is essentially and determinately and vigorously not based on the noun.

Poetry is concerned with using with abusing, with losing with wanting, with denying with avoiding with adoring with replacing the noun. It is doing that always doing that, doing that and doing nothing but that. Poetry is doing nothing but using losing refusing and pleasing and betraying and caressing nouns. That is what poetry does, that is what poetry has to do no matter what kind of poetry it is. And there are a great many kinds of poetry.

When I said.

A rose is a rose is a rose is a rose.

And then later made that into a ring I made poetry and what did I do I caressed completely caressed and addressed a noun.

Now let us think of poetry any poetry all poetry and let us see if this is not so. Of course it is so anybody can know that.

I have said that a noun is a name of anything by definition that is what it is and a name of anything is not interesting because once you know its name the enjoyment of naming it is over and therefore in writing prose names that is nouns are completely uninteresting. But and that is a thing to be remembered you can love a name and if you love a name then saying that name any number of times only makes you love it more, more violently more persistently more tormentedly. Anybody knows how anybody calls out the name of anybody one loves. And so that is poetry really loving the name of anything and that is not prose. Yes any of you can know that.

Poetry like prose has lived through a good deal. Anybody or anything lives through a good deal. Sometimes it included everything and sometimes it includes only itself and there can be any amount of less and more at any time of its existence.

Of course when poetry really began it practically included everything it included narrative and feelings and excitements and nouns so many nouns and all emotions. It included narrative but now it does not include narrative.

I often wonder how I am ever to come to know all that I am to know about narrative. Narrative is a problem to me. I worry about it a good deal these days and I will not write or lecture about it yet, because I am still too worried about it worried about knowing what it is and how it is and where it is and how it is and how it will be what it is. However as I say now and at this time I do not I will not go into that. Suffice it to say that for the purpose of poetry it has now for a long time not had anything to do with being there.

Perhaps it is a mistake perhaps not that it is no longer there.

I myself think that something else is going to happen about narrative and I work at it a great deal at this time not work but bother about it. Bother is perhaps the better word for what I am doing just now about narrative. But anyway to go back to poetry.

Poetry did then in beginning include everything and it was natural that it should because then everything including what was happening could be made real to anyone by just naming what was happening in other words by doing what poetry always must do by living in nouns.

Nouns are the name of anything. Think of all that early poetry, think of Homer, think of Chaucer, think of the Bible and you will see what I mean you will really realize that they were drunk with nouns, to name to know how to name earth sea and sky and all that was in them was enough to make them live and love in names, and that is what poetry is it is a state of knowing and feeling a name. I know that now but I have only come to that knowledge by long writing.

So then as I say that is what poetry was and slowly as everybody knew the names of everything poetry had less and less to do with everything. Poetry did not change, poetry never changed, from the beginning until now and always in the future poetry will concern itself with the names of things. The names may be repeated in different ways and very soon I will go into that matter but now and always poetry is created by naming names the names of something the names of somebody the names of anything. Nouns are the names of things and so nouns are the basis of poetry.

Before we go any further there is another matter. Why are the lines of poetry short, so much shorter than prose, why do they rhyme, why in order to complete themselves do they have to end with what they began, why are all these things the things that are in the essence of poetry even when the poetry was long even when now the poetry has changed its form.

Once more the answer is the same and that is that such a way to express oneself is the natural way when one expresses oneself in loving the name of anything. Think what you do when you do do that when you love the name of anything really love its name. Inevitably you express yourself in that way, in the way poetry expresses itself that is in short lines in repeating what you began in order to do it again. Think of how you talk to anything whose name is new to you a lover a baby or a dog or a new land or any part of it. Do you not inevitably repeat what you call out and is that calling out not of necessity in short lines. Think about it and you will see what I mean by what you feel.

So as I say poetry is essentially the discovery, the love, the passion for the name of anything.

Now to come back to how I know what I know about poetry.

I was writing The Making of Americans, I was completely obsessed by the inner life of everything including generations of everybody's living and I was writing prose, prose that had to do with the balancing the inner balancing of everything. I have already told you all about that.

And then, something happened and I began to discover the names of things, that is not discover the names but discover the things the things to see the things to look at and in so doing I had of course to name them not to give them new names but to see that I could find out how to know that they were there by their names or by replacing their names. And how was I to do so. They had their names and naturally I called them by the names they had and in doing so having begun looking at them I called them by their names with passion and that made poetry, I did not mean it to make poetry but it did, it made the Tender Buttons, and the Tender Buttons was very good poetry it made a lot more poetry, and I will now more and more tell about that and how it happened.

I discovered everything then and its name, discovered it and its name. I had always known it and its name but all the same I did discover it.

I remember very well when I was a little girl and I and my brother found as children will the love poems of their very very much older brother. This older brother had just written one and it said that he had often sat and looked at any little square of grass and it had been just a square of grass as grass is, but now he was in love and so the little square of grass was all filled with birds and bees and butterflies, the difference was what love was. The poem was funny we and he knew the poem was funny but he was right, being in love made him make poetry, and poetry made him feel the things and their names, and so I repeat nouns are poetry.

So then in Tender Buttons I was making poetry but and it seriously troubled me, dimly I knew that nouns made poetry but in prose I no longer needed the help of nouns and in poetry did I need the help of nouns. Was there not a way of naming things that would not invent names, but mean names without naming them.

I had always been very impressed from the time that I was very young by having had it told me and then afterwards feeling it myself that Shakespeare in the forest of Arden had created a forest without mentioning the things that make a forest. You feel it all but he does not name its names.

Now that was a thing that I too felt in me the need of making it be a thing that could be named without using its name. After all one had known its name anything's name for so long, and so the name was not new but the thing being alive was always new.

What was there to do.

I commenced trying to do something in Tender Buttons about this thing. I went on and on trying to do this thing. I remember in writing An

Acquaintance With Description looking at anything until something that was not the name of that thing but was in a way that actual thing would come to be written.

Naturally, and one may say that is what made Walt Whitman naturally that made the change in the form of poetry, that we who had known the names so long did not get a thrill from just knowing them. We that is any human being living has inevitably to feel the thing anything being existing, but the name of that thing of that anything is no longer anything to thrill any one except children. So as everybody has to be a poet, what was there to do. This that I have just described, the creating it without naming it, was what broke the rigid form of the noun the simple noun poetry which now was broken.

Of course you all do know that when I speak of naming anything, I include emotions as well as things.

So then there we were and what were we to do about it. Go on, of course go on what else does anybody do, so I did, I went on.

Of course you might say why not invent new names new languages but that cannot be done. It takes a tremendous amount of inner necessity to invent even one word, one can invent imitating movements and emotions in sounds, and in the poetical language of some languages you have that, the german language as a language suffers from this what the words mean sound too much like what they do, and children do these things by one sort or another of invention but this has really nothing to do with language. Language as a real thing is not imitation either of sounds or colors or emotions it is an intellectual recreation and there is no possible doubt about it and it is going to go on being that as long as humanity is anything. So every one must stay with the language their language that has come to be spoken and written and which has in it all the history of its intellectual recreation.

And so for me the problem of poetry was and it began with Tender Buttons to constantly realize the thing anything so that I could recreate that thing. I struggled I struggled desperately with the recreation and the avoidance of nouns as nouns and yet poetry being poetry nouns are nouns. Let me read you bits of the Portrait of Sherwood Anderson and The Birthplace of Bonnes to show you what I mean.

Can anybody tell by looking which was the towel used for cooking.

PORTRAITS AND PRAYERS. PAGE 162.

Very fine is my valentine.
Very fine and very mine.
Very mine is my valentine very mine and
very fine.
Very fine is my valentine and mine, very fine
very mine and mine is my valentine.

PORTRAITS AND PRAYERS. PAGE 152.

BUNDLES FOR THEM

A HISTORY OF GIVING BUNDLES

We were able to notice that each one in a way carried a bundle, they were not a trouble to them nor were they all bundles as some of them were chickens some of them pheasants some of them sheep and some of them bundles, they were not a trouble to them and then indeed we learned that it was the principal recreation and they were so arranged that they were not given away, and today they were given away.

I will not look at them again.

They will not look for them again.

They have not seen them here again.

They are in there and we hear them again.

In which way are stars brighter than they are. When we have come to this decision. We mention many thousands of buds. And when I close my eyes I see them.

If you hear her snore

It is not before you love her

You love her so that to be her beau is very lovely

She is sweetly there and her curly hair is very lovely.

She is sweetly here and I am very near and that is very lovely.

She is my tender sweet and her little feet are stretched out well which is a treat and very lovely.

Her little tender nose is between her little eyes which close and are very lovely.

She is very lovely and mine which is very lovely.

I found in longer things like Operas and Plays and Portraits and Lucy Church Amiably and An Acquaintance With Description that I could come nearer to avoiding names in recreating something.

That brings us to the question will poetry continue to be necessarily short as it has been as really good poetry has been for a very long time. Perhaps not and why not.

If enough is new to you to name or not name, and these two things come to the same thing, can you go on long enough. Yes I think so.

So then poetry up to the present time has been a poetry of nouns a poetry of naming something of really naming that thing passionately completely passionately naming that thing by its name.

Slowly and particularly during the nineteenth century the English nineteenth century everybody had come to know too well very much too well the name anything had when you called it by its name.

That is something that inevitably happened. And what else could they do. They had to go on doing what they did, that is calling anything by its name passionately but if as I say they really knew its name too well could they call it its name simply in that way. Slowly they could not.

And then Walt Whitman came. He wanted really wanted to express the thing and not call it by its name. He worked very hard at that, and he called it Leaves of Grass because he wanted it to be as little a well known name to be called upon passionately as possible. I do not at all know whether Whitman knew that he wanted to do this but there is no doubt at all but that is what he did want to do.

You have the complete other end of this thing in a poet like Longfellow, I cite him because a commonplace poet shows you more readily and clearly just what the basis of poetry is than a better one. And Longfellow knew all about calling out names, he on the whole did it without passion but he did it very well.

Of course in the history of poetry there have been many who have also tried to name the thing without naming its names, but this is not a history of poets it is a telling what I know about poetry.

And so knowing all this about poetry I struggled more and more with this thing. I say I knew all this about poetry but I did not really know all this then about poetry, I was coming to know then then when I was writing commencing to know what I do now know about prose but

I did not then know anything really to know it of what I now know about poetry.

And so in Tender Buttons and then on and on I struggled with the ridding myself of nouns, I knew nouns must go in poetry as they had gone in prose if anything that is everything was to go on meaning something.

And so I went on with this exceeding struggle of knowing really knowing what a thing was really knowing it knowing anything I was seeing anything I was feeling so that its name could be something, by its name coming to be a thing in itself as it was but would not be anything just and only as a name.

I wonder if you do see what I mean.

What I mean by what I have just said is this. I had to feel anything and everything that for me was existing so intensely that I could put it down in writing as a thing in itself without at all necessarily using its name. The name of a thing might be something in itself if it could come to be real enough but just as a name it was not enough something. At any rate that is the way I felt and still do feel about it.

And so I went through a very long struggle and in this struggle I began to be troubled about narrative a narrative of anything that was or might be happening.

The newspapers tell us about it but they tell it to us as nouns tell it to us that is they name it, and in naming it, it as a telling of it is no longer anything. That is what a newspaper is by definition just as a noun is a name by definition.

And so I was slowly beginning to know something about what poetry was. And here was the question if in poetry one could lose the noun as I had really and truly lost it in prose would there be any difference between poetry and prose. As this thing came once more to be a doubt inside me I began to work very hard at poetry.

At that time I wrote Before the Flowers of Friendship Faded Friendship Faded and there I went back again to a more or less regular form to see whether inside that regular form I could do what I was sure needed to be done and also to find out if eventually prose and poetry were one or not one.

In writing this poem I found I could be very gay I could be very lively in poetry, I could use very few nouns in poetry and call out practically no names in poetry and yet make poetry really feel and sound as poetry, but was it what I wanted that should be done. But it did not decide anything for me but it did help me in my way.

XII

I am very hungry when I drink,
I need to leave it when I have it held,
    They will be white with which they know they see, that darker
makes it be a color white for me, white is not shown when I am
dark indeed with red despair who comes who has to care that they
will let me a little lie like now I like to lie I like to live I like to die
 I like to lie and live and die and live and die and by and by I like to
live and die and by and by they need to sew, the difference is that
sewing makes it bleed and such with them in all the way of seed
and seeding and repine and they will which is mine and not all
mine who can be thought curious of this of all of that made it and
come lead it and done weigh it and mourn and sit upon it know it
for ripeness without deserting all of it of which without which it
has not been born. Oh no not to be thirsty with the thirst of hunger
not alone to know that they plainly and ate or wishes. Any little one
will kill himself for milk.

BEFORE THE FLOWERS OF FRIENDSHIP FADED
FRIENDSHIP FADED (PLAIN EDITION). PAGE 14.

XIV

It could be seen very nicely
That doves have each a heart,
Each one is always seeing that they could not
be apart,
A little lake makes fountains
And fountains have no flow,
And a dove has need of flying
And water can be low,
Let me go.
Any week is what they seek
When they have to halve a beak.
I like a painting on a wall of doves
And what do they do,
They have hearts
They are apart
Little doves are winsome
But not when they are little and left.

I decided and Lucy Church Amiably had been an attempt to do it, I decided that if one definitely completely replaced the noun by the thing in itself, it was eventually to be poetry and not prose which would have to deal with everything that was not movement in space. There could no longer be form to decide anything, narrative that is not newspaper narrative but real narrative must of necessity be told by any one having come to the realization that the noun must be replaced not by inner balance but by the thing in itself and that will eventually lead to everything. I am working at this thing and what will it do this I do not know but I hope that I will know. In the Four In America I have gone on beginning but I am sure that there is in this what there is that it is necessary to do if one is to do anything or everything. Do you see what I mean. Well anyway that is the way that I do now feel about it, and this is all that I do know, and I do believe in knowing all I do know, about prose and poetry. The rest will come considerably later.

Wallace Stevens
"The Noble Rider
and the Sound of Words,"
1942

"I am the necessary angel of earth / Since, in my sight, you see the earth again." What makes a figure that will suffice in modern times, whether the figure of the poem's form or the figurative language used to make the image? Presented as a lecture at Princeton in 1942 and published the same year, "The Noble Rider and the Sound of Words" is the first essay in Wallace Stevens's book-length—and life-long—exploration of the nature of imagination and reality, entitled *The Necessary Angel*.

For Stevens, as for William Carlos Williams in *Spring and All*, the struggle is with reality. But whereas in Williams, reality is form, for Stevens, who writes in a loose iambic, reality is the world pressing against the equally real power of the human mind, a power he calls the imagination. Modern poetry, he claims, must be the arena in which this struggle takes place. The poem as an act of the mind.

Born in Pennsylvania, Stevens was educated at Harvard and spent his adult life in Hartford, Connecticut, where he was an insurance executive. In 1923, when he was forty-four, he published his first collection, *Harmonium,* in which some of his most loved poems were published: "Thirteen Ways of Looking at a Blackbird," "The Snow Man," "The Emperor of Ice Cream." However, it is in his longer poems—"Notes Toward a Supreme Fiction," "The Auroras of Autumn," "An Ordinary Evening at New Haven"—that he concentrates on his true subject, one greatly influenced by his early readings in French symbolism: the poem itself. "Poetry is a part of the structure of reality," Stevens writes in another essay, "Three Academic Pieces," "If this has been demonstrated, it pretty much amounts to saying that the structure of poetry and the structure of reality are one."

❋

The Noble Rider and the Sound of Words

In the *Phaedrus*, Plato speaks of the soul in a figure. He says:

Let our figure be of a composite nature—a pair of winged horses and a chari-oteer. Now the winged horses and the charioteer of the gods are all of them noble, and of noble breed, while ours are mixed; and we have a charioteer who drives them in a pair, and one of them is noble and of noble origin, and the other is ignoble and of ignoble origin; and, as might be expected, there is a great deal of trouble in man-aging them. I will endeavor to explain to you in what way the mortal differs from the immortal creature. The soul or animate being has the care of the inanimate, and traverses the whole heaven in divers forms appearing;—when perfect and fully winged she soars upward, and is the ruler of the universe; while the imperfect soul loses her feathers, and drooping in her flight at last settles on the solid ground.

We recognize at once, in this figure, Plato's pure poetry; and at the same time we recognize what Coleridge called Plato's dear, gorgeous nonsense. The truth is that we have scarcely read the passage before we have identified ourselves with the charioteer, have, in fact, taken his place and, driving his winged horses, are traversing the whole heaven. Then suddenly we remember, it may be, that the soul no longer exists and we droop in our flight and at last settle on the solid ground. The figure be-comes antiquated and rustic.

I

What really happens in this brief experience? Why does this figure, potent for so long, become merely the emblem of a mythology, the rustic memorial of a belief in the soul and in a distinction between good and evil? The answer to these questions is, I think, a simple one.

I said that suddenly we remember that the soul no longer exists and we droop in our flight. For that matter, neither charioteers nor chariots any longer exist. Consequently, the figure does not become unreal because we are troubled about the soul. Besides, unreal things have a reality of their own, in poetry as elsewhere. We do not hesitate, in poetry, to yield ourselves to the unreal, when it is possible to yield ourselves. The existence of the soul, of charioteers and chariots and of winged horses is immaterial. They did not exist for Plato, not even the charioteer and chariot; for certainly a charioteer driving his chariot across the whole heaven was for Plato precisely what he is for us. He was unreal for Plato as he is for us. Plato, however, could yield himself, was free to yield himself, to this gorgeous nonsense. We cannot yield ourselves. We are not free to yield ourselves.

Just as the difficulty is not a difficulty about unreal things, since the imagination accepts them, and since the poetry of the passage is, for us, wholly the poetry of the unreal, so it is not an emotional difficulty. Something else than the imagination is moved by the statement that the horses of the gods are all of them noble, and of noble breed or origin. The statement is a moving statement and is intended to be so. It is insistent and its insistence moves us. Its insistence is the insistence of a speaker, in this case Socrates, who, for the moment, feels delight, even if a casual delight, in the nobility and noble breed. Those images of nobility instantly become nobility itself and determine the emotional level at which the next page or two are to be read. The figure does not lose its vitality because of any failure of feeling on Plato's part. He does not communicate nobility coldly. His horses are not marble horses, the reverence to their breed saves them from being that. The fact that the horses are not marble horses helps, moreover, to save the charioteer from being, say, a creature of cloud. The result is that we recognize, even if we cannot realize, the feelings of the robust poet clearly and fluently noting the images in his mind and by means of his robustness, clearness and fluency communicating much more than the images themselves. Yet we do not quite yield. We cannot. We do not feel free.

In trying to find out what it is that stands between Plato's figure and ourselves, we have to accept the idea that, however legendary it appears to be, it has had its vicissitudes. The history of a figure of speech or the history of an idea, such as the idea of nobility, cannot be very different from the history of anything else. It is the episodes that are of interest, and here the episode is that of our diffidence. By us and ourselves, I mean you and me; and yet not you and me as individuals but as representatives of a state of mind. Adams in his work on Vico makes the remark that the true history of the human race is a history of its progressive mental states. It is a remark of interest in this relation. We may assume that in the history of Plato's figure there have been incessant changes of response; that these changes have been psychological changes, and that our own diffidence is simply one more state of mind due to such a change.

The specific question is partly as to the nature of the change and partly as to the cause of it. In nature, the change is as follows: The imagination loses vitality as it ceases to adhere to what is real. When it adheres to the unreal and intensifies what is unreal, while its first effect may be extraordinary, that effect is the maximum effect that it will ever have. In Plato's figure, his imagination does not adhere to what is real. On the contrary, having created something unreal, it adheres to it and intensifies its unreality. Its first effect, its effect at first reading, is its maximum effect, when the imagination, being moved, puts us in the place of the charioteer, before the reason checks us. The case is, then, that we concede that the figure is all imagination. At the same time, we say that it has not the slightest meaning for us, except for its nobility. As to that, while we are moved by it, we are moved as observers. We recognize it perfectly. We do not realize it. We understand the feeling of it, the robust feeling, clearly and fluently communicated. Yet we understand it rather than participate in it.

As to the cause of the change, it is the loss of the figure's vitality. The reason why this particular figure has lost its vitality is that, in it, the imagination adheres to what is unreal. What happened, as we were traversing the whole heaven, is that the imagination lost its power to sustain us. It has the strength of reality or none at all.

2

What has just been said demonstrates that there are degrees of the imagination, as, for example, degrees of vitality and, therefore, of intensity. It is an implication that there are degrees of reality. The discourse about the two elements seems endless. For my own part, I intend merely to follow, in a very hasty way, the fortunes of the idea of nobility as a characteristic of the imagination, and even as its symbol or alter ego, through several of the episodes in its history, in order to determine, if possible, what its fate has been and what had determined its fate. This can be done only on the basis of the relation between the imagination and reality. What has been said in respect to the figure of the charioteer illustrates this.

I should like now to go on to other illustrations of the relation between the imagination and reality and particularly to illustrations that constitute episodes in the history of the idea of nobility. It would be agreeable to pass directly from the charioteer and his winged horses to Don Quixote. It would be like a return from what Plato calls "the back of heaven" to one's own spot. Nevertheless, there is Verocchio (as one among others) with his statue of Bartolommeo Colleoni, in Venice, standing in the way. I have not selected him as a Neo-Platonist to relate us back from a modern time to Plato's time, although he does in fact so relate us, just as through Leonardo, his pupil, he strengthens the relationship. I have selected him because there, on the edge of the world in which we live today, he established a form of such nobility that it has never ceased to magnify us in our own eyes. It is like the form of an invincible man, who has come, slowly and boldly, through every warlike opposition of the past and who moves in our midst without dropping the bridle of the powerful horse from his hand, without taking off his helmet and without relaxing the attitude of a warrior of noble origin. What man on whose side the horseman fought could ever be anything but fearless, anything but indomitable? One feels the passion of rhetoric begin to stir and even to grow furious; and one thinks that, after all, the noble style, in whatever it creates, merely perpetuates the noble style. In this statue, the apposition between the imagination and reality is too favorable to the imagination. Our difficulty is not primarily with any detail. It is primarily with the whole. The point is not so much to analyze the difficulty as to determine whether we share it, to find out whether it exists, whether we regard this specimen of the genius of Verrocchio and of the Renaissance as a bit of uncommon panache, no longer quite the appropriate thing outdoors, or whether we regard it, in the language of Dr. Richards, as something inexhaustible to meditation or, to speak for myself, as a thing of a nobility responsive to the most minute demand. It seems, nowadays, what it may very well not have seemed a few years ago, a little overpowering, a little magnificent.

Undoubtedly, Don Quixote could be Bartolommeo Colleoni in Spain. The tradition of Italy is the tradition of the imagination. The tradition of Spain is the tradition of reality. There is no apparent reason why the reverse should not be true. If this is a just observation, it indicates that the relation between the imagination and reality is a question, more or less, of precise equilibrium. Thus it is not a question of the difference between grotesque extremes. My purpose is not to contrast Colleoni with Don Quixote. It is to say that one passed into the other, that one became and was the other. The difference between them is that Verrocchio believed in one kind of nobility and Cervantes, if he believed in any, believed in another kind. With Verrocchio it was an affair of the noble style, whatever his prepossession respecting the nobility of man as a real animal may have been. With Cervantes, nobility was not a thing of the imagination. It was a part of reality, it was something that exists in life, something so true to us that it is in danger of ceasing to exist, if we isolate it, something in the mind of a precarious tenure. These may be words. Certainly, however, Cervantes sought to set right the balance between the imagination and reality. As we come closer to our own times in Don Quixote and as we are drawn together by the intelligence common to the two periods, we may derive so much satisfaction from the restoration of reality as to become wholly prejudiced against the imagination. This is to reach a conclusion prematurely, let alone that it may be to reach a conclusion in respect to something as to which no conclusion is possible or desirable.

There is in Washington, in Lafayette Square, which is the square on which the White House faces, a statue of Andrew Jackson, riding a horse with one of the most beautiful tails in the world. General Jackson is raising his hat in a gay gesture, saluting the ladies of his generation. One looks at this work of Clark Mills and thinks of the remark of Bertrand Russell that to acquire immunity to eloquence is of the utmost importance to the citizens of a democracy. We are bound to think that Colleoni, as a mercenary, was a much less formidable man than General Jackson, that he meant less to fewer people and that, if Verrocchio could have applied his prodigious poetry to Jackson, the whole American outlook today might be imperial. This work is a work of fancy. Dr. Richards cites Coleridge's theory of fancy as opposed to imagination. Fancy is an activity of the mind which puts things together of choice, *not* the will, as a principle of the mind's being, striving to realize itself in knowing itself. Fancy, then, is an exercise of selection from among objects already supplied by association, a selection made for purposes which are not then and therein being shaped but have been already fixed. We are concerned then with an object occupying a position as remarkable as any that can be found in the United States in which there is not the slightest trace of the imagination. Treating this work as typical, it is obvious that the American will as a principle of the mind's being is easily satisfied in its efforts to realize itself in knowing itself. The statue may be dismissed, not without speaking of it again as a thing that at least makes us conscious of ourselves as we were, if not as we are. To that extent, it helps us to know ourselves. It helps us to know ourselves as we were and that helps us to know ourselves as we are. The statue is neither of the imagination nor of reality. That it is a work of fancy precludes it from being a work of the imagination. A glance at it shows it to be unreal. The bearing of this is that there can be works, and this includes poems, in which neither the imagination nor reality is present.

The other day I was reading a note about an American artist who was said to have "turned his back on the aesthetic whims and theories of the day, and established headquarters in lower Manhattan." Accompanying this note was a reproduction of a painting called *Wooden Horses*. It is a painting of a merry-go-round, possibly of several of them. One of the horses seems to be prancing. The others are going lickety-split, each one struggling to get the bit in his teeth. The horse in the center of the picture, painted yellow, has two riders, one a man, dressed in a carnival costume, who is seated in the saddle, the other a blonde, who is seated well up the horse's neck. The man has his arms under the girl's arms. He holds himself stiffly in order to keep his cigar out of the girl's hair. Her feet are in a second and shorter set of stirrups. She has the legs of a hammer-thrower. It is clear that the couple are accustomed to wooden horses and like them. A little behind them is a younger girl riding alone. She has a strong body and streaming hair. She wears a short-sleeved, red waist, a white skirt and an emphatic bracelet of pink coral. She has her eyes on the man's arms. Still farther behind, there is another girl. One does not see much more of her than her head. Her lips are painted bright red. It seems that it would be better if someone were to hold her on her horse. We, here, are not interested in any aspect of this picture except that it is a picture of ribald and hilarious reality. It is a picture wholly favorable to what is real. It is not without imagination and it is far from being without aesthetic theory.

3

These illustrations of the relation between the imagination and reality are an outline on the basis of which to indicate a tendency. Their usefulness is this: that they help to make clear, what no one may ever have doubted, that just as in this or that work the degrees of the imagination and of reality may vary, so this variation may exist as between the works of one age and the works of another. What I have said up to this point amounts to this: that the idea of nobility exists in art today only in degenerate forms or in a much diminished state, if, in fact, it exists at all or otherwise than on sufferance; that this is due to failure in the relation between the imagination and reality. I should now like to add that this failure is due, in turn, to the pressure of reality.

A variation between the sound of words in one age and the sound of words in another age is an instance of the pressure of reality. Take the statement by Bateson that a language, considered semantically, evolves through a series of conflicts between the denotative and the connotative forces in words; between an asceticism tending to kill language by stripping words of all association and a hedonism tending to kill language by dissipating their sense in a multiplicity of associations. These conflicts are nothing more than changes in the relation between the imagination and reality. Bateson describes the seventeenth century in England as predominately a connotative period. The use of words in connotative senses was denounced by Locke and Hobbes, who desired a mathematical plainness; in short, perspicuous words. There followed in the eighteenth century an era of poetic diction. This was not the language of the age but a language of poetry peculiar to itself. In time, Wordsworth came to write the preface to the second edition of the *Lyrical Ballads* (1800), in which he said that the first volume had been published, "as an experiment, which, I hoped, might be of some use to ascertain how far, by fitting to metrical arrangement a selection of the real language of man in a state of vivid sensation, that sort of pleasure and that quantity of pleasure may be imparted, which a Poet may rationally endeavour to impart."

As the nineteenth century progressed, language once more became connotative. While there have been intermediate reactions, this tendency toward the connotative is the tendency today. The interest in semantics is evidence of this. In the case of some of our prose writers, as, for example, Joyce, the language, in quite different ways, is wholly connotative. When we say that Locke and Hobbes denounced the connotative use of words as an abuse, and when we speak of reactions and reforms, we are speaking, on the one hand, of a failure of the imagination to adhere to reality, and, on the other, of a use of language favorable to reality. The statement that the tendency toward the connotative is the tendency today is disputable. The general movement in the arts, that is to say, in painting and in music, has been the other way. It is hard to say that the tendency is toward the connotative in the use of words without also saying that the tendency is toward the imagination in other directions. The interest in the subconscious and in surrealism shows the tendency toward the imaginative. Boileau's remark that Descartes had cut poetry's throat is a remark that could have been made respecting a great many people during the last hundred years, and of no one more aptly than of Freud, who, as it happens, was familiar with it and repeats it in his *Future of an Illusion*. The object of that essay was to suggest a surrender to reality. His premise was that it is the unmistakable character of the present situation not that the promises of religion have become smaller but that they appear less credible to people. He notes the decline of religious belief and disagrees with the argument that man cannot in general do without the consolation of what he calls the religious illusion and that without it he would not endure the cruelty of reality. His conclusion is that man must venture at last into the hostile world and that this may be called education to reality. There is much more in that essay inimical to poetry and not least the observation in one of the final pages that "The voice of the intellect is a soft one, but it does not rest until it has gained a hearing." This, I fear, is intended to be the voice of the realist.

A tendency in language toward the connotative might very well parallel a tendency in other arts toward the denotative. We have just seen that that is in fact the situation. I suppose that the present always appears to be an illogical complication. The language of Joyce goes along with the dilapidations of Braque and Picasso and the music of the Austrians. To the extent that this painting and this music are the work of men who regard it as part of the science of painting and the science of music it is the work of realists. Actually its effect is that of the imagination, just as the effect of abstract painting is so often that of the imagination, although that may be different. Busoni said, in a letter to his wife, "I have made the painful discovery that nobody loves and feels music." Very likely, the reason there is a tendency in language toward the connotative today is that there are many who love it and feel it. It may be that Braque and Picasso love and feel painting and that Schönberg loves and feels music, although it seems that what they love and feel is something else.

A tendency toward the connotative, whether in language or elsewhere, cannot continue against the pressure of reality. If it is the pressure of reality that controls poetry, then the immediacy of various theories of poetry is not what it was. For instance, when Rostrevor Hamilton says, "The object of contemplation is the highly complex and unified content of consciousness, which comes into being through the developing subjective attitude of the percipient," he has in mind no such "content of consciousness" as every newspaper reader experiences today.

By way of further illustration, let me quote from Croce's Oxford lecture of 1933. He said: "If . . . poetry is intuition and expression, the fusion of sound and imagery, what is the material which takes on the form of sound and imagery? It is the whole man: the man who thinks and wills, and loves, and hates; who is strong and weak, sublime and pathetic, good and wicked; man in the exultation and agony of living; and together with the man, integral with him, it is all nature in its perpetual labour of evolution. . . . Poetry . . . is the triumph of contemplation. . . . Poetic genius chooses a strait path in which passion is calmed and calm is passionate."

Croce cannot have been thinking of a world in which all normal life is at least in suspense, or, if you like, under blockage. He was thinking of normal human experience.

Quite apart from the abnormal aspect of everyday life today, there is the normal aspect of it. The spirit of negation has been so active, so confident and so intolerant that the commonplaces about the romantic provoke us to wonder if our salvation, if the way out, is not the romantic. All the great things have been denied and we live in an intricacy of new and local mythologies, political, economic, poetic, which are asserted with an ever-enlarging incoherence. This is accompanied by an absence of any authority except force, operative or imminent. What has been called the disparagement of reason is an instance of the absence of authority. We pick up the radio and find that comedians regard the public use of words of more than two syllables as funny. We read of the opening of the National Gallery at Washington and we are convinced, in the end, that the pictures are counterfeit, that museums are impositions and that Mr. Mellon was a monster. We turn to a recent translation of Kierkegaard and we find him saying: "A great deal has been said about poetry reconciling one with existence; rather it might be said that it arouses one against existence; for poetry is unjust to men . . . it has use only for the elect, but that is a poor sort of reconciliation. I will take the case of sickness. Aesthetics replies proudly and quite consistently, 'That cannot be employed, poetry must not become a hospital.' Aesthetics culminates . . . by regarding sickness in accordance with the principle enunciated by Friedrich Schlegel: 'Nur Gesundheit is liebenswürdig.' (Health alone is lovable.)"

The enormous influence of education in giving everyone a little learning, and in giving large groups considerably more: something of history, something of philosophy, something of literature; the expansion of the middle class with its common preference for realistic satisfactions; the penetration of the masses of people by the ideas of liberal thinkers, even when that penetration is indirect, as by the reporting of the reasons why people oppose the ideas that they oppose,—these are normal aspects of everyday life. The way we live and the way we work alike cast us out on reality. If fifty private houses were to be built in New York this year, it would be a phenomenon. We no longer live in homes but in housing projects and this is so whether the project is literally a project or a club, a dormitory, a camp or an apartment in River House. It is not only that there are more of us and that we are actually close together. We are close together in every way. We lie in bed and listen to a broadcast from Cairo, and so on. There is no distance. We are intimate with people we have never seen and, unhappily, they are intimate with us. Democritus plucked his eye out because he could not look at a woman without thinking of her as a woman. If he had read a few of our novels, he would have torn himself to pieces. Dr. Richards has noted "the widespread increase in the aptitude of the average mind for self-dissolving introspection, the generally heightened awareness of the goings-on of our own minds, *merely as goings-on.*" This is nothing to the generally heightened awareness of the goings-on of other people's minds, *merely as goings-on.* The way we work is a good deal more difficult for the imagination than the highly civilized revolution that is occurring in respect to work indicates. It is, in the main, a revolution for more pay. We have been assured, by every visitor, that the American businessman is absorbed in his business and there is nothing to be gained by disputing it. As for the workers, it is enough to say that the word has grown to be literary. They have become, at their work, in the face of the machines, something approximating an abstraction, an energy. The time must be coming when, as they leave the factories, they will be passed through an air-chamber or a bar to revive them for riot and reading. I am sorry to have to add that to one that thinks, as Dr. Richards thinks, that poetry is the supreme use of language, some of the foreign universities in relation to our own appear to be, so far as the things of the imagination are concerned, as Verrocchio is to the sculptor of the statue of General Jackson.

These, nevertheless, are not the things that I had in mind when I spoke of the pressure of reality. These constitute the drift of incidents, to which we accustom ourselves as to the weather. Materialism is an old story and an indifferent one. Robert Wolseley said: "True genius . . . will enter into the hardest and dryest thing, enrich the most barren Soyl, and inform the meanest and most uncomely matter . . . the baser, the emptier, the obscurer, the fouler, and the less susceptible of Ornament the subject appears to be, the more is the Poet's Praise . . . who, as Horace says of Homer, can fetch Light out of Smoak, Roses out of Dunghills, and give a kind of Life to the Inanimate . . ." (Preface to Rochester's *Valentinian*, 1685, *English Association Essays and Studies* 1939). By the pressure of reality, I mean the pressure of an external event or events on the consciousness to the exclusion of any power of contemplation. The definition ought to be exact and, as it is, may be merely pretentious. But when one is trying to think of a whole generation and of a world at war, and trying at the same time to see what is happening to the imagination, particularly if one believes that that is what matters most, the plainest statement of what is happening can easily appear to be an affectation.

For more than ten years now, there has been an extraordinary pressure of news—let us say, news incomparably more pretentious than any description of it, news, at first, of the collapse of our system, or, call it, of life; then of news of a new world, but of a new world so uncertain that one did not know anything whatever of its nature, and does not know now, and could not tell whether it was to be all-English, all-German, all-Russian, all-Japanese, or all-American, and cannot tell now; and finally news of a war, which was a renewal of what, if it was not the greatest war, became such by this continuation. And for more than ten years, the consciousness of the world has concentrated on events which have made the ordinary movement of life seem to be the movement of people in the intervals of a storm. The disclosures of the impermanence of the past suggested, and suggest, an impermanence of the future. Little of what we have believed has been true. Only the prophecies are true. The present is an opportunity to repent. This is familiar enough. The war is only a part of a war-like whole. It is not possible to look backward and to see that the same thing was true in the past. It is a question of pressure, and pressure is incalculable and eludes the historian. The Napoleonic era is regarded as having had little or no effect on the poets and the novelists who lived in it. But Coleridge and Wordsworth and Sir Walter Scott and Jane Austen did not have to put up with Napoleon and Marx and Europe, Asia and Africa all at one time. It seems possible to say that they knew of the events of their day much as we know of the bombings in the interior of China and not at all as we know of the bombings of London, or, rather, as we should know of the bombings of Toronto or Montreal. Another part of the war-like whole to which we do not respond quite as we do to the news of war is the income tax. The blanks are specimens of mathematical prose. They titillate the instinct of self-preservation in a class in which that instinct has been forgotten. Virginia Woolf thought that the income tax, if it continued, would benefit poets by enlarging their vocabularies and I dare say that she was right.

If it is not possible to assert that the Napoleonic era was the end of one era in the history of the imagination and the beginning of another, one comes closer to the truth by making that assertion in respect to the French Revolution. The defeat or triumph of Hitler are parts of a war-like whole but the fate of an individual is different from the fate of a society. Rightly or wrongly, we feel that the fate of a society is involved in the orderly disorders of the present time. We are confronting, therefore, a set of events, not only beyond our power to tranquillize them in the mind, beyond our power to reduce them and metamorphose them, but events that stir the emotions to violence, that engage us in what is direct and immediate and real, and events that involve the concepts and sanctions that are the order of our lives and may involve our very lives; and these events are occurring persistently with increasing omen, in what may be called our presence. These are the things that I had in mind when I spoke of the pressure of reality, a pressure great enough and prolonged enough to bring about the end of one era in the history of the imagination and, if so, then great enough to bring about the beginning of another. It is one of the peculiarities of the imagination that it is always at the end of an era. What happens is that it is always attaching itself to a new reality, and adhering to it. It is not that there is a new imagination but that there is a new reality. The pressure of reality may, of course, be less than the general pressure that I have described. It exists for individuals according to the circumstances of their lives or according to the characteristics of their minds. To sum it up, the pressure of reality is, I think, the determining factor in the artistic character of an era and, as well, the determining factor in the artistic character of an individual. The resistance to this pressure or its evasion in the case of individuals of extraordinary imagination cancels the pressure so far as those individuals are concerned.

4

Suppose we try, now, to construct the figure of a poet, a possible poet. He cannot be a charioteer traversing vacant space, however ethereal. He must have lived all of the last two thousand years, and longer, and he must have instructed himself, as best he could, as he went along. He will have thought that Virgil, Dante, Shakespeare, Milton placed themselves in remote lands and in remote ages; that their men and women were the dead—and not the dead lying in the earth, but the dead still living in their remote lands and in their remote ages, and living in the earth or under it, or in the heavens—and he will wonder at those huge imaginations, in which what is remote becomes near, and what is dead lives with an intensity beyond any experience of life. He will consider that although he has himself witnessed, during the long period of his life, a general transition to reality, his own measure as a poet, in spite of all the passions of all the lovers of the truth, is the measure of his power to abstract himself, and to withdraw with him into his abstraction the reality on which the lovers of truth insist. He must be able to abstract himself and also to abstract reality, which he does by placing it in his imagination. He knows perfectly that he cannot be too noble a rider, that he cannot rise up loftily in helmet and armor on a horse of imposing bronze. He will think again of Milton and of what was said about him: that "the necessity of writing for one's living blunts the appreciation of writing when it bears the mark of perfection. Its quality disconcerts our hasty writers; they are ready to condemn it as preciosity and affectation. And if to them the musical and creative powers of words convey little pleasure, how out of date and irrelevant they must find the . . . music of Milton's verse." Don Quixote will make it imperative for him to make a choice, to come to a decision regarding the imagination and reality; and he will find that it is not a choice of one over the other and not a decision that divides them, but something subtler, a recognition that here, too, as between these poles, the universal interdependence exists, and hence his choice and his decision must be that they are equal and inseparable. To take a single instance: When Horatio says,

> Now cracks a noble heart. Good night, sweet prince,
> And flights of angels sing thee to thy rest!

are not the imagination and reality equal and inseparable? Above all, he will not forget General Jackson or the picture of the *Wooden Horses.*

I said of the picture that it was a work in which everything was favorable to reality. I hope that the use of that bare word has been enough. But without regard to its range of meaning in thought, it includes all its natural images, and its connotations are without limit. Bergson describes the visual perception of a motionless object as the most stable of internal states. He says: "The object may remain the same, I may look at it from the same side, at the same angle, in the same light; nevertheless, the vision I now have of it differs from that which I have just had, even if only because the one is an instant later than the other. My memory is there, which conveys something of the past into the present."

Dr. Joad's comment on this is: "Similarly with external things. Every body, every quality of a body resolves itself into an enormous number of vibrations, movements, changes. What is it that vibrates, moves, is changed? There is no answer. Philosophy has long dismissed the notion of substance and modern physics has endorsed the dismissal. . . . How, then, does the world come to appear to us as a collection of solid, static objects extended in space? Because of the intellect, which presents us with a false view of it."

The poet has his own meaning for reality, and the painter has, and the musician has; and besides what it means to the intelligence and to the senses, it means something to everyone, so to speak. Notwithstanding this, the word in its general sense, which is the sense in which I have used it, adapts itself instantly. The subject-matter of poetry is not that "collection of solid, static objects extended in space" but the life that is lived in the scene that it composes; and so reality is not that external scene but the life that is lived in it. Reality is things as they are. The general sense of the word proliferates its special senses. It is a jungle in itself. As in the case of a jungle, everything that makes it up is pretty much of one color. First, then, there is the reality that is taken for granted, that is latent, and, on the whole, ignored. It is the comfortable American state of life of the eighties, the nineties and the first ten years of the present century. Next, there is the reality that has ceased to be indifferent, the years when the Victorians had been disposed of and intellectual minorities and social minorities began to take their place and to convert our state of life to something that might not be final. This much more vital reality made the life that had preceded it look like a volume of Ackermann's colored plates or one of Töpfer's books of sketches in Switzerland. I am trying to give the feel of it. It was the reality of twenty or thirty years ago. I say that it was a vital reality. The phrase gives a false impression. It was vital in the sense of being tense, of being instinct with the fatal or with what might be the fatal. The minorities began to convince us that the Victorians had left nothing behind. The Russians followed the Victorians, and the Germans, in their way, followed the Russians. The British Empire, directly or indirectly, was what was left and as to that one could not be sure whether it was a shield or a target. Reality then became violent and so remains. This much ought to be said to make it a little clearer that in speaking of the pressure of reality, I am thinking of life in a state of violence, not physically violent, as yet, for us in America, but physically violent for millions of our friends and for still more millions of our enemies and spiritually violent, it may be said, for everyone alive.

A possible poet must be a poet capable of resisting or evading the pressure of the reality of this last degree, with the knowledge that the degree of today may become a deadlier degree tomorrow. There is, however, no point to dramatizing the future in advance of the fact. I confine myself to the outline of a possible poet, with only the slightest sketch of his background.

5

Here I am, well-advanced in my paper, with everything of interest that I started out to say remaining to be said. I am interested in the nature of poetry and I have stated its nature, from one of the many points of view from which it is possible to state it. It is an interdependence of the imagination and reality as equals. This is not a definition, since it is incomplete. But it states the nature of poetry. Then I am interested in the role of the poet and this is paramount. In this area of my subject I might be expected to speak of the social, that is to say sociological or political, obligation of the poet. He has none. That he must be contemporaneous is as old as Longinus and I dare say older. But that he *is* contemporaneous is almost inevitable. How contemporaneous in the direct sense in which being contemporaneous is intended were the four great poets of whom I spoke a moment ago? I do not think that a poet owes any more as a social obligation than he owes as a moral obligation, and if there is anything concerning poetry about which people agree it is that the role of the poet is not to be found in morals. I cannot say what that wide agreement amounts to because the agreement (in which I do not join) that the poet is under a social obligation is equally wide. Reality is life and life is society and the imagination and reality; that is to say, the imagination and society are inseparable. That is pre-eminently true in the case of the poetic drama. The poetic drama needs a terrible genius before it is anything more than a literary relic. Besides the theater has forgotten that it could ever be terrible. It is not one of the instruments of fate, decidedly. Yes: the all-commanding subject-matter of poetry is life, the never-ceasing source. But it is not a social obligation. One does not love and go back to one's ancient mother as a social obligation. One goes back out of a suasion not be denied. Unquestionably if a social movement moved one deeply enough, its moving poems would follow. No politician can command the imagination, directing it to do this or that. Stalin might grind his teeth the whole of a Russian winter and yet all the poets in the Soviets might remain silent the following spring. He might excite their imaginations by something he said or did. He would not command them. He is singularly free from that "cult of pomp," which is the comic side of the European disaster; and that means as much as anything to us. The truth is that the social obligation so closely urged is a phase of the pressure of reality which a poet (in the absence of dramatic poets) is bound to resist or evade today. Dante in Purgatory and Paradise was still the voice of the Middle Ages but not through fulfilling any social obligation. Since that is the role most frequently urged, if that role is eliminated, and if a possible poet is left facing life without any categorical exactions upon him, what then? What is his function? Certainly it is not to lead people out of the confusion in which they find themselves. Nor is it, I think, to comfort them while they follow their readers to and fro. I think that his function is to make his imagination theirs and that he fulfills himself only as he sees his imagination become the light in the minds of others. His role, in short, is to help people to live their lives. Time and time again it has been said that he may not address himself to an élite. I think he may. There is not a poet whom we prize living today that does not address himself to an élite. The poet will continue to do this: to address himself to an élite even in a classless society, unless, perhaps, this exposes him to imprisonment or exile. In that event he is likely not to address himself to anyone at all. He may, like Shostakovich, content himself with pretence. He will, nevertheless, still be addressing himself to an élite, for all poets address themselves to someone and it is of the essence of that instinct, and it seems to amount to an instinct, that it should be to an élite, not to a drab but to a woman with the hair of a pythoness, not to a chamber of commerce but to a gallery of one's own, if there are enough of one's own to fill a gallery. And that élite, if it responds, not out of complaisance, but because the poet has quickened it, because he has educed from it that for which it was searching in itself and in the life around it and which it had not yet quite found, will thereafter do for the poet what he cannot do for himself, that is to say, receive his poetry.

I repeat that his role is to help people to live their lives. He has had immensely to do with giving life whatever savor it possesses. He has had to do with whatever the imagination and the senses have made of the world. He has, in fact, had to do with life except as the intellect has had to do with it and, as to that, no one is needed to tell us that poetry and philosophy are akin. I want to repeat for two reasons a number of observations made by Charles Mauron. The first reason is that these observations tell us what it is that a poet does to help people to live their lives and the second is that they prepare the way for a word concerning escapism. They are: that the artist transforms us into epicures; that he has to discover the possible work of art in the real world, then to extract it, when he does not himself compose it entirely; that he is *un amoureux perpétuel* of the world that he contemplates and thereby enriches; that art sets out to express the human soul; and finally that everything like a firm grasp of reality is eliminated from the aesthetic field. With these aphorisms in mind, how is it possible to condemn escapism? The poetic process is psychologically an escapist process. The chatter about escapism is, to my way of thinking, merely common cant. My own remarks about resisting or evading the pressure of reality mean escapism, if analyzed. Escapism has a pejorative sense, which it cannot be supposed that I include in the sense in which I use the word. The pejorative sense applies where the poet is not attached to reality, where the imagination does not adhere to reality, which, for my part, I regard as fundamental. If we go back to the collection of solid, static objects extended in space, which Dr. Joad posited, and if we say that the space is blank space, nowhere, without color, and that the objects, though solid, have no shadows and, though static, exert a mournful power, and, without elaborating this complete poverty, if suddenly we hear a different and familiar description of the place:

> *This City now doth, like a garment, wear*
> *The beauty of the morning, silent bare,*

Ships, towers, domes, theatres, and temples lie
Open unto the fields, and to the sky;
All bright and glittering in the smokeless air;

if we have this experience, we know how poets help people to live their lives. This illustration must serve for all the rest. There is, in fact, a world of poetry indistinguishable from the world in which we live, or, I ought to say, no doubt, from the world in which we shall come to live, since what makes the poet the potent figure that he is, or was, or ought to be, is that he creates the world to which we turn incessantly and without knowing it and that he gives to life the supreme fictions without which we are unable to conceive of it.

And what about the sound of words? What about nobility, of which the fortunes were to be a kind of test of the value of the poet? I do not know of anything that will appear to have suffered more from the passage of time than the music of poetry and that has suffered less. The deepening need for words to express our thoughts and feelings which, we are sure, are all the truth that we shall ever experience, having no illusions, makes us listen to words when we hear them, loving them and feeling them, makes us search the sound of them, for a finality, a perfection, an unalterable vibration, which it is only within the power of the acutest poet to give them. Those of us who may have been thinking of the path of poetry, those who understand that words are thoughts and not only our own thoughts but the thoughts of men and women ignorant of what it is that they are thinking, must be conscious of this: that, above everything else, poetry is words; and that words, above everything else, are, in poetry, sounds. This being so, my time and yours might have been better spent if I had been less interested in trying to give our possible poet an identity and less interested in trying to appoint him to his place. But unless I had done these things, it might have been thought that I was rhetorical, when I was speaking in the simplest way about things of such importance that nothing is more so. A poet's words are of things that do not exist without the words. Thus, the image of the charioteer and of the winged horses, which has been held to be precious for all of time that matters, was created by words of things that never existed without the words. A description of Verrocchio's statue could be the integration of an illusion equal to the statue itself. Poetry is a revelation in words by means of the words. Croce was not speaking of poetry in particular when he said that language is perpetual creation. About nobility I cannot be sure that the decline, not to say the disappearance of nobility is anything more than a maladjustment between the imagination and reality. We have been a little insane about the truth. We have had an obsession. In its ultimate extension, the truth about which we have been insane will lead us to look beyond the truth to something in which the imagination will be the dominant complement. It is not only that the imagination adheres to reality, but, also, that reality adheres to the imagination and that the interdependence is essential. We may emerge from our *bassesse* and, if we do, how would it happen if not by the intervention of some fortune of the mind? And what would that fortune of the mind happen to be? It might be only commonsense but even that, a commonsense beyond the truth, would be a nobility of long descent.

The poet refuses to allow his task to be set for him. He denies that he has a task and considers that the organization of materia poetica is a contradiction in terms. Yet the imagination gives to everything that it touches a peculiarity, and it seems to me that the peculiarity of the imagination is nobility, of which there are many degrees. This inherent nobility is the natural source of another, which our extremely headstrong generation regards as false and decadent. I mean that nobility which is our spiritual height and depth; and while I know how difficult it is to express it, nevertheless I am bound to give a sense of it. Nothing could be more evasive and inaccessible. Nothing distorts itself and seeks disguise more quickly. There is a shame of disclosing it and in its definite presentations a horror of it. But there it is. The fact that it is there is what makes it possible to invite to the reading and writing of poetry men of intelligence and desire for life. I am not thinking of the ethical or the sonorous or at all of the manner of it. The manner of it is, in fact, its difficulty, which each man must feel each day differently, for himself. I am not thinking of the solemn, the portentous or demoded. On the other hand, I am evading a definition. If it is defined, it will be fixed and it must not be fixed. As in the case of an external thing, nobility resolves itself into an enormous number of vibrations, movements, changes. To fix it is to put an end to it. Let me show it to you unfixed.

Late last year Epstein exhibited some of his flower paintings at the Leicester Galleries in London. A commentator in *Apollo* said: *"How with this rage can beauty hold a plea* . . . The quotation from Shakespeare's 65th sonnet prefaces the catalogue. . . . It would be apropos to any other flower paintings than Mr. Epstein's. His make no pretence to fragility. They shout, explode all over the picture space and generally oppose the rage of the world with such a rage of form and colour as no flower in nature or pigment has done since Van Gogh."

What ferocious beauty the line from Shakespeare puts on when used under such circumstances! While it has its modulation of despair, it holds its plea and its plea is noble. There is no element more conspicuously absent from contemporary poetry than nobility. There is no element that poets have sought after, more curiously and more piously, certain of its obscure existence. Its voice is one of the inarticulate voices which it is their business to overhear and to record. The nobility of rhetoric is, of course, a lifeless nobility. Pareto's epigram that history is a cemetery of aristocracies easily becomes another: that poetry is a cemetery of nobilities. For the sensitive poet, conscious of negations, nothing is more difficult than the affirmations of nobility and yet there is nothing that he requires of himself more persistently, since in them and in their kind, alone, are to be found those sanctions that are the reasons for his being and for that occasional ecstasy, or ecstatic freedom of the mind, which is his special privilege.

It is hard to think of a thing more out of time than nobility. Looked at plainly it seems false and dead and ugly. To look at it at all makes us realize sharply that in our present, in the presence of our reality, the past looks false and is, therefore, dead and is, therefore, ugly; and we turn away from it as from something repulsive and particularly from the characteristic that it has a way of assuming: something that was noble in its day, grandeur that was, the rhetorical once. But as a wave is a force and not the water of which it is composed, which is never the same, so nobility is a force and not the manifestations of which it is composed, which are never the same. Possibly this description of it as a force will do more than anything else I can have said about it to reconcile you to it. It is not an artifice that the mind has added to human nature. The mind has added nothing to human nature. It is a violence from within that protects us from a violence without. It is the imagination pressing back against the pressure of reality. It seems, in the last analysis, to have something to do with our self-preservation; and that, no doubt, is why the expression of it, the sound of its words, helps us to live our lives.

Marianne Moore, "Feeling and Precision," 1944

"I, too, dislike it," Marianne Moore writes in her poem entitled "Poetry." "Reading it, however, with a perfect contempt for it, one discovers in it, after all, a place for the genuine." The geniune, for Moore, often meant not only the raw material of poetry, but an equal emphasis on the crafting of it.

Moore's first poems, championed by Pound, appeared in the *Egoist* and *Poetry* in 1915, and her first book from the Egoist Press in 1921. Critic as well as poet, Moore served as editor of the literary magazine *The Dial* from 1925 to 1929, where she reviewed almost all the modernist poets including H.D., Eliot, Stevens, Pound, Williams, Cummings, and Stein.

Thoroughly modernist in her collagist technique of embedding quotations from other writers in her poetry and her prose, Moore also practiced the qualities of precision and economy professed by the imagists. Her use of syllabics, wherein the rhythm of the poem is determined by an arbitrary number of syllables counted per line—unlike the traditonal accentual method of scanning feet—made her poetry sound very much like prose. "Freedom," she defines in the later essay "Humility, Concentration, and Gusto," is "a discipline imposed by ourselves."

"Feeling and Precision" first appeared in the *Sewanee Review* in 1944 and was subsequently published in her collection of prose pieces entitled *Predilections* in 1951.

❋

Feeling and Precision

Feeling at its deepest—as we all have reason to know—tends to be inarticulate. If it does manage to be articulate, it is likely to seem overcondensed, so that the author is resisted as being enigmatic or disobliging or arrogant.

One of New York's more painstaking magazines asked me, at the suggestion of a contributor, to analyze my sentence structure, and my instinctive reply might have seemed dictatorial: you don't devise a rhythm, the rhythm is the person, and the sentence but a radiograph of personality. The following principles, however, are aids to composition by which I try, myself, to be guided: if a long sentence with dependent clauses seems obscure, one can break it into shorter units by imagining into what phrases it would fall as conversation; in the second place, expanded explanation tends to spoil the lion's leap—an awkwardness which is surely brought home to one in conversation; and in the third place, we must be as clear as our natural reticence allows us to be.

William Carlos Williams, commenting on his poem "The Red Wheelbarrow," said, "The rhythm though no more than a fragment, denotes a certain unquenchable exaltation"; and Wallace Stevens, referring to poetry under the metaphor of the lion says, "It can kill a man." Yet the lion's leap would be mitigated almost to harmlessness if the lion were clawless, so precision is both impact and exactitude, as with surgery; and also in music, the conductor's signal, as I am reminded by a friend, which "begins far back of the beat, so that you don't see when the down beat comes. To have started such a long distance ahead makes it possible to be exact. Whereas you can't be exact by being restrained." When writing with maximum impact, the writer seems under compulsion to set down an unbearable accuracy; and in connection with precision as we see it in metaphor, I think of Gerard Hopkins and his description of the dark center in the eye of a peacock feather as "the color of the grape where the flag is turned back"; also his saying about some lambs he had seen frolicking in a field, "It was as though it was the ground that tossed them"; at all events, precision is a thing of the imagination; and it is a matter of diction, of diction that is virile because galvanized against inertia. In Louis Ginsberg's poem "Command of the Dead," the final stanza reads:

> And so they live in all our works
>> And sinew us to victory.
> We see them when we most are gay;
>> We feel them when we most are free.

The natural order for the two mosts would be

> We see them when we are most gay;
> We feel them when we are most free

but that would mean, being at our gayest makes us think of them, and being free makes us feel them—gross in accuracy since these "mosts" are the essence of compassion.

"Fighting Faith Saves the World," an inadvertent ambiguity, as the title for a review of *Journey Among Warriors* by Eve Curie, seems to mean, fight faith and the world is saved; whereas to say, a fighting faith saves the world, would safeguard the meaning.

Explicitness being the enemy of brevity, an instance of difficult descriptive matter accurately presented is that passage in the Book of Daniel (X: 9, 10, 11) where the writer says: "Then was I in a deep sleep on my face, and my face toward the ground. And, behold, an hand touched me, which set me upon my knees and upon the palms of my hands. And I stood trembling." Think what *we* might have done with the problem if we had been asked to describe how someone was wakened and, gradually turning over, got up off the ground.

Instinctively we employ antithesis as an aid to precision, and in Arthur Waley's translation from the Chinese one notices the many paired meanings —"left and right"; "waking and sleeping"; "one embroiders with silk, an inch a day; of plain sewing one can do more than five feet." Anyone with contemporary pride thinks of W. H. Auden in connection with antithesis, as in *The Double Man* (the *New Year Letter*) he says of the devil:

> For, torn between conflicting needs,
> He's doomed to fail if he succeeds,
> . . . .
> If love has been annihilated
> There's only hate left to be hated.

Nor can we forget Socrates' answer: "I would rather die having spoken in my manner than speak in your manner and live." And there is that very dainty instance of antithesis in Thomas Watson's and William Byrd's madrigal, "A Gratification unto Master John Case":

> Let Enuy barke against the starres,
> Let Folly sayle which way she please,
> with him I wish my dayes to spend, . . .
> whose quill hath stoode fayre Musickes friend,
> chief end to peace, chief port of ease.

When we think we don't like art it is because it is artificial art. "Mere technical display," as Plato says, "is a beastly noise"—in contrast with art, which is "a spiritual magnetism" or "fascination" or "conjuring of the soul."

Voltaire objected to those who said in enigmas what others had said naturally, and we agree; yet we must have the courage of our peculiarities. What would become of Ogden Nash, his benign vocabulary and fearless rhymes, if he wrote only in accordance with the principles set forth by our manuals of composition?

> I love the Baby Giant Panda
> I'd welcome one to my veranda.
> I never worry, wondering maybe
> Whether it isn't Giant Baby;
> I leave such matters to the scientists—
> The Giant Baby—and Baby Giantists.
> I simply want a veranda, and a
> Giant Baby Giant Panda.

This, it seems to me, is not so far removed from George Wither's motto: "I grow and wither both together."

Feeling has departed from anything that has on it the touch of affectation, and William Rose Benét, in his preface to the *Collected Poems of Ford Madox Ford*, says: "Whether or not there is such a thing as poetic afflatus there are certain moments that must be seized upon, when more precise language than at any other time, is ready to hand for the expression of spontaneous feeling." My own fondness for the unaccented rhyme derives, I think, from an instinctive effort to ensure naturalness. "Even elate and fearsome rightness like Shakespeare's is only preserved from the offense of being 'poetic' by his well-nested effects of helpless naturalness."

Chaucer and Henryson, it seems to me, are the perfection of naturalness in their apparently artless art of conveying emotion intact. In "Orpheus and Eurydice," Henryson tells how Tantalus stood in a flood that rose "aboif his chin"; yet

> quhen he gaipit thair wald no drop cum In;
> . . . .
> Thus gat he nocht his thrist [to slake] no[r] mend.
>
> Befoir his face ane naple hang also,
> fast at his mowth upoun a twynid [threid],

quhen he gaipit, It rollit to and fro,
and fled, as it refusit him to feid.
Quhen orpheus thus saw him suffir neid,
he tuk his harp and fast on it can clink;
The wattir stud, and tantalus gat a drink.

One notices the wholesomeness of the uncapitalized beginnings of
lines, and the gusto of invention, with climax proceeding out of climax,
which is the mark of feeling.

We call climax a device, but is it not the natural result of strong feeling? It is, moreover, a pyramid that can rest either on its point or in its
base, witty anticlimax being one of Ludwig Bemelmans' best enticements,
as when he says of the twelve little girls, in his story *Madeline:*

They smiled at the good
and frowned at the bad
and sometimes they were very sad.

Intentional anticlimax as a department of surprise is a subject by itself; indeed, an art, "bearing," as Longinus says, "the stamp of vehement
emotion like a ship before a veering wing," both as content and as sound;
but especially as sound, in the use of which the poet becomes a kind of
hypnotist—recalling Kenneth Burke's statement that "the hypnotist has a
way out and a way in."

Concealed rhyme and the interiorized climax usually please me better
than the open rhyme and the insisted-on climax, and we can readily understand Dr. Johnson's objection to rigmarole, in his takeoff on the ballad:

I put my hat upon my head,
    And went into the Strand.
And there I saw another man,
    With his hat in his hand.

"Weak rhythm" of the kind that "enables an audience to foresee the
ending and keep time with their feet," disapproved by Longinus, has its
subtle opposite in E. E. Cummings' lines about Gravenstein apples—
"wall" and "fall," "round," "sound," and "ground," worked into a hastening
tempo:

But over a (see just
over this) wall

the red and the round
(they're Gravensteins) fall
with a kind of a blind
big sound on the ground

And the intensity of Henry Treece's "Prayer in Time of War" so shapes the lines that it scarcely occurs to one to notice whether they are rhymed or not:

Black Angel, come you down! Oh Purge of God,
By shroud of pestilence make pure the mind,
Strike dead the running panther of desire
That in despair the poem put on wings,
That letting out the viper from the veins
Man rock the mountain with his two bare hands!

With regard to unwarinesses that defeat precision, excess is the common substitute for energy. We have it in our semi-academic, too conscious adverbs—awfully, terribly, frightfully, infinitely, tremendously; in the word "stunning," the phrase "knows his Aristotle," or his Picasso, or whatever it may be; whereas we have a contrastingly energetic usefulness in John Crowe Ransom's term "particularistic," where he says T. S. Eliot "is the most particularistic critic that English poetry and English criticism have met with." Similarly with Dr. Johnson's "encomiastick," in the statement that Dryden's account of Shakespeare "may stand as a perpetual model of encomiastick criticism."

It is curious to see how we have ruined the word "fearful" as meaning full of fear. Thomas Nashe says of his compatriot Barnes—quoting Campion—"hee bragd when he was in France, he slue ten men, when (fearful cowbaby), he never heard a piece shot off but he fell on his face."

One recalls, as a pleasing antidote to jargon, Wyndham Lewis' magazine *The Tyro*, which defined a tyro as "an elementary person, an elemental usually known in journalism as the veriesttyro." "Very," when it doesn't mean true, is a word from which we are rightly estranged, though there are times when it seems necessary to the illusion of conversation or to steady the rhythm; and a child's overstatement of surprise upon receiving a gift—a playhouse—seems valuable, like foreign-language idiom—"This is the most glorious and terrific thing that ever came into this house"; but Sir Francis Bacon was probably right when he said, "Hyperbole is comely only in love."

I have an objection to the word "and" as a connective between adjectives—"he is a crude and intolerant thinker." But note the use of "and" as an ornament in the sonnet (66) in which Shakespeare is enumerating the many things of which he is tired:

> And art made tongue-tied by authority,
> And folly (doctor-like) controlling skill,
> And simple truth miscall'd simplicity,
> And captive good attending captain ill.

Defending Plato against the charge of "allegorical bombast" in his eulogy of man's anatomy and the provision whereby the heart "might throb against a yielding surface and get no damage," Longinus asks, "Which is better, in poetry and in prose, . . . grandeur with a few flaws or mediocrity that is impeccable?" And unmistakably Ezra Pound's instinct against preciosity is part of his instinct for precision and accounts for his "freedom of motion" in saying what he has to say "like a bolt from a catapult"—not that the catapult is to us invariably a messenger of comfort. One of his best accuracies, it seems to me, is the word "general" in the sentence in which he praises "the general effect" of Ford Madox Ford's poem "On Heaven"—avoiding the temptation to be spuriously specific; and although Henry James was probably so susceptible to emotion as to be obliged to seem unemotional, it is a kind of painter's accuracy for Ezra Pound to say of him as a writer, "Emotions to Henry James were more or less things that other people had, that one didn't go into."

Fear of insufficiency is synonymous with insufficiency, and fear of incorrectness makes for rigidity. Indeed, any concern about how well one's work is going to be received seems to mildew effectiveness. T. S. Eliot attributes Bishop Andrewes' precision to "the pure motive," and the fact that when he "takes a word and derives the world from it, . . . he is wholly in his subject, unaware of anything else." Mr. McBride, in the New York *Sun,* once said of Rembrandt and his etching "The Three Crosses": "It was as though Rembrandt was talking to himself, without any expectation that the print would be seen or understood by others. He saw these things and so testified."

This same rapt quality we have in Bach's *Art of the Fugue*—his intensively private soliloquizing continuity that ends, "Behold I Stand before Thy Throne." We feel it in the titles of some of his works, even in translation—"Behold from Heaven to Earth I Come."

Professor Maritain, when lecturing on scholasticism and immortality, spoke of those suffering in concentration camps, "unseen by any star, unheard by any ear," and the almost terrifying solicitude with which he spoke made one know that belief is stronger even than the struggle to survive. And what he said so unconsciously was poetry. So art is but an expression of our needs; is feeling, modified by the writer's moral and technical insights.

William Carlos Williams, "Author's Introduction" to *The Wedge*, 1944

As early as 1918, Williams was distancing himself from the Anglo-American modernism of Pound and Eliot in the prologue of his experimental prose piece *Kora in Hell*, calling them "men content with the connotations of their masters." Although greatly influenced by imagism, and Pound, whom he first met when they were undergraduates at the University of Pennsylvania, as well as the Dada and surrealist visual artists and poets who gathered around Alfred Stieglitz's 291 gallery in Manhattan, Williams wanted to create something new, something that drew on the contemporaerity of America and the speech rhythms of the American idiom. "Nothing is good," he writes, "save the new."

In his early book, *Spring and All* (1923) Williams combines prose with some of the most well-known of his poems, such as "The Red Wheelbarrow," poems that aim at direct statement and the commonplace fused with the energy of the imagination, what he defines as "seeing the thing itself without forethought or afterthought but with great intensity of perception." This essay, which served as an introduction to his 1944 collection of poems, *The Wedge*, is emblematic of this objectivist stance, as well as for his claims for a new prosody. His belief, like Pound's, was that in order to say something new, one must be able to say it in a new way. The poem as a machine. Art as a made thing. "Compose," he wrote in his poem, "A Sort of a Song," written the same year as this essay:

> Compose. (No ideas
> but in things) Invent!

Williams, more than anyone, has changed our idea of the suitable subject matter of a poem. A poem can be made out of anything because (as Mallarmé, a very different sort of poet, said to Degas) it is made out of words.

❋

Author's Introduction to *The Wedge*

The war is the first and only thing in the world today.

The arts generally are not, nor is this writing a diversion from that for relief, a turning away. It *is* the war or part of it, merely a different sector of the field.

Critics of rather better than average standing have said in recent years that after socialism has been achieved it's likely there will be no further use for poetry, that it will disappear. This comes from nothing else than a faulty definition of poetry—and the arts generally. I don't hear anyone say that mathematics is likely to be outmoded, to disappear shortly. Then why poetry?

It is an error attributable to the Freudian concept of the thing, that the arts are a resort from frustration, a misconception still entertained in many minds.

They speak as though action itself in all its phases were not compatible with frustration. All action the same. But Richard Coeur de Lion wrote at least one of the finest lyrics of his day. Take Don Juan for instance. Who isn't frustrated and does not prove it by his actions—if you want to say so? But through art the psychologically maimed may become the most distinguished man of his age. Take Freud for instance.

The making of poetry is no more an evidence of frustration than is the work of Henry Kaiser or of Timoshenko. It's the war, the driving forward of desire to a complex end. And when that shall have been achieved, mathematics and the arts will turn elsewhere—beyond the atom if necessary for their reward and let's all be frustrated together.

A man isn't a block that remains stationary though the psychologists treat him so—and most take an insane pride in believing it. Consistency! He varies; Hamlet today, Caesar tomorrow; here, there, somewhere—if he is to retain his sanity, and why not?

The arts have a *complex* relation to society. The poet isn't a fixed phenomenon, no more is his work. *That* might be a note on current affairs, a diagnosis, a plan for procedure, a retrospect—all in its own peculiarly enduring form. There need be nothing limited or frustrated about that. It may be a throw-off from the most violent and successful action or run parallel to it, a saga. It may be the picking out of an essential detail for memory, something to be set aside for further study, a sort of shorthand of emotional significances for later reference.

Let the metaphysical take care of itself, the arts have nothing to do with it. They will concern themselves with it if they please, among other things. To make two bald statements: There's nothing sentimental about a machine, and: A poem is a small (or large) machine made of words. When I say there's nothing sentimental about a poem I mean that there can be no part, as in any other machine, that is redundant.

Prose may carry a load of ill-defined matter like a ship. But poetry is the machine which drives it, pruned to a perfect economy. As in all machines its movement is intrinsic, undulant, a physical more than a literary character. In a poem this movement is distinguished in each case by the character of the speech from which it arises.

Therefore, each speech having its own character, the poetry it engenders will be peculiar to that speech also in its own intrinsic form. The effect is beauty, what in a single object resolves our complex feelings of propriety. One doesn't seek beauty. All that an artist or a Sperry can do is to drive toward his purpose, in the nature of his materials; not to take gold where Babbit metal is called for; to make: make clear the complexity of his perceptions in the medium given to him by inheritance, chance, accident or whatever it may be to work with according to his talents and the will that drives them. Don't talk about frustration fathering the arts. The bastardization of words is too widespread for that today.

My own interest in the arts has been extracurricular. Up from the gutter, so to speak. Of necessity. Each age and place to its own. But in the U. S. the necessity for recognizing this intrinsic character has been largely ignored by the various English Departments of the academies.

When a man makes a poem, makes it, mind you, he takes words as he finds them interrelated about him and composes them—without distortion which would mar their exact significances—into an intense expression of his perceptions and ardors that they may constitute a revelation in the speech that he uses. It isn't what he *says* that counts as a work of art, it's what he makes, with such intensity of perception that it lives with an intrinsic movement of its own to verify its authenticity. Your attention is called now and then to some beautiful line or sonnet-sequence because of what is said there. So be it. To me all sonnets say the same thing of no importance. What does it matter what the line "says"?

There is no poetry of distinction without formal invention, for it is in the intimate form that works of art achieve their exact meaning, in which they most resemble the machine, to give language its highest dignity, its illumination in the environment to which it is native. Such war, as the arts live and breathe by, is continuous.

It may be that my interests as expressed here are pre-art. If so I look for a development along these lines and will be satisfied with nothing else.

Charles Olson, "Projective Verse," 1950

Four years after William Carlos Williams wrote his introduction to *The Wedge,* he spoke at the University of Washington. In a lecture entitled "The Poem as a Field of Action," Williams said, "I propose sweeping changes from top to bottom of the poetic structure." Whereas Williams believed this new structure might evolve out of attention paid to speech rhythms, Charles Olson claimed it would come from "the act of the composition itself." In this extremely influential essay, published in *New York Poetry* in 1950, Olson proposes a new method for doing so, one based on the rhythms of breath and the projective nature of thought.

"Projective Verse" was written a year before Olson began his years as instructor and director of Black Mountain College, in North Carolina, which had on its faculty such experimental artists as the composer John Cage, choreographer Merce Cunningham, and painters Franz Kline and Robert Rauschenberg. During his tenure there, he met and published Robert Creeley, Robert Duncan, and Denise Levertov (who became known as Black Mountain poets), as well as Louis Zukofsky, Allen Ginsberg, and Jack Kerouac. Promoting a verse that, like Williams's, is active and alive, not reflective or representational, Olson believed that "art doesn't seek to describe but to enact."

✳

Projective   Verse

(projectile   (percussive   (prospective

vs.

The NON-Projective

(or what a French critic calls "closed" verse, that verse which print bred and which is pretty much what we have had, in English & American, and have still got, despite the work of Pound & Williams:

it led Keats, already a hundred years ago, to see it (Wordsworth's, Mil-
ton's) in the light of "the Egotistical Sublime"; and it persists, at this lat-
ter day, as what you might call the private-soul-at-any-public-wall)

Verse now, 1950, if it is to go ahead, if it is to be of *essential* use, must, I
take it, catch up and put into itself certain laws and possibilities of the
breath, of the breathing of the man who writes as well as of his listenings.
(The revolution of the ear, 1910, the trochee's heave, asks it of the younger
poets.)

✻

I want to do two things: first, try to show what projective or OPEN verse
is, what it involves, in its act of composition, how, in distinction from the
non-projective, it is accomplished; and II, suggest a few ideas about what
stance toward reality brings such verse into being, what that stance does,
both to the poet and to his reader. (The stance involves, for example, a
change beyond, and larger than, the technical, and may, the way things
look, lead to new poetics and to new concepts from which some sort of
drama, say, or of epic, perhaps, may emerge.)

I

First, some simplicities that a man learns, if he works in OPEN, or what
can also be called COMPOSITION BY FIELD, as opposed to inherited line,
stanza, over-all form, what is the "old" base of the non-projective.

(1) the *kinetics* of the thing. A poem is energy transferred from where
the poet got it (he will have some several causations), by way of the poem
itself to, all the way over to, the reader. Okay. Then the poem itself must,
at all points, be a high energy-construct and, at all points, an energy-
discharge. So: how is the poet to accomplish same energy, how is he, what
is the process by which a poet gets in, at all points energy at least the
equivalent of the energy which propelled him in the first place, yet an energy which is peculiar to verse alone and which will be, obviously, also different from the energy which the reader, because he is a third term, will
take away?

This is the problem which any poet who departs from closed
form is specially confronted by. And it involves a whole series of new
recognitions. From the moment he ventures into FIELD COMPOSITION

—put himself in the open—he can go by no track other than the one the poem under hand declares, for itself. Thus he has to behave, and be, instant by instant, aware of some several forces just now beginning to be examined. (It is much more, for example, this push, than simply such a one as Pound put, so wisely, to get us started: "the musical phrase," go by it, boys, rather than by, the metronome.)

(2) is the *principle*, the law which presides conspicuously over such composition, and, when obeyed, is the reason why a projective poem can come into being. It is this: FORM IS NEVER MORE THAN AN EXTENSION OF CONTENT. (Or so it got phrased by one, R. Creeley, and it makes absolute sense to me, with this possible corollary, that right form, in any given poem, is the only and exclusively possible extension of content under hand.) There it is, brothers, sitting there, for USE.

Now (3) the *process* of the thing, how the principle can be made so to shape the energies that the form is accomplished. And I think it can be boiled down to one statement (first pounded into my head by Edward Dahlberg): ONE PERCEPTION MUST IMMEDIATELY AND DIRECTLY LEAD TO A FURTHER PERCEPTION. It means exactly what it says, is a matter of, at *all* points (even, I should say, of our management of daily reality as of the daily work) get on with it, keep moving, keep in, speed, the nerves, their speed, the perceptions, theirs, the acts, the split second acts, the whole business, keep it moving as fast as you can, citizen. And if you also set up as a poet, USE USE USE the process at all points, in any given poem always, always one perception must must must MOVE, INSTANTER, ON ANOTHER!

So there we are, fast, there's the dogma. And its excuse, its usableness, in practice. Which gets us, it ought to get us, inside the machinery, now, 1950, of how projective verse is made.

❋

If I hammer, if I recall in, and keep calling in, the breath, the breathing as distinguished from the hearing, it is for cause, it is to insist upon a part that breath plays in verse which has not (due, I think, to the smothering of the power of the line by too set a concept of foot) has not been sufficiently observed or practiced, but which has to be if verse is to advance to its proper force and place in the day, now, and ahead. I take it that PROJECTIVE VERSE teaches, is, this lesson, that that verse will only do in which a poet manages to register both the acquisitions of his ear *and* the pressures of his breath.

Let's start from the smallest particle of all, the syllable. It is the king and pin of versification, what rules and holds together the lines, the larger forms, of a poem. I would suggest that verse here and in England dropped this secret from the late Elizabethans to Ezra Pound, lost it, in the sweetness of meter and rime, in a honey-head. (The syllable is one way to distinguish the original success of blank verse, and its falling off, with Milton.)

It is by their syllables that words juxtapose in beauty, by these particles of sound as clearly as by the sense of the words which they compose. In any given instance, because there is a choice of words, the choice, if a man is in there, will be, spontaneously, the obedience of his ear to the syllables. The fineness, and the practice, lie here, at the minimum and source of speech.

> O western wynd, when wilt thou blow
> And the small rain down shall rain
> O Christ that my love were in my arms
> And I in my bed again

It would do no harm, as an act of correction to both prose and verse as now written, if both rime and meter, and, in the quantity words, both sense and sound, were less in the forefront of the mind than the syllable, if the syllable, that fine creature, were more allowed to lead the harmony on. With this warning, to those who would try: to step back here to this place of the elements and minims of language, is to engage speech where it is least careless—and least logical. Listening for the syllables must be so constant and so scrupulous, the exaction must be so complete, that the assurance of the ear is purchased at the highest—40 hours a day—price. For from the root out, from all over the place, the syllable comes, the figures of, the dance.

> "Is" comes from the Aryan root, *as*, to breathe. The English "not"
> equals the Sanscrit *na*, which may come from the root *na*, to be lost,
> to perish. "Be" is from *bhu*, to grow.

I say the syllable, king, and that it is spontaneous, this way: the ear, the ear which has collected, which has listened, the ear, which is so close to the mind that it is the mind's, that it has the mind's speed . . .

it is close, another way: the mind is brother to this sister and is, because it is so close, is the drying force, the incest, the sharpener . . .

it is from the union of the mind and the ear that the syllable is born.

But the syllable is only the first child of the incest of verse (always, that Egyptian thing, it produces twins!). The other child is the LINE. And together, these two, the syllable *and* the line, they make a poem, they make that thing, the—what shall we call it, the Boss of all, the "Single Intelligence." And the line comes (I swear it) from the breath, from the breathing of the man who writes, at the moment that he writes, and thus is, it is here that, the daily work, the WORK, gets in, for only he, the man who writes, can declare, at every moment, the line its metric and its ending—where its breathing, shall come to, termination.

The trouble with most work, to my taking, since the breaking away from traditional lines and stanzas, and from such wholes as, say, Chaucer's *Troilus* or S's *Lear*, is: contemporary workers go lazy RIGHT HERE WHERE THE LINE IS BORN.

Let me put it baldly. The two halves are:
the HEAD, by way of the EAR, to the SYLLABLE
the HEART, by way of the BREATH, to the LINE

And the joker? that it is in the 1st half of the proposition that, in composing, one lets-it-rip; and that it is in the 2nd half, surprise, it is the line that's the baby that gets, as the poem is getting made, the attention, the control, that it is right here, in the line, that the shaping takes place, each moment of the going.

I am dogmatic, that the head shows in the syllable. The dance of the intellect is there, among them, prose or verse. Consider the best minds you know in this here business: where does the head show, is it not, precise, here, in the swift currents of the syllable? can't you tell a brain when you see what it does, just there? It is true, what the master says he picked up from Confusion: all the thots men are capable of can be entered on the back of a postage stamp. So, is it not the PLAY of a mind we are after, is not that that shows whether a mind is there at all?

And the threshing floor for the dance? Is it anything but the LINE? And when the line has, is, a deadness, is it not a heart which has gone lazy, is it not, suddenly, slow things, similes, say, adjectives, or such, that we are bored by?

For there is a whole flock of rhetorical devices which have now to be brought under a new bead, now that we sight with the line. Simile is only one bird who comes down, too easily. The descriptive functions generally have to be watched, every second, in projective verse, because of their easiness, and thus their drain on the energy which composition by field allows into a poem. *Any* slackness takes off attention, that crucial thing, from the job in hand, from the *push* of the line under hand at the moment, under the reader's eye, in his moment. Observation of any kind is, like argument in prose, properly previous to the act of the poem, and, if allowed in, must be so juxtaposed, apposed, set in, that it does not, for an instant, sap the going energy of the content toward its form.

It comes to this, this whole aspect of the newer problems. (We now enter, actually, the large area of the whole poem, into the FIELD, if you like, where all the syllables and all the lines must be managed in their relations to each other.) It is a matter, finally, of OBJECTS, what they are, what they are inside a poem, how they got there, and, once there, how they are to be used. This is something I want to get to in another way in Part II, but, for the moment, let me indicate this, that every element in an open poem (the syllable, the line, as well as the image, the sound, the sense) must be taken up as participants in the kinetic of the poem just as solidly as we are accustomed to take what we call the objects of reality; and that these elements are to be seen as creating the tensions of a poem just as totally as do those other objects create what we know as the world.

The objects which occur at every given moment of composition (of recognition, we can call it) are, can be, must be treated exactly as they do occur therein and not by any ideas or preconceptions from outside the poem, must be handled as a series of objects in a field in such a way that a series of tensions (which they also are) are made to *hold*, and to hold exactly inside the content and the context of the poem which has forced itself, through the poet and them, into being.

Because breath allows *all* the speech-force of language back in (speech is the "solid" of verse, is the secret of a poem's energy), because, now, a poem has, by speech, solidity, everything in it can now be treated as solids, objects, things; and, though insisting upon the absolute difference of the reality of verse from that other dispersed and distributed thing, yet each of these elements of a poem can be allowed to have the play of their separate energies and can be allowed, once the poem is well-composed, to keep, as those other objects do, their proper confusions.

Which brings us up, immediately, bang, against tenses, in fact against syntax, in fact against grammar generally, that is, as we have inherited it.

Do not tenses, must they not also be kicked around anew, in order that time, that other governing absolute, may be kept, as must the space-tensions of a poem, immediate, contemporary to the acting-on-you of the poem? I would argue that here, too, the LAW OF THE LINE, which projective verse creates, must be hewn to, obeyed, and that the conventions which logic has forced on syntax must be broken open as quietly as must the too set feet of the old line. But an analysis of how far a new poet can stretch the very conventions on which communication by language rests, is too big for these notes, which are meant, I hope it is obvious, merely to get things started.

Let me just throw in this. It is my impression that *all* parts of speech suddenly, in composition by field, are fresh for both sound and percussive use, spring up like unknown, unnamed vegetables in the patch, when you work it, come spring. Now take Hart Crane. What strikes me in him is the singleness of the push to the nominative, his push along that one arc of freshness, the attempt to get back to word as handle. (If logos is word as thought, what is word as noun, as, pass me that, as Newman Shea used to ask, at the galley table, put a jib on the blood, will ya.) But there is a loss in Crane of what Fenollosa is so right about, in syntax, the sentence as first act of nature, as lightning, as passage of force from subject to object, quick, in this case, from Hart to me, in every case, from me to you, the VERB, between two nouns. Does not Hart miss the advantages, by such an isolated push, miss the point of the whole front of syllable, line, field, and what happened to all language, and to the poem, as a result?

I return you now to London, to beginnings, to the syllable, for the pleasures of it, to intermit:

> If music be the food of love, play on,
> give me excess of it, that, surfeiting,
> the appetite may sicken, and so die.
> That strain again. It had a dying fall,
> o, it came over my ear like the sweet sound
> that breathes upon a bank of violets,
> stealing and giving odour.

What we have suffered from, is manuscript, press, the removal of verse from its producer and its reproducer, the voice, a removal by one, by two removes from its place of origin *and* its destination. For the breath has a double meaning which latin had not yet lost.

The irony is, from the machine has come one gain not yet sufficiently observed or used, but which leads directly on toward projective verse and its consequences. It is the advantage of the typewriter that, due to its rigidity and its space precisions, it can, for a poet, indicate exactly the breath, the pauses, the suspensions even of syllables, the juxtapositions even of parts of phrases, which he intends. For the first time the poet has the stave and the bar a musician has had. For the first time he can, without the convention of rime and meter, record the listening he has done to his own speech and by that one act indicate how he would want any reader, silently or otherwise, to voice his work.

It is time we picked the fruits of the experiments of Cummings, Pound, Williams, each of whom has, after his way, already used the machine as a scoring to his composing, as a script to its vocalization. It is now only a matter of the recognition of the conventions of composition by field for us to bring into being an open verse as formal as the closed, with all its traditional advantages.

If a contemporary poet leaves a space as long as the phrase before it, he means that space to be held, by the breath, an equal length of time. If he suspends a word or syllable at the end of a line (this was most Cummings' addition) he means that time to pass that it takes the eye—that hair of time suspended—to pick up the next line. If he wishes a pause so light it hardly separates the words, yet does not want a comma—which is an interruption of the meaning rather than the sounding of the line—follow him when he uses a symbol the typewriter has ready to hand:

"What does not change / is the will to change"

Observe him, when he takes advantage of the machine's multiple margins, to juxtapose:

"Sd he:
    to dream takes no effort
      to think is easy
        to act is more difficult

  but for a man to act after he has taken thought, this!
is the most difficult thing of all"

Each of these lines is a progressing of both the meaning and the breathing forward, and then a backing up, without a progress or any kind of movement outside the unit of time local to the idea.

There is more to be said in order that this convention be recognized, especially in order that the revolution out of which it came may be so forwarded that work will get published to offset the reaction now afoot to return verse to inherited forms of cadence and rime. But what I want to emphasize here, by this emphasis on the typewriter as the personal and instantaneous recorder of the poet's work, is the already projective nature of verse as the sons of Pound and Williams are practicing it. Already they are composing as though verse was to have the reading its writing involved, as though not the eye but the ear was to be its measurer, as though the intervals of its composition could be so carefully put down as to be precisely the intervals of its registration. For the ear, which once had the burden of memory to quicken it (rime & regular cadence were its aids and have merely lived on in print after the oral necessities were ended) can now again, that the poet has his means, be the threshold of projective verse.

II

Which gets us to what I promised, the degree to which the projective involves a stance toward reality outside a poem as well as a new stance towards the reality of a poem itself. It is a matter of content, the content of Homer or of Euripides or of Seami as distinct from that which I might call the more "literary" masters. From the moment the projective purpose of the act of verse is recognized, the content does—it will—change. If the beginning and the end is breath, voice in its largest sense, then the material of verse shifts. It has to. It starts with the composer. The dimension of his line itself changes, not to speak of the change in his conceiving, of the matter he will turn to, of the scale in which he imagines that matter's use. I myself would pose the difference by a physical image. It is no accident that Pound and Williams both were involved variously in a movement which got called "objectivism." But that word was then used in some sort of a necessary quarrel, I take it, with "subjectivism." It is now too late to be bothered with the latter. It has excellently done itself to death, even though we are all caught in its dying. What seems to me a more valid formulation for present use is "objectism," a word to be taken to stand for the kind of relation of man to experience which a poet might state as the necessity of a line or a work to be as wood is, to be as clean as wood is as it issues from the hand of nature, to be shaped as wood can be when a man has had his hand to it. Objectism is the getting rid of the lyrical interference of the individual as ego, of the "subject" and his soul, that peculiar presumption by which western man has interposed himself between what he is as a creature of nature (with certain instructions to carry out) and those other creatures of nature which we may, with no derogation, call objects. For a man is himself an object, whatever he may take to be his advantages, the more likely to recognize himself as such the greater his advantages, particularly at that moment that he achieves an humilitas sufficient to make him of use.

It comes to this: the use of a man, by himself and thus by others, lies in how he conceives his relation to nature, that force to which he owes his somewhat small existence. If he sprawl, he shall find little to sing but himself, and shall sing, nature has such paradoxical ways, by way of artificial forms outside himself. But if he stays inside himself, if he is contained within this nature as he is participant in the larger force, he will be able to listen, and his hearing through himself will give him secrets objects share. And by an inverse law his shapes will make their own way. It is in this sense that the projective act, which is the artist's act in the larger field of objects, leads to dimensions larger than the man. For a man's problem, the moment he takes speech up in all its fullness, is to give his work his seriousness, a seriousness sufficient to cause the thing he makes to try to take its place alongside the things of nature. This is not easy. Nature works from reverence, even in her destructions (species go down with a crash). But breath is man's special qualification as animal. Sound is a dimension he has extended. Language is one of his proudest acts. And when a poet rests in these as they are in himself (in his physiology, if you like, but the life in him, for all that) then he, if he chooses to speak from these roots, works in that area where nature has given him size, projective size.

It is projective size that the play, *The Trojan Women*, possesses, for it is able to stand, is it not, as its people do, beside the Aegean—and neither Andromache or the sea suffer diminution. In a less "heroic" but equally "natural" dimension Seami causes the Fisherman and the Angel to stand clear in *Hagoromo*. And Homer, who is such an unexamined cliche that I do not think I need to press home in what scale Nausicaa's girls wash their clothes.

Such works, I should argue—and I use them simply because their equivalents are yet to be done—could not issue from men who conceived verse without the full relevance of human voice, without reference to where lines come from, in the individual who writes. Nor do I think it accident that, at this end point of the argument, I should use, for example, two dramatists and an epic poet. For I would hazard the guess that, if projective verse is practiced long enough, is driven ahead hard enough along the course I think it dictates, verse again can carry much larger material than it has carried in our language since the Elizabethans. But it can't be jumped. We are only at its beginnings, and if I think that the *Cantos* make more "dramatic" sense than do the plays of Mr. Eliot, it is not because I think they have solved the problem but because the methodology of the verse in them points a way by which, one day, the problem of larger content and of larger forms may be solved. Eliot is, in fact, a proof of a present danger, of "too easy" a going on the practice of verse as it has been, rather than as it must be, practiced. There is no question, for example, that Eliot's line, from "Prufrock" on down, has speech-force, is "dramatic," is, in fact, one of the most notable lines since Dryden. I suppose it stemmed immediately to him from Browning, as did so many of Pound's early things. In any case Eliot's line has obvious relations backward to the Elizabethans, especially to the soliloquy. Yet O.M. Eliot is *not* projective. It could even be argued (and I say this carefully, as I have said all things about the non-projective, having considered how each of us must save himself after his own fashion and how much, for that matter, each of us owes to the non-projective, and will continue to owe, as both go alongside each other) but it could be argued that it is because Eliot has stayed inside the non-projective that he fails as a dramatist—that his root is the mind alone, and a scholastic mind at that (no high *intelletto* despite his apparent clarities)—and that, in his listenings he has stayed there where the ear and the mind are, has only gone from his fine ear outward rather than, as I say a projective poet will, down through the workings of his own throat to that place where breath comes from, where breath has its beginnings, where drama has to come from, where, the coincidence is, all act springs.

selected bibliography

ANTHOLOGIES

Apollonio, Umbro, ed. *Futurist Manifestos*. London: Thames and Hudson, 1973.
Caws, Mary Ann, ed. *Manifesto: A Century of Isms*. Lincoln: University of Nebraska Press, 2001.
Motherwell, Robert, ed. *The Dada Painters and Poets*. 2d ed. Cambridge: Harvard University Press, 1981.
Richardson, Michael, and Krzysztof Fijalkowski, eds. *Refusal of the Shadow: Surrealism and the Caribbean*. London: Verso, 2001.

PROSE WORKS BY POETS INCLUDED IN THIS BOOK

Baudelaire, Charles. *The Painter of Modern Life and Other Essays*. Translated by Jonathan Mayne. New York: DaCapo P, 1986.
———. *Selected Writings on Art and Artists*. Translated by P. E. Charvet. New York: Penguin, 1972.
Breton, André. *Manifestoes of Surrealism*. Edited by Richard Seaver and Helen R. Lane. Ann Arbor: University of Michigan Press, 1972.
Césaire, Aimé. *Lyric and Dramatic Poetry, 1946–1982*. Translated by Clayton Eshleman and Annette Smith. Charlottesville: University of Virginia Press, 1990.
Coleridge, Samual Taylor. *Biographia Literaria, or Biographical Sketches of My Literary Life*. Edited by George Watson. London: J. M. Dent, 1965.
Dickinson, Emily. *Letters of Emily Dickinson*. Edited by Thomas H. Johnson. Cambridge: Harvard University Press, 1986.
Eliot, T. S. *Selected Essays*. New York: Harcourt, Brace and World, 1960.
———. *Selected Prose*. Edited by Frank Kermode. New York: Harcourt Brace Jovanovich, 1975.
Emerson, Ralph Waldo. *The Selected Writings of Ralph Waldo Emerson*. New York: Modern Library, 1992.
Hopkins, Gerard Manley. *A Hopkins Reader*. Edited by John Pick. Garden City, N.Y.: Doubleday, 1966.
Hughes, Langston. *A Langston Hughes Reader*. New York: Braziller, 1971.
Keats, John. *Letters of John Keats*. Edited by Robert Gittings. Oxford: Oxford University Press, 1970.

Lorca, Federico García. *In Search of Duende: Federico García Lorca*. Edited by Christopher Mauer. New York: New Directions, 1988.

Loy, Mina. *The Lost Lunar Baedeker*. Edited by Roger L. Conover. New York: Noonday, 1996.

Mallarmé, Stéphane. *Selected Prose Poems, Essays and Letters*. Translated by Bradford Cook. Baltimore: John Hopkins University Press, 1956.

Moore, Marianne. *Complete Prose of Marianne Moore*. Edited by Patricia C. Willis. New York: Elisabeth Sifton, 1986.

Olson, Charles. *Selected Writings*. Edited by Robert Creeley. New York: New Directions, 1966.

Pound, Ezra. *ABC of Reading*. New York: New Directions, 1960.

———. *Literary Essays*. Edited by T. S. Eliot. New York: New Directions, 1968.

———. *Selected Prose, 1909–1965*. Edited by William Cookson. New York: New Directions, 1973.

———. *The Spirit of Romance*. New York: New Directions.

Rimbaud, Arthur. *Collected Poems*. Translated by Oliver Bernard. London: Penguin, 1997.

———. *Selected Prose*. Edited by Frank Kermode. Harmondsworth: Penguin, 1965.

Shelley, Percy Bysshe. *Shelley's Literary and Philosophical Criticism*. Edited by John Shawcross. Folcroft, Pa.: Folcroft Library, 1977.

Stein, Gertrude. *How to Write*. Edited by Patricia Meyerowitz. New York: Dover, 1975.

———. *Lectures in America*. New York: Vintage, 1975.

Stevens, Wallace. *The Necessary Angel: Essays on Reality and the Imagination*. New York: Vintage, 1951.

Valéry, Paul. *An Anthology*. Edited by James Lawler. Princeton: Princeton Univesity Press, 1977.

Whitman, Walt. *Leaves of Grass and Other Writings*. Edited by Michael Moon. New York: Norton, 2002.

Williams, William Carlos. *Imaginations*. Edited by Webster Schotl. New York: New Directions, 1971.

———. *Selected Essays*. New York: New Directions, 1969.

Wordsworth, William. *The Major Works*. Edited by Stephen Gill. Oxford: Oxford University Press, 2000.

Zukofsky, Louis. *Prepositions +: The Collected Critical Essays*. Middletown: Wesleyan University Press , 2000.

Apollinaire, Guillaume. *Selected Writings.* Translated by Roger Shattuck. New York: New Directions, 1971.

Auden, W. H. *The Dyers Hand and Other Essays.* New York: Vintage, 1968.

H.D. *Notes on Thought and Vision.* San Francisco: City Lights, 1982.

Frost, Robert. *Selected Prose.* Edited by Hyde Cox and Edward Connery Lathem. New York: Holt, 1966.

Jacob, Max. *Introduction, Dice Cup: Selected Prose Poems.* Edited by Michael Brownstein. New York: Sun, 1980.

Machado, Antonio. *Juan de Mairena: Epigrams, Maxims, Memoranda and Memoirs of an Apocryphal Professor.* Translated by Ben Belitt. Berkeley: University of California Press, 1963.

Mandelstam, Osip. *Complete Critical Prose and Letters.* Translated by Jane Gray Harris and Constance Link. Dana Point: Ardis, 1997.

Pessoa, Fernando. *Selected Prose of Fernando Pessoa.* Edited by Richard Zenith. New York: Grove, 2001.

Poe, Edgar Allen. *Selected Writings: Poems, Tales, Essays and Reviews.* Edited by David Galloway. Harmondsworth: Penguin, 1967.

Rilke, Rainer Maria. *Letters on Cezanne.* Edited by Clara Rilke; translated by Joel Agee. New York: Fromm International, 1985.

―――. *Letters to a Young Poet.* Translated by M. D. Hector Norton. New York: Norton, 1962.

Rukeyser, Muriel. *A Muriel Rukeyser Reader.* Edited by Jan Heller Levi. New York: Norton, 1994.

Sénghor, Leopold Sédar. *Prose and Poetry.* Translated by John Reed and Clive Wake. London: Heinemann Educational, 1976.

Tzara, Tristan. *Seven Dada Manifestos and Lampsteries.* Translated by Barbara Wright. London: John Calder, 1977.

Yeats, William Butler. *Essays and Introductions.* New York: Macmillan, 1971.

about the editor

Melissa Kwasny was born in LaPorte, Indiana. She graduated from the University of Montana in 1977 where she studied with Richard Hugo and Madeline Defrees. After spending ten years in San Francisco, teaching in the California Poets in the Schools program, she returned to Montana where she received her MFA in Poetry in 1999.

Kwasny is the author of two novels, *Modern Daughters and the Outlaw West* (1990) and *Trees Call for What They Need* (1993), as well as one book of poetry, *The Archival Birds* (2000). Her poems and essays have appeared in numerous publications including *Ploughshares*, *Poetry Northwest*, *Threepenny Review*, *American Voice*, *Bellingham Review*, and *Willowsprings*. She is currently teaching as Visiting Writer at the University of Wyoming.